A NEW EUSEBIUS

SPCK Large Paperbacks

A NEW EUSEBIUS

*Documents illustrative of the history of the
Church to A.D. 337*

edited by

J. STEVENSON

Based upon the collection edited by the late B. J. Kidd

LONDON
S·P·C·K

First published in 1957
Reprinted with corrections, 1960, 1965, 1968
Seventh impression 1977
S.P.C.K.
Holy Trinity Church
Marylebone Road
London, NW1 4DU
Made and printed by offset in Great Britain by
The Camelot Press Ltd, Southampton

ISBN 0 281 00802 7

CONTENTS

Note: Where two or more sources are given, and one or more of these is in brackets, this indicates that, while the first is the actual source, the passage consists of, or embodies quotation from, the others. If, however, this fact is sufficiently indicated in the title, no author except the original source is named.

CONTENTS   XV

SARMATIA

ΟΝΙΑ

MURSA

CIBALE · SINGIDUNUM

DACIA

CRIMEA

R. Danube

ΤΙΑ

MOESIA

·NAïSSUS

BLACK SEA

ADRIANOPLE

MACEDONIA PHILIPPI THRACE BYZANTIUM (AFT. CONSTANTINOPLE) SINOPE

THESSALONICA PAPHLAGONIA

·NICOMEDIA PONTUS

LAMPSACUS NICAEA BITHYNIA ·NEOCAESAREA ARMENIA

·ANCYRA

ASIA PHRYGIA CAPPADOCIA

GREECE SMYRNA SARDIS HIEROPOLIS

CORINTH ·ATHENS EPHESUS 5 ·PHILOMELIUM CAESAREA SAMOSATA

·OLYMPIA 3 TRALLES ·ANTIOCH ANAZARBUS EDESSA NISIBIS

PATMOS ICONIUM ·TARSUS OSRHOËNE

·CYRRHUS MESOPOTAMIA

RHOSSUS R.Tigris

CRETE ARYCANDA ·ANTIOCH

·LAODICEA R.Euphrates

TRIPOLI SYRIA DURA

NEAN CYPRUS ·BERYTUS ·PALMYRA

SEA

·TYRE SELEUCIA-CTESIPHON

PTOLEMAIS ·CYRENE PALESTINE SAMARIA ·BOSTRA

CYRENAICA ALEXANDRIA CAESAREA 1

LYDDA 2 JERUSALEM

MARMARICA MAREOTIS ·GAZA

·THMUIS

·PHAENO

EGYPT ALEXANDER'S ISLE

R.Nile

·L·Q·T

ACKNOWLEDGEMENTS

Thanks are due to the following for permission to include copyright material:

The Cambridge University Press (F. C. Burkitt: *The Religion of the Manichees*; H. Chadwick: *Origen Contra Celsum*; and B. S. Easton: *The Apostolic Tradition of Hippolytus*).

The Clarendon Press (A. S. L. Farquharson: *The Meditations of the Emperor Marcus Aurelius*; and R. Walzer: *Galen on Jews and Christians*).

The English Universities Press (A. H. M. Jones: *Constantine and the Conversion of Europe*).

The Harvard University Press (R. P. Casey: *Excerpta ex Theodoto*, from *Studies and Documents*; and J. P. Knipfing's translations of *Libelli* of the persecution of Decius, from the *Harvard Theological Review*).

The Trustees of the Loeb Classical Library (G. W. Butterworth: *Clement of Alexandria*; T. R. Glover: *Tertullian's Apology*; A. M. Harmon: *Lucian*; K. Lake: *Apostolic Fathers*; J. C. Rolfe: *Suetonius*; and C. R. Woodward and H. Mattingly: *St John Damascene, Barlaam and Ioasaph*).

Longmans, Green and Company (J. N. D. Kelly: *Early Christian Creeds*).

The Princeton University Press (Clyde Pharr: *The Theodosian Code*).

The Trustees of the British Museum (H. I. Bell: *Jews and Christians in Egypt*).

The Executors of the late Reverend H. M. Gwatkin (*Selections from Early Christian Writers*).

ABBREVIATIONS

A.-N. C. L. . .	Ante-Nicene Christian Library
C.A.H. . . .	*Cambridge Ancient History*
C.I.L. . . .	*Corpus Inscriptionum Latinarum*
C.S.E.L. . . .	*Corpus Scriptorum Ecclesiasticorum Latinorum*
D.C.B. . . .	*Dictionary of Christian Biography*
G.C.S.	*Die griechischen christlichen Schriftsteller der ersten drei Jahrhunderte*
Irenaeus, Harvey .	*Sancti Irenaei libros quinque adversus Haereses,* ed. W. W. Harvey
J.E.H.	*Journal of Ecclesiastical History*
J.R.S.	*Journal of Roman Studies*
J.T.S.	*Journal of Theological Studies*
Lawlor and Oulton, Eusebius . .	Eusebius, *The Ecclesiastical History and the Martyrs of Palestine*, translated with introduction and notes by H. J. Lawlor and J. E. L. Oulton
L.F.	Library of the Fathers
N. & P.-N. F. .	Nicene and Post-Nicene Fathers
Opitz	*Athanasius Werke*, ed. H. G. Opitz (Berlin 1934, etc.)
P.G.	Migne, *Patrologia Graeca*
P.L.	Migne, *Patrologia Latina*
R.S.V. . . .	Revised Standard Version
T.U.	Texte und Untersuchungen zur Geschichte der altchristlichen Literatur

Square brackets indicate paraphrased passages

PREFACE

IN 1920 and 1923 the Society for Promoting Christian Knowledge published Volumes I and II of *Documents Illustrative of the History of the Church* edited by the late B. J. Kidd, and covering the period down to A.D. 461, the dividing point between the volumes being A.D. 313. As source books these have served students of Early Church History well. They are now out of print, and the present book aims at being a successor to the earlier part of Kidd's work. In the process of selection some of the passages used by Kidd have been dropped, and a number of others added. It is hoped that the notes, in which numerous further passages are incorporated, the chronological tables, and the notes on sources will be found useful.

The debt which the study of Early Church History owes to the work of Eusebius of Caesarea, the earliest Church historian, need not be reiterated here, and it may not be inappropriate to commemorate him in the title of a book dealing with the whole period for which he is a chief primary authority.

I wish to thank my friend and colleague, the Reverend Henry Chadwick, Fellow of Queens' College, for his kindness in helping me at various points in my work, particularly with Celsus and Paul of Samosata, and in reading the proofs of the whole. His suggestions have enabled me to introduce a number of improvements. I wish also to thank the publishers and the printers for their help during the preparation and production of the book.

Downing College, Cambridge   J. STEVENSON
    May 1957

NOTE TO SECOND AND THIRD IMPRESSIONS

Some minor corrections have been made in the second and third impressions.

                                J. S.

1. MARTYRDOM OF JAMES, THE LORD'S BROTHER, 62

(Josephus, *Antiquities of the Jews*, XX.9.1)

But this younger Ananus, who, as we have told you already, took the High Priesthood, was a bold man in his temper and very insolent. He was also of the sect of the Sadducees, who are very rigid in judging offenders above all the rest of the Jews, as we have already observed. When therefore Ananus was of this disposition, he thought he had now a proper opportunity (to exercise his authority). Festus was now dead, and Albinus was but upon the road. So he assembled the sanhedrin of judges, and brought before them the brother of Jesus who was called Christ, whose name was James, and some others. And when he had formed an accusation against them as breakers of the law, he delivered them to be stoned. But those who seemed the most equitable of the citizens, and accurate in legal matters, disliked what was done. They also sent to the King (Agrippa), desiring him to send to Ananus that he should act so no more; for that what he had already done was not to be justified. Nay, some of them went also to meet Albinus, as he was upon his journey from Alexandria, and informed him that it was not lawful for Ananus to assemble a sanhedrin without his consent. Albinus was persuaded by what they said, and wrote in anger to Ananus, and threatened that he would bring him to punishment for what he had done. On which account King Agrippa took the High Priesthood from him when he had ruled but three months, and made Jesus the son of Damneus High Priest. (William Whiston, *The Works of Josephus*, altered.)

Albinus became procurator in 62. There is a much longer and more elaborate account of James' martyrdom in Eusebius, *H.E.* II.23, derived from Hegesippus.

2. EXPULSION OF THE JEWS FROM ROME, *c.* 49

(Suetonius, *Life of Claudius*, XXV.4.)

Since the Jews constantly made disturbances at the instigation of Chrestus, he expelled them from Rome.... (J. C. Rolfe, *Suetonius* (Loeb Library), II, p. 53.)

In this chapter Suetonius is dealing with actions of Claudius towards various foreign races. Aquila and Priscilla moved to Corinth in consequence of this edict (Acts 18.2). The words *at the instigation of Chrestus* may well refer to disturbances caused by the preaching of Christianity among the Jews, and these disturbances could become serious in so large a Jewish community. The garbled form *Chrestus* might be taken by the authorities as the name of a contemporary individual, particularly as his supporters would insist that he was still alive. Justin (*Apol.* I.4), Tertullian (*Apol.* 3.5) and Lactantius (*Inst.* IV.7.5) show that "Christus" and "Chrestus" were pronounced in much the same way. "Chraestus" was quite common as a personal name.

3–7. THE NERONIAN PERSECUTION

The Great Fire of Rome took place in July 64. Only four of the fourteen wards of the city escaped damage. Nero was suspected of having caused the fire. Of our ancient authorities Tacitus is non-committal, while Pliny the Elder, Suetonius, and Dio Cassius attribute the fire to the agency of the Emperor. Whatever the truth, the Emperor found the accusation awkward, particularly at a time when through his crimes and follies his own popularity was at a low ebb.

3.

(Tacitus, *Annals*, XV.44.2–8.)

2   But all human efforts, all the lavish gifts of the emperor, and the propitiations of the gods, did not banish the sinister belief that
3 the conflagration was the result of an order. Consequently, to get rid of the report, Nero fastened the guilt and inflicted the most exquisite tortures on a class hated for their abominations, called
4 Christians by the populace. Christus, from whom the name had its origin, suffered the extreme penalty during the reign of Tiberius at the hands of one of our procurators, Pontius Pilatus, and a deadly superstition, thus checked for the moment, again broke out not only in Judaea, the first source of the evil, but also in the City, where all things hideous and shameful from every part of
5 the world meet and become popular. Accordingly, an arrest was first made of all who confessed; then, upon their information, an immense multitude was convicted, not so much of the crime of
6 arson, as of hatred of the human race. Mockery of every sort was added to their deaths. Covered with the skins of beasts, they were torn by dogs and perished, or were nailed to crosses, or were doomed to the flames. These served to illuminate the night when

7 daylight failed. Nero had thrown open his gardens for the spectacle, and was exhibiting a show in the circus, while he mingled with the people in the dress of a charioteer or drove about in a 8 chariot. Hence, even for criminals who deserved extreme and exemplary punishment, there arose a feeling of compassion; for it was not, as it seemed, for the public good, but to glut one man's cruelty, that they were being destroyed. (Church and Brodribb, *The Annals of Tacitus*, p. 304f., altered.)

The evidence of Tacitus is not contemporary, but dates from about 50 years after the event. By that time Christians must have increased considerably in numbers, and Tacitus, as governor of Asia *c.* 112, must have been perfectly familiar with them. As can be seen from the above passage, he regards them as scum.

5. *who confessed*—(?) to Christianity or to arson. While it is possible that a few Christians set fire to Rome, it is much more likely that the confession was to Christianity. We need not be surprised that Nero made the Christians scapegoats. They believed that the end of the world would come in a great conflagration (cf. 2 Pet. 3.10) in which the destruction by fire of the City was to be a leading feature (cf. Rev. 18.8–10; 19.3). It is not impossible that joy at the burning of Rome caused attention to be drawn to them. But even if a few Christians had set Rome on fire, many were punished simply as members of an unpopular group.

hatred of the human race (*odium humani generis*). The important Medicean manuscript reads, not *was convicted* (*convicti sunt*) but "were indicted on a double charge" (*coniuncti sunt*). Thus *odium humani generis* may be a real charge. It was a charge brought against magicians, and the penalty was death by burning. The early Christians were frequently reproached with being magicians (Jesus being a chief magician), cf. 119, 193. Tacitus believes that the Christians were criminals, *who deserved extreme and exemplary punishment*.

No other ancient source pagan or Christian connects the Christians with the fire, till we reach Sulpicius Severus (cf. 7). But Nero was universally recognized as the first persecutor.

4.

(Suetonius, *Life of Nero*, XVI.2.)

Punishment was inflicted on the Christians, a class of men given to a new and wicked superstition. (J. C. Rolfe, *Suetonius* (Loeb Library), II, p. 111, altered.)

This reference comes in a list of miscellaneous legislative provisions: it is preceded by one concerning the sale of food in taverns, and followed by one concerning the behaviour of charioteers. Suetonius does not connect the punishment of the Christians with the Great Fire, for causing which he blames Nero quite unequivocally.

wicked (*maleficus*). The noun *maleficus* means "magician", cf. 265, p. 306.

5.

(Clement of Rome, *First Epistle to the Corinthians*, V–VI.)

In Ch. IV Clement, using examples from the Old Testament, has been setting forth the dreadful effects of jealousy. He then turns to his own times.

V.1 But, to finish with these ancient examples, let us come to the athletes of the recent past; let us take the noble examples of our
2 own generation. Through jealousy and envy the greatest and most righteous pillars (of the Church) were persecuted, and contended
3 unto death. Let us set before our eyes the good (i.e. heroic)
4 Apostles: Peter, who through unrighteous jealousy endured not one or two but many labours, and so having borne witness pro-
5 ceeded to his due place of glory. Through jealousy and strife
6 Paul displayed the prize of endurance; seven times in bonds, driven into exile, stoned, appearing as a herald in both the East
7 and the West he won noble fame for his faith; he taught righteousness to the whole world, and after reaching the limits of the West bore witness before the rulers. Then he passed from the world and went to the holy place, having shown himself the greatest pattern of endurance.
VI.1 Associated with these men of holy life is a great multitude of the elect, who because of jealousy have suffered many indignities and tortures and have set a very noble example in our midst.
2 Because of jealousy women were persecuted, who as Danaids and Dircae suffered terrible and impious indignities and thereby safely completed the race of faith and, thought weak in body, received a noble reward of honour. (W. K. Lowther Clarke, *The First Epistle of Clement to the Corinthians*, pp. 51–2.)

Clement, looking at the persecution from within the Church, regards *jealousy and strife* as leading causes (cf. St Paul, Phil. 1.15). This may correspond to Tacitus' statement *upon their information, an immense multitude was convicted*. Such feelings were a part of the bitter hostility between strict Jewish and other Christians.

V. 7 *the limits of the West*, i.e. Spain, cf. St Paul, Rom. 15.24,28, and 124 below. "A Roman could not have thought of his city as being on the Western boundary of the world. A Spanish journey was contemplated by Paul. Such a journey is difficult to reconcile with the date of the N.T. We must conclude either that tradition assumed the intention was carried out, the true facts having been forgotten, or that Clement refers to a matter of common knowledge, our ignorance of which is a salutary reminder of the limits of the N.T. evidence." (Lowther Clarke, op. cit., pp. 89, 90.)

On the deaths of the Apostles see notes on the two following passages.

VI. 2 *Danaids and Dircae.* "The traditional punishment of the daughters of Danaus in the underworld was eternally to fill with water a cask with holes in it; some more cruel variation is probably meant. Dirce was tied to the horns of a bull and dragged to death." (Lowther Clarke, op. cit., p. 91.)

The Greek text is corrupt, and for "Danaids" we should perhaps read "Danaae". The story of Danae would afford material for *terrible and impious indignities.*

6.

(Eusebius, *H.E.* II.25.5–8; including quotations from Gaius, a Roman Christian writer, and from Dionysius, Bishop of Corinth.)

5 Thus, then, was Nero the first to be heralded as above all an antagonist of God and stirred up to murder the apostles. It is related that in his day Paul was beheaded at Rome itself, and that Peter likewise was crucified, and this story is accredited by the

6 attachment, which prevails to this day, of the names of Peter and Paul to the cemeteries there; and in no less degree also by a churchman, named Gaius, who lived in the time of Zephyrinus, bishop of the Romans. Gaius, in a written discussion with Proclus, a champion of the heresy of the Phrygians, speaks thus of the places where the sacred tabernacles of the said apostles have been laid:

7 But I can point out the trophies of the apostles. For if you would go to the Vatican, or to the Ostian Way, you will find the trophies of those who founded this church.

8 And that they were martyred both on the same occasion, Dionysius, bishop of the Corinthians, writing to the Romans, affirms as follows:

In these ways you also, by such an admonition, have united the planting that came from Peter and Paul, of both the Romans and the Corinthians. For indeed both planted also in our Corinth, and likewise taught us; and likewise they taught together also in Italy, and were martyred on the same occasion.

These quotations I have made, in order to accredit still further the facts of the history. (Lawlor and Oulton, *Eusebius*, I, p. 60, altered.)

5. John 21.18–19 is early evidence for the crucifixion of Peter. Tertullian (*De Praescriptione Haereticorum* 36) mentions the method of the Apostles' deaths (148).

6. *the heresy of the Phrygians*, i.e. Montanism, see 85–92. The sites mentioned by Gaius are, of course, those traditionally associated with the sepulture of the Apostles, though *trophies* means no more than "memorials". "It (i.e. the shrine of St Peter) was a modest version of a type of martyr-shrine that is already familiar from other sites, and took the form of a small open courtyard, with an altar resting on two colonnettes set against an apsidal niche in the west face. The form was borrowed from pagan practice and would have attracted no attention in any second- or third-century cemetery." (J. B. Ward Perkins, "The Shrine of St Peter and its twelve spiral columns", *J.R.S.*, XLII (1952), p. 21 and p. 21n.)

7.

(Sulpicius Severus, *Chronica*, 29.3.)

Thus a beginning was made of violent persecution of the Christians. Afterwards also laws were enacted and the religion was forbidden. Edicts were publicly published: "No one must profess Christianity." Then Paul and Peter were condemned to death. The former was beheaded, Peter was crucified.

laws were enacted. First-century documents like the First Epistle of Peter and the Book of Revelation show that Christians were persecuted. But it is unlikely that a "law" was enacted for the whole Empire. On this question, see A. N. Sherwin-White, "The early Persecutions and Roman Law again", *J.T.S.* (N.S.), III.2 (1952), pp. 199ff.

Sulpicius apparently places the deaths of the Apostles later than that of the others who died under Nero. There is nothing improbable in this, as there is no reason why the Christian leaders should have been at hand awaiting arrest.

8. FLIGHT OF THE CHRISTIANS FROM JERUSALEM, *c.* 66

(Eusebius, *H.E.* III.5.3.)

Moreover, the people of the church at Jerusalem, in accordance with a certain *oracle* that was vouchsafed by way of revelation to approved men there, had been commanded *to depart from the city* before the war, and *to inhabit a certain city of Peraea.* They called it *Pella.* And when *those who believed in Christ* had removed from Jerusalem, as if holy men had utterly deserted both the royal metropolis of the Jews itself and the whole land of Judaea, the Justice of God then visited upon them all their acts of violence to

Christ and his apostles, by destroying that generation of wicked persons *root and branch* from among men. (Lawlor and Oulton, *Eusebius*, I, p. 68.)

Epiphanius also records this flight. A comparison of his account with that of Eusebius shows a common source, which is undoubtedly Hegesippus. The words in italics appear to come from him.

Pella was beyond Jordan, and was then in the dominions of Herod Agrippa II. The Christians in Jerusalem could not be expected to show any sympathy to, or receive any from Jewish nationalists, cf. 17. For difficulties about a flight to Pella see S. G. F. Brandon, *The Fall of Jerusalem and the Christian Church*, pp. 169-73.

9. THE ROTAS-SATOR SQUARE

```
R O T A S
O P E R A
T E N E T
A R E P O
S A T O R
```

Of this word square seven examples which date from Roman times have been found, two at Pompeii, one at Cirencester, and four at Dura-Europos in Mesopotamia. These are not formal inscriptions, but are scratched on walls or pillars. The Pompeian examples must date from before 79, when the city was overwhelmed in the great eruption of Mount Vesuvius, and the other examples belong to the third century A.D., those at Dura being anterior to 256 when the city was destroyed by the Persians. The meaning, if any, of the words is difficult to determine, but the square as a whole must have meaning.

```
          A
          P
          A
          T
          E
          R
A PATERNOSTER O
          O
          S
          T
          E
          R
          O
```

(F. Grosser, *Archiv. f. Religionswissenschaft*, XXIV (1926), pp. 165-9.)

(de Jerphanion, "Academie des Inscriptions et Belles-Lettres", *Comptes Rendus*, 1937, p. 86.)

If these or similar interpretations are correct the interesting problem is raised of Christians who, before 79, used Latin, AO as a description of God, and a cryptic rendering of the cross as a Christian symbol. Two *graffiti* from Pompeii mention Christians.

On the problems raised by this inscription see Hugh Last, *The Rotas-Sator Square: present position and future prospects*. (*J.T.S.* (N.S.), III (1952), pp. 92–7.) For another interpretation of the square see P. Grosjean in *J.T.S.* (N.S.) III (1952), pp. 97–8.

10–11. PERSECUTION BY DOMITIAN, 96

10.

(Dio Cassius, *Epitome*, LXVII.14.)

And in the same year Domitian slew amongst many others Flavius Clemens in his consulship, though he was his cousin and had to wife his own kinswoman, Flavia Domitilla. Against them both was brought a charge of atheism: and on this many others who made shipwreck on Jewish customs were condemned, of whom some were put to death, while others were at the least deprived of their property; but Domitilla was only banished to Pandateria. Glabrio, however, who had been consul with Trajan, he also slew, partly on the same charges as the rest, and partly because he fought with beasts. (H. M. Gwatkin, *Selections from Early Christian Writers*, p. 11.)

Domitian was rigorous in his treatment of the Jews, and insistent on the payment by them of the temple tax, which, after the destruction of the temple in 70, his father Vespasian had diverted to the use of Jupiter Capitolinus.

On the death of Flavius Clemens and Acilius Glabrio, cf. Suetonius, *Life of Domitian*, 37, 38. Suetonius says that Glabrio was condemned as a revolutionary; he describes Flavius Clemens as a man of the "most contemptible inertia" and states that he was killed "on the slenderest suspicion". These descriptions and the attribution of "atheism and of Jewish customs" are not inapt as applied to Christians, but the literary evidence certainly does not prove that these men were so. In Christian tradition Domitilla is counted a Christian, as the following passage from Eusebius shows, but the existence of the (Christian) Cemetery of Domitilla outside Rome by itself proves no more than that from about 150 onwards, the Christians constructed a cemetery on land that had belonged to Domitilla half a century before. According to Dio, Nerva forbade the bringing of accusations of *maiestas* (treason) or "Jewish life".

11.

(Eusebius, *H.E.* III.17–20.)

17   [The reign of terror under Domitian in which the Roman aristocracy suffered severely (cf. Tacitus, *Agricola*, 2–3, 44–5), culminated in his becoming successor (διάδοχος) of Nero in hostility to God.]

18.1 It is recorded that at that time *the apostle and evangelist John,* being still alive, was condemned to dwell in the island of *Patmos* for his testimony to the divine word.

2   Indeed, Irenaeus, in writing about the number of the name of the Antichrist which is to be found in the Apocalypse of John,[1] as it is called, uses these very words in the fifth book of his work Against the Heresies, with reference to John:

3   But if it were necessary that his name should be announced openly at this present time, it would have been stated by him who also saw the revelation. For it was seen not long ago, but almost in our own generation, at the close of the principate of Domitian.

4   So conspicuous, then, had the teaching of our faith become at the time of the persons just mentioned, that even those writers who stood far apart from our doctrine did not hesitate to record in their histories both the persecution and the martyrdoms that took place in it. Yes, and they also gave an exact indication of the date, for they have placed it on record that in the fifteenth year of Domitian, in company with *many* others, *Flavia Domitilla, the daughter of a sister of Flavius Clemens* who was one of the *consuls* at Rome at that time, was committed by way of punishment *to the island of Pontia because of her testimony* for Christ.

19   Now when this Domitian gave orders that those who were of the family of David should be put to death, it is recorded in an ancient authority that some heretics brought an accusation against the descendants *of Jude,* who was the Saviour's *brother after the flesh, on the ground that* they were of *the family of David,* and that they bore kinship to Christ Himself. This is shown by Hegesippus, who speaks as follows in these very words:

20.1 But there still survived of the family of the Lord the grandsons of Jude, His brother after the flesh, as he was called. These they informed against, as being of the family of David; and the *evocatus* brought them before Domitian Caesar. For he feared

2 the coming of the Christ, as did also Herod. And he asked them if they were of David's line, and they acknowledged it. Then he asked them what possessions they had or what fortune they owned. And they said that between the two of them they had only nine thousand denarii, half belonging to each of them; and this they asserted they had not in money, but only in thirty-nine plethra of land, so valued, from which by their own labours they both paid the taxes and supported themselves.

(Lawlor and Oulton, *Eusebius*, I, p. 79–80.)

[1] Rev. 13.18.

20.3–5 [The accused explained that Christ's kingdom was not of this world and Domitian dismissed them with contempt.]

Words in italics in 18.1–3 and in 19 come from Hegesippus, in 18.4 from "Brettius" (see following note).

We do not know to what pagan writers Eusebius refers in 18.4. In his *Chronicle* he refers to "Brettius" as a source, but the later chronicler John Malalas speaks of B. in such a way that he must have been a Christian. Eusebius is also wrong in his statement that Domitilla was niece of Flavius Clemens.

18.4. *Pontia* (?) Pandateria cf. 10.

20.1. *the* "evocatus". "The *evocati* were soldiers who had served their term, and were called upon again for military service. Here perhaps the reference is to the guardians of Domitian's bed-chamber, *the evocatus* being the one who was on duty at the moment. Hegesippus seems to have supposed that the grandsons of Jude were brought to Rome." (Lawlor and Oulton, *Eusebius*, II, p. 89.)

For the story of the grandsons of Jude, it is clear that Hegesippus is Eusebius' authority. There is no other evidence to confirm the story, but it fits well with Domitian's suspicious temper and anti-Jewish policy.

12. THE BEGINNING OF CLEMENT'S *FIRST EPISTLE TO THE CORINTHIANS*, *c.* 96

(I–III.3.)

A schism had arisen in Corinth and this letter, written by Clement in the name of the Church at Rome, was designed to attempt to end it. The first sentence of the letter may refer to persecution at the end of Domitian's reign.

I.1   Owing to the sudden and repeated misfortunes and calamities which have befallen us, brethren, we are somewhat late, we think, in concerning ourselves with the matters disputed among you, beloved, and with the sedition, so alien and out of place in God's elect, so abominable and impious, which a few impetuous and obstinate persons have enkindled to such a pitch of frenzy that your revered and famous name, deservedly loved of all men, has
2 been greatly reviled. For who that stayed with you did not make proof of your virtuous and firm faith? did not marvel at your discreet and gentle piety in Christ? did not proclaim the magnificent character of your hospitality? did not praise your perfect and secure knowledge? (Lowther Clarke, *First Epistle of Clement to the Corinthians*, p. 49.)

I.3–II.8 [Clement goes on to praise the Christian virtues of the Corinthians.]

III.1 Fame and enlargement were given you in full measure, and
the saying was fulfilled: *My beloved ate and drank and was enlarged
and waxed fat and kicked.*[1]

2   Thence came jealousy and envy, strife and sedition, persecution
3 and disorder, war and captivity. So *the dishonoured* rose up *against
the honoured,* those of no repute, against those of repute, the
foolish against the prudent, *the young against the elders.*[2] (Lowther
Clarke, op. cit., p. 50.)

On jealousy and envy, cf. 5.

13. THE CHRISTIAN MINISTRY, c. 96

(Clement, *First Epistle to the Corinthians,* XL–XLII, XLIV.)

XL.1 Now that all these things are clear to us, and we have studied
the depths of divine knowledge, we ought to do in due order all
things which the Lord hath commanded us to perform at ap-
2 pointed times. The offerings and services he has commanded to
be performed carefully, and not to be done in a haphazard or
3 disorderly way, but at fixed times and seasons. Where and by
whom he desires them to be performed he has himself fixed
according to his most excellent counsel, in order that all things
may be done in holy wise according to his good pleasure and be
4 acceptable to his will. They then who at the appointed time make
their offerings are acceptable and blessed, for following the ordi-
5 nances of the Lord they err not. For the high priest has been given
his own proper services, and the priests have been assigned their
own place, and Levites have their own ministrations. The lay man
is bound by the lay ordinances.

XLI.1 Let each of you, brethren, *in his own order*[3] give thanks to
God, with a good conscience, not exceeding the fixed rule of his
2 ministration, and with reverence. Not everywhere, brethren, are
offered the daily sacrifices or the freewill offerings, or the offerings
for sin and trespass, but in Jerusalem only. And even there they
are not offered in every place, but before the shrine at the altar,
after the offering has been examined for defects by the high priest
3 and the aforesaid ministers. Those who do anything contrary to
4 what befits his will incur death as the penalty. You see, brethren,
the greater the knowledge of which we have been accounted
worthy, the greater the danger to which we are exposed.

XLII.1 The Apostles received the Gospel for our sakes from the
2 Lord Jesus Christ; Jesus the Christ was sent from God. Christ

[1] Deut. 32.15.   [2] Isa. 3.5.   [3] 1 Cor. 15.23.

3 therefore is from God, and the Apostles are to God's will. So when
they had received their orders and had been filled with confidence
by the resurrection of our Lord Jesus Christ, and confirmed in
faith by the word of God, they went out in the confidence of the
Holy Spirit, preaching the Gospel, that the Kingdom of God was
4 about to come. So, preaching in country and city, they appointed
their firstfruits, having tested them by the Spirit, to be bishops
5 and deacons of those who should believe. And this was no novelty,
for long ago it had been written concerning bishops and deacons.
For the Scripture says in one place: *I will establish their bishops in
righteousness and their deacons in faith.*[1]

*   *   *

XLIV.1 Our Apostles also knew through our Lord Jesus Christ
2 that there would be strife over the name of the bishop's office. So
for this reason, since they had perfect foreknowledge, they appointed the aforesaid persons and subsequently gave them perma-
nence, so that, if they should fall asleep, other approved men
3 should succeed to their ministry. Men, therefore, who were
appointed by the Apostles, or subsequently by other eminent men,
with the approval of the whole Church, and have ministered
blamelessly to the flock of Christ in a humble, peaceable, and
worthy way, and have had testimony borne to them by all for
long periods—such men we consider are unjustly deposed from
4 their ministry. For it will be no small sin on our part, if we
depose from the episcopal office those who have in blameless and
5 holy wise offered the gifts. Blessed are the presbyters who have
gone before in the way, who came to a fruitful and perfect end;
for they need have no fear lest anyone depose them from their
6 assigned place. For we see that you have removed certain men of
good behaviour from a ministry blamelessly and honourably
fulfilled. (W. K. Lowther Clarke, *The First Epistle of Clement*,
pp. 71-2, 73-4, slightly altered.)

The dispute at Corinth (cf. 12) had been occasioned by the deposition of
certain ministers from their office. Clement is concerned to show how the
Christian observances must be conducted in perfect order in the proper place
and by the proper persons, even as the Jewish ones had been.

XLII. The only Christian ministers to be recognized were those appointed
by the Apostles or by their successors. There appear to be two ranks of minister, (1) elders (πρεσβύτεροι) or bishops (ἐπίσκοποι), (2) deacons. On the
succession of teachers going back to the Apostles, cf. 96, 148, 150.

The quotation of Isa. 60.17 is not in accordance with any other version. The
Revised Standard Version has, *I will make your overseers peace, and your task-
masters righteousness.*

[1] Isa. 60.17

14. THE CHRISTIANS IN BITHYNIA: PLINY'S DILEMMA, *c.* 112

(Pliny, *Epp.* X.96.)

Pliny was sent to Bithynia, instead of the usual Senatorial governor, *c.* 112 by Trajan to reorganize the affairs of the province, particularly those of the self-governing cities, which had fallen into a deplorable state through the mismanagement of "local authorities". The extant correspondence between him and the Emperor shows Pliny to be "upright and conscientious, but irresolute, pedantic, and totally unable to think and act for himself in any unusual circumstances" (Mackail, *Latin Literature*, p. 225). The Christians were one of the unusual circumstances.

1   It is my custom, lord emperor, to refer to you all questions whereof I am in doubt. Who can better guide me when I am at a stand, or enlighten me if I am in ignorance? In investigations of Christians I have never taken part; hence I do not know what is the crime usually punished or investigated, or what allowances
2   are made. So I have had no little uncertainty whether there is any distinction of age, or whether the very weakest offenders are treated exactly like the stronger; whether pardon is given to those who repent, or whether a man who has once been a Christian gains nothing by having ceased to be such; whether punishment attaches to the mere name apart from secret crimes, or to the secret crimes connected with the name. Meantime this is the course I have taken with those who were accused before me as
3   Christians. I asked them whether they were Christians, and if they confessed, I asked them a second and third time with threats of punishment. If they kept to it, I ordered them for execution; for I held no question that whatever it was that they admitted, in any case obstinacy and unbending perversity deserve to be
4   punished. There were others of the like insanity; but as these were Roman citizens, I noted them down to be sent to Rome.

Before long, as is often the case, the mere fact that the charge was taken notice of made it commoner, and several distinct cases
5   arose. An unsigned paper was presented, which gave the names of many. As for those who said that they neither were nor ever had been Christians, I thought it right to let them go, since they recited a prayer to the gods at my dictation, made supplication with incense and wine to your statue, which I had ordered to be brought into court for the purpose together with the images of the gods, and moreover cursed Christ—things which (so it is

said) those who are really Christians cannot be made to do.
6 Others who were named by the informer said that they were
Christians and then denied it, explaining that they had been, but
had ceased to be such, some three years ago, some a good many
years, and a few even twenty. All these too both worshipped your
statue and the images of the gods, and cursed Christ.

7   They maintained, however, that the amount of their fault or
error had been this, that it was their habit on a fixed day to
assemble before daylight and recite by turns a form of words to
Christ as a god; and that they bound themselves with an oath,
not for any crime, but not to commit theft or robbery or adultery,
not to break their word, and not to deny a deposit when demanded. After this was done, their custom was to depart, and
to meet again to take food, but ordinary and harmless food; and
even this (they said) they had given up doing after the issue of
my edict, by which in accordance with your commands I had
8 forbidden the existence of clubs. On this I considered it the more
necessary to find out from two maid-servants who were called
deaconesses, and that by torments, how far this was true: but I
discovered nothing else than a perverse and extravagant superstition. I therefore adjourned the case and hastened to consult you.
9 The matter seemed to me worth deliberation, especially on
account of the number of those in danger; for many of all ages
and every rank, and also of both sexes are brought into present or
future danger. The contagion of that superstition has penetrated
not the cities only, but the villages and country; yet it seems pos-
10 sible to stop it and set it right. At any rate it is certain enough that
the almost deserted temples begin to be resorted to, that long dis-
used ceremonies of religion are restored, and that fodder for
victims finds a market, whereas buyers till now were very few.
From this it may easily be supposed, what a multitude of men can
be reclaimed, if there be a place of repentance. (H. M. Gwatkin,
Selections from Early Christian Writers, pp. 27–31, altered.)

We have no information about the early propagation of Christianity in
Bithynia. The province is included in the list in 1 Pet. 1.1.

Notwithstanding Pliny's diffidence, he knew quite well what to do with
Christians, i.e. have them executed. As time went on however, being "upright
and conscientious", he naturally felt doubts because some of those accused
must have appeared such unlikely people to be guilty of something wicked,
or of the "crimes attached to the name". But he had already condemned those
who were obstinate Christians.

3. *I asked them a second and third time* . . . "Roman law did not accept a *single*
confession of a prisoner as proof of guilt, unless the confession was supported

by external proof, but required the confession to be repeated." (Pritchard and Bernard, *Pliny's Selected Letters*, ad loc.)

obstinacy and unbending perversity: "The feature of Christianity which Pliny here points out as his personal reason for punishing, was exactly the point which, as Christianity grew, made it seem politically dangerous to the authority of the empire . . ." (E. G. Hardy, *Pliny's Correspondence with Trajan*, ad loc.), cf. 112.

7. The information given by the apostates shows that the Christians met regularly on two separate occasions:

(1) *before daylight*: the meetings had got to take place before work started for the day, or after it had ceased. The first meeting mentioned was for worship: "to recite a form of words" (*carmen dicere*) may mean "to sing a hymn".

they bound themselves with an oath (*sacramentum*). Pliny understands the apostates thus, but in using *sacramentum* they may quite well have meant "sacrament".

(2) Later, probably in the evening, for the *Agape*, now distinct from the Eucharist, which was no longer taken at a meal time. (Pritchard and Bernard, op. cit., ad loc.) From the apostates Pliny discovered that reports of cannibalism among Christians were unfounded.

Some of Pliny's informants must have apostatized within the period of his governorship, or else they must have remained in close touch with the Christians, as they knew that the Christians, to avert suspicion from themselves, had given up their *Agape*.

clubs (*Hetaeriae* (Greek) or *Collegia* (Latin)). "The right of voluntary association for some purpose of common interest not inconsistent with good citizenship was freely recognized in the Roman realm. Such organizations might be for business, social, charitable, or religious purposes" (Merrill, *Essays in Early Christian History*, p. 52f.). Some *collegia* were *licita*, i.e. authorized, they had received official sanction: most were *illicita*, unauthorized. That does not mean "prohibited", but it does mean that action might be taken against them if they proved centres of political disaffection as happened on various occasions in Roman history (Hardy, op. cit., ad loc.). Other correspondence of Pliny and Trajan shows that the *collegia* had a bad reputation in Bithynia, and were probably in no small degree responsible for the rotten condition of the province. (*Epp.* XXXII and XXXIII, XCII and XCIII.)

Many have thought that the Christians were punished for being a *collegium illicitum*; this idea may cover part of the truth, but quite clearly it was not for this reason that Pliny condemned Christians.

8. *deaconesses* (*Ministrae*), cf. Rom. 16.1.

10. *fodder for victims*: "the farmers who brought into the various markets food for the temple victims were in danger of being ruined" (Hardy, op. cit., ad loc.); cf. Acts 19.23ff. for another instance of Christianity being bad for business. But G. E. M. de Ste Croix in *Past and Present*, No. 27, 1964, translates, "the flesh of the sacred victims" finds etc., which makes excellent sense.

15. TRAJAN'S REPLY TO PLINY
(Pliny, *Ep.* X.97.)

1 You have adopted the proper course, my dear Secundus, in your examination of the cases of those who were accused to you as Christians, for indeed nothing can be laid down as a general
2 ruling involving something like a set form of procedure. They are not to be sought out; but if they are accused and convicted, they must be punished—yet on this condition, that whoso denies himself to be a Christian, and makes the fact plain by his action, that is, by worshipping our gods, shall obtain pardon on his repentance, however suspicious his past conduct may be. Papers, however, which are presented unsigned ought not to be admitted in any charge, for they are a very bad example and unworthy of our time. (Gwatkin, *Selections from Early Christian Writers*, p. 31, slightly altered.)

1. *Nothing can be laid down as a general rule* . . . Trajan used this policy in dealing with other matters (*Ep.* LXVI, CXIII).
2. *They are not to be sought out.* . . . "What a decision, how inevitably entangled! He says they must not be sought out, implying they are innocent; and he orders them to be punished, implying they are guilty. He spares them and rages against them, he pretends not to see and punishes." (Tertullian, *Apology*, 2.8, Tr. T. R. Glover (Loeb Library).) Tertullian's conclusion is a natural one, but there was a great deal of sense in Trajan's decision. It avoided constant difficulties such as those with which Pliny had been faced, while retaining sanctions that could be imposed if necessary. The pardon granted to apostates shows that it was the "name" that was attacked.

Trajan's decision, in so far as it released Christians from anonymous accusations, worked in their favour.

16. *RESCRIPT* OF HADRIAN TO CAIUS MINUCIUS FUNDANUS, PROCONSUL OF ASIA, *c.* 125
(From the original Latin as given by Rufinus, in his translation of Eusebius, *H.E.* IV.9.)

1 I received the letter written to me by your predecessor, the most illustrious Serenius Granianus, and it is not my pleasure to pass by without inquiry the matter referred to me, lest both the innocent should be disturbed, and an opportunity for plunder

2 afforded to slanderous informers. Now, if our subjects of the Provinces are able to sustain by evidence this their petition against the Christians, so as to accuse them before a Court of Justice, I have no objection to their taking this course. But I do not allow them to use mere clamorous demands and outcries for this purpose. For it is much more equitable, if any one wishes to accuse them, for you to take cognizance of the matters laid to their 3 charge. If therefore any one accuses and proves that the aforesaid men do anything contrary to the laws, you will also determine their punishments in accordance with their offences. You will on the other hand, by Hercules, take particular care that if any one demand a writ of accusation against any of these Christians, merely for the sake of libelling them, you proceed against that man with heavier penalties, in accordance with his heinous guilt. (*L.F.*, altered.)

The increase in numbers and popularity of a religious sect which did not afford reciprocal toleration to the pagan deities, and was (unlike the Jews) international, caused the pagans to raise tumults against them, particularly in times of public stress (cf. 21 (Eusebius, *H.E.* V.1.4–7)). Naturally such disturbances would cause great anxiety to provincial governors. Unfortunately we do not possess the letter of Granianus to Hadrian, but it is clear that the Emperor preserves the principle laid down by Trajan; nothing was to be allowed against the Christians except on regular accusation. It looks as though Granianus had written to Hadrian after being faced with tumultuous demands for action.

3. Granianus may have raised the question, "They say that Christians commit cannibalism, incest, sacrilege, etc." Hadrian replies, "if found guilty of these crimes they are to be punished in accordance with their offences." Justin (*Apol.* I.68) regards this rescript as securing the Christians from persecution, as does Melito of Sardis (44).

The position of an accusation of Christianity alone is left obscure. Clearly non-Christians had been accused of Christianity, cf. 14 (sect. 5), and Hadrian is anxious to safeguard these.

17. JEWISH PERSECUTION OF CHRISTIANS IN THE LAST JEWISH REVOLT, 132–135

(Justin, *Apology*, I.31.)

For in the Jewish war which lately raged, Barcochba, the leader of the revolt of the Jews, gave orders that Christians alone should be led to cruel punishments, unless they would deny Jesus Christ and utter blasphemy. (A.-N. C. L.)

The Christians could not support the Messianic pretensions of Barcochba, cf. Eusebius, *Chronicle*, ad ann. Abr. 2149.

A brief letter of Barcochba found in 1952 at Murabba'at, about 16 miles S.E. of Jerusalem, deals with the Galileans, and the attitude of some of his followers to them. But the letter is variously interpreted. (See *Revue Biblique*, 60 (1953) pp. 276–94; ibid. 61 (1954) pp. 191–2; ibid. 63 (1956) pp. 44–8.) For the letter itself see, e.g., J. M. Allegro, *The Dead Sea Scrolls*, illustration no. 7.

18. THE MARTYRDOM OF POLYCARP, 22 FEBRUARY 156

(*The Martyrdom of Polycarp*. Text in Lightfoot, *Apostolic Fathers*, II.iii, pp. 363–401: Lake, *Apostolic Fathers* (Loeb Library), II, pp. 312–45.)

The Church of God sojourning at Smyrna to the Church of God sojourning at Philomelium, and to all the sojournings of the Holy Catholic Church in every place, mercy and peace and love of God the Father and of our Lord Jesus Christ be multiplied.

I.1 We write to you, brethren, the account of the martyrs and of the blessed Polycarp, who, by his martyrdom set his seal as it were upon the persecution, and put an end to it. For nearly all the preceding events came to pass in order that to us the Lord might once again give an example of the martyrdom which resembles the Gospel story.

2 For he waited that he might be betrayed, just as was the Lord, that we too may become imitators of Him, regarding not only what concerns ourselves but also what concerns our neighbours.[1]

For it is the part of true and constant love that a man should wish not only himself, but also all the brethren to be saved.

II.1 Now blessed and noble are all the martyrdoms which have taken place in accordance with the will of God; for we are bound to be very reverent and to ascribe the power over all things to

2 God. And who could fail to admire their nobility and endurance and love for their Master? Some were so torn by the scourges that the structure of their flesh to the inner veins and arteries was exposed to view; but they endured it, so that even the bystanders were moved to pity and lamentation. Some reached such a pitch of noble endurance that not one of them let cry or groan escape him, showing to us all that in the hours of their torture Christ's martyrs were absent from the flesh, or rather that standing by

[1] Cf. Phil. 2.4.

3 their side their Lord conversed with them. So, giving heed to the grace of Christ, they despised the torments of the world, by a single hour purchasing eternal life. Cold to them was the fire of the cruel tormentors; for they kept before their eyes their escape from the fire that is everlasting and is never quenched, while with the eyes of the heart they looked up at the good things reserved for them that have endured, which *neither ear hath heard nor eye seen, neither have entered into the heart of man*,[1] but were being shown by the Lord to those who were now already no 4 longer men but angels. In like manner they that were condemned to the beasts underwent awful punishments, being stretched on sharp shells and punished with various other forms of torture, that, if it were possible, by means of protracted punishment the tyrant might induce them to denial. For the devil devised many wiles against them.

III.1 But thanks be to God, for he did not prevail against any. For the right noble Germanicus, by means of his endurance, turned their cowardice into courage. With signal distinction did he fight against the beasts. While the Proconsul, wishing to persuade him, was urging him to have compassion on his youth, in his eagerness to be released the sooner from their unrighteous and lawless mode of life he used force to the wild beast and pulled it on himself. 2 Now it was on this that all the multitude, amazed at the noble conduct of the Godloving and Godfearing race of the Christians, shouted out, "Away with the Atheists. Search for Polycarp."

IV.1 But one of them, Quintus by name, a Phrygian, lately arrived from Phrygia, when he saw the beasts, was afraid. It was he who had forced both himself and certain others to come forward of their own accord. After very earnest entreaty he had been persuaded by the Proconsul to take the oath and offer incense. Therefore brethren, we do not commend those who surrender themselves, for not such is the teaching of the Gospel.[2]

V.1 Now the most admirable Polycarp so soon as he heard the news showed no dismay, but wished to remain in town. The majority, however, prevailed on him to withdraw. And withdraw he did, to a little farm not far from the city. There he spent his time with a few companions, occupied night and day in nothing but prayer for all men, and for the Churches throughout the world, as indeed was his constant habit. And while praying he 2 fell into a trance three days before his apprehension, and he saw his pillow being burned by fire. And he turned and said to his companions, "I must needs be burned alive."

[1] 1 Cor. 2.9.   [2] Cf. Matt. 10.23.

VI.1   As his pursuers were persistent, he shifted his quarters to another farm. Immediately the pursuers arrived (i.e. at his first hiding
place) and, on failing to find him, they seized two slave-boys. One

2 of these confessed under torture. For indeed it was impossible for
him to evade pursuit, since they that betrayed him were of his own
household.[1] And the Chief Constable, who, as it befell, bore the
same name as Herod, made haste to bring Polycarp into the
stadium, that he might be made a partner of Christ, and so fulfil
his own appointed lot, and that his betrayers might undergo the
punishment of Judas himself.

VII.1   Accordingly, having the lad with them, on Friday at about
supper-time there went out constables and mounted men, with
their usual equipment, hurrying as *against a thief*.[2] Late in the day
they came up in a body and found him in a cottage lying in an
upper room. He could have escaped thence to another place,

2 but he refused, saying, *God's will be done*.[3] So, on hearing of their
arrival, he came down and conversed with them, while they
wondered at his age and his constancy, and at there being so
much haste about the arrest of such an old man. Upon this he
gave orders for something to be served for them to eat and drink,
at that hour, as much as they wanted. He asked them to give him

3 an hour, that he might pray undisturbed. On their granting him
this he stood up and prayed, being so full of the grace of God, that
for the space of two hours he could not hold his peace, and the
hearers were astonished, and many were sorry that they had
come after so venerable an old man.

VIII.1   After remembering all, both small and great, high and low,
who had ever come his way, and all the Catholic Church throughout the world, at last he brought his prayer to an end. The time
had come for departure. They set him on an ass and brought him

2 into the city, it being a high Sabbath. He was met by the Chief
Constable Herod and Nicetes, his father, who shifted him into
their carriage, and tried to persuade him as they sat by his side,
urging, "Why, what harm is there in saying 'Caesar is Lord,' and
sacrificing, and the rest of it, and so saving yourself?" At first he
made no reply, but, as they were persistent, he said, "I do not

3 intend to do what you advise me." On their failing to persuade
him they began to use terrible language and pushed him out so
hastily that as he was getting down from the carriage he scraped
his shin. Without turning round, as though he had suffered no
hurt, he walked on with speed, and was taken to the stadium,
where there was so great a din that it was impossible for any one
to be heard.

[1] Cf. Matt. 10.36.   [2] Matt. 26.55.   [3] Cf. Acts 21.14; Matt. 6.10.

IX.1 As Polycarp was entering the stadium, there came a voice to him from heaven, *Be strong*, Polycarp, *and play the man.*[1] The speaker indeed no one saw, but the voice was heard by those of our friends who were present. Then he was brought forward, and great was the din as they heard that Polycarp was arrested.

2 So he was brought before the Proconsul, who asked him if he were Polycarp? He said "Yes," and the Proconsul tried to persuade him to deny his faith, urging, "Have respect to your old age," and the rest of it, according to the customary form, "Swear by the genius of Caesar; change your mind; say, 'Away with the Atheists!'" Then Polycarp looked with a stern countenance on the multitude of lawless heathen gathered in the stadium, and waved his hands at them, and looked up to heaven with a groan,

3 and said, "Away with the Atheists." The Proconsul continued insisting and saying, "Swear, and I release you; curse Christ." And Polycarp said, "Eighty-six years have I served Him, and He has done me no wrong: how then can I blaspheme my King who saved me?"

X.1 The Proconsul continued to persist and to say, "Swear by the genius of Caesar;" he answered, "If you vainly imagine that I would 'swear by the genius of Caesar', as you say, pretending that you are ignorant who I am, hear plainly that I am a Christian. And if you are willing to learn the doctrine of Christianity,

2 appoint a day, and listen." The Proconsul said, "Persuade the people." Polycarp then said, "You, indeed, I should have deemed worthy of argument, for we have been taught to render to authorities and powers ordained by God, honour as is meet, so long as it does us no harm, but as for those, I do not think them worthy of my making my defence to them."

XI.1 The Proconsul said, "I have wild beasts; if you will not change your mind I will throw you to them." Then he said, "Bid them be brought: change of mind from better to worse is not a change that we are allowed; but to change from wrong to right

2 is good." Then again said the Proconsul to him, "If you despise the beasts, unless you change your mind, I shall have you burnt," But Polycarp said: "You threaten the fire that burns for an hour, and after a little while is quenched; for you are ignorant of the fire of the judgement to come, and of everlasting punishment reserved for the ungodly. But why delay? Do what you wish."

XII.1 While speaking these words and many more he was filled with courage and gladness: his face grew full of grace, so that not only did it not fall, agitated at all that was being said to him, but on the contrary the Proconsul was amazed, and sent his own

[1] Josh. 1.6,7,9.

herald to make proclamation in the middle of the stadium thrice,
2 "Polycarp has confessed himself to be a Christian." No sooner
was this proclaimed by the herald than the whole multitude, both
of Gentiles and of Jews dwelling at Smyrna, with ungovernable
rage and a loud voice began to yell—"This is the teacher of Asia,
the father of the Christians, the destroyer of our Gods, the man
who teaches many not to sacrifice or worship." With these words
they kept up their shout and continued asking Philip the Asiarch
3 to let loose a lion at Polycarp. But he said he could not as he had
closed the games. Thereupon they thought good to yell with one
accord that he should burn Polycarp alive. For the vision about
his pillow must needs be fulfilled, when he saw it burning while
he was at prayer, and he turned round and said prophetically to
the faithful who were with him, "I must needs be burnt alive."

XIII.1 This then happened with great speed; the mob in a moment
got together logs and faggots from the workshops and baths;
2 the Jews as usual showed themselves specially zealous in the work.
When the pyre had been made ready, Polycarp took off all his
upper garments, and untied his girdle. He endeavoured also to
take off his shoes, though he had never been in the habit of doing
this, because every one of the faithful was eager to be the first to
touch his bare body. Because of the goodness of his life he had
been treated with every honour even before his head was white.
3 Forthwith then all the gear adapted for the pyre was put about
him. They were on the point of fastening him with nails, but he
said, "Let me be as I am: He that gives me power to abide the
fire will grant me too without your making me fast with nails to
stay at the pyre unflinching."

XIV.1 So they did not nail him, but they bound him. He put his
hands behind him and was bound, like a goodly ram out of a great
flock for an offering, a whole burnt offering made ready and
acceptable to God. Then he looked up to heaven and said, "O
Lord God Almighty, Father of Thy beloved and blessed child
Jesus Christ, through whom we have received our knowledge of
Thee, God of Angels and Powers and of all creation and of the
2 whole race of the righteous who live before Thy face, I bless Thee
in that Thou hast deemed me worthy of this day and hour; that I
might take a portion among the martyrs in the cup of Christ, *to
the resurrection* of eternal *life*[1] both of soul and body in the incorruption of the Holy Ghost. Among these may I to-day be
welcome before Thy face as a rich and acceptable sacrifice as Thou
didst prepare and manifest beforehand and didst fulfil, Thou the
3 faithful and true God. For this cause, and for all things I praise
[1] John 5.29.

Thee, I bless Thee, I glorify Thee through the everlasting and heavenly High Priest Jesus Christ Thy beloved Son, through Whom to Thee with Him and with the Holy Ghost be glory now and for the ages to come. Amen."

XV.1 When he had offered up his Amen and completed his prayer, those in charge kindled the fire. A great flame flashed out, and we to whom the sight was granted, saw a marvel; and we moreover were preserved to the end that we might tell to the rest what came
2 to pass. The fire made the appearance of a vaulted roof, like a ship's sail filling out with the wind, and it walled about the body of the martyr in a ring. There was it in the midst, not like flesh burning, but like a loaf baking, or like gold and silver being refined in a furnace. Moreover we caught a fragrance as of the breath of frankincense or some other precious spice.

XVI.1 In the end, when the lawless mob had seen that his body could not be consumed by the fire they commanded an executioner to go and stab him with a dagger. He did this and there came out [a dove and] so much blood that it put out the fire, and all the multitude marvelled at the mighty difference between the
2 unbelievers and the elect, of whom one was this man, the most admirable Polycarp, who in our times was an apostolic and prophetic teacher, bishop of the Holy Church in Smyrna; for every word which he uttered from his mouth was accomplished and will be accomplished.

XVII.1 But when the jealous, envious evil one, the adversary of the race of the righteous, saw both the majesty of his martyrdom and his blameless career from the beginning, and that he was crowned with the crown of incorruption and had carried off a prize which could not be gainsaid, he contrived that not even his poor body should be taken up by us, though many were desirous
2 to do so and to come into communion with his holy flesh. So he prompted Nicetes, father of Herod and brother of Alce, to entreat the magistrate not to grant his body, lest, as he said, we should forsake the Crucified, and begin to worship this man. They said this through the prompting and persistence of the Jews, who even kept watch, when we were about to try to take him out of the fire, ignorant that it will never at any time be possible for us to abandon Christ—who, blameless on behalf of sinners, suffered for the salvation of them that are being saved, throughout the
3 whole world—and to worship some other. For Him, as Son of God, we adore; the martyrs, as disciples and imitators of the Lord, we reverence as they deserve on account of their unsurpassable loyalty to their own King and Teacher. God grant us to be made sharers alike of their lot and of their discipleship.

XVIII.1   When the centurion saw the contentiousness caused by the Jews, he put him in the midst, and, as their custom is, burned 2 him. So we afterwards took up his bones, more valuable than precious stones and finer than gold, and laid them where it was 3 fitting. There the Lord will permit us, as shall be possible to us, to assemble ourselves together in joy and gladness, and to celebrate the birthday of his martyrdom, alike in memory of them that have fought before, and for the training and preparation of them that are to fight hereafter.

XIX.1   Thus it befell the blessed Polycarp, who was martyred with them that came from Philadelphia, himself and eleven others, in Smyrna, and is himself alone held in all men's memory, so that even by the heathen he is everywhere spoken of as one who was not merely an illustrious teacher, but also a conspicuous martyr. His martyrdom all men are eager to copy, in that it came to pass 2 according to the Gospel of Christ. Through his patience he overcame the unrighteous ruler, and thus received the crown of incorruption. Rejoicing with Apostles and all just men, he glorifies our Almighty God and Father, and blesses our Lord Jesus Christ, Saviour of our souls, and Helmsman of our bodies, and Shepherd of the Catholic Church throughout the world.

*   *   *

XXI.1   The blessed Polycarp was martyred on the second day of the first part of the month Xanthicus, on the seventh day before the Kalends of March, at the eighth hour, on a great Sabbath. He was arrested by Herod in the Chief Priestship of Philip of Tralles, in the proconsulship of Statius Quadratus, but in the everlasting reign of Jesus Christ; to Whom be honour, glory, dominion and an everlasting throne from generation to generation. Amen. (B. Jackson, *St Polycarp*, 49–74, much altered, chiefly from the versions of Lake (Loeb Library) and E. C. E. Owen, *Some Authentic Acts of the Early Martyrs*.)

The date of the martyrdom:

"The date of the martyrdom of Polycarp is fixed by the chronicle of Eusebius as 166–167, but this date has now been almost universally abandoned, as according to the letter to the church at Smyrna, Polycarp's martyrdom was on Saturday, Xanthicus 2, that is Feb. 23, in the proconsulship of Statius Quadratus, and from a reference in Aelius Aristides, Waddington (*Mémoire sur la chronologie de la vie du rhéteur, Aelius Aristide*, Paris, 1864) showed that Quadratus became proconsul of Asia in 153–4. Now, Feb. 23 fell on a Saturday in 155. It is therefore suggested that Feb. 23, 155, was the date of the martyrdom. The question however is complicated by the statement in the letter that the day of the martyrdom was a great Sabbath. This may mean the Jewish feast Purim, and Purim in 155 was not on Feb. 23. Mr C. H. Turner has argued in *Studia Biblica*, II, pp. 105ff., that Purim, Feb. 22, 156, is the real date and that the Roman reckoning which regards Xanthicus 2 as equivalent to Feb. 23 is a mistake due to neglect to consider fully the complicated system of intercalation in the Asian calendar. More recently Prof. E. Schwartz has argued in the *Abhandlungen der königlichen Gesellschaft der Wissenschaften zu Göttingen*, VIII (1905), 6, pp. 125ff., that the 'great Sabbath' can only mean the Sabbath after the Passover (cf. John 19.31), and that owing to the local customs of the Jews in Smyrna this was on Feb. 22 in the year 156 A.D. He thus reaches the same result as Turner, but by a different method." (K. Lake, *Apostolic Fathers* (Loeb Library), II, pp. 310–11.)

But it should be noted that the above sketch of the problem does not provide a final solution and that Grégoire (*Analecta Bollandiana*, Tom. LXIX (1951), pp. 1–38) makes the date 177, and W. Telfer (*J.T.S.* (N.S.), III.1 (1952), pp. 79–83) suggests 168. Eusebius places Polycarp's martyrdom, in his *Church History* and in his *Chronicle*, under Marcus Aurelius.

Some reject Ch. XXI as a trustworthy historical source. If it is rejected the reference to the governorship of Statius Quadratus is worthless.

Philomelium is a town in Phrygia.

I.1. *which resembles the Gospel story*: "The writer desires to bring out the points of resemblance to the Passion of Christ. The coincidences are remarkable, but none are in themselves at all improbable." (Lake, *Apostolic Fathers* (Loeb Library), II, p. 319n.)

IV.1. In general the Church opposed the idea that Christians should, of their own volition, court martyrdom, cf. 142.

VIII.2. *Caesar is Lord*: "In a certain sense κύριος Καῖσαρ might have been said innocently, but as intended, it was a direct negation of κύριος Ἰησοῦς and a virtual deification of the emperor." (Lightfoot, *Apostolic Fathers*, II. 3, p. 375.)

IX.2. *Swear by the genius of Caesar*: "genius"=fortune, tutelary spirit: "The *genius* as such is always good, and the source of the good gifts and hours which brighten the life of the individual man, and also the source of his physical and mental health, in a word, his good spirit: hence the oaths and conjurings by one's own genius or that of another." (Preller, *Rom. Myth.*, p. 567, quoted by Wilkins on Horace, *Epistles*, I.7.94.)

3. *Eighty-six years*: in the ancient world the age of old men was often not known accurately: the birthday was known, but the actual age was forgotten. So the age of Polycarp must remain problematical.

X.2. *Persuade the people*: "it is not clear with what motive the proconsul says this: whether (1) like Pilate, with a sincere desire to release the prisoner, or (2) as an excuse for his execution, knowing such an appeal to be useless." (Lightfoot, op. cit., p. 381.)

XII.2. *Jews dwelling at Smyrna*: Jews took a prominent part in persecution of the Christians. A well-known reference is in Tertullian, *Scorp.* 10, "synagogues of the Jews, sources of persecutions". Cf. also 17 above. For Jews at Smyrna, cf. Lightfoot, op. cit., pp. 382–3.

Philip the Asiarch: Philip (of Tralles, cf. XXI below) was one of the most prominent provincials of this time, cf. Lightfoot's note: "The Asiarch was the head of the *Commune Asiae*, the confederation of the provincial cities of the Roman province of Asia. As such he was the 'chief-priest' of Asia (XXI below) and president of the games." (Lightfoot, op. cit., p. 383.)

XVI.1. [*a dove and*]: "Whether this formed part of the original text or not, it must be explained by the belief that the human soul departed from the body at death in the form of a bird." (Lightfoot, op. cit., p. 390.)

XVII.2. *Alce*: Ignatius twice mentions a Christian of Smyrna of this name, and the mention of Alce in this passage must surely refer to a Christian.

It is natural that the pagans should misunderstand the honour shown to the martyrs.

XXI.1. *in the everlasting reign of Jesus Christ*: "this phrase is pointedly inserted instead of a reference to the reigning Emperor". (Lake, op. cit., p. 341n.)

19. THE MARTYRDOM OF PTOLEMY AND LUCIUS, *c.* 160 (?)

(Justin, *Apology*, II.2.)

A certain woman lived with a licentious husband; she herself had formerly been licentious too. But when she came to the knowledge of the teachings of Christ she became sober-minded, and endeavoured to persuade her husband likewise to be temperate, citing the teaching of Christ, and assuring him that there shall be punishment in eternal fire inflicted upon those who do not live temperately and with right reason. But he continued in the same excesses and alienated his wife by his actions. For she, considering it wicked to live any longer as a wife with a husband who sought in every way means of indulging in pleasure contrary to the law of nature and in violation of what is right, wished to be divorced from him. And when she was over-persuaded by her friends, who advised her still to continue with him, in the idea that some time or other her husband might give hope of amendment, she did violence to her own feeling and remained with him. But when her husband had gone to Alexandria, and was reported to be conducting himself worse than ever, she—that she might not, by continuing in matrimonial connection with him, and by sharing his bed and his board, become a partaker also in his wickednesses and impieties—gave him what you call a bill of divorce, and was separated from him. But this "gentleman" her husband—while he ought to have been rejoicing that she had now given up those actions which formerly she unhesitatingly committed with the slaves and hirelings, when she delighted in drunkenness and every vice, and desired that he too should give up the same,—when she had gone from him without his desire, brought an accusation against her, affirming that she was a Christian. And she presented a petition to you, the Emperor, requesting that first she be permitted to arrange her affairs, and afterwards to make her defence against the accusation, when her affairs were set in order. And this you granted. And her quondam husband, since he was now no longer able to prosecute her turned on a man named Ptolemy, whom Urbicus punished, and who had been her teacher in the Christian doctrines. And this he did in the following way. He persuaded a centurion—who had cast Ptolemy into prison, and who was friendly to himself—to take Ptolemy and interrogate him on this sole point: whether he were a Christian? And Ptolemy, being a lover of truth, and not of a deceitful or false disposition, when he confessed himself to be a Christian, was bound by the centurion, and for a long time punished in the prison. And, at last, when the man was brought before Urbicus, just as before he was asked this one question only: whether he was a Christian? And again, being conscious of the benefits that had accrued to him through the teaching of Christ, he confessed his discipleship in the divine virtue. For he who denies anything, either denies it because he condemns the thing itself, or he shrinks from confession because he is conscious of his own unworthiness or alienation from it; neither of which cases is that of the true Christian. And when Urbicus ordered him to be led away to punishment, one Lucius, who was also himself a Christian, seeing the unreasonable judgement that had thus been given, said to Urbicus: "What is the ground of this judgement? Why have you punished this man, not as an adulterer, nor fornicator, nor murderer, nor thief, nor robber, nor convicted of any crime at all, but who has only confessed that he is called by the name of Christian? This judgement of yours, O Urbicus, does not become the Emperor Pius, nor the philosopher, the son of Caesar, nor the sacred senate." And he said nothing else in answer to Lucius than this: "You also seem to me to be such an one." And when Lucius answered, "Most certainly I am," he ordered him also to be led away. And he professed his thanks, knowing that he was delivered from such wicked rulers, and was going to the Father and King of the heavens. And still a third having come forward was condemned to be punished. (A.-N. C. L., altered.)

This passage shows well the disabilities of a "mixed" marriage (cf. Tertullian, *To his wife*, 2.3–6), the power of private hatred in attacks on Christians, and the summary method of condemnation adopted by a hostile judge who gave no opportunity for recantation.

The date is uncertain; Justin's *Second Apology* was clearly written soon after these events. It may be as early as 152, or as late as 161.

20. THE MARTYRDOM OF JUSTIN AND HIS COMPANIONS, 165

(*Acta Sancti Justini et sociorum*: Text in O. von Gebhardt, *Acta Martyrum Selecta*, pp. 18–21; Knopf-Krüger, *Ausgewählte Märtyrerakten*, ed. 3, pp. 15–17.)

1   In the time of the wicked defenders of idolatry impious decrees were issued in town and country against the pious Christian folk to compel them to offer libations to vain idols. So the saints were seized and brought before the prefect of Rome, by name Rusticus.

2   When they were brought before the judgement seat, Rusticus the prefect said to Justin: "First of all obey the gods, and make submission to the Princes."

Justin said: "To obey the commands of our Saviour Jesus Christ is not worthy of blame or condemnation."

The prefect Rusticus said: "What doctrines do you hold?"

Justin said: "I have endeavoured to make myself acquainted with all doctrines, but I have given my assent to the true doctrines of the Christians, whether they please the holders of false beliefs or no."

The prefect Rusticus said: "Do those doctrines please you, you wretch?"

Justin said: "Yes, for the belief in accordance with which I follow them is right."

The prefect Rusticus said: "What belief do you mean?"

Justin said: "That which we religiously profess concerning the God of the Christians, in whom we believe, one God, existing from the beginning, Maker and Artificer of the whole creation, seen and unseen; and concerning our Lord Jesus Christ, the Son of God, who has also been proclaimed aforetime by the prophets as about to come to the race of men for herald of salvation and for master of true disciples. And I, being but a man, regard what

I say to be of little worth in comparison of His infinite God-head, but there is a power in prophecy, and that I acknowledge; therein hath proclamation been made aforetime of Him of whom I just spoke as the Son of God. For I know that from the beginning the prophets foretold His coming among men."

3 The prefect Rusticus said: "Where do you meet together?" Justin said: "Where each wills and can. Do you really think that we all meet in the same place? Not so: for the God of the Christians is not confined by place, but being unseen fills heaven and earth, and is worshipped and glorified by the faithful everywhere."

The prefect Rusticus said: "Tell me, where do ye meet, or in what place do you gather your disciples?"

Justin said: "I lodge above in the house of Martin, near the baths of Timothy,[1] and during all this time (this is my second visit to Rome) I have known no other place of meeting but his house. And if any wished to come to me, I imparted to him the word of truth."

Rusticus said: "To come to the point then, are you a Christian?"

Justin said: "Yes, I am a Christian."

4 The prefect Rusticus said to Chariton: "Tell me further, Chariton, are you also a Christian?"

Chariton said: "I am a Christian by God's command."

The prefect Rusticus said to Charito: "What do you say, Charito?"

Charito said: "I am a Christian by God's gift."

Rusticus said to Euelpistus: "And what are you?"

Euelpistus, a slave of Caesar, answered: "I also am a Christian, freed by Christ, and share by the grace of Christ in the same hope."

The prefect Rusticus said to Hierax: "Are you also a Christian?"

Hierax said: "Yes, I am a Christian, for I worship and adore the same God."

The prefect Rusticus said: "Did Justin make you Christians?"

Hierax said: "I was, and shall ever be, a Christian."

A man called Paeon stood up and said: "I also am a Christian."

The prefect Rusticus said: "Who taught you?"

Paeon said: "I received from my parents this good confession."

Euelpistus said: "I listened indeed gladly to the words of Justin, but I too received Christianity from my parents."

[1] The text is corrupt; and the location of Justin's meeting place wholly uncertain.

The prefect Rusticus said: "Where are your parents?"

Euelpistus said: "In Cappadocia."

Rusticus said to Hierax: "Where are your parents?"

He answered, saying: "Our true father is Christ, and our mother our faith in Him. My earthly parents are dead, and I was dragged away from Iconium in Phrygia before coming hither."

The prefect Rusticus said to Liberian: "And what do you say? Are you a Christian? Are you an unbeliever like the rest?"

Liberian said: "I also am a Christian; for I am a believer and adore the only true God."

5   The prefect said to Justin: "Listen, you that are said to be a learned man, and think that you are acquainted with true doctrine, if you shall be scourged and beheaded, are you persuaded that you will ascend to heaven?"

Justin said: "I hope to have His gifts if I endure these things. For I know that for all who so live there abides until the consummation of the whole world the free gift of God."

The prefect Rusticus said: "Do you then think that you will ascend to heaven, to receive certain rewards?"

Justin said: "I do not think, I know and am fully persuaded."

The prefect Rusticus said: "Let us now come to the pressing matter in hand. Agree together and sacrifice with one accord to the gods.'

Justin said: "No one who is rightly minded turns from true belief to false."

The prefect Rusticus said: "If you do not obey, you shall be punished without mercy."

Justin said: "If we are punished for the sake of our Lord Jesus Christ we hope to be saved, for this shall be our salvation and confidence before the more terrible judgement-seat of our Lord and Saviour which shall judge the whole world." So also said the other martyrs: "Do what you will. For we are Christians and offer no sacrifice to idols."

Rusticus the prefect gave sentence: "Let those who will not sacrifice to the gods and yield to the command of the Emperor be scourged and led away to be beheaded in accordance with the laws."

6   The holy martyrs went out glorifying God to the customary place and were beheaded, and fulfilled their testimony by the confession of their Saviour. And some of the faithful took their bodies by stealth and laid them in a convenient place, the grace of our Lord Jesus Christ working with them, to whom be glory for ever and ever. Amen. (E. C. E. Owen, *Some authentic Acts of the early Martyrs*, pp. 48–52, very slightly altered.)

6. *In a convenient place*: the site of their burial is not known to us.

21. THE MARTYRS OF LYONS AND VIENNE, 177

(Letter of the Churches in Eusebius, *H.E.* V.1.3–63.)

3   The servants of Christ who sojourn at Vienne and Lyons in Gaul to the brethren in Asia and Phrygia *who* have the same *faith* and hope *as we* of redemption: *peace and grace* and glory *from God the Father, and* Christ *Jesus our Lord.*[1]

4   ... Indeed we are unable, and it is beyond the power of pen, to state with exactitude the greatness of the affliction here, the mighty rage of the heathen against the saints, and all that the blessed

5   martyrs endured. For the adversary fell upon us with all his might, and gave us *already* a foretaste of what *his coming* in the future without restraint would be[2]; he left nothing undone to train and exercise beforehand his own against the servants of God, insomuch that not only were we excluded from houses and baths and market-place, but they even forbade any of us to be seen at all in any place

6   whatsoever. Nevertheless the grace of God was our captain on the other side, rescued the weak, and ranged against the foe firm pillars,[3] able by their endurance to draw upon themselves the whole attack of the evil one. And these joined battle, enduring every kind of reproach and punishment; yea, regarding their many trials as little, they hastened to Christ, truly showing *that the sufferings of this present time are not worthy to be compared with the glory which shall be revealed to us-ward.*[4]

7   First of all they nobly endured the attacks which the whole mass of the people heaped upon them, clamours, blows, halings, plunderings, stonings and confinements, and all that an infuriated

8   mob is wont to employ against foes and enemies. Then they were conducted to the market-place by the tribune and the authorities presiding over the city; and when they had been questioned before the whole multitude, and given their testimony, they were

9   shut up in prison until the governor's arrival. But afterwards, when they were brought before the governor, who used all the usual savagery against us, Vettius Epagathus, one of the brethren, a man filled with the fulness of love towards God and his neighbour, came forward. His conduct had reached such a degree of perfection that, young though he was, his reputation equalled

---

[1] Cf. 2 Pet. 1.1,2.   [2] Cf. 2 Thess. 2.7–9.   [3] Cf. 1 Tim. 3.15; Gal. 2.9.
[4] Rom. 8.18.

that of the elder Zacharias; for he had *walked in all the command-ments and ordinances of the Lord blameless*[1]; in every service to his neighbour he was untiring, *having a great zeal for God*[2] and *fervent in spirit*.[3] Such a man could not endure the passing of so groundless a judgement against us; but was exceeding angry, and requested that he himself might be heard in defence of the brethren, that
10 there is nothing godless or impious among us. Those around the tribunal cried out against him (for he was indeed a man of note), and the governor would not listen to the just request he had thus put forward, but asked him this one question, if he too were a Christian. And having confessed in a very clear voice, he also attained to the inheritance of the martyrs, being called the advo-cate of Christians, but having the *Advocate*[4] *in* himself, *the Spirit* of *Zacharias*[5]; which Spirit he showed in the fulness of *his love*, in that he was *well pleased* to *lay down even* his *own life for* the defence of *the brethren.*[6] For he was and is a true disciple of Christ, *following the Lamb whithersoever he goeth.*[7]

11   Henceforward the rest were divided; some were manifestly ready for martyrdom, and fulfilled with all zeal the confession wherein they gave witness; but others were manifestly unready and untrained and still weak, unable to bear the strain of a mighty conflict: of which number some ten proved abortions. These last wrought in us great sorrow and immeasurable mourning, and hindered the zeal of the remainder who had not yet been seized, and who in spite of every terrible suffering nevertheless attended
12 the martyrs and would not leave them. But then we were all greatly affrighted at the uncertainty of confession; not that we feared the punishments inflicted, but we looked to the issue and
13 dreaded lest any should fall away. Nevertheless those who were worthy were seized day by day, thus filling up the number of the former class, so that from the two churches were gathered all the zealous members, by whose means our position here had been
14 mainly established. And there were seized also certain of our heathen household servants, since the governor gave an official order that we should all be sought out. And they too, thanks to *the snares* of Satan,[8] in their fear of the tortures which they saw the saints enduring, and at the instigation of the soldiers, falsely accused us of Thyestean banquets and Oedipodean intercourse, and things of which it is not right for us to speak or think, nay,
15 not even to believe that the like was ever done by man. But these

---

[1] Luke 1.6.   [2] Rom. 10.2.   [3] Acts 18.25; Rom. 12.11.
[4] παράκλητος (comforter).   [5] John 14.16f.,26; Luke 1.67.
[6] 1 John 3.16; 1 Thess. 2.8.   [7] Rev. 14.4.
[8] Ign. *Trall.* 8; *Philad.* 6.

rumours spread, and all were infuriated at us, insomuch that those who had formerly acted with moderation, on the ground of friendship, were now greatly incensed and *cut to the heart*[1] against us. Thus was fulfilled that which was said by the Lord: *The* time will *come*, when *whosoever killeth you shall think that he offereth*

16 *service unto God*.[2] From that time on the holy martyrs endured punishments beyond all description, Satan earnestly endeavouring to elicit from their lips also some of the slanders.

17 But the entire fury of the crowd, governor and soldiers fell upon Sanctus, the deacon from Vienne, and upon Maturus, a noble combatant though but lately baptized, and upon Attalus, a native of Pergamum, of which church he had been always *the pillar and ground*,[3] and upon Blandina, through whom Christ showed that things which appear mean and unsightly and despicable in the eyes of men are accounted worthy of great glory in the sight of God,[4] through love towards Him, a love which

18 showed itself in power and did not boast itself in appearance.[5] For when we were all afraid, and her mistress according to the flesh[6] (who was herself also a combatant in the ranks of the martyrs) was in a state of agony, lest the weakness of her body should render her unable even to make a bold confession, Blandina was filled with such power that those who by turns kept torturing her in every way from dawn till evening were worn out and exhausted, and themselves confessed defeat from lack of aught else to do to her; they marvelled that the breath still remained in a body all mangled and covered with gaping wounds, and they testified that a single form of torture was sufficient to render life extinct, let

19 alone such and so many. But the blessed woman, like a noble champion, in confession regained her strength; and for her, to say "I am a Christian, and with us no evil finds a place" was refreshment and rest and insensibility to her lot.

20 Now as for Sanctus, he also nobly endured with surpassing and superhuman courage all the torments that human hands could inflict, and though the wicked men hoped that the continuance and severity of the tortures would cause him to utter something that he ought not, he set the battle against them with such firmness that he would not state even his own name, or the people or city whence he came, or whether he were bond or free. But to every question he replied in Latin: "I am a Christian." This he confessed again and again, instead of name and city and race and all else,

21 and no other word did the heathen hear from his lips. Hence there actually arose great contention on the part of the governor and

---

[1] Acts 5.33; 7.54.   [2] John 16.2.   [3] 1 Tim. 3.15.
[4] Cf. 1 Cor. 1.28.   [5] Cf. 2 Cor. 5.12.   [6] Cf. Eph. 6.5; Col. 3.22.

the torturers against him, with the result that finally, when
nothing else was left to inflict upon him, they applied red-hot

22 brazen plates to the most tender parts of his body. And though
these were burning, Sanctus himself remained unbending and
unyielding, and firm in his confession; for he was bedewed and
strengthened by the heavenly *fountain of the water of life*[1] which

23 issues from the bowels of Christ.[2] But his poor body was a witness
to what he had undergone—one whole wound and bruise, con-
tracted, having lost the outward form of a man—in which body
Christ suffered and accomplished mighty wonders, bringing the
adversary to nought and *showing* for the *ensample* of those that
remained[3] that nothing is to be feared where the love of the

24 Father is,[4] nothing is painful where there is the *glory of Christ*.[5]
For the wicked men after certain days again tortured the martyr,
thinking to overcome him when they applied the same instruments to limbs so swollen and enflamed that he could not bear
even the hand to touch them; or that he would die under the
tortures and so cause terror to the rest. Yet not only did nothing
of the kind occur in this case, but, contrary to all human expectation, the poor body actually arose and became erect under the
subsequent tortures, and regained its former shape and the use of
its limbs. Thus by the grace of Christ the second torturing proved

25 for him not punishment but healing. And Biblis too, one of those
who had denied, *the devil* supposed that he had already *devoured*[6];
but wishing to use her slander as a further ground of condemnation, he brought her to punishment, that he might compel an
already fragile and craven woman to state impieties concerning

26 us. She, however, regained her senses under the torture and awoke,
so to speak, out of a deep sleep, when the passing retribution
recalled to her mind the *eternal punishment*[7] in hell; and she directly
contradicted the slanderers, saying: "How could they eat their
children, who may not eat blood even of creatures without
reason?"[8] And henceforth she confessed herself a Christian, and
joined the inheritance of the martyrs.

27   Now when the tyrant's instruments of torture were brought to
nought by Christ through the endurance of the blessed ones, the
devil began to invent other devices: close confinement in prison,
in darkness and its most noisome spot; stretching the feet in the
stocks, and keeping them stretched five holes apart; and all those
other torments which his servants when enraged—aye, and filled
with their master—are wont to inflict upon prisoners. So that the

[1] Rev. 21.6.   [2] Cf. John 7.38; 19.34.   [3] Cf. 1 Tim. 1.16.
[4] Cf. 1 John 4.18. [5] 2 Cor. 8.23.   [6] 1 Pet. 5.8.
[7] Matt. 25.46.   [8] Cf. Acts 15.29.

more part were stifled in the prison, as many as the Lord willed
28 thus to depart, that He might manifest *His glory*.[1] For some,
though tortured so cruelly that it seemed they could no longer
live even with every attention, remained alive in the prison,
destitute indeed of human care, but fortified afresh by *the Lord*
and *strengthened*[2] both in body and soul, cheering on and en-
couraging the rest. But others who were young and just recently
apprehended, whose bodies had not been previously tortured,
could not endure the rigour of their confinement, and died within
29 its walls. Now the blessed Pothinus, to whom had been committed
the ministry of the bishopric at Lyons, was above ninety years of
age, and very weak in body. He was scarcely breathing because
of the bodily *weakness* which was laid upon him, but the earnest
desire for martyrdom filled him with that renewed strength which
a *willing spirit*[3] supplies. He too was haled to the tribunal, and
though his body was weakened both by age and disease, his life
was preserved within him, that through it Christ might *triumph*.[4]
30 He was conveyed to the tribunal by the soldiers, escorted by the
city authorities and *the whole multitude*,[5] who gave utterance to all
sorts of cries, as if he were Christ Himself[6]; and so he gave *the*
31 *good* witness.[7] Being examined by the governor as to who the
God of the Christians was, he replied, "If thou art worthy, thou
shalt know"; and thereupon he was haled without mercy, and
received blows of every kind: those close by heaped on him all
manner of insult with blows of hands and feet, regardless of his
age, while those at a distance made him the object of whatever
missile came to their hand; and all considered it a grievous fault
and impiety to be behindhand in their wanton violence to him.
For thus indeed they thought to avenge their gods. Scarcely
breathing he was cast into prison, and after two days gave up the
ghost.
32   Then in truth a mighty dispensation of God came to pass, and
the measureless compassion of Jesus was displayed, in a manner
rarely vouchsafed among the brethren, but not beyond the art of
33 Christ. For they who had denied when the Christians were first
arrested were also confined with [the others] and shared their
sufferings; for on this occasion their denial had profited them
nothing. On the contrary, those who confessed what they really
were, were confined as Christians, no other charge being brought
against them; while the others were detained thenceforward as
murderers and scoundrels, and were punished twice as much as

---

[1] Cf. John 2.11.   [2] 2 Tim. 4.17.   [3] Cf. Mark 14.38.
[4] Cf. 2 Cor. 2.14; Col. 2.15.   [5] Luke 23.1.
[6] Cf. Luke 23.18ff.   [7] Cf. 1 Tim. 6.13.

34 the rest. For the burden of the confessors was lightened by the joy
of martyrdom, the hope of the promises, their love to Christ, and
the Spirit of the Father; but the others were grievously tormented
by their conscience, insomuch that their countenances could be
35 clearly distinguished from all the rest as they passed by. For they
went forth with joy, great glory and grace blended on their
countenances, so that even their *chains* hung around them like a
goodly ornament,[1] as a bride adorned *with golden fringes of divers
colours*,[2] perfumed the while with the *sweet savour of Christ*[3];
hence some supposed that they had been anointed with earthly
ointment as well. But the others were dejected, downcast, unsightly and covered with every kind of confusion; reproached,
moreover, by the heathen for baseness and cowardice; under the
charge of murder, and having lost the one precious, glorious and
life-giving Name. The rest beholding this were stablished, and
those who were apprehended confessed without doubting, nor
did they bestow even a thought upon the persuasion of the devil.
36 ... After this their martyrdoms henceforth embraced every different form of death. For having *woven* a single *crown*[4] of divers
colours and variegated flowers they offered it to the Father. And
so it was fitting that the noble champions, after having endured a
varied conflict and mightily conquered, should receive as their
37 due the mighty *crown* of incorruptibility.[5] Maturus, then, and
Sanctus and Blandina and Attalus were led to contend with wild
beasts to the amphitheatre, and to the public spectacle of heathen
inhumanity, a day for contests with wild beasts being granted of
38 set purpose for our benefit. And Maturus and Sanctus passed once
more through every kind of torture in the amphitheatre, as if they
had suffered absolutely nothing before, or rather as if they had
already vanquished their antagonist in many rounds, and were
now contending for the crown itself. Again they ran the gauntlet
of scourges, as is the custom of the place; they were dragged by
wild beasts; they endured all that the cries of a maddened populace
ordered, now from this side, now from that; and last of all, the
iron chair, which fried their bodies and choked them with smoke.
39 Nor even at this point did the heathen stop, but were still further
maddened, in their desire to conquer the Christians' endurance;
nevertheless nothing escaped the lips of Sanctus save that word of
confession which it had been his wont from the very first to utter.
40 So then, these men, whose life had lasted long through a mighty
conflict, were finally sacrificed, being *made* throughout that day

---

[1] Cf. Ign., *Eph.* 11.   [2] Ps. 45.13 (LXX).
[3] 2 Cor. 2.15.   [4] Cf. Ign., *Magn.* 13 (Phil. 4.1; 1 Thess. 2.19).
[5] 1 Cor. 9.25.

a spectacle unto the world[1] in place of all the varied show that single combats offered.

41   Now Blandina, suspended on a stake, was exposed as food to wild beasts which were let loose against her. Even to look on her, as she hung cross-wise in earnest prayer, wrought great eagerness in those who were contending, for in their conflict they beheld with their outward eyes in the form of their sister Him who was crucified for them, that He might persuade those who believe in Him that all who suffer for the glory of Christ have unbroken

42   fellowship with the living God. And as none of the wild beasts then touched her, she was taken down from the stake and cast again into prison, being kept for another conflict, that she might conquer in still further contests, and so both render irrevocable the sentence passed on *the crooked serpent*,[2] and encourage the brethren—she the small, the weak, the despised, who had *put on Christ*[3] the great and invincible Champion, and who in many rounds vanquished the adversary and through conflict was crowned with the *crown* of incorruptibility.[4]

43   As for Attalus, he too was loudly called for by the crowd (for he was well known), and entered the arena a ready combatant by reason of his good conscience, since he had been truly exercised in the Christian discipline, and always a *witness* among us of *truth*.[5]

44   He was conducted round the amphitheatre, preceded by a board, on which was written in Latin "This is Attalus the Christian," the people bursting with vehement indignation against him. But when the governor learnt that he was a Roman, he ordered him to be taken back to the prison, where also were the others concerning whom he wrote to Caesar and was awaiting his sentence.

45   But the intervening time proved *not idle nor unfruitful*[6] in their case; nay, through their endurance the measureless compassion of Christ was displayed. For by the living the dead were quickened, and martyrs forgave those who were not martyrs, and the virgin mother rejoiced greatly to receive alive those whom her womb

46   had brought forth dead. For by their means the more part of those who had denied were brought again to birth,[7] were conceived again, were rekindled into life, and learnt to confess; full now of life and vigour they approached the tribunal, for their trial was made sweet by God, who *hath no pleasure in the death of the sinner, but is kind towards repentance*[8]; that they might be again

47   questioned by the governor. For Caesar had written that they

---

[1] 1 Cor. 4.9.   [2] Isa. 27.1.   [3] Rom. 13.14; Gal. 3.27.
[4] 1 Cor. 9.25.   [5] Cf. John 18.37.   [6] 2 Pet. 1.8.
[7] "The Greek text is meaningless" (Lake). Schwartz's emendation is translated.
[8] Ezek. 33.11; 2 Pet. 3.9.

should be tortured to death,[1] but that any who denied should be set free. And as the national festival held in that place was then at its commencement—a festival largely attended by visitors from all the tribes—the governor had the blessed ones conducted to the tribunal, to make of them a spectacle, and to form a procession for the benefit of the crowds. Therefore he again examined them; and those who appeared to possess Roman citizenship he beheaded, 48 but sent the others to the wild beasts. And Christ was mightily glorified in those who formerly denied Him, but then confessed, contrary to the expectation of the heathen. Indeed they were examined by themselves, presumably as a prelude to their release; but confessing, were added to the inheritance of the martyrs. And there remained outside those who had never even a trace of faith, or an idea of the marriage *garment*,[2] or a thought for the fear of God, nay rather, *blaspheming the Way* by their manner of life[3]— 49 in fact, *the sons of perdition*.[4] But all the rest *were added*[5] to the Church.

While these were being examined, a certain Alexander, a Phrygian by race and a physician by profession, who had lived for many years in the Gauls, and was known almost to everyone for his love to God and *boldness* for *the word* (for he too was not destitute of the apostolic gift),[6] stood by the tribunal and by signs encouraged them to confess. To the bystanders there he appeared 50 to be, as it were, in travail. The crowd were enraged that those who had formerly denied should afterwards confess, and cried out against Alexander as the cause of this. Thereupon the governor summoned him and asked him who he was; and angry at his reply "A Christian," condemned him to the wild beasts. And on the following day he entered [the amphitheatre] in the company of Attalus as well; for indeed the governor, to please the crowd, 51 had delivered Attalus too again to the wild beasts. These men experienced in turn every instrument that has been devised for torture in the amphitheatre, and, having endured a mighty conflict, at last were sacrificed like the rest. Alexander *neither groaned nor uttered* the slightest *cry*,[7] but held converse with God in his 52 heart. But Attalus, when he was placed in the iron chair and scorched, so that the fumes rose from his body, addressed the multitude in Latin: "Behold, this which ye do is devouring men; but we neither devour men nor practise any other wickedness." And on being asked the name of God, he replied, "God has not 53 a name as a man has." And after all these, finally on the last day

---

[1] Cf. Heb. 11.35.   [2] Cf. Matt. 22.11.   [3] Cf. 2 Pet. 2.2; Acts 19.9, etc.
[4] John 17.12; 2 Thess. 2.3.   [5] Acts 2.41.   [6] Cf. Acts 4.29–31.
[7] *Mart. Pol.* 2.

of the single combats Blandina was again brought in, in the company of Ponticus, a lad about fifteen years old. They had also been fetched in every day to view the tortures of the others. The heathen tried to force them to swear by their idols, and as they remained firm and set them at nought, the multitude was so infuriated at them that it had neither compassion for the youth of the

54 boy nor respect for the sex of the woman. Nay, they exposed them to every cruelty and brought them through the entire round of tortures, again and again trying to force them to swear. But this they were unable to accomplish; for Ponticus, encouraged by his sister (so that the heathen themselves saw that it was she who was urging him on and strengthening him), having nobly endured every kind of torture *gave up his spirit*.[1] But the blessed

55 Blandina last of all, having, like a high-born mother, exhorted her children and sent them forth victorious to the King,[2] travelled herself along the same path of conflicts as they did, and hastened to them, rejoicing and exulting at her departure, like one *bidden to*

56 a marriage *supper*,[3] rather than cast to the wild beasts. And after the scourging, after the wild beasts, after the frying-pan, she was at last thrown into a basket and presented to a bull. For a time the animal tossed her, but she had now lost all perception of what was happening, thanks to the hope she cherished, her grasp of the objects of her faith, and her intercourse with Christ. Then she too was sacrificed, and even the heathen themselves acknowledged that never in their experience had a woman endured so many terrible sufferings.

57 Nevertheless not even thus were their madness and cruelty towards the saints satisfied. For wild and barbarous tribes when incited by a wild beast were not easily checked; and their wanton violence found another distinct outlet with regard to the corpses.

58 That they had been worsted did not put them out of countenance, since for them man's gift of reason did not exist; nay rather, in them as in a wild beast the fact inflamed anger, and the governor and people were at one in displaying an unjust hatred towards us, that the Scripture might be fulfilled: *He that is lawless, let him do lawlessness still: and he that is righteous, let him be accounted righteous*

59 *still*.[4] For indeed they cast those suffocated in prison to the dogs, and kept a careful guard by night and day lest any should receive funeral rites at our hands. And then they actually exposed what the wild beasts and the fire had left behind—mangled or charred, as the case might be—and the heads of the others together with their severed trunks, and guarded them likewise from burial, with

[1] John 19.30.   [2] Cf. 2 Macc. 7.20–23,27–29,41.   [3] Rev. 19.9.
[4] Rev. 22.11: for the unusual reading in this text, cf. Dan. 12.10 (Theod.).

60 a military watch, for many days. And some were moved with indignation and *gnashed on* them *with their teeth*,[1] seeking to take still further vengeance upon them; while others laughed and jeered, at the same time exalting their own idols, to whom they attributed the punishment of the Christians; others again, of a more forbearing nature and seeming to extend to them a measure of fellow-feeling, uttered many reproaches, saying, "*Where is their god?*[2] and what profit has their religion brought them, which
61 they have preferred to their own life?" So varied, then, was their attitude; but as for us, we were plunged in great grief, in that we could not bury the bodies in the earth. For neither did night avail us for this purpose, nor did money persuade or prayers move them. But in every possible way they kept guard, as if the prevention of burial would bring them great gain.
62 . . . The bodies, then, of the martyrs, which for six days were displayed and exposed to the elements in every way possible, the lawless men afterwards burnt and reduced to ashes. Then they swept them down into the river Rhone which flows close by, so that not even a trace of them might remain upon the earth. And
63 this they did, thinking that they could conquer God and deprive them of *the regeneration*,[3] "in order," as they themselves said, "that they may not even have hope of a resurrection, in faith of which they introduce into our midst a certain strange and new-fangled cult, and despise dread torments, and are ready to go to their death, and that too with joy. Now let us see if they will rise again, and if their *god can* help them, and *deliver them out of* our *hands*."[4]
(Lawlor and Oulton, *Eusebius,* I, pp. 140–7, slightly altered.)

Christianity in Gaul first began among the Greek communities of the south, some of which, e.g. Marseilles, were planted *c.* 600 B.C. in the great age of Greek colonization, largely from Asia. The Asian connection was alive and vigorous; this letter is addressed to the churches of the mother country, and some of the martyrs came from there, as did Irenaeus, who succeeded Pothinus as bishop. Those who perished in this persecution, as can be seen from various lists of later date, numbered 47 or 48 (see e.g. Lawlor and Oulton, *Eusebius,* II, p. 160), but the total number of those who suffered some form of punishment was greater.

Lyons was the capital of the province Gallia Lugdunensis, but was also "the capital of Imperial Gaul, and in the time of Marcus Aurelius was the greatest city in Europe after Rome" (Lawlor and Oulton, op. cit., II, p. 154).

Vienne, in Gallia Narbonensis, about 16 miles S. of Lyons. It is possible that there was no actual outbreak of persecution there, but the two churches are coupled because Christians from Vienne (13 and 17) suffered.

[1] Acts 7.54.   [2] Ps. 42.3,10.   [3] Matt. 19.28.   [4] Dan. 3.15; 6.20 (Theod.)

4-7. It is clear that persecution began "unofficially" through disorderly mobs; then (8) the city authorities investigated, and held the prisoners until the governor arrived. If there is any truth in Irenaeus' account (I.7, Harvey, 1.13 A.-N. C. L.) of the doings of the heretic Marcus in Gaul, the heathen had much whereof they could accuse Christians in general.

9. *the elder Zacharias*, cf. Luke 1.6,67.

10. *the advocate of Christians*: "Rufinus takes this to mean that he was so named by the governor, which seems to be right" (Lawlor and Oulton, *Eusebius*, II, p. 155).

11ff. The apostates were not released: this was natural as the heathen were obsessed [with the question of "crimes". The information gained from slaves (14) appeared to reveal a situation that demanded action. Therefore the governor did not follow the principle laid down by Trajan, which may, however, have already undergone modification under Marcus Aurelius (cf. 44, 112).

44. *But when the governor learnt that he was a Roman*: the governor now wrote to Caesar about the whole matter, probably because he felt that he had such proof of "crimes" that apostates could not be pardoned. The Emperor's answer was a re-affirmation of Trajan's principle.

45. *the martyrs forgave*: cf. the trouble which arose later when this practice became abused in the Decian persecution (203-6).

47. *the national festival*: held annually about the end of July or the beginning of August. At this assembly sacrifice was offered to the goddess Roma and to the genius of Augustus, the distribution of taxes was settled, and complaints lodged against imperial officials.

59ff. For the refusal of the heathen to allow Christians to recover the bodies of the martyrs, cf. the *Martyrdom of Polycarp*, XVII, XVIII (18). The belief of the heathen that by destruction of the bodies they could stop resurrection (i.e. of the body) shows the importance of this part of Christian doctrine.

22. THE MARTYRS OF SCILLI IN AFRICA PROCONSULARIS, 17 JULY 180

(*Passio Sanctorum Scillitanorum*: Text in O. von Gebhardt, *Acta Martyrum Selecta*, pp. 22-7; Knopf-Krüger, *Ausgewählte Mär-tyrerakten*, ed. 3 pp. 28-9.)

In the consulship of Praesens, then consul for the second time, and Claudian, on the 17th of July, Speratus, Nártzalus and Cit-tinus, Donata, Secunda, Vestia were brought to trial at Carthage in the council-chamber. The proconsul Saturninus said to them: "You may merit the indulgence of our Lord the Emperor, if you return to a right mind."

Speratus said: "We have never done harm to any, we have never lent ourselves to wickedness; we have never spoken ill of any, but have given thanks when ill-treated, because we hold our own Emperor in honour."

The proconsul Saturninus said: "We also are religious people, and our religion is simple, and we swear by the genius of our Lord the Emperor, and pray for his safety, as you also ought to do."

Speratus said: "If you will give me a quiet hearing, I will tell you the mystery of simplicity."

Saturninus said: "If you begin to speak evil of our sacred rites, I will give you no hearing; but swear rather by the genius of our Lord the Emperor."

Speratus said: "I do not recognize the empire of this world; bur rather I serve that God, whom no man has seen nor can see. I have not stolen, but if I buy anything, I pay the tax, because I recognize my Lord, the King of kings and Emperor of all peoples."

The proconsul Saturninus said to the rest: "Cease to be of this persuasion."

Speratus said: "The persuasion that we should do murder, or bear false witness, that is evil."

The proconsul Saturninus said: "Have no part in this madness."

Cittinus said: "We have none other to fear save the Lord our God who is in heaven."

Donata said: "Give honour to Caesar as unto Caesar, but fear to God."

Vestia said: "I am a Christian."

Secunda said: "I wish to be none other than what I am."

The proconsul Saturninus said to Speratus: "Do you persist in remaining a Christian?"

Speratus said: "I am a Christian." And all were of one mind with him.

The proconsul Saturninus said: "Do you desire any space for consideration?"

Speratus said: "When the right is so clear, there is nothing to consider."

The proconsul Saturninus said: "What have you in your case?"

Speratus said: "The Books, and the letters of a just man, one Paul."

The proconsul Saturninus said: "Take a reprieve of thirty days and think it over.'

Speratus again said: "I am a Christian." And all were of one mind with him.

The proconsul Saturninus read out the sentence from his note-book: "Whereas Speratus, Nartzalus, Cittinus, Donata, Vestia, Secunda, and the rest have confessed that they live in accordance with the religious rites of the Christians, and, when an opportunity was given them of returning to the usage of the Romans, persevered in their obstinacy, it is our pleasure that they should suffer by the sword."

Speratus said: "Thanks be to God."

Nartzalus said: "To-day we are martyrs in heaven: thanks be to God!"

The proconsul Saturninus commanded that proclamation be made by the herald: "I have commanded that Speratus, Nart-zalus, Cittinus, Veturius, Felix, Aquilinus, Laetantius, Januaria, Generosa, Vestia, Donata, Secunda be led forth to execution."

They all said: "Thanks be to God!"

And so all were crowned with martyrdom together, and reign with the Father and Son and Holy Spirit for ever and ever. Amen. (E. C. E. Owen, *Some authentic Acts of the early Martyrs*, pp. 71-3, very slightly altered.)

Tertullian informs us (*To Scapula*, 3) that Saturninus was the first governor to persecute Christians in Africa. This *Passio* gives the account of the appearance of a second batch of Christians before the Proconsul, as others are mentioned in the sentence, both collectively and by name. These may have been remitted to prison to await the arrival of the group headed by Speratus.

23. THE THUNDERING LEGION, *c.* 171-177

(Eusebius, *H.E.* V.5.1-4.)

5.1 ... It is recorded that his brother Marcus Aurelius Caesar, when about to engage in battle with the Germans and Sarmatians, was in despair because his army was in great distress with thirst; but that the soldiers of the legion of Melitene, as it is called, with a faith that has subsisted from that day until now, when they were drawn up before the enemy, kneeled on the ground, as is our familiar custom in prayer, and turned to God in supplication.

2 And it is recorded that, though a sight like this appeared marvellous to the enemy, a still more marvellous thing followed immediately: that a thunderbolt drove the enemy to flight and destruction, while a shower descended on the army of those who

had called upon the Divine Being, and refreshed it when just on the point of entirely perishing with thirst. Now this story is to
3 be found even in writers alien to our faith, whose care it has been to write the history of the times of the said emperors; but it has also been told by our own writers. Pagan historians, however, being strangers to the faith, have stated the marvellous occurrence without acknowledging that it was in answer to the prayers of Christians; but ours, being lovers of truth, have told the event in a simple and artless manner.
4 To this latter class belongs Apollinarius, who said that from that time the legion which had wrought the marvel by its prayers received from the emperor a title appropriate to the event, being styled, in Latin, the Thundering Legion.

The source of this story is clearly the *Apology* of Apollinarius, addressed to Marcus Aurelius. Its prevalence is shown by Tertullian's reference to it (*Apology*, 5.6 (140 below)), and by the fact that a Christian forged a letter for Marcus, in which he recounted the miracle. The letter is preserved in the manuscript of Justin's *Apologies*. The incident (without of course any reference to Christianity) is related to Dio Cassius, *Epitome LXXI* 8-10.

"The curious legend of the 'Thundering Legion' arose in connection with a great victory over the Quadi. A storm seems to have burst over the armies during battle, and while a grateful shower of rain fell upon the Romans, the enemy were disconcerted by thunder and lightning. The event was considered miraculous, and was said to be the answer of Heaven to the prayers of a legion consisting of Christians. That some such occurrence did take place is confirmed by a sculpture on the Column of Aurelius, but of course at this time there was no such thing as a Christian legion; and the legion *Fulminata* existed under Augustus." (Bury, *The Student's Roman Empire*, p. 545.)

For a full discussion see A. B. Cook, *Zeus, III*, i, pp. 324-33. The word *fulminatus* means either "struck by a thunderbolt", as a mark of divine favour (Cook op. cit., II, i, pp. 22ff., 33ff.) or "hurled like a thunderbolt, quick as a thunderbolt" (ibid., III, i, p. 325).

Whatever be the basis of the story, it shows that by 170-200 many Christians were serving in the army; Apollinarius and Tertullian find no difficulty in this; the former in fact assumes that a whole legion consisted of Christian soldiers. It should be noted that in the forged letter of Marcus, the Christians, however inappositely, are stated not to be armed.

1. *his brother*: As McGiffert shows (*The Church History of Eusebius* (N. & P.-N. F.) pp. 390-1.) Eusebius was completely confused about the names of the two successors of Antoninus Pius, whom we call Marcus Aurelius and Lucius Verus.

24. IGNATIUS OF ANTIOCH ON HIS WAY TO MARTYRDOM, c. 110–115

(Ignatius, *To the Romans*, V.)

From Syria unto Rome I am fighting with wild beasts by land and sea, by night and day, bound to ten leopards, that is, a bunch of soldiers, whose usage grows still harsher when they are liberally treated. Yet through their unjust doings I am more truly learning
2 discipleship. *Yet am I not hereby justified.*[1] May I have joy of the beasts that are prepared for me. I pray too that they may prove prompt with me. I will even entice them to devour me promptly, and not to refrain, as they have refrained from some, through fear. And even though they are not willing without constraint, I will
3 force them. Pardon me. I know what is expedient for me. Now I am beginning to be a disciple. May naught of things visible or invisible seek to allure me, that I may attain unto Jesus Christ. Let there come on me fire and cross and conflicts with wild beasts, wrenching of bones, mangling of limbs, crushing of the whole body, grievous torments of the devil may I but attain to Jesus Christ. (J. H. Srawley, *Epistles of St Ignatius*, 3 ed., pp. 75–6, altered.)

Ignatius wrote to the Roman Church largely in order that they might not take any steps to save him from martyrdom. We know nothing of the circumstances of his arrest, but prisoners were sometimes sent to Rome, cf. 14.

2. *May I have joy of the beasts*, cf. Ignatius, *To the Ephesians*, I 2, and the *Martyrdom of Polycarp*, III 1 (18 above).

25. THE PERSON OF CHRIST

(Ignatius, *To the Ephesians*, VII.)

1 For some are wont, out of malicious cunning, to bear about with them the Name, while they practise certain other deeds unworthy of God. These you must needs avoid as wild beasts. For they are mad dogs, biting stealthily, against whom you must be
2 on your guard, for their bite is hard to heal. There is one Physician, of flesh and of Spirit, originate and unoriginate, God in man, true Life in death, son of Mary and Son of God, first passible and then impassible, Jesus Christ our Lord. (J. H. Srawley, *Epistles of St Ignatius*, 3 ed., pp. 42–3.)

1. The opponents are Docetic teachers, whose morals were as weak as their theology.

[1] 1 Cor. 4.4.

2. *There is one physician*, i.e. "who can cope with it" (Lightfoot). "The anti-thesis of flesh and spirit is intended to express the human and the Divine nature of Christ respectively" (Lightfoot, *Apostolic Fathers*, II.2, pp. 47, 48).

originate and unoriginate: "Ignatius is using the words to express little more than "created and uncreate" (Srawley, op. cit., p. 43n). *Originate* refers to Christ's human nature.

first passible and then impassible: in his letter *To Polycarp*, III.2, Ignatius puts the antithesis the other way round.

26. JEWISH ERROR AND CHRISTIAN TRUTH

(Ignatius, *To the Magnesians*. VIII, IX, X.)

VIII.1　Be not deceived by strange doctrines nor by ancient fables, seeing that they are profitless. For if, until now, we live according
2　to Judaism, we confess that we have not received grace. For the divine prophets lived in accordance with Christ Jesus. For this cause too they were persecuted, being inspired by [His] grace, so that the disobedient might be fully convinced that there is One God, who manifested Himself through Jesus Christ His Son, who is His Word, coming forth from silence, who in all things did the good pleasure of Him that sent Him.

IX.1　If therefore those who lived in ancient observances attained unto newness of hope, no longer keeping the Sabbath, but living a life ruled by the Lord's day, whereon our life too had its rising
2　through Him and His death—which some deny, a mystery through which we have received the power to believe, and there-fore we endure, that we may be found disciples of Jesus Christ, our only Teacher—how shall we be able to live apart from Him? For the prophets also became His disciples, and awaited in the spirit His coming to teach them. And therefore He, for whom they rightly waited, came and raised them from the dead.

X.1-2　[Ignatius goes on to appeal to his readers to cling to Christ, to turn to the new leaven and to the salt with savour.]

3　It is outrageous to utter the name of Jesus Christ and live in Judaism. For Christianity believed not in Judaism, but Judaism in Christianity, in which every *tongue* believing in God *was brought together*.[1] (J. H. Srawley, *Epistles of St Ignatius*, 3 ed., pp. 57-60, altered.)

[1] Cf. Isa. 66.18.

"The heresy which Ignatius has in mind belongs to the same category with the heresy of the Colossian Church, of the Pastoral Epistles, of the Apocalypse, of the Catholic Epistles, and of the Corinthians. It is Judaism crossed with Gnosticism." (Lightfoot, *Apostolic Fathers*, II.2, p. 124.)

VIII.2. *the divine prophets*: "Ignatius maintains that the teaching of the prophets anticipated, and was completed by, the perfect revelation of God in Christ" (Srawley, op. cit., p. 58n).

coming forth from silence: Word implies previous silence. "As Logos implies the manifestation of deity whether in His words or in His works, so *Sige* (silence) is the negation of this. Hence the expression, 'coming forth from silence' might be used at any point where there is a sudden transition from non-manifestation to manifestation." (Lightfoot, op. cit., II.2, p. 127.)

27. DOCETISM

(Ignatius, *To the Trallians*, IX, X.)

IX.1 Be deaf, therefore, when any one speaks unto you apart from Jesus Christ, who was of the race of David, the child of Mary, who was truly born, and ate and drank, was truly persecuted under Pontius Pilate, was truly crucified and died, before the eyes of those in heaven and those on earth and those under the earth;

2 who also was truly raised from the dead, since His Father raised Him up, who in like manner will also raise up us who believe on Him—even His Father will raise us in Christ Jesus, apart from whom we have not true life.

X.1 But if it be, as some godless men, i.e. unbelievers, assert, that He suffered in phantom only—it is they that are phantoms— why am I in bonds? Why, moreover, do I pray that I may fight with the wild beasts? Then I die for naught. Then I lie against the Lord. (J. H. Srawley, *Epistles of St Ignatius*, 3 ed., pp. 66–7, altered.)

"The stumbling-block of that age was not so much the Lord's divinity as his crucifixion. Because he suffered, said the Jew, he was not divine. Because he was divine, replied the Gnostic, he did not suffer. Thus the Judaizers and the Gnostics had a common interest in explaining away his sufferings, for they were agreed that divinity and suffering are inconsistent with each other. So they introduced a higher power as the real Christ. The Ebionites made the Spirit of the Lord (in the Jewish sense) light on a common man. The Gnostics clothed a heavenly power with the appearance of manhood, so that those sufferings were only in appearance. In either case, it is denied that the Redeemer suffered at all." (H. M. Gwatkin, *Early Church History to A.D. 313*, Vol 1, p. 11.)

Docetism is attacked by Ignatius in this letter and in his letters to the Smyrnaeans, Magnesians, and Philadelphians.

X.1. *I lie against the Lord*, i.e. "my life and my preaching alike are a falsehood against Him, for they assume that Christ really did rise" (Lightfoot, *Apostolic Fathers*, II.2, p. 176).

28. THE MINISTRY AND THE SACRAMENTS

(Ignatius, *To the Smyrnaeans*, VIII.)

1 Avoid divisions, as the beginning of evil. Follow, all of you, the bishop, as Jesus Christ followed the Father; and follow the presbytery as the Apostles. Moreover, reverence the deacons as the commandment of God. Let no man do aught pertaining to the Church apart from the bishop. Let that eucharist be considered valid which is under the bishop or him to whom he commits it.

2 Wheresoever the bishop appears, there let the people be, even as wheresoever Christ Jesus is, there is the Catholic Church. It is not lawful apart from the bishop either to baptize, or to hold a love-feast. But whatsoever he approves, that also is well-pleasing to God, that everything which you do may be secure and valid. (J. H. Srawley, *Epistles of St Ignatius*, 3 ed., p. 96–8.)

Ignatius is the earliest author who insists on the threefold ministry. The above passage may be taken merely as an example of a theme that runs through all his epistles except that to the Romans. On the Ministry, cf. 13, 29, 33, 224, 228, 308.

2. *the Catholic Church*: this is the earliest example of this expression: "Catholic" means "universal".

love-feast (*Agape*): "the name was given to the social meals, in which the early church sought to give expression to the amity and brotherly love of its members." (Srawley, op. cit., p. 30n), cf. 14 (sect. 7).

29. THE PROPHETIC INSPIRATION OF IGNATIUS

(Ignatius, *To the Philadelphians*, VII.)

1 For even if after the flesh some wished to lead me astray, yet the Spirit is not deceived since it is from God. For it knoweth whence it cometh and whither it goeth, and it convicts the things

which are in secret. I cried aloud, when I was among you, I spake
with a loud voice, with the voice of God, "Give heed unto the
2 bishop and the presbytery and deacons." But they suspected that
I said this because I knew beforehand the division caused by
some; yet He is my witness, Whose prisoner I am, that I learned
it not from human flesh. But it was the Spirit Who kept preaching
in these words: "Do nothing without the bishop. Keep your
flesh as a shrine of God. Love union. Flee divisions. Become
followers of Jesus Christ as He also was of the Father." (J. H.
Srawley, *Epistles of St Ignatius*, 3 ed., p. 86.)

For other passages dealing with the ministry, see note to 28.
Ignatius is an inspired prophet whose words must find acceptance in the
community in which his prophecies are uttered.

30. POLYCARP OF SMYRNA ON IGNATIUS

(Polycarp, *To the Philippians*, XIII.)

Both you and Ignatius have written to me that, if any one go
to Syria, he is to convey the letter also from you. I shall carry
out your wish, if I find a favourable opportunity; whether I go
myself, or find some one to act the envoy also for you. The
letters of Ignatius sent to us by him, and all the rest which we had
by us, we have sent to you, as you enjoined. They are attached to
this letter. From them you will be able to be greatly benefited,
for they embrace faith, patience, and every kind of edification
which regards our Lord. If ye have any more certain knowledge
concerning Ignatius himself, and those with him, inform us. (B.
Jackson, *St Polycarp*, pp. 46–7.)

In his letter to Polycarp (Ch. VIII) Ignatius writes that he was due to sail
suddenly from Troas to Neapolis (Cavalla in Macedonia). We can see that he
reached Philippi, and after that we lose sight of him. This extract shows the
close association that already existed between the churches of different cities
and provinces: it also shows us how collections of letters written by prominent
Christians were formed. "It is interesting to notice that the one Epistle which
neither Polycarp nor the Philippians could easily obtain would be that to the
Romans, and that it is this letter which in the Ignatian MSS seems to have
had a different textual history from that of the other six." (K. Lake, *Apostolic
Fathers* (Loeb Library), I, p. 280f.)

31. PAPIAS OF HIERAPOLIS (*c.* 130), AND THE COMMENTS OF EUSEBIUS UPON HIM

(Eusebius, *H.E.* III.39.)

1   But of Papias there are five treatises extant, which also have been entitled *Expositions of the Dominical Oracles*. These Irenaeus also mentions as his only writings, saying somewhat as follows:

> And these things Papias also, who was a hearer of John and a companion of Polycarp, a man of primitive times, attests in writing in the fourth of his books. For there are five books composed by him.[1]

2   So, indeed, says Irenaeus. Nevertheless Papias himself, in the preface to his discourses, makes it plain that he was in no sense a hearer and eye-witness of the holy apostles; but tells us, by the language he uses, that he had received the things pertaining to the faith from those who were their pupils:

3   But I will not hesitate also to set down for thy benefit, along with the interpretations, all that ever I carefully learnt and carefully recalled from the elders, guaranteeing its truth. For I did not take delight, as most men do, in those who have much to say, but in those who teach what is true; not in those who recall foreign commandments, but in those who recall the commandments given by the Lord to faith, and reaching us from the truth
4   itself. And if anyone chanced to come who had actually been a follower of the elders, I would inquire as to the discourses of the elders, what Andrew or what Peter said, or what Philip, or what Thomas or James, or what John or Matthew or any other of the Lord's disciples; and the things which Aristion and John the elder, disciples of the Lord, say. For I supposed that things out of books did not profit me so much as the utterances of a voice *which liveth and abideth*.[2]

5   Here it is worth while noting that twice in his enumeration he mentions the name John: the former of these Johns he puts in the same list with Peter and James and Matthew and the other apostles, clearly indicating the evangelist; but the latter he places with others, in a separate clause,[3] outside the number of the apostles, placing Aristion before him; and he clearly calls him "elder".
6   So that he hereby also proves their statement to be true who have

---

[1] Iren. V. 33.4.   [2] 1 Pet. 1.23.   [3] Or "with a distinction in the phrase".

said that two persons in *Asia* have borne the same name, *and that there were two tombs at Ephesus, each of which is* still to this day *said to be John's*.[1] And to these details one must needs pay attention, for it is likely that the second (if one is unwilling to admit that it was the first) saw the Revelation which is extant under the name

7 of John. And Papias, of whom we are now speaking, acknowledges that he received *the discourses of the* apostles from those *who had been* their *followers*, but says that he was himself an actual hearer of *Aristion and* of *John the elder*.[2] Certainly he mentions them by name frequently in his treatises and sets forth their traditions.

8   So much, then, for these points which, it is hoped, we have not adduced to no purpose. But it is right to add to the words of Papias which we have quoted other sayings, in which he relates some other miraculous events likewise, as having come down to

9 him by tradition. It has been shown, indeed, by what has gone before, that Philip the apostle resided in Hierapolis with his daughters; but now it must be pointed out that Papias, their contemporary, mentions that he had a wonderful story from *the daughters of Philip*. For he relates that the *resurrection* of a dead body took place in his day; and, on the other hand, he tells of another miraculous happening, concerned with *Justus who was* surnamed *Barsabbas*: that he *drank* a deadly poison[3] and, by the grace of the Lord, suffered no unpleasant effects.

10   [A reminder, quoting Acts 1.17,23,24, that Justus had been put forward, with Matthias, to fill the place of Judas.]

11   And the same writer has quoted other things also, as coming to him from unwritten tradition; for instance, certain strange parables of the Saviour and teachings of His, and some other

12 things of a rather mythical character. And among these is his statement that there will be a certain period of a thousand years after the resurrection from the dead, when the kingdom of Christ will be set up in a material order upon this earth. I imagine that he got these ideas through a misinterpretation of the apostolic accounts, for he did not understand what they said mystically and

13 in figurative language. For he evidently was a man of exceedingly small intelligence, as one might say judging from his discourses; nevertheless it was owing to him that so very many churchmen after him adopted a like opinion, taking their stand on the fact

---

[1] Dion. Alex., *Prom.* VII.25.16, see 237, p. 272.   [2] Papias in sect. 4 above.
[3] See Philip of Side in *T.U.* V.2, p. 170; cf. [Mark] 16.18.

that he was a man of primitive times: as, for example, Irenaeus and all others who have given evident expression to like views.

14 And, besides, Papias gives us in his work accounts of the aforesaid Aristion of the sayings of the Lord, and traditions of John the elder.

While we refer scholars to these, we shall now of necessity add to the words of his already quoted a tradition which he has set forth concerning Mark who wrote the Gospel. It is in these words:

15   This also the elder used to say. Mark, indeed, having been the interpreter of Peter, wrote accurately, howbeit not in order, all that he recalled of what was either said or done by the Lord. For he neither heard the Lord, nor was he a follower of His, but, at a later date (as I said), of Peter; who used to adapt his instructions to the needs [of the moment], but not with a view to putting together the Dominical oracles in orderly fashion: so that Mark did no wrong in thus writing some things as he recalled them. For he kept a single aim in view: not to omit anything of what he heard, nor to state anything therein falsely.

16   Such, then, is Papias' account of Mark. But the following is the statement concerning Matthew:

So then, Matthew compiled the oracles in the Hebrew language; but everyone interpreted them as he was able.

17   And the same writer has used testimonies drawn from the former epistle of John, and likewise from that of Peter; and he has set forth, as well, another story about a woman accused falsely of many sins before the Lord, which the Gospel of the Hebrews contains. (Lawlor and Oulton, *Eusebius*, I, pp. 99–101.)

For a succinct commentary on the whole passage, see Lawlor and Oulton, *Eusebius*, II, pp. 112–16.

The passage well illustrates the methods of transmission of the Christian "tradition", and the confusions, e.g. about who exactly were "elders" (cf. sect. 4 with sect. 7) which quite naturally existed.

32. SIN AND REPENTANCE

(1. Hermas, *The Shepherd*, Vis. II.ii.1–6.)

Hermas received the following teaching about sin and repentance from a little book handed to him by the old lady (the Church), which she bade him copy (33). He had initially great difficulty in understanding the script.

1 But after fifteen days, when I had fasted and prayed greatly to the Lord, the knowledge of the writing was revealed to me.

2 And these things were written: Your seed, Hermas, have set God at naught, and have blasphemed the Lord, and have betrayed their parents in great wickedness, and they are called the betrayers of parents, and their betrayal has not profited them, but they have added to their sins wanton deeds and piled up wickedness, and so

3 their crimes have been made complete. But make these words known to all your children and to your wife, who shall in future be to you as a sister. For she also does not refrain her tongue, with which she sins; but when she has heard these words she will refrain

4 it, and will obtain mercy. After you have made known these words to them, which the Master commanded me to reveal to you, all the sins which they have formerly committed shall be forgiven them, and they shall be forgiven to all the saints who have sinned up to this day, if they repent with their whole

5 heart, and put aside double-mindedness from their heart. For the Master has sworn to his elect by his glory that if there be still sin after this day has been fixed, they shall find no salvation; for repentance for the just has an end; the days of repentance have been fulfilled for all the saints, but for the heathen repentance is

6 open until the last day. You shall say, then, to the leaders of the Church, that they reform their ways in righteousness, to receive in full the promises with great glory. (Lake, *Apostolic Fathers* (Loeb Library), II, pp. 19–21.)

(2. Hermas, *The Shepherd*, Mand. IV.iii.1–2,6.)

On this occasion Hermas is taught by "The Shepherd".

1 "I have heard, sir," said I, "from some teachers that there is no second repentance beyond the one given when we went down into the water and received remission of our former sins."

2 He said to me, "You have heard correctly, for that is so. For he who has received remission of sin ought never to sin again,

6 but to live in purity. . . . "But I tell you," said he, "after that great and holy calling, if a man be tempted by the devil and sin, he has one repentance, but if he sin and repent repeatedly it is unprofitable for such a man, for scarcely shall he live." (Lake, ibid., II, pp. 83–5.)

In Heb. 6.4–8 no opportunity of repentance was given to those who had been baptized and then committed sin. On the situation at Rome about the end of the second century, cf. 137, 160.

33. THE CHURCH

(Hermas, *The Shepherd*, Vis. II.iv.1–3.)

One of the informants from whom the prophet Hermas gained his revelations was an ancient lady whose identity is disclosed to him in the following passage:

1   And a revelation was made to me, brethren, while I slept, by a very beautiful young man who said to me, "Who do you think that the ancient lady was from whom you received the little book?" I said, "The Sibyl." "You are wrong," he said, "she is not." "Who is she, then?" I said. "The Church," he said. I said to him, "Why then is she old?" "Because," he said, "she was created the first of all things. For this reason is she old; and for her
2 sake was the world established." And afterwards I saw a vision in my house. The ancient lady came and asked me if I had already given the book to the elders. I said that I had not given it. "You have done well," she said, "for I have words to add. When, therefore, I have finished all the words they shall be made known
3 by you to all the elect. You shall therefore write two little books and send one to Clement and one to Grapte. Clement then shall send it to the cities abroad, for that is his duty; and Grapte shall exhort the widows and orphans; but in this city you shall read it yourself with the elders who are in charge of the church." (Lake, *Apostolic Fathers* (Loeb Library), II, p. 25.)

Hermas was on his way to Cumae on the two occasions that he had met the lady, and as Cumae was the home of the Sibyl, it was natural to suppose that the lady was she. Many Christians in the early centuries believed the Sibyl to be a true prophetess, and this belief persisted, as the opening lines of the *Dies irae* show.

1. *she was created the first of all things*: this conception of a spiritual church that had been the first created thing is found in II Clement also (Ch. 14.1–4). But in Hermas, who is a moral reformer, the antique feebleness of the Church is due to the faults of Christians: "Why did she appear to you in the first vision as old and seated on a chair? Because your spirit is old and already fading away, and has no power through your weakness and double-mindedness." (Vis. III.xi.2, tr. Lake, op. cit., p. 55.)

As Christians grew better, so the Church became younger and more beautiful. "Church" was also one of the Gnostic aeons, which existed before the world (65 below).

3. Section 3 shows that this part of the *Shepherd* was contemporary with

Clement, and that it was not uncommon for letters to be written by the Roman church to other churches.

the elders: this fits in with the conception of the ministry that we find in Clement's *Epistle to the Corinthians* (13).

34. THE APOLOGISTS QUADRATUS AND ARISTEIDES

(Eusebius, *H.E.* IV.3.)

1 To him (i.e. Hadrian) Quadratus dedicated and addressed a discourse, which he had composed in defence of our religion, because certain wicked men were endeavouring to molest our people. The treatise is still to be found in the hands of very many of the brethren, as indeed it is in ours also. From it we may gather striking proofs of the author's understanding and of his apostolic 2 soundness in the faith. But he himself reveals the early date at which he lived in the following account, given by him in these very words:

But the works of our Saviour were always present (for they were genuine): namely, those who were healed, those who rose from the dead; who were not only seen in the act of being healed or raised, but were also always present; and not merely when the Saviour was in earth, but after his departure as well, they lived for a considerable time; insomuch that some of them survived even to our own day.

3 Such a one was he. And Aristides too, a faithful follower of our religion, has left behind him an Apology which, like Quadratus, he dedicated to Hadrian on behalf of the faith. And his book also is to this day preserved in the hands of very many. (Lawlor and Oulton, *Eusebius*, I, p. 106.)

From an anonymous writer against the Montanists, quoted by Eusebius (V.17), we find that Quadratus was a prophet, a generation earlier than the Montanist prophetesses (89). The anonymous writer obviously regards him as belonging to Asia Minor. Jerome's identification of him (*De Vir. Ill.* 19; *Ep.* LXX.4) with a Bishop of Athens, *c.* 170, is almost certainly erroneous.

The *Apology* of Aristeides was probably presented to Antoninus Pius, not to Hadrian.

35. CHRISTIAN THEOLOGY AND ETHICS,
c. 150

(Aristeides, *Apology*, XV, XVI.)

(Text from the Greek and Syriac, as arranged by Geffcken, *Zwei griechische Apologeten*, pp. 24ff. Parts of the passage derived from the Syriac are in italics, probable additions to the original Greek are bracketed.)

XV.1 "As for the Christians, they trace their line from the Lord Jesus Christ. He is confessed to be the Son of the most high God, who came down from heaven, by the Holy Ghost, (for the salvation of mankind,) and was born of a (pure) Virgin, (without seed of man, and without defilement,) and took flesh, *and in a daughter of man there dwelt the Son of God. This is taught from that Gospel which a little while ago was spoken among them as being preached; wherein if ye also will read, ye will comprehend the power*
2 *that is upon it. This Jesus, then, was born of the tribe of the Hebrews; and He had twelve disciples, in order that a certain dispensation of His might be fulfilled. He was pierced by the Jews; and He died and was buried; and they say that after three days He rose and ascended to heaven; and then these twelve disciples went forth* into all the kingdoms of the world, telling of his greatness *with all humility and sobriety*; whence they who still serve the righteousness of his preaching are called Christians, *who are well known.*
3 *Now the Christians, O king, by going about and seeking have found the truth, and as we have comprehended from their writings they are nearer to the truth and to exact knowledge than the rest of the peoples.* For they acknowledge God the Creator and Maker of all things, *in whom are all things and from whom are all things*: (in the only-begotten Son, and in the Holy Ghost,) and other God than him they worship none. They have the commandments of the Lord Jesus Christ himself engraven on their hearts, and these they observe, looking for the resurrection of the dead and the life of
4 the world to come. They commit neither adultery nor fornication; nor do they bear false witness, *they do not deny a deposit*, nor covet other men's goods: they honour father and mother, and love their neighbours: they give right judgement; *and they do not*
5 *worship idols in the form of man.* They do not unto other that which they would not have done unto themselves. They comfort such as wrong them, and make friends of them: they labour to do good
6 to their enemies: (they are meek and gentle.) *And their wives, O*

king, are pure as virgins, and their daughters modest: and their men refrain themselves from all unlawful intercourse and all uncleanness, in the hope of the recompense that is to come in another world: but as for their servants or handmaids, or their children if any of them have any, they persuade them to become Christians for the love that they have towards them; and when they have become so, they call
7 *them without distinction brethren: they do not worship strange gods:* and they walk in all humility and kindness, and falsehood is not found among them, and they love one another. They despise not the widow, and grieve not the orphan. He that hath distributeth liberally to him that hath not. If they see a stranger, they bring him under their roof, and rejoice over him, as it were their own brother: for they call themselves brethren, not after the flesh, but after the
8 spirit *and in God: but when one of their poor passes away from the world, and any of them sees him, then he provides for his burial according to his ability; and if they hear that any of their number is imprisoned or oppressed for the name of their Messiah, all of them provide for his needs, and if it is possible that he may be delivered, they deliver him.*
9 *And if there is among them a man that is poor and needy, and they have not an abundance of necessaries, they fast two or three days that*
10 *they may supply the needy with their necessary food.* For Christ's sake they are ready to lay down their lives: they keep his commandments faithfully, living righteous and holy lives, as the Lord commanded them, giving him thanks *every morning and* every
11 hour, *for meat and drink and every blessing. And if any righteous person of their number passes away from the world they rejoice and give thanks to God, and they follow his body, as if he were moving from one place to another: and when a child is born to any one of them, they praise God, and if again it chance to die in its infancy, they praise God mightily, as for one who has passed through the world without sins. And if again they see that one of their number has died in his iniquity or in his sins, over this one they weep bitterly and sigh, as over one who*
12 *is about to go to punishment: such is the ordinance of the law of the Christians, O king, and such their conduct.*
XVI.1 *As men who know God, they ask from Him petitions which are proper for Him to give and for them to receive: and thus they accomplish the course of their lives. And because they acknowledge the goodnesses of God towards them, lo! on account of them there flows forth the beauty that is in the world. And truly they are of the number of those that have found the truth by going about and seeking it, and as far as we have comprehended, we have understood that they only are near to the knowledge of the truth.*
2 *But the good deeds which they do, they do not proclaim in the ears of the multitude, and they take care that no one shall perceive them, and*

*hide their gift, as he who has found a treasure and hides it. And they
labour to become righteous as those that expect to see their Messiah and
receive from Him the promises made to them with great glory.*

3   *But their sayings and their ordinances, O king, and the glory of their
service, and the expectation of their recompense of reward, according to
the doing of each one of them, which they expect in another world, thou*
4   *art able to know from their writings. It sufficeth for us that we have
briefly made known to your majesty concerning the conversation and
the truth of the Christians. For truly great and wonderful is their teaching to him that is willing to examine and understand it. And truly this*
5   *people is a new people, and there is something divine mingled with it.
Take now their writings and read in them, and lo! ye will find that not
of myself have I brought these things forward nor as their advocate have
I said them, but as I have read in their writings, these things I firmly
believe, and those things also that are to come. And therefore I was constrained to set forth the truth to them that take pleasure therein and seek
after the world to come.*

6   *And I have no doubt that the world stands by reason of the intercession
of Christians.* But all other nations are deceived, and deceive
themselves, *rolling themselves before the elements of the world,
according as the sight of their understanding is unwilling to pass by them.*
Walking in darkness *because they are unwilling to know the truth*
they stagger one against another like drunken men *and fall down.*
(Translation of the Greek from Woodward and Mattingly, *St
John Damascene, Barlaam and Ioasaph* (Loeb Library), pp. 421-5,
of the Syriac from J. Rendel Harris, *The Apology of Aristides*,
pp. 36-7, 48-51.)

XV.1.   *trace their line*: Aristeides divides mankind into four races, Barbarians
and Greeks, Jews and Christians.

From the first part of the above passage one can trace most of the articles of
Christian belief, which became embodied in creeds, cf. 106, and in rules of
faith, cf. 93.

For the description of Christian life, cf. that given in *The Epistle to Diognetus*
(36).

The "king" addressed is the Emperor Antoninus Pius.

36. CHRISTIAN LIFE IN THE SECOND CENTURY

(*The Epistle to Diognetus*, V, VI, VII.)

V.1 For Christians are not distinguished from the rest of man-
2 kind by country, or by speech, or by dress. For they do not dwell

in cities of their own, or use a different language, or practise a
3 peculiar life. This knowledge of theirs has not been proclaimed
by the thought and effort of restless men; they are not champions
4 of a human doctrine, as some men are. But while they dwell in
Greek or barbarian cities according as each man's lot has been
cast, and follow the customs of the land in clothing and food,
and other matters of daily life, yet the condition of citizenship
5 which they exhibit is wonderful, and admittedly strange. They
live in countries of their own, but simply as sojourners; they
share the life of citizens, they endure the lot of foreigners; every
foreign land is to them a fatherland, and every fatherland a foreign
6 land. They marry like the rest of the world, they breed children,
7 but they do not cast their offspring adrift. They have a common
8 table, but yet not common. They exist in the flesh, but they live
9 not after the flesh. They spend their existence upon earth, but their
10 citizenship is in heaven. They obey the established laws, and in
11 their own lives they surpass the laws. They love all men, and are
12 persecuted by all. They are unknown, and they are condemned;
13 they are put to death, and they gain new life. They are poor, and
make many rich; they lack everything, and in everything they
14 abound. They are dishonoured, and their dishonour becomes their
15 glory; they are reviled, and are justified. They are abused, and
16 they bless; they are insulted, and repay insult with honour. They
do good, and are punished as evil-doers; and in their punishment
17 they rejoice as gaining new life therein. The Jews war against them
as aliens, and the Greeks persecute them; and they that hate them
can state no ground for their enmity.

VI.1 In a word, what the soul is in the body Christians are in the
2 world. The soul is spread through all the members of the body,
3 and Christians through all the cities of the world. The soul dwells
in the body, but it is not of the body, Christians dwell in the world,
4 but they are not of the world. The soul, itself invisible, is detained
in a body which is visible; so Christians are recognized as being
in the world, but their religious life remains invisible.

5–8 [The author develops his theme of the antithesis between soul
and body, between the Christians and the world.]

9 The soul when it is stinted of food and drink thrives the better;
so Christians when they are punished increase daily all the more.
10 So great is the position to which God has appointed them, and
which it is not lawful for them to refuse.

VII.1 For this is no earthly discovery, as I said, which was delivered
into their charge; it is no mortal idea which they regard themselves
bound so diligently to guard; it is no stewardship of merely human

2 mysteries with which they have been entrusted. But God Himself in very truth, the almighty and all-creating and invisible God, Himself from heaven planted among men and established in their hearts the Truth and the Word, the holy, incomprehensible Word, sending to men not a servant, as one might imagine, or an angel or ruler, or one of those who administer earthly things, or of those who have been entrusted with the ordering of things in heaven, but the very Artificer and Maker of the universe Himself, by whom He made the heavens, . . .

[For the rest of section 2 the author expatiates on the work of the Word in creation.]

3 Did He send Him, as a man might think, on a mission of
4 domination and fear and terror? Indeed He did not, but in gentleness and meekness He sent Him, as a king sending his own son who is himself a king; He sent Him as God, He sent Him as man to men, He sent Him with the idea of saving, of persuading, not of forcing; for force is no part of the nature of God. He sent Him as
5 inviting, not as pursuing man; He sent Him in love, not in judge-
6 ment. For He will send Him in judgement; and who shall en-
7 dure His coming? . . . (Do you not see them) flung to the wild
8 beasts, to make them deny their Lord, and yet unconquered? Do you not see that the more of them are punished the more their
9 numbers increase? These things do not look like the achievements of man; they are the power of God; they are the proofs of His presence. (L. B. Radford, *The Epistle to Diognetus*, pp. 61ff., altered.)

With this account of Christian life, cf. that in *The Apology* of Aristeides (35).
V.7. *not common*, i.e. not polluted, the reference is probably to the calumnies circulated about Christian "love-feasts": but many accept the conjecture κοίτη, "bed".

17. *and they that hate them can state no ground*: "Besides the hatred which knew its own reasons—the hatred of the Jew for believers in the Christhood of the Nazarene, and the hatred of the pagan for the scorners of his gods—there was the hatred of the world, Jewish and pagan alike, for the Christianity which rebuked its ways; and this was the hatred which could not or would not give an account of itself." (Radford, op. cit., p. 66.)
VII.9. *they are the proofs of His presence*: In section 6 παρουσία was translated "coming" because the context was one of judgement. There is a lacuna after 6 and the ideas in 7ff. refer to what is happening in the course of history. The word may apply to Christ's *first* coming, or to His continuing presence with His followers.

37. WHY PEOPLE BECOME CHRISTIANS

(Justin, *Apology*, I.16.)

[After quoting Christ's words, based on Luke 6.29, Matt. 5.22, 41,16, Justin goes on:]

For we ought not to be contentious; neither has He (Christ) desired us to be imitators of wicked men, but He exhorted us to lead all men, by patience and gentleness, from shame and the love of evil. For we can prove this even in the case of many who once were of your way of thinking, but have changed their violent and tyrannical disposition, being overcome either by the constancy which they have witnessed in their neighbours' lives, or by the extraordinary forbearance they have observed in their fellow-travellers when defrauded, or by the honesty of those with whom they transacted business. (A.-N. C. L., altered.)

In the second century the Christians lived down the slanderous accusations made against them.

38. CONVERSION

(Justin, *Dialogue with Trypho*, 110, 3–4.)

3   And we who were filled full of war, and slaughter one of another, and every kind of evil, have from out of the whole earth each changed our weapons of war, our swords into ploughshares and our pikes into farming tools, and we farm piety, righteousness, the love of man, faith, and hope which comes from the father Himself through Him who was crucified, each of us dwelling under his own vine, that is, each enjoying only his own wedded wife. For ye know the word of prophecy, *and his wife*
4   *as a thriving vine.*[1] And that there is *none that maketh afraid*,[2] and leadeth into captivity us who throughout all the earth have set our faith on Jesus, is evident. For though we are beheaded, and crucified, and exposed to beasts and chains and fire and all other forms of torture, it is plain that we do not forsake the confession of our faith, but the more things of this kind happen to us so much the more are there many others who become believers and truly religious through the name of Jesus. Just as when one cuts away the parts of a vine that have borne fruit, it so bursts

[1] Ps. 128.3.   [2] Mic. 4.4.

forth that other flourishing and fruitbearing branches shoot up—
in that very way is it also with us. For the vine that has been planted
by God, and Christ the Saviour, is His people. (A. Lukyn
Williams, *The Dialogue with Trypho*, pp. 226-7.)

On Christian bravery in martyrdom as an impulse to conversion, cf. Justin,
Apology, II.12, and Tertullian, *Apology*, 50.12-16.

39. CHRISTIANS CHARGED WITH ATHEISM, AT THE INSTIGATION OF DEMONS

(Justin, *Apology*, I.5-6.)

5   Why, then, should this be? In our case, though we declare that
we do no wickedness, and that we do not hold these atheistic
opinions, you do not examine the charges made against us; but,
impelled by unreasoning passion, and by the instigation of evil
demons, you punish us without examination. For the truth shall
be spoken; because of old evil demons, effecting apparitions, both
defiled women and corrupted boys, and showed such terrifying
sights to men, that those who did not use reason in judging of the
actions that were done, were struck with terror; but being carried
away by fear, and not knowing that these were evil demons,
they called them gods, and called each by the name which each
of the demons gave for himself. And when Socrates endeavoured,
by true reason and examination, to bring these things to light, and
deliver men from the demons, then the demons themselves, by
means of men who rejoiced in iniquity, compassed his death, as
an atheist and a profane person, on the charge that "he was introducing new divinities"; and in our case they display a similar
activity. For not only among the Greeks did reason (Logos) prevail to condemn these things through Socrates, but also among
the Barbarians were they condemned by Reason (or the Word,
the Logos) Himself, who took shape, and became man, and was
called Jesus Christ; and in obedience to Him, we not only deny
that they who did such things as these are really gods, but assert
that they are wicked and impious demons, whose actions will
not bear comparison with those even of men desirous of virtue.

6   Hence are we called atheists. And we confess that we are
atheists, so far as gods of this sort are concerned, but not with
respect to the most true God, the Father of righteousness and
temperance and the other virtues, who is free from all impurity.

But both Him, and the Son who came forth from Him and taught us these things, and the host of the other good angels who follow and are made like to Him, and the prophetic Spirit, we worship and adore, knowing them in reason and truth, and declaring without grudging to every one who wishes to learn, as we have been taught. (A.-N. C. L., altered.)

λόγος in Justin has sometimes to be translated "reason", and sometimes "Reason, or Word" according to the context.

The Christians were often called "Atheists", cf. 10, 18 (*Martyrdom of Polycarp*, III.2, IX.2), 110.

the host of the other good angels . . .: "The only natural translation of the text, as it stands, commits Justin to the worship of angels" (B. L. Gildersleeve, *The Apologies of Justin Martyr*, p. 117).

40. CHRISTIANS BEFORE CHRIST

(Justin, *Apology*, I.46.)

But lest some should, without reason, and for the perversion of what we teach, maintain that we say that Christ was born one hundred and fifty years ago under Quirinius, and taught what we say He taught subsequently in the time of Pontius Pilate; and should urge against us as though all men who were born before Him were irresponsible—let us anticipate and solve the difficulty. We have been taught that Christ is the first-born of God, and we have declared above that He is the Word of whom every race of men were partakers; and those who lived with reason are Christians, even though they were thought atheists; as, among the Greeks, Socrates and Heraclitus, and men like them; and among the barbarians, Abraham, and Ananias, and Azarias, and Misael, and Elias, and many others whose actions and names we decline for the present to recount, because we know it would be tedious.

The question "Why did not Christ come sooner?" was one which the early Christians had to face, and this is Justin's answer, cf. *Epistle to Diognetus*, 9.

Justin compares Christ with Socrates in *Apology*, II.10: his regard for Heracleitus comes from that philosopher's attachment to the λόγος, cf., e.g., Adam, *The Religious Teachers of Greece*, p. 216ff. His liking for Heracleitus was not shared by his pupil Tatian (*Oration to the Greeks*, 3).

Eusebius, the Church Historian, held the view that "the teaching of Christianity was neither new nor strange. What was new was the Church, the race of Christians. Their corporate existence, their general piety, and their increasing influence were indeed new, but their teaching was not. It had been followed centuries before them by Abraham and Moses and the later prophets; and the religion of the patriarchs was identical with that of the Christians. All history was a contest between God, acting through Patriarchs, Prophets, and the Church on the one hand, and the Devil, instigating Jews, Persecutors, and Heretics, on the other. It is a contest in which the Devil always gets the worst of it in the long run, but the righteous suffer considerably in the process." (Lake, *Eusebius*, *Ecclesiastical History* (Loeb Library), I, pp. xv–xvi.)

41. THE LIGHT THAT LIGHTETH EVERY MAN

(Justin, *Apology*, II.13.)

For I myself, when I discovered the wicked disguise which the evil spirits had thrown around the divine doctrines of the Christians, to turn aside others from joining them, laughed both at those who framed these falsehoods, and at the disguise itself, and at popular opinion; and I confess that I both boast and with all my strength strive to be found a Christian; not because the teachings of Plato are different from those of Christ, but because they are not in all respects similar, as neither are those of the others, Stoics, and poets and historians. For each man spoke well in proportion to the share he had of the generative word (or reason), seeing what was related to it. But they who contradict themselves on the more important points appear not to have possessed the wisdom that is infallible, and the knowledge which is irrefutable. Whatever things were rightly said among all teachers, are the property of us Christians. For next to God, we worship and love the Word who is from the Unbegotten and Ineffable God, since also He became man for our sakes, that, becoming a partaker of our sufferings, He might also bring us healing. For all the writers were able to see realities darkly through the sowing of the implanted word that was in them. For the seed and imitation imparted according to capacity is one thing, and quite another is the thing itself, of which there is the participation and imitation according to the grace which is from Him. (A.-N. C. L., altered.)

the generative word (or reason): a Stoic term. "In action as the creative force in nature, this universal Reason also bears the name of Generative Reason (σπερματικὸς λόγος). It bears this name more immediately in relation to the universe, not only as being the generating power by which all things are produced from primary fire as from seed according to an inner law, but because in the present condition of things all form and shape, all life and reason grow out of it, in short, because primary fire and reason contain in themselves the germ of all things: In the same sense generative powers in the plural, or σπερματικοὶ λόγοι denote the generative powers as part of the soul, and must be thought of as bearing the same relation to the individual soul that the generative powers of Nature do to the soul of nature. By the term generative reason, therefore must be understood the creative and forming forces in nature, which have collectively produced the Universe, and particular exercises of which produce individual things." (Zeller, *Stoics, Epicureans and Sceptics*, E. Tr. (revised ed.), pp. 172-3.)

42. CHRISTIAN BAPTISM AND CHRISTIAN WORSHIP

(Justin, *Apology*, I, 61-7.)

The secretiveness of the Christians as to their rites and ceremonies was one of the reasons for public distrust of their morals: some of the Apologists do little to dispel this distrust: naturally they did not wish to reveal what was known only to the faithful. Justin however came out into the open.

61   I will explain how we also dedicated ourselves to God when we were made new through Christ; lest, if we omit this, we seem to be in any way unfair in our explanation. As many as are persuaded and believe that the things are true which are taught by us and said to be true, and undertake to be able to live accordingly, are instructed to pray and to entreat God with fasting, for the remission of their past sins, and we pray and fast with them. Then they are brought by us where there is water, and are born again in the same manner in which we were ourselves born again. For, in the name of God, the Father and Lord of the universe, and of our Saviour Jesus Christ, and of the Holy Spirit, they then receive the washing with water.

[Justin then quotes John 3.5 (*Except ye be born again . . .*) and Isa. 1.16-20 (*Wash you, make you clean . . .*).]

And for this rite we have learned the following reason from the apostles. Since at our first birth we were born without our own knowledge or choice, by our parents coming together, and were brought up in bad habits and wicked training; in order that we may not remain the children of necessity and of ignorance, but may become the children of choice and knowledge, and may obtain the remission of sins formerly committed, there is pronounced in the water over him who has chosen to be born again, and has repented of his sins, the name of God the Father and Lord of the universe; he who leads to the laver the person that is to be washed calling Him by this name alone. For no one can give a name to the ineffable God; and if any one dare to say that it is possible to do so, he raves with the so-called hopeless madness. And this washing is called illumination, because they who learn these things are illuminated in their understandings. And in the name of Jesus Christ, who was crucified under Pontius Pilate, and in the name of the Holy Ghost, who through the prophets foretold all things about Jesus, he who is illuminated is washed.

62   [Justin points out that the evil demons instigate a parody of baptism in *their* rites, and cause their worshippers to "put off their shoes" in parody of the command given to Moses.
63, 64   A digression on how God appeared to Moses, and on further misrepresentations by the demons.
65   Justin returns to the subject of Christian initiation, and describes the first Eucharist of the newly baptized, and the weekly worship of Christians.]

But we, after we have thus washed him who has been convinced and has assented to our teaching, bring him to the place where those who are called brethren are assembled, in order that we may offer earnest prayers in common for ourselves and for the newly enlightened person, and for all others in every place, that we may be counted worthy, now that we have learned the truth, by our works also to be found good citizens and keepers of the commandments, so that we may be saved with an everlasting salvation. At the end of the prayers, we salute one another with a kiss. There is then brought to the president of the brethren bread and a cup of wine mixed with water; and he taking them, offers up praise and glory to the Father of the universe, through the name of the Son and of the Holy Ghost, and gives thanks at considerable length for our being counted worthy to receive these things at His hands. When he has concluded the prayers and thanksgivings, all the people present express their joyful assent by saying Amen. (Amen in the Hebrew language means "so be it".) And when the president has given thanks, and all the people have expressed their joyful assent, those who are called by us deacons give to each of those present to partake of the bread and wine mixed with water over which the thanksgiving was pronounced, and to those who are absent they carry away a portion.

66   And this food is called among us "Eucharist", of which no one is allowed to partake but the man who believes that the things which we teach are true, and who has been washed with the washing that is for remission of sins and unto a second birth, and who is so living as Christ has enjoined. For not as common bread and common drink do we receive these; but in like manner as Jesus Christ our Saviour, having been made flesh by the word of God, had both flesh and blood for our salvation, so likewise have we been taught that the food which is blessed by the word of prayer transmitted from Him, and by which our blood and flesh by assimilation are nourished, is the flesh and blood of that Jesus who was made flesh. For the apostles, in the memoirs composed by them, which are called Gospels, have thus delivered unto us what was enjoined upon them; that Jesus took bread, and when He had given thanks, said, *This do in remembrance of me, this is my body*[1]; and that, after the same manner, having taken the cup and given thanks, He said, *This is my blood*[2]; and gave it to them alone. This the wicked demons in imitation, in the mysteries of Mithras, delivered the command to do. For that bread and a cup of water are placed with certain formulae in the mystic rites of one who is being initiated, you either know or can learn. (A.-N. C. L., altered from Gwatkin, *Selections from early Christian Writers*, and from other sources.)

67   [Justin goes on to describe the weekly Eucharist held each Sunday.]

61.   The baptismal formula is in the threefold name: the characterization of God as *Father and Lord of the universe* excludes heretical conceptions of a second god; the characterization of Jesus Christ, as *crucified under Pontius Pilate*, is in opposition to docetic ideas. On Baptism, cf. 103, 107, 130, 156–7.

65.   *with a kiss:* cf. 168 below.

66.   *For not as common bread*, etc. "This passage is claimed alike by Calvinists, Lutherans and Romanists; and, indeed, the language is so inexact that each party may plausibly maintain that their own opinion is advocated by it" (M. Dods, in A.-N. C. L.).

the word of prayer transmitted from Him, i.e. from the institution of the Eucharist.

Tertullian also mentions this Mithraic communion in *De Praescriptione Haereticorum*, 40.

On Christian Worship, see also 13, 14, 103, 147.

[1] Luke 22.19.   [2] Matt. 26.28; Mark 14.24.

43. JUDAISTIC CHRISTIANITY

(Justin, *Dialogue with Trypho*, 47.1-4.)

1   Trypho inquired again: If a man, aware that this is so, after he has also plainly known that this is the Christ, and believed and obeyed Him, wishes to keep these precepts also—shall he be saved?

And I: In my opinion, Trypho, I say that such a man will be saved, unless he strenuously does his very utmost to persuade others—I mean those of the Gentiles who have been circumcised by Christ from their error—to keep the commandments that he does, saying that they will not be saved unless they keep them. For this is what you yourself did at the beginning of our discussion, declaring that I shall not be saved unless I keep them.

2   He answered: Why then do you say: "In my opinion such a man shall be saved?" Are there any who say that such persons shall not be saved?

There are, Trypho, was my reply, and persons who are bold enough not even to join with such in conversation or meals; with whom I myself do not agree. But if they, because of the weakness of their mind, desire to keep such of the sayings of Moses as are now possible—which we perceive were appointed because of the hardness of the people's heart—while they still hope on this Christ of ours, and also desire to keep those ordinances of the practice of righteousness and of piety which are everlasting and in accordance with nature, and choose to live with Christians and believers, as I said before, without persuading them either to receive circumcision like themselves, or to keep sabbath, or to observe other things of the same kind—I declare that we must fully receive such, and have communion with them in all

3   respects, as being of one family and as brothers. But if, Trypho, I said, they who are of your race say they believe on this Christ of ours, and in every way compel those who are of Gentile birth and believe on this Christ to live in accordance with the law appointed by Moses, or choose not to have communion with them that have such a life in common—these also in like manner I do not

4   accept. Now they that follow their advice, and live under the law, as well as keep their profession in the Christ of God, will, I suppose, perhaps be saved. But they that once professed and recognized that this is the Christ, and for some cause or other passed over into the life under the Law, denying that this is the

Christ, and do not repent before death, cannot, I declare, in any wise be saved. (A. Lukyn Williams, *The Dialogue with Trypho*, pp. 93-4, slightly altered.)

[In the rest of Ch. 47 Justin declares that Jews cannot be saved, particularly those who curse the Christians in their synagogues (cf. Lukyn Williams, op. cit., p. 33, n.3), and repeats what he had said about apostates to Judaism, concluding with a saying that he attributes to Christ, "In whatsoever I overtake you, in that will I also judge you". (Cf. Lukyn Williams, op. cit., p. 95, n.2.)]

1. *Trypho inquired again*: he had originally asked about the salvation of Jewish Christians who kept the Law in Ch. 46.

2. Justin's charitable view of Jewish Christianity was not, as we see from the above passage, shared by all Christians. Later on Jewish Christians were regarded as heretical: Jerome writing to Augustine, regards them as neither Jews nor Christians. (*Ep.* 112.13 (75 in C. S. E. L. edition of Augustine's letters).)

4. Conversion from Christianity to Judaism was not unknown through the whole period of early church history.

44. THE APOLOGY OF MELITO OF SARDIS, c. 175

(Eusebius, *H.E.* IV.26.5-11.)

In the earlier sections of Ch. 26, Eusebius gives a list of Melito's works, and quotes his work *On the Passover* (see 125nn.). He then proceeds to quote from his *Apology* addressed to Marcus Aurelius, a work now lost.

5 And in the petition addressed to the emperor, Melito records that under him the following misfortunes befell us:

For the race of the godly—a thing that never before happened—is now persecuted, being harassed in Asia by recent decrees. For the shameless informers and lovers of other men's goods, taking advantage of the ordinances, plunder openly, day and night pillaging innocent persons.

6   *   *   *

And if this action is taking place at thy bidding, well and good. For a just emperor would never make an unjust decision; and we for our part gladly accept the honour of such a death. Howbeit. this request only we present to thee, that thou wouldest thyself first note the workers of such strife, and so judge aright as to whether they are worthy of death and punishment, or of safety and quiet. But if this decision and this fresh ordinance—not fit for use even against barbarian enemies—come not from thee, we beseech thee all the more earnestly not to abandon us to such spoliation at the hands of the people.

7   *   *   *

For our philosophy at first flourished among barbarians; but after it had appeared among thy peoples during the mighty principate of thy ancestor Augustus, it became to thy Empire especially an auspicious boon. For from that time the power of the Romans increased to something great and splendid. And to this thou hast become the successor whom men desired; yea, and such shalt thou continue to be, along with thy son, if thou protectest the philosophy which goes with the Empire and began with Augustus, which also thy ancestors honoured, as they did the other religions.
8 And this is the greatest proof of the fact that it was for the good that our doctrine flourished alongside of the Empire in its happy inception: that from the time of the principate of Augustus no evil has befallen it, but, on the contrary, all things have been
9 splendid and glorious in accordance with the prayers of all. Nero and Domitian, alone of all [the emperors], persuaded by certain malignant persons, desired to bring our doctrine into ill repute; and since their day, by an unreasonable custom, lying information
10 about the Christians has come to be prevalent. But thy pious fathers have corrected their ignorance, many a time rebuking in writing as many as dared to raise disturbances concerning them. Thus it is clear that thy grandfather Hadrian wrote to the proconsul Fundanus, governor of Asia, as well as to many others besides; and thy father, when thou also wast ruling the world with him, wrote to the cities, and, among others, to the people of Larissa and Thessalonica and Athens, and to all the Greeks,
11 that they should raise no disturbances concerning us. But as for thee, we are the more persuaded that thou wilt do all whatsoever we ask of thee, inasmuch as thou art of the same mind on these matters as they; aye, and with a far greater love for mankind and for wisdom. (Lawlor and Oulton, *Eusebius*, I, pp. 132–3, slightly altered.)

5.   *by recent decrees*: Melito appears to regard the situation as having changed for the worse, cf. 21.

10.   *Hadrian wrote to the proconsul Fundanus*: see 16.

New points that appear in Melito are his ideas that church and empire rose and prospered together, and that only bad emperors were active persecutors.

This idea is correct in that only Nero and (?) Domitian adopted a positive policy, but the difficulties attending the position of the Christians are revealed by the succession of imperial rescripts about them. Cf. also Tertullian, *Apology*, 5.6–8 (140).

45. THE CHARGES BROUGHT AGAINST THE CHRISTIANS, c. 177

(Athenagoras, *Legatio pro Christianis*, 1–3.)

1   [Athenagoras argues that the Emperors grant toleration to all religions,]

. . . deeming on the one hand, that to believe in no god at all is impious and wicked, and on the other that it is necessary for each man to worship the gods he prefers, in order that, through fear of the deity, men may be kept from wrongdoing. But in our case—and do not like the multitude to be led astray by hearsay—we are hated for our name.

. . . Names are not deserving of hatred: it is the unjust act that calls for penalty and punishment. And accordingly, with admiration of your mildness and gentleness, and your peaceful and benevolent disposition towards every man, individuals live in the possession of equal rights; and the whole empire, under your intelligent sway, enjoys profound peace. But for us who are called Christians you have not in like manner cared; but although we commit no wrong—nay, as will appear in the sequel of this discourse, are of all men most piously and righteously disposed towards the Deity and towards your government—you allow us to be harassed, plundered and persecuted, the multitude making war upon us for our name alone. We venture therefore to lay a statement of our case before you . . . and we beseech you to bestow some consideration upon us also, that we may cease at length to be slaughtered at the instigation of false accusers.

[Athenagoras proceeds to show that Christians despise attacks on their property or on worldly possessions, but that the attacks do not stop there and are directed against their persons: their opponents "pour upon us wholesale charges of crime of which we are guiltless even in thought."

Chapter 2 is a plea that Christians should not be judged merely by their name, but by their crimes, if any.]

3   Three things are alleged against us: atheism, Thyestean feasts,

Oedipodean intercourse. But if these charges are true, spare no
class; proceed at once against our crimes; destroy us root and
branch, with our wives and children, if any man is found to live
like the brutes.

But, if these things are only idle tales and empty slanders,
originating in the fact that virtue is opposed by its very nature
to vice, and that contraries war against one another by a divine law
(and you are yourselves witnesses that no such iniquities are
committed by us, for you forbid informations to be laid against
us), it remains for you to make inquiry concerning our life, our
opinions, our loyalty and obedience to you and your house and
government, and thus at length to grant to us the same rights
(we ask nothing more) as to those who persecute us. For we shall
then conquer them, unhesitatingly surrendering, as we now do,
our very lives for the truth's sake. (A.-N. C. L., slightly altered.)

Persecution "for the name" was a policy that perplexed both Christians and
pagans.

46. ATHENAGORAS FLATTERS THE EMPERORS

(Athenagoras, *Legatio pro Christianis*, 6.)

Then there are Plato and Aristotle—not that I am about to go
through all that the philosophers have said about God, as if I
wished to exhibit a complete summary of their opinions; for I
know that, as you excel all men in intelligence and in the power
of your rule, in the same proportion do you surpass them all in
an accurate acquaintance with all learning, cultivating as you do
each several branch with more success than even those who have
devoted themselves exclusively to any one. (A.-N. C. L.)

Towards the end of Ch. 7 Athenagoras refers to the Emperors as "excelling
all others in intelligence and in piety towards the true God". He cannot be
acquitted of flattery, and the existence of this tendency shows that how much
even a Christian could be affected by current rhetorical methods of address.

47. HEGESIPPUS

(Eusebius, *H.E.* IV.22.)

1   Now Hegesippus, in the five Memoirs which have come down
to us, has left behind a very complete record of his personal views.
And in his Memoirs he tells us that on a journey as far as *Rome* he

associated with very many bishops, and that he had received the same teaching from all. In fact, we may listen to what he says, when, after some remarks on the epistle of Clement to the Corinthians, he adds as follows:

2   And the church of the Corinthians continued in the true doctrine until Primus was bishop at Corinth.. . . . With them I associated on my voyage to Rome, and I abode with the Corinthians many days; during which we were refreshed together in
3   the true doctrine. But when I came to Rome, I made for myself a succession-list as far as Anicetus; whose deacon was Eleutherus. And from Anicetus Soter received the succession; after whom came Eleutherus. And in every succession and in every city that which the Law and the Prophets and the Lord preach is faithfully followed.

4-6 [Eusebius quotes Hegesippus on the succession of Symeon, cousin of Christ, as bishop of Jerusalem, on the origin of heresy,
7   which he traces to jealousy on the part of Thebuthis, a defeated candidate, and on the sects among the Jews.]

8   And he wrote very much else besides, which in part we have already mentioned previously, giving the accounts at suitable points. And he sets down certain things from the Gospel of the Hebrews and the Syriac [Gospel] and, in particular, from [writings in] the Hebrew tongue, thus showing that he was himself a believer of Hebrew origin. And he relates other matters as well,
9   on the strength of unwritten Jewish tradition. And not only he, but Irenaeus also and the whole company of the ancients, used to call the Proverbs of Solomon "All-virtuous Wisdom." And in treating of the Apocryphal [books], as they are called, he records that some of them were fabricated by certain heretics in his own time. (Lawlor and Oulton, *Eusebius*, I, p. 127-8.)

3.   *I made for myself a succession-list* (διαδοχὴν): this list was identified by Lightfoot with one found in Epiphanius *Haer.* 27.6. But the following objections have been brought against this rendering: (1) Why does Eusebius, who is greatly interested in episcopal succession, not give the list? (2) Can the word διαδοχή mean, in the time of Hegesippus, a "list"? (3) Why does Rufinus translate the Greek by "permansi ibi", "I stayed there"? Hence Harnack and others prefer the emendation διατριβὴν or διαγωγὴν, "stay". Cf. Eus. *H.E.* IV.11.7. "Hegesippus records that he himself took up his abode at Rome in his (Anicetus') day, and remained (permansisse, Rufinus) there until the episcopate of Eleutherus." (Lawlor and Oulton, op. cit., I.113.)
The following replies may be made to these arguments: (1) The "argument

from silence" is a very dangerous one; (2) In Eus. *H.E.* V.5.9, 12.2, διαδοχὴ can bear the meaning "list". "There is evidence that even in pre-Christian writers it might possibly be used of a series of names. It is impossible therefore absolutely to rule out such a meaning here, however unlikely it may be." (Jalland, *The Church and the Papacy*, p. 87); (3) Rufinus is by no means an accurate translator.

9. *"All-virtuous Wisdom"*: used, e.g., by Clement, *Epistle to the Corinthians*, LVII. On designations of the Book of Proverbs see Lightfoot's note in *St Clement of Rome*, II, pp. 166–7.

On the dates of the Roman Bishops, see 96 (notes).

48. SIMON MAGUS

(Justin, *Apology*, I.26.)

There was a Samaritan, Simon, a native of the village called Gitto, who in the reign of Claudius Caesar, and in your royal city of Rome, did mighty acts of magic, by virtue of the art of the devils operating in him. He was considered a god, and as a god was honoured by you with a statue, which statue was erected on the river Tiber, between the two bridges, and bore this inscription, in the language of Rome:

"Simoni Deo Sancto,"
"To Simon the holy God."

And almost all the Samaritans, and a few even of other nations, worship him, and acknowledge him as the first god; and a woman, Helena, who went about with him at that time, and had formerly been a prostitute, they say is the first idea generated by him. (A.-N. C. L.)

Whether Simon is the same as the person of that name in Acts 8.9–24 is uncertain. Justin regarded him as merely a pretender to divine honours; but he certainly links him with heresy: shortly after the above passage he mentions Marcion (74). It was as the *fons et origo* of heresy that the Church remembered Simon throughout the early centuries, cf. Irenaeus (who mentions the statue —"he is said to have been honoured . . ."—), I.16.1, Harvey; I.23.1, A.-N. C. L.; "Simon, from whom all sorts of heresies derive their origin . . ." .

Justin was quite mistaken about the statue. A base was found in 1574 in the island in the Tiber but the inscription reads SEMONI SANCO DEO FIDIO etc. SEMO SANCUS was an Italian deity and the dedication was misread by Justin or his informant.

49. THE CONTENT OF GNOSIS

(Clement of Alexandria, *Excerpta ex Theodoto*, 78.2.)

... who we were, and what we have become, where we were, where we were placed, whither we hasten, from what we are redeemed, what birth is, what rebirth. (R. P. Casey, *Studies and Documents*, I, p. 89, slightly altered.)

Cf. the Valentinian *Gospel of Truth*, "He who thus is going to have knowledge knows whence he came and whither he is going" (R. M. Grant, *Gnosticism, an Anthology*, p. 150).

50. BASILEIDES: THE ALLEGED TRADITION

(Hippolytus, *Refutation of all Heresies*, VII.20.1 (A.-N. C. L. VII.8).)

Basileides, therefore, and Isidorus, the true son and disciple of Basileides, say that Matthias communicated to them secret discourses, which, being specially instructed, he heard from the Saviour. Let us, then, see how clearly Basileides, simultaneously with Isidorus, and the entire band of their followers, not only tell lies about Matthias, but even about the Saviour Himself. (A.-N. C. L., altered.)

On tradition as establishing doctrine, cf. 69, 96.

51. BASILEIDES: "IN THE BEGINNING"

(Hippolytus, *Refutation of all Heresies*, VII.20.2 (A.-N. C. L. VII.8).)

There was [a time] says Basileides, when there was "nothing". Not even, however, did that "nothing" constitute anything of existent things; but, to express myself undisguisedly and candidly, and without any quibbling, there was absolutely not one single thing. But when, he says, I employ the expression "was", I do not say that it was, but in order to signify the meaning of what I wish to elucidate, namely that there was "absolutely nothing". (A.-N. C. L., altered.)

52. BASILEIDES: THE ABSOLUTE TRANS-CENDENCE OF "GOD"

(Hippolytus, *Refutation of all Heresies*, VII.21.1-2,4 (A.-N. C. L. VII.9).)

1   Since, therefore, "nothing" existed,—not matter, nor substance, nor what is insubstantial, nor simple, nor composite, nor uncompounded, nor devoid of senses, nor man, nor angel, nor god, nor,

in short, any of those things that have names, or are apprehended by sense, or that are cognized by intellect, but when all things have been thus, and even with greater minuteness, absolutely removed, God, "non-existent" (whom Aristotle styles "conception of conception", but these (heretics) "non-existent"), inconceivably, insensibly, indeterminately, involuntarily, im-
2 passively, and unactuated by desire, willed to create a world. Now I employ, he says, the expression "willed" for the purpose of expressing my meaning, for he did so involuntarily, and inconceivably and insensibly. And by the expression "world" I do not mean that which was subsequently formed according to breadth and division, and which stood apart; nay, far from this, for I mean the germ of a world. The germ, however, of the world had all things in itself.

* * *

4 In this way, "non-existent" God made the world out of "non-existents", casting and depositing some one Seed that contained in itself a conglomeration of the germs of the world. (A.-N. C. L., altered.)

53. BASILEIDES: CREATION

(Hippolytus, *Refutation of all Heresies*, VII.22.3—25 (A.-N. C. L. VII.10–13)).

22.3 Whence, he says, came the light? From nothing. For it has not been written, he says, whence, but only from the voice of him who speaks the word. And he who speaks the word, he says, was non-existent; nor was that existent which was being produced.
4 The seed of the cosmical system was generated, he says, from non-existents, i.e. the word which was spoken, *Let there be light.*[1] And this, he says, is that which has been stated in the Gospels: *He was the true light, which lighteth every man that cometh into the world.*[2] He derives his originating principles from that Seed, and is enlightened. This is that seed which has in itself the entire conglomeration of germs. (A.-N. C. L., altered.)

5 [Hippolytus goes on to relate this (cosmic) Seed to the thought of Aristotle; it is the "genus" from which infinite "species" are derived.

* * *

[1] Gen. 1.3.   [2] John 1.9.

7 In this Seed existed the principle of Sonship, in a triple sense. The First Sonship was subtle in substance, the Second more
8 opaque or coarse, the Third required purification. The First on bursting forth from the Seed flew upward to the "non-existent"
9– God, the Second desired to do so; but could reach the "non-
16 existent" only by the help of a "wing" which Basileides called "Holy Spirit": the latter could not itself reach this sphere, but became the firmament, separating what was below (the Cosmos) from the sphere of the "non-existent". The Third Sonship remained in the Seed.

* * *

23.3 There next burst forth from the Seed the Great Archon, the
–6 head of the Cosmos: he soared aloft as far as the firmament, which blocked his course, but he believed that nothing lay beyond, and that he himself was the sole god. He therefore began to create the Cosmos, but first he created a son, who was superior to his father in intelligence and wisdom (this had been pre-determined by the "non-existent" God), and with him, he proceeded to the work of creation.]

23.7 This is, according to them, what is denominated the Ogdoad, where the Great Archon has his throne. The entire celestial creation, then, that is, the Aether, the Great Wise Creator Himself formed. The Son, however, begotten of this Archon, operates in him, and offered him suggestions, being endued with far greater wisdom than the Creator Himself. (A.-N. C. L.)

* * *

25.3 [The Great Archon imagined that he was the Supreme Being, as he was unable to penetrate into the realm of the "non-existent" God.
24.3–4 The heavenly Cosmos extending as far as the moon was thus created. A similar process produced the sub-lunary Cosmos, called the Hebdomad. A second Archon arose from the Cosmic Seed, far inferior to the First, and he also produced a son superior to himself, and went on to the work of creation. He is the God of the Old Testament.
25.1, 5 Meanwhile, the Third Sonship had been left behind in the Cosmic Seed, still the domain of formlessness. To illuminate this the Gospel came.]

54. BASILEIDES: THE GOSPEL

(Hippolytus, *Refutation of all Heresies*, VII.26.1–4,7 (A.-N. C. L. VII.14).)

1   The Gospel then came, says Basileides, first from the Sonship through the Son, that was seated beside the Archon, to the Archon, and the Archon learned that He was not God of the universe, but was begotten; and had above himself the deposited treasure of that Ineffable and Unnameable and Non-existent One, and of the Sonship; he both repented and feared when he understood in

2   what ignorance he was. This, he says, is what has been declared: *The fear of the Lord is the beginning of wisdom.*[1] For, being orally instructed by Christ, who was seated near, he began to acquire wisdom, learning who is the Non-Existent One, what the Sonship is, what the Holy Spirit, what the constitution of all things, and where the restoration of these will occur. This is the wisdom spoken in a mystery, concerning which, says Basileides, Scripture uses the following expressions: *Not in words taught of human wisdom, but in those taught of the Spirit.*[2] The Archon, then, being orally instructed, and taught, and being thereby filled with fear, proceeded to make confession concerning the sin which He had

4   committed in magnifying Himself. This, he says, is what has been declared: *I have recognized my sin, and I know my transgression, and about this I shall confess for ever.*[3] When, then, the Great Archon had been orally instructed, and the whole creation of the Ogdoad had been orally instructed and taught, and the mystery became known to the celestial powers, it was also necessary that afterwards the Gospel should come to the Hebdomad, in order likewise that the Archon of the Hebdomad might be similarly instructed and indoctrinated into the Gospel. (A.-N. C. L., altered.)

[A similar process enlightened the Hebdomad, and . . .]

7   . . . it was necessary, likewise, that afterwards the Formlessness existent in our quarter of creation should be enlightened, and that the mystery should be revealed to the Sonship, which had been left behind in Formlessness, just like an abortion. (A.-N. C. L., altered.)

---

[1] Ps. 111.10.   [2] 1 Cor. 2.13.   [3] Ps. 32.5.

55. BASILEIDES: JESUS

(Hippolytus, *Refutation of all Heresies*, VII.26.8,10 (A.-N. C. L. VII.14).)

8 The light, therefore, which came down from the Ogdoad above to the Son of the Hebdomad, descended from the Hebdomad upon Jesus the son of Mary, and he was enlightened being illuminated with the light that shone upon him. (A.-N. C. L., altered.)

10 [As a result the Third Sonship was redeemed from the sphere of Formlessness, and hastened upward to the sphere of Sonship.]

56. BASILEIDES: THE INCARNATION

(Hippolytus, *Refutation of all Heresies*, VII.27.8–12 (A.-N. C. L. VII.15).)

8 Jesus, however, was born, according to these heretics, as we have already declared. And when the generation which has been previously explained took place, all the events in the Saviour's life occurred, according to them, in the same manner as they have been written in the Gospels. And these things happened, he says, in order that Jesus might become the firstfruit of a distinction of the different orders that had been confused together. (A.-N. C. L., altered.)

9–11 [Jesus contained in himself something from all parts of the creation and performed a separating process which clearly distinguished the separate parts of creation.]

For the whole doctrine of these heretics is the confusion as it were of the cosmic seed; and the distinction and restoration of the things which were in confusion to their proper spheres.
12 Jesus has become the firstfruit of the distinction and his passion has taken place for no other cause than to bring distinction to things that had been confused. For Basileides says that in this way all the Sonship that had been left in Formlessness in order to give and receive benefits had to be distinguished as Jesus also had been distinguished (i.e. by the different elements in him separating into the different parts of creation). (A.-N. C. L., altered.)

57. BASILEIDES: THE CONSUMMATION OF ALL THINGS

(Hippolytus, *Refutation of all Heresies*, VII.27.1–4 (A.-N. C. L. VII.15).)

1   When, therefore, he says, the entire Sonship shall have come, and shall be above the boundary, i.e. the Spirit, then the creation will become the object of mercy. For *the creation groans until now,* and is tormented, and waits for *the manifestation of the sons of God,*[1] in order that all the men of the Sonship may ascend from thence. When this takes place, God, he says, will bring upon the whole Cosmos enormous ignorance, that all things may continue according to their nature, and that nothing may desire
2   anything of the things that are contrary to their nature. But all the souls of this quarter of creation, as many as possess the nature of remaining immortal in this region only, continue in it, aware of nothing different or better. And there will not prevail any rumour or knowledge in regions below concerning superior regions, lest subjacent souls should be wrung with torture from longing after impossibilities.

*   *   *

3   All things, therefore, that abide in their own peculiar locality are incorruptible, but corruptible if they are disposed to wander and cross over from the things that are according to their nature. In this way the Archon of the Hebdomad will know nothing of superjacent entities. For enormous ignorance will lay hold on him likewise, in order that sorrow, and grief and groaning may depart from him; for he will not desire aught of impossible things,
4   nor will he be visited with anguish. In like manner, however, this ignorance will lay hold also on the Great Archon of the Ogdoad, and similarly on all the creatures that are subject unto him, in order that in no respect anything may desire aught of those things that are contrary to its nature, and may not thus be overwhelmed with sorrow. And so there will be the restitution of all things which, in conformity with their nature, have in the beginning a foundation in the Cosmic Seed, but will be restored at their proper periods. (A.-N. C. I., altered.)

[1] Rom. 8.22,19.

58. THE TEACHING OF BASILEIDES, c. 130, ACCORDING TO IRENAEUS

(Irenaeus, I.19.1–4 Harvey; 24.3–7 A.-N. C. L.[1])

1
(3)   Basileides again, that he may appear to have discovered something more sublime and plausible, (i.e. than Satorninus, who has
just been mentioned), gives an immense development to his doctrines. He sets forth that Mind was first born of the unborn Father,
that from him, again, was born Logos, from Logos Prudence,
from Prudence Wisdom and Power, and from Power and
Wisdom the powers, and princes, and angels, whom he also calls
the *first*; and that by them the first heaven was made. Then other
powers, being formed by emanation from these, created another
heaven similar to the first; and in like manner, when others,
again, had been formed by emanation from them, corresponding
exactly to those above them, these, too, framed another third
heaven; and then from this third, in downward order, there was
a fourth succession of descendants; and so on, after the same
fashion, they declare that more and more princes and angels were
formed, and three hundred and sixty-five heavens. Wherefore
the year contains the same number of days in conformity with the
number of the heavens.

2
(4)   Those angels who occupy the lowest heaven, that, namely,
which is visible to us, formed all the things which are in the
world, and made allotments among themselves of the earth and of
those nations which are upon it. The chief of them is he who is
thought to be the God of the Jews; and inasmuch as he desired to
render the other nations subject to his own people, that is, the
Jews, all the other princes resisted and opposed him. Wherefore
all other nations rushed upon his nation. But the Father without
birth and without name, perceiving that they would be destroyed,
sent his own first-begotten Mind (he it is who is called Christ)
to bestow deliverance on them that believe in him, from the power
of those who made the world. He appeared, then, on earth as a
man, to the nations of these powers, and wrought miracles.
Wherefore he did not himself suffer death, but a certain Simon of
Cyrene, being compelled, bore the cross in his stead; Simon was
transfigured by him, that he might be thought to be Jesus, and

[1] Chapter and section references in A.-N. C. L. follow those of Massuet's
edition (1712). Where it is necessary to give references to Harvey and to
A.-N. C. L., those for the latter are placed in parentheses.

was crucified, through ignorance and error, while Jesus himself received the form of Simon, and, standing by, laughed at them. For since he was an incorporeal power, and the Mind of the unborn Father, he transfigured himself as he pleased, and thus ascended to him who had sent him, deriding them, inasmuch as he could not be laid hold of, and was invisible to all. Those, then, who know these things have been freed from the princes who formed the world; so that one must not confess him who was crucified, but him who came in the form of a man, and was thought to be crucified, and was called Jesus, and was sent by the Father, that by this dispensation he might destroy the works of the makers of the world. If any one, therefore, he declares, confesses the crucified, that man is still a slave, and under the power of those who formed our bodies; but he who denies him has been freed from these beings, and is acquainted with the dispensation of the unborn Father.

3
(5) Salvation belongs to the soul alone, for the body is by nature subject to corruption. He declares, too, that the prophecies were derived from those princes who were the makers of the world, but the law was specially given by their chief, who led the people out of the land of Egypt. He attaches no importance to meats offered to idols, thinks them of no consequence, and makes use of them without any hesitation; he holds also the practice of other religious rites (?), and of every kind of lust, a matter of perfect indifference.

(6) [Irenaeus then goes on to comment on their use of magic, and of mysterious names for the heavenly powers, including Caulacau, the name under which the Saviour went.

They practise secrecy, and do not disclose membership of the sect.]

"Do thou," they say, "know all, but let nobody know thee." For this reason, persons of such a persuasion are also ready to recant, or rather it is impossible that they should suffer on account of a mere name, since they are like to all. The multitude, however, cannot understand these matters, but only one out of a thousand, or two out of ten thousand. They declare that they are no longer Jews, and that they are not yet Christians; and that it is not at all fitting to speak openly of their mysteries, but right to keep them secret by preserving silence.

4
(7) They make out the local positions of the three hundred and sixty-five heavens in the same way as do astrologers. For, accepting the propositions of these latter, they have transferred them to

their own type of doctrine. They hold that their chief is Abraxas; and, on this account, that word contains in itself the numbers amounting to three hundred and sixty-five. (A.-N. C. L., altered.)

This account does not tally with the account of Hippolytus given in 50 to 57. It represents what Irenaeus believed about Basileides, and may represent "in substance the creed of the Basileidians not half a century after Basileides had written". (Hort, *D.C.B.*, s.v. Basilides.)

59. BASILEIDES ON THE PROBLEM OF EVIL

(Basileides, *Exegetica*, XXIII, in Clement of Alexandria, *Stromateis*, IV.12.81.2–82.2.)

2   For I say that those who fall into the so-called afflictions, because they unknowingly sinned in other faults, are brought to this good end by the kindness of him who brings them. Though they may be accused on other grounds, they do not suffer like criminals condemned for what are admitted to be offences, nor are they cursed as adulterers or murderers, but as accused of being Christians. This will encourage them so that they will not
3 seem to suffer. And if anyone who has not sinned at all happens to suffer (though this is unusual), such a man does not suffer through the machinations of power, but will suffer as a child
82.1 would, who seems not to have sinned. . . . As then a child who, has neither sinned before nor has committed any actual sin now, but has sinfulness in him, receives good when subjected to suffering and reaps much benefit from difficulties, so even if a perfect man happen not to have sinned in any way, but suffers, he suffers his afflictions as a child does. Though he has within him the sinful principle he does not seize the opportunity to commit sin. He does not sin; but he is not to be reckoned as without sinfulness.
2 For just as the man who desires to commit adultery is an adulterer, even if he does not succeed in commiting adultery, and he who wants to do murder is a murderer, even if he is unable to kill; so also if I see the man without sin whom I mentioned suffering, even if he has done nothing wrong I should say that he is wicked because of his desire to sin. For I will say anything rather than call Providence evil. (Grant, *Second-century Christianity*, pp. 19–20, altered.)

60. AGRIPPA CASTOR, AN OPPONENT OF BASILEIDES

(Eusebius, *H.E.* IV.7.6–8.)

6   Among those which have come down to us, there is a most powerful refutation of Basileides by a writer of the greatest renown at that time, Agrippa Castor, which unmasks the man's 7 cunning imposture. In exposing his hidden mysteries, he says that Basileides composed four and twenty books on the Gospel, and on the other hand that he named Barcabbas and Barcoph as his prophets, providing himself likewise with certain others who never existed, whom he called by barbarous names in order to strike amazement into those who marvel at such things; that he taught that to taste meat offered to idols, and to renounce without reservation the faith in times of persecution, were matters of indifference; and that he imposed upon his followers a five years' 8 silence after the manner of Pythagoras. And the writer of whom we have spoken has collected other similar facts about Basileides, and thus openly laid bare the error of the said heresy in no unworthy fashion. (Lawlor and Oulton, *Eusebius,* I, p. 109.)

7. *four and twenty books on the Gospel*: it would appear that Basileides was the most active Christian thinker of his time. But we know very little about his thought or his "curious speculations" (Burkitt, *Church and Gnosis,* p. 86) in which magic was mingled.

Barcoph: called Parchor by Clement of Alexandria, *Stromateis,* VI.6.52–3.

61. VALENTINUS

(Tertullian, *Against the Valentinians,* 4.)

Valentinus had expected to become a bishop, because he was an able man both in genius and eloquence. Being indignant, however, that another obtained the dignity by reason of a claim which confessorship had given him, he broke with the church o the true faith. Just like those restless spirits which, when roused by ambition, are usually inflamed with the desire of revenge, he applied himself with all his might to exterminate the truth; and finding the by-way of a certain old opinion, he marked out a highway for himself with the subtlety of a serpent. Ptolemy afterwards entered on the same highway, by distinguishing the names and the numbers of the Aeons into personal substances, which, however, he kept apart from God. Valentinus had included these in the very essence of the Deity, as senses and affections of motion. Sundry lanes were then struck off therefrom, by Heracleon and Secundus and the magician Marcus. (A.-N. C. L., altered.)

62. VALENTINUS: GOD

(Irenaeus, I.1.1.)

They say that in the invisible and ineffable heights above there exists a certain perfect, pre-existent Aeon, whom they call Before-the-beginning, Primal-father, and Abyss. . . . He is invisible and incomprehensible, eternal and unbegotten, and he remained throughout innumerable cycles of ages in profound serenity and quiescence. There existed along with him Thought, whom they also call Grace and Silence. At last this Abyss determined to send forth from himself the beginnings of all things, and deposited this production (which he had resolved to bring forth) in the co-existent Silence, even as seed is deposited in the womb. She then, having received this seed, and becoming pregnant, gave birth to Mind, who was both similar and equal to him who had produced him, and was alone capable of comprehending his father's greatness. This Mind they call also Only-begotten, and Father, and the Beginning of all Things. Along with him was also produced Truth; and these four constituted the first and first-begotten Pythagorean Tetrad, which they also denominate the root of all things. For there are first Abyss and Silence, and then Mind and Truth. And Only-begotten, perceiving for what purpose he had been produced, also himself sent forth Word and Life, being the father of all those who were to come after him, and the beginning and fashioning of the entire Pleroma. (A.-N. C. L., altered.)

Irenaeus proceeds to relate the production of thirty Aeons in all in groups of eight, ten, and twelve. The last pair were Design and Wisdom. These aeons complete the Pleroma, the truly divine world.

incomprehensible means "that cannot be grasped".

63. VALENTINUS: LIFE AMONG THE AEONS

(Irenaeus, I.1.2 Harvey; I.2.1 A.-N. C. L.)

2   They proceed to tell us that the Primal-Father of their scheme
(1) was known only to Only-begotten, who sprang from him; in
other words, only to Mind, while to all the others he was invisible
and incomprehensible. And, according to them, Mind alone took
pleasure in contemplating the Father, and exulted in considering
his immeasurable greatness; while he also meditated how he might
communicate to the rest of the Aeons the greatness of the Father,
revealing to them how vast and mighty he was, and how he was
without beginning, beyond comprehension, and altogether incapable of being seen. But, in accordance with the will of the
Father, Silence restrained him, because it was his design to lead
them all to an acquaintance with the aforesaid Primal-Father, and
to create within them a desire of investigating his nature. In like
manner, the rest of the Aeons also, in a kind of quiet way, had a
wish to behold the Author of their being, and to contemplate that
First Cause which had no beginning. (A.-N. C. L., altered.)

64. VALENTINUS: THE FALL OF "WISDOM"

(Irenaeus, I.1.2–3 Harvey; I.2.2–4 A.-N. C. L.)

Irenaeus gives two accounts of this regrettable occurrence; the second
appears to belong to the Italic School of Valentinians, cf. Quispel, *Vigiliae
Christianae*, I.1 (1947), p. 43ff., *The Original Doctrine of Valentine*.

2   But there rushed forth in advance of the rest that Aeon who
was much the latest of them, namely Wisdom, and suffered passion
apart from the embrace of her consort Design. This passion,
indeed, first arose among those who were connected with Mind
and Truth, but passed as by contagion to this degenerate Aeon,
who acted under a semblance of love, but was in reality influenced
by temerity, because she had not, like Mind, enjoyed communion
with the perfect Father. This passion, they say, consisted in a
desire to search into the nature of the Father; for she wished,
according to them, to comprehend his greatness. When she could
not attain her end, inasmuch as she aimed at an impossibility, and

thus became involved in an extreme agony of mind, while both on account of the vast profundity as well as the unsearchable nature of the Father, and on account of the love she bore him, she was ever stretching herself forward, there was danger lest she should at last have been absorbed by his sweetness, and resolved into his absolute essence, unless she had met with that Power which supports all things, and preserves them outside of the unspeakable greatness. This power they term Boundary. (A.-N. C. L., altered.)

Boundary (Horos) appears twice in Irenaeus' narrative. Here he is "a perpetual function of Mind" (Quispel, op. cit., p. 45). His duty was to restrain and support Wisdom; she became convinced that the Father was incomprehensible, and gave up her passion.

The second account is as follows:

3   But some of them fabulously describe the passion and change of mind of Wisdom as follows: They say that she, having engaged in an impossible and impracticable attempt, brought forth an amorphous substance, such as her female nature enabled her to produce. When she looked upon it, her first feeling was one of grief, on account of the imperfection of its generation, and then of fear lest this should end her own existence. Next she lost, as it were, all command of herself, and was in the greatest perplexity while endeavouring to discover the cause of all this, and in what way she might conceal what had happened. Being greatly harassed by these passions, she at last changed her mind, and endeavoured to return anew to the Father. When, however, she in some measure made the attempt, strength failed her, and she became a suppliant of the Father. The other Aeons, Mind in particular, presented their supplications along with her. And hence they declare that matter had its beginning from ignorance and grief, and fear and bewilderment.

(4)   The Father afterwards produces, in his own image, by means of Only-begotten, the above-mentioned Boundary, without conjunction, masculo-feminine. For they maintain that sometimes the Father acts in conjunction with Silence, but that at other times he shows himself independent both of male and female. They term this Boundary (Horos) both Cross and Redeemer, and Emancipator and Boundary-fixer, and Bringer-back. And by this Boundary they declare that Wisdom was purified and established, while she was also restored to her proper conjunction. For her inborn idea having been taken away from her, along with its supervening passion, she herself certainly remained within the

Pleroma; but her conception with its attendant passion, was separated from her by Boundary, fenced off, and expelled outside Boundary. This conception was, no doubt, a spiritual substance, possessing some of the natural tendencies of an Aeon, but at the same time shapeless and without form, because it had received nothing. And on this account they say that it was a weak and female fruit. (A.-N. C. L., altered.)

"As we are soon to learn Sophia's conduct was not marked by true Wisdom: what in modern terminology would be a much nearer equivalent is *Philosophy*." (F. C. Burkitt, *Church and Gnosis*, p. 44.)

3. *lest this should end her own existence*: Hippolytus, *Refutation of all Heresies*, VI.31, tells us that this fear extended to all the Aeons, and that they supplicated the Father for the deliverance of "Wisdom", who continued to weep because of the abortion to which she had given birth. So the Father ordered a new emanation, from Mind and Truth, namely Christ and the Holy Spirit, to give a distinctive form to the abortion, and comfort Wisdom and stop her wailing. Cf. the next passage.

On Jewish Christians see, e.g., Schoeps, *Ebionite Christianity* (*J.T.S.* (N.S.) iv (1953), pp. 219 ff).

65. VALENTINUS: JESUS IS PRODUCED BY THE WHOLE PLEROMA

(Irenaeus, I.4.1 Harvey, I.2.5–6 A.-N. C. L.)

1   [After the restoration of "Wisdom", and the expulsion of her (5) offspring from the Pleroma Only-Begotten produced one final pair of Aeons, Christ and the Holy Spirit. The "mission" of Christ to the Aeons was to teach them about their own nature, and their relation to the Father (Abyss).]

6   But the Holy Spirit taught them to give thanks on being all rendered equal among themselves, and led them to a state of true repose. Thus, then, they tell us that the Aeons were constituted equal to each other in form and sentiment, so that all became as Mind, and Word, and Man, and Christ. The female Aeons, too, became all as Truth, and Life, and Spirit, and Church. Everything, then, being thus established, and brought into a state of perfect rest, they next tell us that these beings sang praises with great joy to the Primal-Father, who himself shared in the abounding exaltation. Then, out of gratitude for the great benefit which had been conferred on them, the whole Pleroma of the Aeons, with one design and desire, and with the concurrence of Christ and

the Holy Spirit, their Father also setting the seal of his approval on their conduct, brought together whatever each one had in himself of the greatest beauty and preciousness; and uniting all these contributions so as skilfully to blend the whole, they produced, to the honour and glory of Abyss, a being of most perfect beauty, the very star of the Pleroma, and the perfect fruit, namely Jesus. Him they also speak of under the name of Saviour, and Christ, and patronymically, Word, and Everything, because He was formed from the contributions of all. (A.-N. C. L., altered.)

66. THE THREE "PRINCIPLES" OF VALENTINUS

(Irenaeus, I.1.11 Harvey; I.6.1 A.-N. C. L.)

11 There being thus three principles, they declare of all that is
(1) material (which they also describe as being "on the left hand") that it must of necessity perish, inasmuch as it is incapable of receiving any breath of incorruption. As to every animal existence (which they also denominate "on the right hand"), they hold that, inasmuch as it is a mean between the spiritual and the material, it passes to the side to which inclination draws it. Spiritual substance, again, they describe as having been sent forth for this end, that, being here united with that which is animal, it might assume shape, the two elements being simultaneously subjected to the same discipline. And this they declare to be *the salt* and *the light of the World*.[1] For the animal substance had need of training by means of the outward senses; and on this account they affirm that the world was created, as well as that the Saviour came to the animal substance (which was possessed of free-will), that He might secure for it salvation. For they affirm that He received the first-fruits of those whom He was to save, from Achamoth that which was spiritual, from the Demiurge He was invested with the animal Christ, but from a special dispensation was begirt with a body endowed with an animal nature, yet constructed with unspeakable skill, so that it might be visible and tangible, and capable of enduring suffering. At the same time, they deny that He assumed anything material, since indeed matter is incapable of salvation. They further hold that the consummation of all things will take place when all that is spiritual has been

[1] Matt. 5.13,14.

formed and perfected by Knowledge; and by "all that is spiritual" they mean spiritual men who have attained to the perfect knowledge of God, and been initiated into these mysteries by Achamoth. And they represent themselves to be these persons. (A.-N. C. L., altered.)

The docetism inherent in Gnostic Christology is shown by the above passage.

67. VALENTINUS: ANIMAL AND SPIRITUAL MEN

(Irenaeus, I.1.11–12 Harvey; I.6.2–4 A.-N. C. L.)

11 (2)   For animal men are instructed in animal things; such men, namely, as are established by their works, and by a mere faith, while they have not perfect knowledge. We of the church, they say, are these persons. Wherefore also they maintain that good works are necessary to us, for that otherwise it is impossible to be saved. But as to themselves, they hold that they shall be entirely and undoubtedly saved, not by means of conduct, but because they are spiritual by nature. For, just as it is impossible that material substance should partake of salvation (since, indeed, they maintain that it is incapable of receiving it), so again it is impossible that spiritual substance (by which they mean themselves) should ever come under the power of corruption, whatever the sort of actions in which they indulged. For even as gold, when submersed in mud, loses not on that account its beauty, but retains its own native qualities, the mud having no power to injure the gold, so they affirm that they cannot in any measure suffer hurt, or lose their spiritual substance, whatever the material actions in which they may be involved.

12 (3)   Wherefore also it comes to pass, that the "most perfect" among them addict themselves without fear to all those kinds of forbidden deeds of which the Scriptures assure us that *they who do such things shall not inherit the kingdom of God*.[1] For instance, they make no scruple about eating meats offered in sacrifice to idols, imagining that they can in this way contract no defilement. Then, again, at every heathen festival celebrated in honour of the idols, these men are the first to assemble; and to such a pitch do they go, that some of them do not even keep away from that bloody spectacle hateful both to God and men, in which gladiators either fight with wild beasts, or singly encounter one another.

[1] Gal. 5.21.

[Irenaeus then goes on to deal with the sexual immorality of these heretics.]

(4)   And committing many other abominations and impieties, they run us down (who from the fear of God guard against sinning even in thought and word) as utterly contemptible and ignorant persons, while they highly exalt themselves, and claim to be perfect, and the elect seed. For they declare that we simply receive grace for use, wherefore also it will again be taken away from us; but that they themselves have grace as their own special possession, which has descended from above by means of an unspeakable and indescribable conjunction; and on this account more will be given them. (A.-N. C. L., altered.)

The immoralities of certain Gnostics were a fruitful source of ill-will against Christians in general. But we may be quite sure that great Gnostic leaders, like Basileides and Valentinus were immune from such practices.

Later in I.7 Harvey; I.13 A.-N. C. L., Irenaeus has much to say of this in connection with Marcus, a Gnostic with whose immoralities he had met in his own district of Gaul.

68. VALENTINUS: THE "INCARNATION"

(Clement of Alexandria, *Stromateis*, III.7.59.3.)

Having endured everything he was continent; thus Jesus exercised his divinity. He ate and drank in a peculiar manner, not evacuating his food. So much power of continence was in him that in him food was not corrupted, since he himself had no corruptibility. (Grant, *Second-century Christianity*, pp. 25–6.)

69. LETTER OF PTOLEMY TO FLORA

(Epiphanius, *Haer*, 33.3–7: G. Quispel, *Ptolémée, Lettre à Flora* (Sources chrétiennes); Völker, *Quellen zur Geschichte der Christlichen Gnosis*, pp. 87–93. The text of the letter is frequently corrupt and has been the subject of considerable emendation. In general Quispel's text has been followed.)

3.1   My dear sister Flora, since many do not understand the law given through Moses, and have got accurate knowledge neither of who gave it nor of its commandments, I think you too will easily understand it if you learn the varying opinions about it.

2 There are those who say that it was ordained by God the Father; others follow a totally opposite view and assert that it was enacted by the hostile and corrupting devil, just as they attribute to him the creation of the world, calling him father and creator of this

3 universe. But in their dissonant singing to one another they constantly stammer, and both parties go utterly astray from the truth

4 of the subject. For it appears that the law was not established by the perfect God and Father—for it is a secondary thing—it is imperfect and in need of fulfilment by another, and has com-

5 mandments alien to the nature and thought of such a God; nor again is the law which destroys injustice to be attributed to the unrighteousness of the adversary. That is what happens to people who do not see what follows from the words of the Saviour. For *a house or city divided against itself cannot stand*,[1] our Saviour

6 declared. Furthermore the apostle says that the creation of the world was peculiar to Him and that *all things were made through him, and apart from him nothing was made*,[2] refuting the flimsy wisdom of these liars; not the creation of a god who corrupts, but of a just God who hates evil. That is the opinion of heedless men who do not understand the cause of the providence of the Demiurge, who are blind not only in the eye of the soul but also in that of the body.

7 How they have strayed from the truth is clear to you from what has been said. Two groups have gone astray each in their peculiar fashion, the one through ignorance of the God of justice,

8 the other through ignorance of the Father of All, whom only he who alone knew him revealed at his coming. Now it remains for us who have been granted the knowledge of both of these, to explain the Law to you with accuracy, what its nature is and the one by whom it has been given, the Lawgiver, proving our demonstrations from the words of our Saviour, through which alone it is possible without error to travel toward the comprehension of reality.

4.1 First one must learn that that whole Law which is contained in the Pentateuch of Moses has not been decreed by some one person, I mean by God alone; but there are also some commandments in it given by men; and that it is tripartite the words of the

2 Saviour teach us. For one part is ascribed to God himself and his legislation; another is ascribed to Moses, not meaning that God gave the law through him, but that Moses legislated starting from his own understanding; and the third is ascribed to the elders of the people, who are themselves found from the beginning intro-

3 ducing ordinances of their own. How this came about you may

[1] Matt. 12.25.   [2] John 1.3.

4 learn from the words of the Saviour. When the Saviour was talking somewhere to those arguing with him about divorce, which was allowed by the Law, he said to them, *Moses because of the hardness of your hearts permitted a man to put away his wife; from the beginning it was not so.*[1] For God joined them together, and

5 *what God has joined, let not a man,* he said, *put asunder.*[2] Here he shows that the law of God is one thing—it forbids a woman to be divorced by her husband—and the law of Moses is another—it permits this bond to be sundered because of hardness of heart.

6 So in this way Moses ordains a law contrary to God, for divorce is contrary to no divorce.

7-9 [Ptolemy points out that Moses had a difficult choice, to allow divorce, or owing to the "moral failure" of the people to allow them to fall into greater wrongdoing.]

10 This was his intention, according to which he is found legislating against God.

11- [Next he deals with the "traditions of the elders" quoting
13 Matt. 15.4-9 (the Corban story).]

14 Clearly then from these examples the whole Law is proved to be divided into three parts; we found in it the legislation of Moses himself, and of the elders, and of God Himself. And this division of ours of the whole Law, has shown us the truth that is in the law.

5.1 Again that one part of the Law which is from God Himself is divided into three parts, into pure legislation, free from evil, which is rightly called Law and which the Saviour *did not come to destroy but to fulfil*[3] (for that which he fulfilled was not alien to him, but required fulfilment; for it did not possess perfection); and into that part bound up with lower things and injustice, a law which the Saviour abrogated as alien to his nature; and it is

2 divided also into that part which is typical and symbolical, legislated as images of higher spiritual things; the Saviour transformed this from the sensible and phenomenal into the spiritual and invisible.

3-4 [The divisions of the part of the law which is from God are: (1) The "pure" (but "imperfect") legislation is the Decalogue which yet lacked perfection till "fulfilled" by the Saviour: (2) Rules about retribution, e.g. "an eye for an eye, etc. . . .".]

For the second wrongdoer is not less unrighteous: he differs

---

[1] Matt. 19.8.   [2] Matt. 19.6.   [3] Matt. 5.17.

5 only in sequence, while he does the same deed. But this commandment was and is just, in so far as it is necessary for the weakness of
those for whom the legislation was made, though it deviates from
the pure Law, and is alien to the nature and goodness of the Father
of all.

*   *   *

8 [(3) Rules about circumcision, fasting, the Sabbath, etc., which
are images and symbols.]

9 All these things, being images and symbols, were transformed
when the truth was made manifest. The material performance
according to appearance was taken away, but revealed according
to the spiritual—the names remained the same but the deeds were
different. For the Saviour commanded us to offer sacrifices, but
not of irrational animals or incense but of spiritual praises and
gloryings and thanksgiving, and through fellowship and beneficence toward neighbours.

*   *   *

6.5 For the images and symbols which were representative of
other things were good, as long as the truth had not yet appeared;
but as the truth is now present, one must do the deeds of the
truth, not those of the image.

*   *   *

7.1 Thus in brief then, I think that I have shown you sufficiently
both the legislation introduced by men and the threefold division
2 of the Law of God. There remains for us the question, Who is
this God who gave the Law? But I think this also has been shown
3 you from what I have said, if you have paid close attention. For if
the Law has not been given by the perfect God himself, as we
have taught, and certainly not by the devil, a thing which it is
not right to say, someone other than these two must have given
4 the Law. He is the *Demiurge* and creator of this whole universe
and what is in it, and he is different in essence from these two;
standing in the midst between them, he should rightly bear the
name of "the Intermediary". And if the perfect God is good in
5 his essence, as he actually is (*For one only is the good God*,[1] our
Saviour said of his Father whom he revealed), and if the evil and
wickedness of the adversary's nature is characterized by injustice,
then he who stands between them in the middle, and is neither
good nor bad nor unjust, may specifically be called just, since he
6 is the arbiter of the justice which proceeds from him. And this
god will be lower than the perfect God and less than *his* justice,

[1] Matt. 19.17.

for indeed he is also begotten and not unbegotten—for one is the unbegotten *Father, of whom is everything*,[1] since everything was specifically fashioned by him, but he will be greater and more powerful than the adversary, and will have a different essence and

7 nature from the other two. For the essence of the adversary is corruption and darkness, for he is material and divided into many parts. The essence of the unbegotten Father of everything is incorruption and self-sufficient light, single and uniform. The essence of this God (i.e. the *Demiurge*) has brought forth two

8 powers; he himself however is an image of the supreme God. Do not let this disturb you now in your desire to learn how from one simple beginning of everything, which we confess and believe, unbegotten and incorrupt and good, there came these two natures, one of corruption and one of the middle, both entirely different in nature, since it is in the nature of the good to beget and bring forth

9 things like itself and consubstantial to it. For with God's help you will learn in order the beginning and the begetting of these, if you are deemed worthy of knowing the apostolic tradition which we too have received from a succession together with the confirma-

10 tion of all our words by the teaching of the Saviour. It has been no inconvenience to me, my dear sister Flora, to make this brief exposition for you; though I have written a short summary, yet I have handled the question sufficiently. My account will be a very great help to you in the future if through this discussion you will bring forth fruit as fair and good land is productive by means of fertile seed. (Grant, *Second-century Christianity*, pp. 30–7, altered, with acknowledgements to the French translation of Quispel, op. cit.)

"Ptolemaeus (about 160) is the Valentinian whose fragments impress the modern reader most favourably. His letter to Flora, . . . reflects careful thought and a clear understanding of the problems presented by the Old Testament to the new Christianity. Had his threefold division been accepted by the early Church the problem of modern criticism might have been much less pressing." (Grant, op. cit., p. 30.)

Irenaeus, *Against Heresies*, I, *Praef.* 2, refers to the disciples of Ptolemy as being particularly active in his time.

70. CERINTHUS

(Irenaeus, I.21 Harvey; I.26.1 A.-N. C. L.)

1 Cerinthus, again, a man who was educated in the wisdom of the Egyptians, taught that the world was not made by the primary

[1] 1 Cor. 8.6.

God, but by a certain power far separated from him, and at a distance from that Authority who is supreme over the universe, and ignorant of the God who is above all. He represented Jesus as having not been born of a virgin, but as being the son of Joseph and Mary according to the ordinary course of human generation, while he nevertheless was more righteous, prudent, and wise than other men. Moreover, after his baptism, Christ descended upon him in the form of a dove from the Supreme Ruler, and that then he proclaimed the unknown Father, and performed miracles. But at last Christ departed from Jesus, and that then Jesus suffered and rose again, while Christ remained impassible, inasmuch as he was a spiritual being. (A.-N. C. L., altered.)

Cerinthus was regarded in second-century tradition as having been an opponent of St John (cf. 96) "a belief curiously travestied by the counter assertion that not St John but Cerinthus himself was the author not only of the Gospel but of the Apocalypse". (D.C.B. s.v. Cerinthus.) He differs from Basileides and Valentinus in that his heresy had a Jewish background. "He refused in the spirit of a true Jew to consider the 'God of the Jews' identical with that author of the material world who was alleged by Gnostic teachers to be inferior and evil. He preferred to identify him with the Angel who delivered the law." (D.C.B. s.v.)

71. THE ESCHATOLOGY OF CERINTHUS

(Gaius in Eusebius, H.E. III.28.2.)

2 Yea, Cerinthus also, by means of revelations purported to be written by a great apostle, fraudulently foists marvellous tales upon us, on the ground that they were shown him by angels. He says that after the resurrection the kingdom of Christ will be on earth, and that the flesh, dwelling at Jerusalem, will once more *serve lusts and pleasures*.[1] And—enemy that he is of God's Scriptures—in his wish to deceive he says that there will be a period of a thousand years, to be spent in wedding festivities. (Lawlor and Oulton, *Eusebius*, I, p. 89.)

revelations purported to be written by a great apostle: i.e. our Book of Revelation, cf. 138.

72. THE EBIONITES

(Irenaeus, I.22 Harvey; I.26.2 A.-N. C. L.)

2 Those who are called Ebionites agree that the world was made by God; but their opinions with respect to the Lord are similar

[1] Tit. 3.3.

to those of Cerinthus and Carpocrates. They use the Gospel according to Matthew only, and repudiate the Apostle Paul, maintaining that he was an apostate from the law. As to the prophetical writings, they endeavour to expound them in a somewhat singular manner: they practise circumcision, persevere in the observance of those customs which are enjoined by the law, and in their Judaic style of life, that they even adore Jerusalem as if it were the house of God. (A.-N. C. L., slightly altered.)

This passage follows immediately after Irenaeus' account of Cerinthus (70). Carpocrates was another Gnostic leader (Iren., I.20 Harvey; I.25 A.-N. C. L.).

This is the earliest passage in which Jewish Christians (cf. 43) are called Ebionites, but the idea that they had a personal founder "Ebion" is a mere supposition. The word means "poor"; and to the Ebionite it was the literal meaning that was the true one. Origen regarded the name as given them because of the poverty of their understanding (*De Principiis*, iv.3.8), or because of their poor and low opinions about Christ (*Comm. in Matt.* XVI.12), or because of the poverty of their interpretation of the law (*Contra Celsum*, II.1).

On Jewish Christians see Schoeps, *Ebionite Christianity* (J.T.S. (N.S.) IV (1953) pp. 219ff.).

73. THE THEOLOGY OF MARCION

(Irenaeus, I.24,25.1 Harvey; I.27.1–2 A.-N. C. L.)

24 Cerdon was one who took his system from the followers of
(1) Simon, and came to live at Rome in the time of Hyginus, who held the ninth place in the episcopal succession from the apostles downwards. He taught that the God proclaimed by the law and the prophets was not the father of our Lord Jesus Christ. For the former was known, but the latter unknown; and the one was righteous, but the other good.

25.1 Marcion of Pontus succeeded him, and developed his school,
(2) advancing the most daring blasphemy against Him who is proclaimed as God by the law and the prophets, declaring Him to be the author of evils, a lover of war, inconstant in judgement, and contrary to Himself. But Jesus being derived from that father who is above the God that made the world, and coming into Judaea in the times of Pontius Pilate the governor, who was procurator of Tiberius Caesar, was manifested in the form of a man to those who were in Judaea, abolishing the prophets and the law, and all the works of that God who made the world, whom also he calls "Ruler of the World". Besides this, he mutilates the Gospel which is according to Luke, removes all that is written respecting the generation of the Lord, and sets aside a great deal of the

teaching of the Lord's discourses, in which the Lord is recorded as most clearly confessing that the Maker of this universe is His Father. He likewise persuaded his disciples that he himself was more worthy of credit than are those apostles who have handed down the gospel to us, delivering to them not the gospel, but merely a fragment of it. In like manner, too, he dismembered the epistles of Paul, removing all that is said by the apostle respecting that God who made the world, to the effect that He is the Father of our Lord Jesus Christ, and also those passages from the prophetical writings which the apostle quotes, in order to teach us that they announced beforehand the coming of the Lord. (A.-N. C. L., altered.)

On Simon, cf. 48.
On Marcion's conception of God, cf. 77–80.

74. MARCION

(Justin, *Apology*, I.26.)

And there is Marcion, a man of Pontus, who is even at this day alive, and teaching his disciples to believe in some other god greater than the Creator. And he, by the aid of the devils, has caused many of every nation to speak blasphemies, and to deny that God is the maker of this universe, and to assert that some other, being greater than He, has done greater works. (A.-N. C. L.)

The date of Justin's *First Apology* is *c.* 155.
This passage shows how fast the teaching of Marcion spread, as Justin is writing only about ten years after Marcion's breach with the Roman church (75).

75. MARCION AND THE ROMAN CHURCH

(Tertullian, *De Praescriptione Haereticorum*, 30.)

In Ch. 30 Tertullian is discussing the comparative lateness of the heresies, compared to the Catholic Church.

For it is evident that those men lived not so long ago,—about the reign of Antoninus—and that they at first were believers in the doctrine of the Catholic Church, in the Church of Rome under the episcopate of the blessed Eleutherus, until (on account of their ever restless curiosity, with which they even infected the brethren) they were more than once expelled,—Marcion, indeed, with the two hundred thousand sesterces which he had brought into the church—and, when banished at last to a permanent excommunication, they scattered abroad the poisons of their doctrines. The same Marcion afterwards professed repentance, and agreed to the conditions granted to him—that he should receive reconciliation if he restored to the church all the others whom he had been training for perdition: he was forestalled, however, by death. (A.-N. C. L., altered.)

Eleutherus was bishop of Rome from c. 175–189 (cf. 47, 96), and Tertullian is mistaken in placing Marcion's breach with the Church so late. Marcionites were already a prosperous sect in Justin's time (74), and Tertullian himself points out (*Against Marcion*, I.19) that there are about one hundred and fifteen years and six and a half months between Tiberius and Antoninus Pius. "Just such an interval do they place between Christ and Marcion", i.e. the date of Marcion's apostasy is c. 144.

76. THE *ANTITHESES* OF MARCION
(Tertullian, *Against Marcion*, I.19.)

Marcion's special and principal work is the separation of the law and the gospel; and his disciples will not be able to deny that their supreme authority has its basis in this (separation), an authority by which they initiate and confirm themselves in his heresy. This is Marcion's *Antitheses*, or contradictory propositions, which aim at committing the gospel to a variance with the law, in order that from the diversity of the two documents which contain them, they may contend for a diversity of gods also. (A.-N. C. L., altered.)

On the *Antitheses*, see, e.g., Fliche et Martin, *Histoire de l'Église*, E. Tr., Vol. III, pp. 525–7, John Knox, *Marcion and the New Testament*, esp. p. 6f.

77. MARCION'S TWO GODS
(Irenaeus, III.40.2 Harvey; III.25.3 A.-N. C. L.)

2   Marcion therefore himself, by dividing God into two, main-
(3) taining one to be good and the other judicial, does in fact, on both sides, put an end to deity. For he that is the judicial one, if he be not good, is not God, because he from whom goodness is absent is not God; and again, he who is good, if he be not judicial, suffers

the same loss as the former, by being deprived of his character of deity. And how can they call the Father of all wise, if they do not assign to Him a judicial faculty? For if He is wise, He is also one who tests [others]; but the judicial power belongs to him who tests, and justice follows the judicial faculty, that it may reach a just conclusion; justice calls forth judgement, and judgement, when it is executed with justice, will pass on to wisdom. (A.-N. C. L., altered.)

This passage is not consistent with 73, and some think that Irenaeus is here confusing the views of Cerdo with those of Marcion. Tertullian, *Against Marcion*, I.6, V.13, indicates that Marcion taught a "just" creator.

78. THE THEOLOGICAL CAVILS OF MARCION

(Tertullian, *Against Marcion*, II.5.)

Now then, you dogs, whom the apostle puts outside, and who yelp at the God of truth, let us come to your various questions. These are the bones of contention, which you are perpetually gnawing! If God is good, and prescient of the future, and able to avert evil, why did He permit man, the very image and likeness of Himself, and, by the origin of his soul, His own substance too, to be deceived by the devil, and fall from obedience of the law into death? For if He had been good, and so unwilling that such a catastrophe should happen, and prescient, so as not to be ignorant of what was to come to pass, and powerful enough to hinder its occurrence, that issue would never have come about, which should be impossible under these three conditions of the divine greatness. Since, however, it has transpired, the contrary proposition, is most certainly true, that God must be deemed neither good, nor prescient, nor powerful. For as no such issue could have happened had God been such as He is reputed—good, and prescient, and mighty—so has this issue actually happened, because He is not such a God. (A.-N. C. L.)

79. TERTULLIAN'S CRITICISM OF MARCION'S "GOOD GOD"

(Tertullian, *Against Marcion*, I.27.)

Listen, you sinners; and you who have not yet come to this, hear, that you may attain to sinfulness! A better god has been discovered, who never takes offence, is never angry, never inflicts punishment, who has prepared no fire in hell, no gnashing of teeth in the outer darkness! He is purely and simply good. He indeed forbids all delinquency, but only in word. He is in you, if you are willing to pay him homage, for the sake of appearances, that you may seem to honour God; for your fear he does not want. And so satisfied are the Marcionites with such pretences, that they have no fear of their god at all. They say it is only an evil being who will be feared, a good one will be loved. Foolish man, do you say that he whom you call Lord ought not to be feared, whilst the very title you give him indicates a power which must itself be feared? . . . Come, then, if you do not fear God as being good, why do you not boil over into every kind of lust, and so realize that which is, I believe, the main enjoyment of life to all who fear not God? Why do you not frequent the customary pleasures of the maddening circus, the bloodthirsty arena, and the lascivious theatre? Why in persecutions also do you not, when the censer is presented, at once redeem your life by the denial of your faith? God forbid, you say with redoubled emphasis (Absit, inquis, absit). So you do fear sin, and by your fear prove that He is an object of fear Who forbids the sin. (A.-N. C. L., altered.)

"To the question of Tertullian to Marcion, why he did not sin if his God was not to be feared and did not punish, one reads the amazingly simple answer 'Absit, absit'. This simply means, that Marcion perceived no necessity in the case of believers to add a further foundation for morality. Seized by compassionate love, and giving himself to it in belief, the redeemed person is raised to a sphere to which the contagion of matter and the lower form of law do not attain. He therefore requires no moral principles, and no foundation for them; it is established that belief is enough since God through belief makes good out of evil. That 'Absit absit' is a document of first rate importance in religious history." (Harnack, *Marcion*, ed. 2, pp. 135-6.)

80. MARCION'S CHRIST

(Tertullian, *Against Marcion*, III.8.)

Now, the more firmly the antichrist Marcion had seized this assumption, i.e. the incredibility of an incarnate God, the more prepared was he, of course, to reject the bodily substance of Christ, since he had introduced his own peculiar god to our notice as neither the author nor the resuscitator of the flesh; and for this very reason, to be sure, as pre-eminently good, and most remote from the deceits and fallacies of the Creator. His Christ, therefore, in order to avoid all such deceits and fallacies, and the imputation, if possible, of belonging to the Creator, was not what he appeared to be, and gave a false account of who he was—flesh and yet not flesh, man and yet not man—likewise God and yet not God! Why should he not have carried also a mere phantom appearance of God? Can I believe him on the subject of the internal substance, who was a deceiver touching the external? How will it be possible to believe him true on a hidden matter, when he has been found so false on a plain fact? (A.-N. C. L., altered.)

With this passage, cf. Tertullian, op. cit. IV.7: "In the fifteenth year of the reign of Tiberius (for such is Marcion's proposition) he came down on to the Galilaean city of Capernaum."

81. REDEMPTION ACCORDING TO MARCION

(Irenaeus, 1.25.2 Harvey; I.27.3 A.-N. C. L.)

2   Salvation will be the attainment only of those souls which had
(3) learned his doctrine; while the body, as having been taken from the earth, is incapable of sharing in salvation. In addition to his blasphemy against God Himself, he advanced this also, truly speaking as with the mouth of the devil, and saying all things in direct opposition to the truth—that Cain, and those like him, and the Sodomites, and the Egyptians, and others like them, and all the nations generally who walked in all sorts of abomination, were saved by the Lord, on His descending into Hades, and on their running unto Him, and that He took them into His kingdom. But the serpent which was in Marcion declared that Abel, and Enoch and Noah, and the patriarchs of the line of Abraham, with all the prophets, and those who were pleasing to God, did not partake in salvation. For since these men, he says, knew that their God was constantly tempting them, so now they suspected that He was tempting them, and did not run to Jesus, or believe His announcement: and for this reason he declared that their souls remained in Hades. (A.-N. C. L., altered.)

In Irenaeus this passage follows directly after 73.

82. THE DIVISIONS OF THE MARCIONITES

(Rhodo in Eusebius, *H.E.* V.13.2–7.)

2   Therefore disagreement has broken out even among themselves, since they contend for an inconsistent opinion. For one of their herd Apelles, he who plumes himself on his mode of life and old age, acknowledges a single principle, but says that the prophecies come from an enemy spirit—putting his trust in the utterances of
3   a maiden possessed of a devil, named Philumene. But others, as also the sailor Marcion himself, introduce two principles; of
4   whom are Potitus and Basilicus. These last, having followed the wolf of Pontus, and failing, as he did, to find the division of things, became reckless, and without any proof baldly asserted two principles. While others, again, of their number, drifting into a worse error, assume not only two, but even three natures. Their leader and chief is Syneros, according to those who shelter themselves behind his school.

*   *   *

5   For the old man Apelles, when he talked with us, was refuted in many wrong statements. Therefore he went on to allege that one ought not to examine doctrine at all, but that everyone should remain in his own belief. For he asserted that they who have placed their hopes in the Crucified will be saved, if only they be found in good works. But he held that the most obscure thing of all was, as I have said, the question of God. For he spoke of a single principle, as also our doctrine does.

*   *   *

6   But when I said to him, "Whence do you get this proof? or how can you say that there is a single principle? tell us," he replied that the prophecies refute themselves, being absolutely devoid of truth; for they are inconsistent and lying and self-contradictory. But as to how there is a single principle, he said he did not know,
7   but that it was merely his impression.[1] Then, on my adjuring him to tell what was true, he swore that he was speaking the truth when he said that he did not understand how there was one uncreated God, but that this was his belief. For my part I laughed, and reproved him, because he said he was a teacher, and yet was unable to establish what he taught. (Lawlor and Oulton, *Eusebius*, I, pp. 157–8.)

[1] οὕτως δὲ κινεῖσθαι μόνον : the meaning is doubtful.

Though the Marcionites were the heretics most dangerous to the Catholic church, for the very reasons that they started from Christian foundations and themselves established a church, we find from Rhodo that they also had their sects.

Apelles was a well-known heretic, to whom Tertullian devoted a treatise (now lost), and to whom Tertullian and Hippolytus refer in extant works. Nothing further is known of the other Marcionites mentioned by Rhodo.

To Apelles the creator was an angel, a created agent of the good God; the "three natures" supported by others are God, the Creator, and Satan.

5. *who have placed their hopes on the Crucified . . . good works*: "This is a truly Christian sentiment, and Apelles should be honoured for the expression of it. It reveals clearly the religious character of Marcionism in distinction from the speculative and theological character of the Gnostics, and indeed of many of the Fathers.

The latter clause, taken as it stands, would seem to indicate an elevation of good works to the level of faith; but though it is possible that Apelles may have intended to express himself thus, it is more probable, when we remember the emphasis which Marcion laid upon Paul's doctrine of salvation by the grace of God alone, that he meant to do no more than emphasize good works as a natural result of true faith, as we do to-day." (McGiffert, *The Church History of Eusebius* (N. & P.-N. F.), p. 228n.)

83. EXAMPLES OF APELLES' CRITICISM OF THE OLD TESTAMENT

1. THE ARK

(Origen, *Hom. in Gen.* II.2 (from the Latin).)

Certain persons raise objections to the ark, and especially Apelles, who was the disciple of Marcion but established another heresy rather than adopted the one he received from his master. Now when he wanted to prove that the writings of Moses contain no divine wisdom and none of the work of the Holy Spirit, he exaggerates the things said of this kind and says that in no way could it have been accomplished that so small an area (as the ark) could contain so many kinds of animals and their foods, which were to last for a whole year. For when two by two the impure animals, i.e. two male and two female of each—this is what the repeated word means—but seven by seven the pure animals, that is seven pairs, are described as led into the ark, how, he says, could that space which is described be made big enough to take even four elephants alone? And afterwards he continues his contradiction, with illustrations from individual species (of animals), and concludes the matter as follows: It is clear that the story is false; but if this be so, it is clear that this scripture is not from God. (Grant, *Second-century Christianity*, p. 84, altered.)

2. GOD AND ADAM

(Ambrose, *De Paradiso*, VIII.38.)

(Ambrose is using Origen, not quoting Apelles directly.)

7 Did God know that Adam would transgress his commandments or did he not? If he did not know, the mark of divine power is absent from such a declaration; if however he knew and nevertheless gave orders which had to be neglected, it is not godlike to give a superfluous command; yet he gave a superfluous command to that first-formed Adam, which he knew he would not keep at all; yet God does nothing superfluous; therefore the writing is not of God. (Grant, *Second-century Christianity*, p. 86, altered.)

"Apelles, looking upon two adverse angels as the authors of the book, i.e. the O.T., regarded it as in great part false." (McGiffert, *The Church History of Eusebius* (N. & P.-N. F.), p. 227n.)

84. AN OPHITE LITURGY

(Origen, *Against Celsus*, VI.31.)

31 If anyone wishes to learn even the inventions of those sorcerers, which they use with the aim of leading men astray by their teaching, pretending to the possession of certain secret truths, though they have met with little success, let him hear what they are taught to say at the eternally chained gates of the Archons after passing through what they call "the Barrier of Evil".

Solitary King, bond of blindness, unconscious oblivion, I hail thee, the supreme Power, preserved by the spirit of providence and wisdom; from thee I am sent in purity, being already part of the light of Son and Father. May grace be with me; yea, father, let it be with me.

And they say that the Powers of the Ogdoad come from him. Then as they pass through the one they call Ialdabaoth they are taught to say next:

And thou, Ialdabaoth, first and seventh, born to have power with boldness, being ruling Word of a pure mind, a perfect work for Son and Father, I bear a symbol marked with a picture of life, and, having opened to the world the gate which thou didst close for thine eternity, I pass by thy power free again. May grace be with me, father, let it be with me.

And they say that the star Saturn is in sympathy with the lion-like Archon. Then they think that the person who has passed through Ialdabaoth and reached Iao must say:

And thou, Archon of the hidden mysteries of Son and Father, who shinest by night, thou Iao, second and first, lord of death, portion of the guiltless, I bear already thine own . . . as a symbol, and am ready to pass by thy power; for by a living word I have prevailed over him that was born of thee. May grace be with me, father, let it be with me.

Then next comes Sabaoth, to whom they think one should say:

Archon of fifth authority, mighty Sabaoth, defender of the law of thy creation which grace is destroying, by a more potent pentad, look upon a blameless symbol of thine art, and let me pass by, preserved by the image of a picture, a body set free by the pentad. May grace be with me, father, let it be with me.[1]

And after him comes Astaphaeus, to whom they believe one should say the following formula:

Archon of the third gate, Astaphaeus, overseer of the original source of water, look on one initiate, and let me pass who have been cleansed by a virgin's spirit, and see the world's essence. May grace be with me, father, let it be with me.

And after him comes Ailoaeus, to whom they think it right to speak as follows:

Archon of the second gate, Ailoaeus, let me pass as I bring to thee a symbol of thy mother, a grace hidden by the powers of the principalities. May grace be with me, father, let it be with me.

Finally they mention Horaeus, and think fit to say to him:

Thou who hast fearlessly passed beyond the wall of fire, who hast been assigned the power over the first gate, Horaeus, look

[1] The password for Adonai has fallen out of the text.

upon a symbol of thy power vanquished by a picture of the tree of life, taken by an image, made in the likeness of a guiltless man, and let me pass by. May grace be with me, father, let it be with me. (H. Chadwick, *Origen*, "*Contra Celsum*", pp. 346–8.)

The Ophites: "Besides these there are those heretics who are called Ophites. For they exalt the serpent to such a degree that they even prefer him to Christ himself. For it was he, they say, who originally gave us the knowledge of good and evil." (Ps.-Tertullian, *Adv. Omn. Haer.* 6.)

"There is a certain sect which does not admit a convert unless he pronounces anathemas on Jesus; and that sect is worthy of the name which it has chosen; for it is the sect of the so-called Ophites, who utter blasphemous words in praise of the serpent." (Origen, *Catena fragm.* 47 in I Cor. 12.3, ed. Jenkins, *J.T.S.* X (1909), p. 30.) (Passages from Chadwick, op. cit., p. 334, nn. 1 and 2.)

The theme of the liturgy is the ascent of the soul through the heavenly spheres. For a detailed commentary see Chadwick's notes on VI.29–33: the "Barrier of Evil" is the "Boundary" set below the true spiritual world, e.g. Horus in the Valentinian system, cf. 64. Each sphere is guarded by an Archon and it is necessary to know the proper formula with which to address him. "It appears that Origen's list of passwords start at the top with the eighth and supreme sphere, not at the bottom, so that he has the Ophite liturgy in the reverse order. The first power to be met would be Horaeus." (Chadwick, op. cit., p. 346, n. 3.)

85. MONTANISM: ARGUMENT AND COUNTER-ARGUMENT

(The "Anonymous" in Eusebius, *H.E.* V.16.3–5.)

3   It is a very long and considerable time, beloved Avircius Marcellus, since I was charged by thee to write some kind of treatise against the heresy of the followers of Miltiades, as they are called. Yet I have somehow held back until now, not through lack of ability to refute falsehood and bear witness to the truth, but from fear and extreme caution, lest perchance I might seem to some to be *adding* a new article or clause to the word of the New Covenant[1] of the Gospel, to which no one who has purposed to *live* according to *the* simple *Gospel*[2] may add, from which no
4   one may *take away*.[3] But when I recently came to Ancyra in Galatia, and found the local church ringing with the noise of this new (not, as they themselves say, prophecy; but much rather, as will be shown) false prophecy: with the help of the Lord we

[1] Gal. 3.15.   [2] Phil. 1.27.   [3] Cf. Rev. 22.18,19.

discoursed, to the best of our ability, for many days in the church on every one of these same points, as well as on those which they put forward; insomuch that the church rejoiced exceedingly and was confirmed in the truth, while they of the contrary part were for the moment discomfited, and the opposers put to grief.

5 So when the local presbyters requested us to leave behind some memorandum of what had been said against *them that oppose themselves*[1] to the word of truth (and there was present also our fellow-presbyter Zoticus of Otrus), though we did not do this, we promised to write it here, should the Lord permit us, and send it to them speedily. (Lawlor and Oulton, *Eusebius*, I, p. 159.)

3. Avircius Marcellus, see 123.

Miltiades: nothing further is known of this Montanist leader, cf. 124.

As prophecy had always been recognized in the Church as a special "gift", the appearance of new revelations given by the Paraclete in the form of prophecy, raised a difficult problem.

5. *our fellow-presbyter*: "This phrase is commonly used by bishops addressing presbyters" (Lawlor and Oulton, *Eusebius*, II, p. 173), but the exact ecclesiastical status of the "Anonymous" is not certain.

86. MONTANISM: THE BEGINNINGS,
c. 157
(The "Anonymous" in Eusebius, *H.E.* V.16.6ff.)

Their opposition, then, and their recent schismatical heresy as 7 regards the Church, arose thus. There is reported to be a certain village in that Mysia which borders on Phrygia, called by the name of Ardabau. There it is said that a certain recent convert to the faith named Montanus (while Gratus was proconsul of Asia), in the immeasurable longing of his soul for the pre-eminence, first gave the adversary a passage into his heart; and that moved by the spirit he suddenly fell into a state of possession, as it were, and abnormal ecstasy, insomuch that he became frenzied and began to babble and utter strange sounds, that is to say, prophesying contrary to the manner which the Church had received from 8 generation to generation by tradition from the beginning. Some of those who heard at that time his spurious utterances were incensed at him, as at one possessed and tormented with a devil, the prey of a *spirit of error*[2] and a disturber of the people. So they rebuked and strove to check his babblings, mindful of the injunction and warning of the Lord to guard watchfully against the

[1] 2 Tim. 2.25.   [2] 1 John 4.6.

coming of *false prophets*.[1] But others were puffed up, as if at a prophetical gift of the Holy Spirit, and filled with no mean conceit, and forgetful of the injunction of the Lord. Therefore they called forth this maddening and cajoling spirit which was deceiving the people, by which they were beguiled and deceived, so

9 that it could no longer be checked to silence. And by some art, or rather by the employment of such an evil artifice, the devil secretly stirred up and enflamed the minds, which had lost in sleep the true faith, of those disobedient persons whose ruin he had devised, and by whom—a strange requital!—he was honoured. So that he raised up two women as well, and so filled them with the spurious spirit that they too chattered in a frenzied, inopportune and unnatural fashion, like him whom we mentioned above. And the spirit pronounced them blessed who rejoiced and prided themselves in him, and puffed them up with the greatness of his promises; yet at times he would administer shrewd and plausible rebukes to their face, that he might seem capable of reproving also. Howbeit there were few who were thus deceived by the Phrygians. Moreover, this arrogant spirit taught them to blaspheme the entire universal Church under heaven, because the spirit of false prophecy received neither honour nor admission

10 into it. For when the faithful throughout Asia had met frequently and at many places in Asia for this purpose, and on examination of the new-fangled teachings had pronounced them profane, and rejected the heresy, these persons were thus expelled from the Church and shut off from its communion. (Lawlor and Oulton, *Eusebius*, I, pp. 159–60.)

The date of the proconsulship of Gratus is not known.

Eusebius' account in his *Church History* occurs in the reign of Commodus: in his *Chronicle* he places the beginning of this heresy in 172: Epiphanius *Haer.* 48.1 places it about 156–157. Epiphanius' date appears to be the most likely: otherwise it is difficult to explain why this heresy spread so rapidly.

9. *Howbeit there were few who were thus deceived by the Phrygians*: Lake (Loeb Library) translates, "though but few of the Phrygians were deceived": this is more in accordance with the Greek.

10. These are the earliest known church councils (except for that in Acts 15).

87. MONTANISM AND MARTYRDOM

((1) The "Anonymous" in Eusebius, *H.E.* V.16.12–13.)

12 Since, therefore, they also used to dub us *slayers* of the *prophets*[2] because we did not receive their *prophets* of unbridled tongue (for

[1] Matt. 7.15. [2] Matt. 23.31.

these, they say, are they whom the Lord promised to send to the people), let them answer us before God: Is there a single one, my good sirs, of these followers of Montanus or of the women who began to chatter, who was *persecuted* by Jews or *killed* by lawless men? Not one. Or, were any of them seized and *crucified*[1] *for the sake of the Name?*[2] Not so. Or even, were any of the women ever *scourged in the synagogues* of the Jews or *stoned?*[3] Never, in any wise. Nay, it was another death that Montanus and Maximilla are reported to have died. (Lawlor and Oulton, *Eusebius*, I, p. 160.)

14 [The Anonymous states that report had it that they committed suicide by hanging themselves, as Judas had done, and that Themiso, "the first steward, as it were, of their so-called prophecy", had been lifted from the ground in ecstasy, but had 15 crashed and so met his end. But he admits that he is not sure of the reliability of this information.]

((2) The "Anonymous" in Eusebius, *H.E.* V.16.20–22.)

20 So then, when worsted in all their arguments they are at a loss, they endeavour to take refuge in the martyrs, saying that they have many martyrs, and that this is a reliable proof of the power of that which is called among them the prophetical spirit. But 21 this, as it appears, proves to be absolutely untrue. For it is a fact that some of the other heresies have immense numbers of martyrs, yet surely we shall not for this reason give them our assent, nor acknowledge that they possess the truth. To take them first, those called Marcionites from the heresy of Marcion say that they have immense numbers of martyrs of Christ, but as regards Christ Himself they do not truly acknowledge Him.

*　　*　　*

22 It is doubtless for this reason that, whenever those called from the Church to martyrdom for the true faith meet with any so-called martyrs from the heresy of the Phrygians, they sever themselves from them and are perfected, without holding communion with them, for they do not wish to assent to the spirit [that spoke] through Montanus and the women. And that this is true, and that it took place in our time at Apamea on the Maeander among those martyrs of Eumenia who were the companions of Gaius and Alexander, is an evident fact. (Lawlor and Oulton, *Eusebius*. I, pp. 161–2.)

[1] Matt. 23.34.　　[2] 3 John 7.　　[3] Matt. 23.34,37.

The Anonymous returned to the subject of martyrdom after dealing with the attempts to exorcise the spirit and the falsity of the new prophecy.

Eagerness for martyrdom was not a mark of Phrygian Montanism (see Lawlor and Oulton's note, *Eusebius*, II, p. 175).

Apollonius was writing in the fortieth year after Montanus began prophesying (Eus. *H.E.* V.18.12), i.e. *c.* 196. But when the Anonymous wrote *c.* 192 there were no Montanist prophets (Eus. *H.E.* V.16.19,17.4). Therefore there seems to have been a recrudescence of prophecy.

88. MONTANIST ETHICS

(Apollonius in Eusebius, *H.E.* V.18.2–11.)

2–4 [Apollonius vigorously attacked the morals of the Montanists, Montanus for his dissolutions of marriages, for his laws on fasting, for his financial schemes and salaried emissaries, the prophetesses for leaving their husbands, for receiving gifts of money and for ostentation.

Then he proceeds to deal with Themiso and Alexander.]

5 Moreover, Themiso also, he who is clothed with plausible covetousness, who did not bear the sign of confession, but put off his chains, thanks to a large sum of money, and (though this fact should have made him humble) boasts himself a martyr—this man, aping the Apostle, dared to compose a "catholic epistle", and therein to instruct those whose faith has surpassed his, to contend with empty-sounding words, and to utter blasphemy against the Lord, the apostles and the holy Church.

* * *

6 But not to speak of many, let the prophetess tell us about Alexander, who calls himself a martyr, with whom she banquets, to whom also many do reverence. It is not for us to speak of his robberies, and the other deeds of daring for which he has been 7 punished; nay, the record office preserves their tale. Which, then, of the two forgives the other's sins? Does the prophet forgive the martyr his robberies, or the martyr the prophet his deeds of covetousness? For though the Lord has said, *Get you no gold, nor silver, neither two coats*,[1] they, in complete contradiction, have transgressed as regards the getting of these forbidden things. For we shall show that they whom they call prophets and martyrs get their petty gains not only from the rich but also from poor

[1] Matt. 10.9,10.

8 people and orphans and widows. And if they are confident, let them take their stand on this, and come to a definite agreement on this understanding, that if convicted they may at least for the future cease to transgress. For one ought to prove the fruits of the

9 prophet: *for the tree is known by its fruit.*[1] But, that those who wish may know about Alexander, he has been judged by Aemilius Frontinus, proconsul at Ephesus, not because of the Name, but because of the robberies he committed, being already an apostate. Next, he made a false appeal to the Name of Christ and was released, having deceived the faithful in that city. And his own community, whence he came, would not receive him, because he was a robber. Those who have a mind to learn about him have

10 the public archives of Asia. And yet the prophet knows nothing of him with whom he associated many years! In exposing this man we also expose, by means of him, his claim to be a prophet. We can show the same in the case of many; and, if they have the courage, let them stand the exposure! (Lawlor and Oulton, *Eusebius*, I, pp. 163–4, slightly altered.)

11   [Apollonius attacks the pretensions of the prophets, showing that their characteristics (receiving gifts, personal adornment, secular avocations) make them false prophets.]

9. It was hard for the Catholics to attack the principles of prophecy, so they attacked persons. The career of Alexander shows interesting parallels with that of Peregrinus (111).

The date of the proconsulship of Aemilius Frontinus is not known.

The prophetess concerned in sections 6–10 is not one of the original trio of prophets.

89. TRUE AND FALSE PROPHETS

(The "Anonymous" in Eusebius, *H.E.* V.17.2–3.)

2 ... but the false prophet in abnormal ecstasy, upon whom follow licence and fearlessness. For while he begins with voluntary ignorance, he ends with involuntary madness of soul, as has been

3 stated. But they cannot show any prophet under either the Old or the New [Covenant] who was moved by the Spirit after this manner, neither Agabus nor Judas nor Silas nor the daughters of Philip, nor Ammia in Philadelphia nor Quadratus, nor can they make their boast of any others whatever not belonging to their number. (Lawlor and Oulton, *Eusebius*, I, p. 162.)

[1] Matt. 12.33.

2. *in abnormal ecstasy*:"Apparently the Montanist prophets spoke while they were in the ecstatic state, while the Catholics argued that the true prophets said nothing till they regained their normal faculties." (Lawlor and Oulton, *Eusebius*, II, p. 176.)

90. MONTANIST UTTERANCES

(From Epiphanius, *Haer.*, 48,49, and Eusebius, *H.E.* V.16.17.)

1   Behold a man is as a lyre, and I fly over it like a plectrum. The man sleeps, and I remain awake. Behold it is the Lord that stirs the hearts of men, and gives men hearts. (Montanus.) 48.4.

2   I am the Lord God Almighty, dwelling in man. It is neither angel nor ambassador, but I, God the Father, who am come. (Montanus.) 48.11.

3   Hear not me, but hear Christ. (Maximilla.) 48.12.

4   After me shall be no prophetess any more, but the consummation. . . . (Maximilla.) 48.2.

5   The Lord sent me to be the party-leader, informer, interpreter of this task, profession, and covenant, constrained, whether he will or nill, to learn the knowledge of God. (Maximilla.) 48.13.

6   Christ came to me in the likeness of a woman, clad in a bright robe, and He planted wisdom in me and revealed that this place (Pepuza) is holy, and that here Jerusalem comes down from heaven. (Priscilla.) 49.1.

(Swete, *The Holy Spirit in the ancient Church*, p. 69.)

7   I am driven as a wolf from the sheep. I am not a wolf. I am word and *spirit and power*.[1] (Maximilla.) (Lawlor and Oulton, *Eusebius*, I, p. 161.)

3.   Epiphanius adds: "She speaks truth in her lying words, though against her will. For often unclean spirits are compelled to overthrow themselves, not being spirits of truth, and to recognize their Lord of necessity, willy nilly" (quoting Acts 16.16, Matt. 8.29).

4.   "She found consolation, as such sufferers, i.e. those expelled from the fold, often do, in the belief that the end was at hand, and regarded herself as the last of the goodly fellowship of the Prophets." (Swete, op. cit., p. 71.)

91. MONTANISM: THE ACCOUNT OF HIPPOLYTUS, c. 220

(Hippolytus, *Refutation of all Heresies*, VIII.19.1–3 (A.-N. C. L. VIII.12.))

1   But there are others who themselves are even more heretical in nature [than the Quartodecimans], Phrygians by birth. These

[1] Cor. 2.4.

have been captivated and deceived by wretched women, called
a certain Priscilla and Maximilla, whom they supposed prophetesses. And they assert that into these the Paraclete Spirit had
departed; and previous to them, they consider in like manner a
certain Montanus as a prophet. And being in possession of an
infinite number of their books, the Phrygians are deluded; and
they do not judge whatever statements are made by them
according to reason; nor do they give heed unto those who are
competent to decide; but they are heedlessly swept onwards, by
the faith which they place in these impostors. And they allege
that they have learned something more through these than from
2 law and prophets and the Gospels. But they magnify these
wretched women above the Apostles and every gift of Grace, so
that some of them presume to assert that there is in them something
superior to Christ. These acknowledge God to be the Father of
the Universe, and Creator of all things, similarly with the Church,
and receive as many things as the Gospel testifies concerning
Christ. They introduce, however, the novelties of fasts, and feasts,
and meals of parched food, and repasts of radishes, alleging that
3 they have been instructed by the women. And some of these
assent to the heresy of the Noëtians, and affirm that the Father
Himself is the Son, and that He came under generation, and
suffering, and death. (A.-N. C. L., altered.)

Catholic writers generally agree that the Montanists were orthodox except
in their addiction to their prophets.
On the heresy of Noëtus, cf. 133.

92. MONTANISM IN GAUL, 177

(Eusebius, *H.E.* V.3.4.)

Eusebius shows that Montanism had reached Gaul by this date. This was a
very natural development, for, as we have seen, (21, p. 40), the Church in
Gaul was closely linked with the Churches in Asia.

And, when a dissension arose about these said persons, the
brethren in Gaul once more submitted a pious and most orthodox
judgement of their own on this matter also, issuing as well various
letters of martyrs who had been perfected among them—letters
that they penned while still in bonds to the brethren in Asia and
Phrygia, and moreover to Eleutherus the then bishop of the

Romans, negotiating for the peace of the churches. (Lawlor and Oulton, *Eusebius*, I, p. 149.)

It is clear that, as the letter from Gaul was *pious and most orthodox*, this heresy had not been successful there. On Montanism at Rome, cf. 152.

93. THE RULE OF FAITH
(Irenaeus, I.2–3 Harvey; I.10,1–2 A.-N. C. L.)

2
(1)
For the Church, though dispersed throughout the whole world, even to the ends of the earth, has received from the apostles and their disciples this faith: in one God, the Father Almighty, who made the heaven and the earth and the seas and all things that are in them; and in one Christ Jesus, the Son of God, who became incarnate for our salvation; and in the Holy Spirit, who proclaimed through the prophets the dispensations and the advents, and the birth from a virgin, and the passion, and the resurrection from the dead, and the incarnate ascension into heaven of the beloved Christ Jesus, our Lord, and His future manifestation from heaven in the glory of the Father *to sum up all things*[1] and to raise up anew all flesh of the whole human race, in order that to Christ Jesus, our Lord and God and Saviour and King, according to the will of the invisible Father, *every knee should bow, of things in heaven, and things in earth, and things under the earth, and that every tongue should confess*[2] to Him, and that He should execute just judgement towards all; that He may send *spiritual wickednesses*,[3] and the angels who transgressed and came into a state of rebellion together with the ungodly, and unrighteous, and wicked, and profane among men, into the everlasting fire; but may, as an act of Grace, confer immortality on the righteous and holy, and those who have kept His commandments, and have persevered in His love, some from the beginning, and others from their repentance, and may surround them with everlasting glory.

3
(2)
As I have already observed, the Church, having received this preaching, and this faith, although scattered throughout the whole world, yet, as if occupying but one house, carefully preserves it. She also believes these points of doctrine just as if she had but one soul, and one and the same heart, and she proclaims them, and teaches them, and hands them down, with perfect harmony, as if she possessed only one mouth. For, although the languages of the world are dissimilar, yet the import of the tradition is one and the

[1] Eph. 1.10.   [2] Phil. 2.10–11.   [3] Eph. 6.12.

same. For the churches which have been planted in Germany have not believed or handed down anything different, nor do those in Spain, nor those in Gaul, nor those in the East, nor those in Egypt, nor those in Libya, nor those which have been established in the central regions of the world. . . . Nor will any one of the rulers in the churches, however highly gifted he may be in point of eloquence, teach doctrines different from these (for no one is greater than the Master); nor, on the other hand, will he who is deficient in power of expression inflict injury on the tradition. For the faith being ever one and the same, neither does one who is able to discourse at great length regarding it, make any addition to it, nor does one, who can say little, diminish it. (A.-N. C. L., altered.)

This is a statement of the essential faith of the Church, put not in a simple credal form, but with additional phrases added: the rule is in direct opposition to the conceptions of the Gnostics. Cf. Hegesippus in 47 above.

3. The Churches in *the central regions of the world*; probably Rome, though Palestine has been suggested.

94. THE TRADITION IS PERPETUALLY REVIVIFIED IN THE CHURCH

(Irenaeus, III.38.1 Harvey; III.24.1 A.-N. C. L.)

But it has been shown that the preaching of the church is everywhere consistent, and continues in an even course, and receives testimony from the prophets, the apostles, and all the disciples—as I have proved—through those in the beginning, the middle, and the end, and through the entire dispensation of God, and that well-founded system which tends to man's salvation, namely, our faith; which, having been received from the church, we do preserve, and which always, by the Spirit of God, renewing its youth, as if it were some precious deposit in an excellent vessel, causes the vessel itself containing it to renew its youth also. For this gift of God has been entrusted to the church, as breath was to the first created man, for this purpose, that all the members receiving it may be vivified; and the means of communion with Christ, that is, the Holy Spirit, has been distributed throughout it, the earnest of incorruption, the means of confirming our faith, and the ladder of ascent to God. For *in the church*, it is said, *God hath set apostles, prophets, teachers*,[1] and all the other means through

[1] I Cor. 12.28.

which the Spirit works; of which all those are not partakers who do not join themselves to the church, but defraud themselves of life through their perverse opinions and infamous behaviour. For where the church is, there is the Spirit of God; and where the Spirit of God is, there is the church, and every kind of grace; but the Spirit is truth. Those, therefore, who do not partake of Him, are neither nourished into life from the mother's breasts, nor do they enjoy that most limpid fountain which issues from the body of Christ; but they dig for themselves *broken cisterns*[1] out of earthly trenches, and drink putrid water out of the mire, fleeing from the faith of the church lest they be convicted; and rejecting the Spirit, that they may not be instructed. (A.-N. C. L., altered.)

95. FAITH SUPERIOR TO KNOWLEDGE

(Irenaeus, II.39.1 Harvey; A.-N. C. L., II.26.1.)

It is therefore better, as I have said, that one should have no knowledge whatever of any one reason why a single thing in creation has been made, but should believe in God, and continue in His love, than that, puffed up through knowledge of this kind, he should fall away from that love which is the life of man; and that he should search after no other knowledge except the knowledge of Jesus Christ the Son of God, who was crucified for us, than that by subtle questions and hairsplitting expressions he should fall into impiety. (A.-N. C. L., altered.)

96. THE ARGUMENT FROM TRADITION

(Irenaeus, III.3,4.)

[In Ch. 2 Irenaeus argues that the heretics, refuted from scripture, fall back on "tradition": when they are referred to the tradition preserved in the successions of presbyters in the churches, they say "that they themselves are wiser not merely than the presbyters, but even than the Apostles, because they have discovered the unadulterated truth". (A.-N. C. L.)]

3.1 The tradition of the Apostles, therefore, manifested in the entire world it is possible for all, who wish to see the truth, to

[1] Jer. 2.13.

contemplate clearly in every church; and we are in a position to enumerate those who were by the apostles instituted bishops in the churches, and the successions of these men to our own times; those who neither taught nor knew anything like the ravings of the heretics. And in fact if the apostles had known hidden mysteries, which they were in the habit of imparting to "the perfect" apart and privily from the rest, they would have delivered them especially to those to whom they were also committing the churches themselves. For they were desirous that these men should be very perfect and blameless in all things, whom also they were leaving behind as their successors, delivering up their own place of government to these men, who if they discharged their functions honestly, would be a great boon to the church, but if they should fall away, the direst calamity.

(2)   Since, however, it would be very tedious, in such a volume as this, to reckon up the successions of all the churches, we do put to confusion all those who, in whatever manner, whether by an evil self-pleasing, by vainglory, or by blindness and perverse opinion, assemble in unauthorized meetings, by indicating that tradition derived from the apostles, of the very great, the very ancient, and universally known church founded and organized at Rome by the two most glorious apostles, Peter and Paul; and also by pointing out the faith preached to men, which comes down to our time by means of the successions of the bishops. For it is necessary that every church, that is, the faithful everywhere, should resort to (? agree with) this church, on account of its pre-eminent authority, in which the apostolical tradition has been preserved continuously by those who exist everywhere.

2   The blessed apostles, then, having founded and built up the
(3) church, committed into the hands of Linus the office of the episcopate. Of this Linus, Paul makes mention in the Epistles to Timothy. To him succeeded Anacletus; and after him, in the third place from the apostles, Clement was allotted the bishopric, who had seen the blessed apostles, and had associated with them, and had the preaching of the apostles still echoing in his ears, and their tradition before his eyes. Nor was he alone in this, for there were many still remaining who had received instruction from the apostles. In the time of this Clement, no small dissension having occurred among the brethren at Corinth, the church in Rome despatched a most powerful letter to the Corinthians, exhorting them to peace, renewing their faith, and declaring the tradition which it had lately received from the apostles. . . . From this document itself, whosoever chooses to do so, may learn that He, the Father of our Lord Jesus Christ, was preached by the churches.

and may also understand the apostolical tradition of the church, since this epistle is of older date than these men who are now propagating falsehood, and who fake up another god beyond the

3 Creator and the Maker of all existing things. To this Clement there succeeded Evarestus. Alexander followed Evarestus; then sixth from the apostles, Sixtus was appointed; after him Telesphorus, who was gloriously martyred; then Hyginus; after him, Pius; then after him Anicetus. Soter having succeeded Anicetus, Eleutherus now, in the twelfth place from the apostles, holds the inheritance of the episcopate. In this order, and by this succession, the ecclesiastical tradition from the apostles, and the preaching of the truth, have come down to us. And this is most abundant proof that there is one and the same vivifying faith, which has been preserved in the church from the apostles until now, and handed down in truth.

4   But Polycarp also was not only instructed by apostles, and conversed with many who had seen Christ, but was also, by apostles in Asia, appointed bishop of the church in Smyrna, whom I also saw in my early youth, for he tarried on earth a very long time, and, when a very old man, gloriously and most nobly suffering martyrdom, departed this life, having always taught the things which he had learned from the apostles, and which the church hands down, which also alone are true. To these things all the Asian churches testify, as do also those men who have succeeded Polycarp down to the present time,—a man who was a far more reliable and more stedfast witness of truth, than Valentinus, and Marcion, and the rest of the evil-minded. He it was who, coming to Rome in the time of Anicetus, caused many to turn away from the aforesaid heretics to the church of God, proclaiming that he had received this one and sole truth from the apostles, —that, namely, which is handed down by the church. There are also those who heard from him that John, the disciple of the Lord, going to bathe at Ephesus, and perceiving Cerinthus within, rushed out of the bath-house without bathing, exclaiming, "Let us fly, lest even the bath-house fall down, because Cerinthus, the enemy of the truth, is within". And Polycarp himself replied to Marcion, who met him on one occasion, and said, "Do you recognize me?" "I do recognize you, the first-born of Satan." Such was the caution which the apostles and their disciples used against holding even a verbal communication with any corrupters of the truth; as Paul also says, *A man that is an heretic, after the first and second admonition, reject; knowing that he that is such is perverted, and sinneth, being condemned of himself.*[1] There

[1] Tit. 3.10,11.

is also a very powerful epistle of Polycarp written to the Philippians, from which those who wish to do so, and are anxious about their salvation, can learn the character of his faith, and the preaching of the truth. Then, again, the church in Ephesus, founded by Paul, and having John remaining among them permanently until the times of Trajan, is a true witness of the tradition of the apostles.

4.1   Since therefore we have such proofs, we ought not to seek the truth among others which it is easy to obtain from the church; since the apostles, like a rich man depositing his money in a bank, delivered into her hands in the fullest measure the whole truth: so that every man, whosoever will, can draw from her the water of life. For she is the entrance to life; all others are thieves and robbers. On this account are we bound to avoid *them*, but to make choice of the things pertaining to the church with the utmost diligence, and to lay hold of the tradition of the truth. For how stands the case? Suppose there arise a dispute relative to some important question among us, should we not have recourse to the most ancient churches with which the apostles held constant intercourse, and learn from them what is certain and clear on the question at issue? For how should it be if the apostles themselves had not left us writings? Should we not in that case, follow the course of the tradition which they handed down to those to whom they committed the churches?

(2)   [Irenaeus proceeds to point to the witness of the "barbarian" churches, which do not possess the written scriptures in their own language. He goes over the articles of their rule of faith and then continues:]

Those who, in the absence of written documents, have believed this faith, are barbarians, so far as regards our language; but as regards doctrine, manners and conversation, they are, because of faith, very wise indeed; and they please God, ordering their conversation in all righteousness, chastity and wisdom. If any one were to preach to these men the inventions of the heretics, speaking to them in their own language, they would at once stop their ears, and flee as far off as possible, not enduring even to listen to the blasphemous address. Thus, by means of that ancient tradition of the apostles, they do not suffer their mind to conceive anything of the portentous language of these teachers, among whom neither church nor doctrine has ever been established. (A.-N. C. L., altered.)

3.1.   *For it is necessary*, etc. The Latin translation reads:

Ad hanc enim ecclesiam propter potentiorem (or *potiorem*) *principalitatem necesse est omnem convenire ecclesiam, hoc est, eos qui sunt undique fideles, in qua semper ab his qui sunt undique conservata est ea quae est ab apostolis traditio.*

It is quite impossible in a book such as this to enter into a discussion of this passage.

The list of Roman Bishops (cf. 47): Down to Clement the order is variously given, cf., e.g., the lists in McGiffert, *Eusebius*, p. 401 (N. & P.-N. F.). It is impossible to offer any reliable dates till we reach Telesphorus. The dates from Telesphorus to Eleutherus, as given by Fliche et Martin, *Histoire de l'Église*, Vol. I, Appendix, are:

> Telesphorus, d. *c.* 136
> Hyginus, *c.* 136–*c.* 140
> Pius, *c.* 140– before 154
> Anicetus, *c.* 154–?
> Soter, ?–175
> Eleutherus, 175–189.

3.4. Polycarp's visit to Rome is usually dated *c.* 154. Whether his encounter with Marcion was at Rome or not we cannot be certain.

The story of St John and Cerinthus is apocryphal.

4.1. The barbarian churches: Irenaeus I *Praef.* 3 speaks of himself as accustomed in speech to use Celtic for the most part.

97. "WHAT WAS GOD DOING BEFORE HE MADE THE WORLD?"

(Irenaeus, II.41.4 Harvey; II.28.3 A.-N. C. L.)

If, for instance, any one asks, "What was God doing before He made the world?" we reply that the answer to such a question lies with God Himself. For that this world was formed perfect by God, receiving a beginning in time, the Scriptures teach us; but no Scripture reveals to us what God was employed about before this event. The answer therefore to that question remains with God, and it is not proper for us to aim at bringing forward foolish, rash, and blasphemous explanations; so that by imagining that one has discovered the explanation of matter, he should in reality set aside God Himself who made all things. (A.-N. C. L., altered.)

Irenaeus is arguing that perfect knowledge cannot be attained in this life: we must investigate scripture, but even so, some things must be left in God's hands. What God has not revealed we are not meant to know.

98. FOUR GOSPELS ONLY

(Irenaeus III.11.11 Harvey; III.11.8 A.-N. C. L.)

But it is not possible that the Gospels can be either more or fewer in number than they are. For, since there are four zones of the world in which we live, and four principal winds, while the church has been scattered throughout all the world, and the *pillar and ground*[1] of the church is the gospel and the spirit of life; it is fitting that she should have four pillars, breathing incorruption on every side, and vivifying men afresh. From this fact, it is evident that the Word, the Artificer of all, He that sitteth upon the cherubim, and holds together all things, when He was manifested to men, gave us the gospel under four forms but bound together by one Spirit. As also David says, when entreating His presence, *Thou that sittest upon the cherubim, shine forth.*[2] For the cherubim, too, were four-faced, and their faces were images of the dispensation of the Son of God. For, it (i.e. the Scripture) says, *The first living creature was like a lion*, symbolizing His effectual working, His supremacy and royal power [Mark], *the second was like a calf*, signifying His sacrificial and sacerdotal order [Luke]; but the *third had the face as of a man*—an evident description of His advent as a human being [Matthew]; *the fourth was like a flying eagle*,[3] pointing out the gift of the Spirit hovering with His wings over the church [John]. And therefore the Gospels are in accord with these things, among which Christ Jesus is seated. For that according to John relates His supreme, effectual, and glorious generation from the Father, thus declaring, *In the beginning was the Word, and the Word was with God, and the Word was God.* Also, *all things were made by Him, and without Him was nothing made.*[4] For this reason, too, is that Gospel full of all confidence, for such is His person. But that according to Luke, taking up His priestly character, commenced with Zacharias the priest offering sacrifice to God. For now was made ready the fatted calf, about to be immolated for the finding again of the younger son. Matthew, again, relates His generation as a man, saying, *The book of the generation of Jesus Christ, the son of David, the son of Abraham*; and also *The birth of Jesus Christ was on this wise.*[5] This Gospel then is in human form; for which reason it is, too, that the character of a humble and meek man is kept up through the whole Gospel. Mark, on the other hand, commences with the prophetical spirit

[1] 1 Tim. 3.15.   [2] Ps. 80.1.   [3] Rev. 4.7.
[4] John 1.1,3.   [5] Matt. 1.1,18.

coming down from on high to men, saying, *The beginning of the gospel of Jesus Christ, as it is written in Esaias the prophet*[1]—pointing to the winged form of the Gospel; and on this account he made a compendious and cursory narrative, for such is the prophetical character. (A.-N. C. L., altered.)

The arguments used by Irenaeus for the establishing of four gospels only cannot be taken seriously by us, though no doubt they had force in his own time. There was an urgent necessity to establish the authority of the four: Irenaeus points out that a Valentinian "Gospel of Truth" had recently been composed (III.11.12 Harvey; 9 A.-N. C. L.); on Gnostic scriptures cf. 124, p. 146. The "Gospel of Truth" has recently been re-discovered. Pagans were aware of discrepancies between Gospels, cf. Origen, *Contra Celsum*, II.27.

99. UNITY OF GOD AND MAN SECURED BY THE INCARNATION

(Irenaeus, III.19.6 Harvey; III.18.7 A.-N. C. L.)

Therefore, as I have already said, He caused man to become one with God. For unless a man had overcome the enemy of man, the enemy would not have been legitimately vanquished. And again: unless God had freely given salvation, we would not now possess it securely. And unless man had been joined to God, he could never have become a partaker of incorruptibility. For it was incumbent upon the Mediator between God and men, by His relationship to both, to bring both to friendship and concord, and present man to God, while He revealed God to man. For, in what way could we be partakers of the adoption of sons, unless we had received from Him through the Son that fellowship which refers to Himself, unless His Word, made flesh, had entered into communion with us? Wherefore also He passed through every stage of life, restoring to all communion with God. (A.-N. C. L., altered.)

100. THE SALVATION OF THE FLESH

(Irenaeus, V.2.1–2 Harvey; V.2.2–3 A.-N. C. L.)

1
(2)   But vain in every respect are they who despise the entire dispensation of God, and disallow the salvation of the flesh, and treat with contempt its regeneration, maintaining that it is not capable of incorruption. But if this indeed do not attain salvation, then

[1] Mark 1.1,2.

neither did the Lord redeem us with His blood, nor is the cup of the Eucharist the communion of His blood, nor the bread which we break the communion of His body.

* * *

2 He acknowledged the cup (which is a part of the creation) as His own blood, from which He bedews our blood; and the bread (also a part of the creation) He affirmed to be His own body, from which He gives increase to our bodies.

(3)   When, therefore, the mingled cup and the manufactured bread receive the Word of God, and the Eucharist becomes the body of Christ, from which things the substance of our flesh is increased and supported, how can they affirm that the flesh is incapable of receiving the gift of God, which is life eternal, the flesh which is nourished from the body and blood of the Lord, and is a member of Him? (A.-N. C. L., altered.)

101. THE DOCTRINE OF RECAPITULATION

(Irenaeus, *Demonstration of the Apostolic Preaching*, 32–34.)

32   Whence then is the substance of the first-formed man? From the Will and the Wisdom of God, and from the virgin earth. *For God had not sent rain,* the Scripture says, *upon the earth,* before man was made; *and there was no man to till the earth.*[1] From this, then, whilst it was still virgin, God took dust of the earth and formed the man, the beginning of mankind. So then the Lord, summing up afresh this man, took the same dispensation of entry into flesh, being born from the Virgin by the Will and the Wisdom of God; that He also should show forth the likeness of Adam's entry into flesh, and there should be that which was written in the beginning, *man after the image and likeness*[2] of God.

33   And just as through a disobedient virgin man was stricken down and fell into death, so through the Virgin who was obedient to the Word of God man was reanimated and received life. For the Lord came to seek again the sheep that was lost; and man it was that was lost: and for this cause there was not made some other formation, but in that same which had its descent from Adam He preserved the likeness of the first formation. For it was necessary that Adam should be summed up in Christ, that mortality might be swallowed up and overwhelmed by immortality;

[1] 1 Gen. 2.5.   [2] Gen. 1.26.

and Eve summed up in Mary, that a virgin should be a virgin's intercessor, and by a virgin's obedience undo and put away the disobedience of a virgin.

34   And the trespass which came by the tree was undone by the tree of obedience, when, hearkening unto God, the Son of man was nailed to the tree; thereby putting away the knowledge of evil and bringing in and establishing the knowledge of good: now evil it is to disobey God, even as hearkening unto God is good. And for this cause the Word spake by Isaiah the prophet, announcing beforehand that which was to come—for therefore are they prophets, because they proclaim what is to come: by him then spake the Word thus: *I refuse not, nor gainsay: I gave my back to scourging, and my cheeks to smiting; and my face I turned not away from the shame of spitting.*[1] So then by the obedience wherewith He obeyed *even unto death,*[2] hanging on the tree, He put away the old disobedience which was wrought in the tree. (Robinson, *St Irenaeus, The Apostolic Preaching*, pp. 98–101.)

This is a theme which Irenaeus uses in his work *Against Heresies*, cf., e.g., III.30.1, 32.1, Harvey; III.21.10, 22.4 A.-N. C. L.; V.19.1; Justin works out the parallel between Eve and Mary in *Dialogue with Trypho*, 100.

102. IRENAEUS' LETTER TO FLORINUS
(Eusebius, *H.E.* V.20.4–8.)

These opinions, Florinus, to say no more, are not of sound judgement; these opinions are not in harmony with the Church, involving those who adopt them in the greatest impiety; these opinions not even the heretics outside the Church ever dared to espouse openly; these opinions the elders before us, who also
5   were disciples of the apostles, did not hand down to you. For when I was still a boy I saw you in lower Asia in the company of Polycarp, faring brilliantly in the imperial court and endeavouring to secure his favour. For I distinctly recall the events of that
6   time better than those of recent years (for what we learn in childhood keeps pace with the growing mind and becomes part of it), so that I can tell the very place where the blessed Polycarp used to sit as he discoursed, his goings out and his comings in, the character of his life, his bodily appearance, the discourses he would address to the people, how he told of his intercourse with John and with the others who had seen the Lord, how he

[1] Isaiah 50.5f.   [2] Phil. 2.8.

remembered their words, and what the things were which he had
heard from them concerning the Lord, His mighty works and
His teaching, and how Polycarp, as having received them from the
eye-witnesses of the life of the Word,[1] related everything in accord-
7 ance with the Scriptures. To these things I used to listen diligently
even then, by the mercy of God which was upon me, noting
them down not on paper but in my heart. And by the grace of
God I constantly ruminate upon them faithfully; and I can testify
before God that if that blessed and apostolic elder had heard the
like, he would have cried aloud and stopped his ears and said, as
was his wont: "Good God, for what sort of times hast Thou
kept me, that I should endure these things?" and he would have
fled the very place where, sitting or standing, he had heard such
8 words. And this can be shown from his letters too which he wrote,
whether to the neighbouring churches, confirming them, or to
some of the brethren, admonishing and exhorting them. (Lawlor
and Oulton, *Eusebius*, I, p. 166, altered slightly.)

The date of this letter is uncertain. Some place it *c.* 180, others *c.* 190. From a
fragment of a letter from Irenaeus to Victor, Bishop of Rome (Harvey,
Irenaeus, II, p. 457) it appears that Florinus was a presbyter at Rome.

103. THE *TEACHING OF THE TWELVE APOSTLES* ON BAPTISM, FASTING, AND THE EUCHARIST; ON PROPHETS AND THE MINISTRY

(Didache VII–XV.2.)

As the date and provenance of the *Didache* are uncertain, the value of this
passage is doubtful. The passage on Baptism and the Eucharist should be compared with 42, those on Prophets and the Ministry with 29, 85–91.

VII.1   And concerning baptism, baptize thus. Having first recited
all these things, baptize *in the name of the Father, and of the Son*
2 *and of the Holy Spirit*[2] in running water. But if thou hast not
running water, baptize in other water; and, if thou canst not in
3 cold, in warm. But if thou hast neither, pour water thrice upon
4 the head in the name of Father, Son and Holy Spirit. And before
the baptism let the baptizer and him that is baptized fast, and such
others as can: and thou shalt bid the person to be baptized to fast
for one or two days before.

[1] Cf. 1 John 1.1,2; Luke 1.2.   [2] Matt. 28.19.

VIII.1 And let not your fasts be with *the hypocrites:*[1] for they fast on the second and fifth days of the week: but do ye fast on the
2 fourth and on the Preparation (i.e. on Friday). Neither pray ye *as do the hypocrites,*[2] but as the Lord commanded in His gospel, *so pray ye; Our Father which art in heaven, hallowed be thy name, thy kingdom come, thy will be done as in heaven, so on earth. Give us this day our daily bread, and forgive us our debt, as we also forgive our debtors, and lead us not into temptation, but deliver us from evil. For*
3 *thine is the power and the glory for ever.*[3] Thrice in the day pray thus.
IX.1 And concerning the Eucharist, give thanks in this manner.
2 First concerning the cup. We thank thee, our Father, for the holy vine of David, thy son, which thou didst make known to us
3 through Jesus, thy son. Glory be to thee for ever. And concerning the broken bread. We thank thee, our Father, for the life and knowledge which thou didst make known to us through Jesus,
4 thy son. Glory be to thee for ever. As this bread that is broken was scattered upon the mountains, and gathered together, and became one, so let thy Church be gathered together from the ends of the earth into thy kingdom: for thine is the glory and the power
5 through Jesus Christ for ever. And let none eat or drink of your Eucharist, but they that have been baptized into the name of the Lord; for concerning this the Lord hath said: *Give not that which is holy to the dogs.*[4]
X.1, 2 And, after you are filled, give thanks thus. We thank thee, Holy Father, for thy holy name, which thou hast made to dwell in our hearts, and for the knowledge, faith, and immortality, which thou didst make known to us through Jesus, thy son. Glory be to thee for ever.
3 Thou, Almighty Lord, *didst create all things*[5] for thy name's sake, and gavest meat and drink for men to enjoy, that they might give thanks unto thee, and to us didst vouchsafe spiritual meat and
4 drink and life eternal, through thy son. Above all we thank thee
5 because thou art mighty. Glory be to thee for ever. Remember, Lord, thy Church, to deliver her from all evil, and to perfect her in thy love, and gather together from *the four winds*[6] her that is sanctified into thy kingdom which thou didst prepare for her.
6 For thine is the power and the glory for ever. Let grace come, and let this world pass away. Hosanna to the God of David. If any is holy, let him come: if any is unholy let him repent.

[1] Matt. 6.16.   [2] Matt. 6.5.
[3] Matt. 6.9–13, with certain variants.   [4] Matt. 7.6.
[5] Cf. Wisd. 1.14; Ecclus. 18.1; Rev. 4.11.
[6] Cf. Matt. 24.31.

7 *Maranatha*.[1] Amen. But suffer the prophets to give thanks as much as they will.

XI.1 Whosoever then shall come and teach you all these things 2 aforesaid, receive him. But, if the teacher himself is perverse and teach another doctrine to destroy these things, hear him not. But if he teach unto the increase of righteousness and of the knowledge 3 of the Lord, receive him as the Lord. And concerning the apostles 4 and prophets, according to the decree of the gospel, so do. But let 5 every apostle that cometh unto you be received as the Lord. And he shall stay one day, and, if need be, the next also, but, if he stay 6 three, he is a false prophet. And, when the apostle goeth forth, let him take nothing save bread, till he reach his lodging, but if 7 he asks money, he is a false prophet. And every prophet that speaketh in the spirit ye shall not try nor judge: for every sin shall 8 be forgiven, but this sin shall not be forgiven.[2] But not every one that speaketh in the spirit is a prophet, but if he have the ways of the Lord, by their ways then shall the false prophet and the 9 prophet be known. And any prophet that orders a table in the 10 spirit shall not eat of it, else is he a false prophet. And every prophet that teaches the truth if he does not what he teaches is a false 11 prophet. But every approved true prophet, who enacts a worldly mystery of the church, but teaches not others to do what he himself doeth, shall not be judged among you, for he has his 12 judgement with God: for even so did the ancient prophets also. But whosoever shall say in the spirit: Give me money, or any other thing, ye shall not listen to him: but, if he bid you give for others that are in need, let no man judge him.

XII.1 Let every one *that cometh in the name of the Lord*[3] be received, and then, when you have proved him, you shall know, for you shall have understanding [to distinguish] between the 2 right hand and the left. If he that cometh is a passer-by, succour him as far as you can; but he shall not abide with you longer than 3 two or three days unless there be necessity. But if he be minded to settle among you, being a craftsman, let him work and eat. 4 But, if he hath no trade, according to your understanding provide that he shall not live idle among you, being a Christian. 5 But, if he will not do this, he is a Christmonger: of such beware.

XIII.1 But every true prophet, who is minded to settle among you, 2 is *worthy of his food*.[4] In like manner a true teacher also is worthy, 3 like the workman, of his maintenance. Thou shalt take, therefore, all first fruits of the produce of winepress and threshing floor, of oxen and sheep, and give them to the prophets; for they are your

[1] Cf. 1 Cor. 16.22.   [2] Cf. Matt. 12.31.   [3] Ps. 118.26; Matt. 21.9.
[4] Matt. 10.10.

4 high priests. But if you have no prophet, give to the poor.
5 If thou art making bread, take the first fruits and give according
to the commandment. In like manner, when thou openest a jar
7 of wine or oil, take the first fruits and give to the prophets. And
of money, and raiment, and of every chattel, take the first fruits,
as seemeth thee good, and give according to the commandment.
XIV.1 And on the Lord's day of the Lord come together and
break bread and give thanks, having first confessed your trans-
2 gressions, that your sacrifice may be pure. But whoso hath a dispute with his fellow, let him not come together with you, until
3 they be reconciled, that your sacrifice be not polluted. For this is
that which was spoken of by the Lord. *In every place and time
offer me a pure sacrifice: for I am a great King, saith the Lord, and
my name is wonderful among the Gentiles.*[1]
XV.1 Elect therefore for yourselves bishops and deacons worthy
of the Lord, men meek and not covetous, and true and approved:
for they also minister unto you the ministry of the prophets and
2 teachers. Therefore despise them not: for these are they which
are honoured of you with the prophets and teachers. (C. Bigg,
The Doctrine of the Twelve Apostles, pp. 45ff., altered.)

VII.1.   *Having first recited all these things*: i.e. concerning the Way of Life and
the Way of Death, which form the subject of the early chapters of the *Didache*.
VIII.1.   *the hypocrites*, i.e. the Jews.
IX.1.   *First concerning the cup*: cf. St Luke's account of the Last Supper. The
Eucharist is not brought into relation with the death of Christ, cf. Justin's
account (42).
IX.4.   The prayer is based on a Jewish prayer for the restoration of Israel.
XI.3.   The *decree of the gospel* cannot be identified.
XI.4–6.   show that *apostle* and *prophet* are different names for the same
person.
XI.11.   The meaning of the phrase *who enacts a worldly mystery of the church*
cannot be determined.

104. TATIAN AND THE ENCRATITES,
c. 170

(Irenaeus I.26 Harvey; I.28.1 A.-N. C. L., quoted in Eusebius
H.E. IV.29.2–3.)

(1) [Irenaeus explains that the heresies split into different sects,
through the desire of individuals to be themselves reckoned as
"teachers".]

[1] Mal. 1.10,14.

To give an example:

2   . . . from Satorninus and Marcion those who are called Encra-
tites preached celibacy, setting at naught the primitive creation of
God, and tacitly censuring Him who *made male and female*[1] for
the generation of mankind; and they introduced abstinence from
such things as they call "animate", thus showing ingratitude to
God who has made all things.[2] And they deny the salvation of the
3 first-created man. And this last point was a recent invention of
theirs, a certain Tatian having first introduced this blasphemy.
He had been a hearer of Justin, and, as long as he was with him,
gave vent to no such doctrine; but after Justin's martyrdom he
broke away from the Church, and, elated at the thought of being
a teacher and puffed up with the idea that he was superior to the
rest, formed a school with a distinctive character of its own. For
while he invented certain invisible aeons, as did the followers of
Valentinus; while he proclaimed marriage to be corruption and
fornication, in a manner similar to Marcion and Satorninus: his
own contribution was to deny the salvation of Adam. (Lawlor
and Oulton, *Eusebius*, I, p. 134.)

With this passage, cf. Irenaeus, III.37 Harvey; III.23.8 A.-N. C. L., where
Irenaeus argues against Tatian's denial of Salvation to Adam: "let them wrangle
about Adam, as if some great gain were to accrue to them, if he be not saved".
    2. *Encratites*: The name is derived from the Greek ἐγκράτεια, "contin-
ence."

105. *THE DIATESSARON* AND OTHER WORKS OF TATIAN

(Eusebius, *H.E.* IV.29.6–7.)

6   Their former leader, however, Tatian, arranged a kind of
joining together and compilation of the Gospels, I know not how,
to which he gave the title The Diatessaron; and it is still to this
day to be found in the hands of some. But it is said that he dared
to alter certain of the apostle's expressions, with a view to correct-
7 ing the style in which they were composed. Now this writer has
left behind him a great number of treatises, of which his famous
book Against the Greeks is chiefly remembered by many. Speaking in it of primitive times, he has shown that Moses and the
prophets of the Hebrews were earlier than all *the* famous men

[1] Gen. 1.27.   [2] Cf. 1 Tim. 4.3,4.

among the Greeks.[1] And this work also seems to be the best and most useful of all his treatises. (Lawlor and Oulton, *Eusebius*, I, p. 135.)

6. *The Diatessaron*: "This work is a harmony of the four Gospels, as Eusebius says and as its title ('Through Four') implies." (Lawlor and Oulton, *Eusebius*, II, p. 151.)

The expression *I know not how* indicates that Eusebius either had not seen *The Diatessaron*, or was contemptuous of it.

in the hands of some: in the fifth century Theodoret found in the churches of his diocese of Cyrrhus more than two hundred copies of the *Diatessaron*, which he destroyed.

7. To prove that Moses and the prophets were earlier in date than the Greek poets and philosophers was a task to which the early church addressed itself assiduously by the production of chronological tables, of which the *Chronicle* of Eusebius is the best example.

106. EARLY CREEDS

(1. From *The Epistle of the Apostles* 5 (16), *c.* 180.)

(I believe) in (the Father) the ruler of the universe,
 and in Jesus Christ (our Redeemer)
 and in the Holy Spirit (the Paraclete)
 and in the holy Church,
 and in the forgiveness of sins.
   (J. N. D. Kelly, *Early Christian Creeds*, p. 82.)

The words in brackets are not found in all MSS.

"The disciples explain that the Five Loaves of the miraculous feeding are a symbol of our Christian belief. . . . Almost certainly it is a three-clause formulary, modelled on the baptismal interrogations, which has been expanded to five clauses by the tacking on of additional articles at the end." (Kelly, loc. cit.)

(2. From the *Dêr Balyzeh Papyrus*.)

. . . confesses the faith, saying
I believe in God the Father almighty,
 and in His only-begotten Son
  our Lord Jesus Christ,
 and in the Holy Spirit, and in the resurrection of the flesh, and the holy Catholic Church.
   (Kelly, *Early Christian Creeds*, p. 88.)

[1] Tat., *Oratio ad Graec.* 31,36–41.

Who is supposed to make the declaration is uncertain. It should be noted that the date of the liturgy contained in this papyrus is very variously estimated from the latter part of the second century onwards. The creed may be much older than the liturgy: "it was almost certainly a baptismal creed in origin." (Kelly, loc. cit.)

107. A GNOSTIC BAPTISM

(Irenaeus, I.14.2 Harvey; I.21.3 A.-N. C. L.)

[Irenaeus goes over the initiation rites of the Marcosians, (1) a symbolic marriage, after the likeness of the conjunctions of the aeons in the Pleroma, (2) baptism.]

Others lead them to water, and baptize them, with the utterance of these words over them, "Into the name of the unknown Father of the universe—into truth, the mother of all things, into Him who descended on Jesus, into union, and redemption, and communion with the powers." (A.-N. C. L.)

The object of the Gnostic baptism was regeneration "into the power that is above all" (Irenaeus, I.1.14. Harvey; I.21.2 A.-N. C. L.). Hence the terms "union" and "communion".
Truth is one of the chief Aeons of the Marcosians.

108. THE FAITH OF JEWS AND CHRISTIANS

(From an Arabic quotation of a lost work of Galen.)

"If I had in mind people who taught their pupils in the same way as the followers of Moses and Christ teach theirs—for they order them to accept everything on faith—I should not have given you a definition." (R. Walzer, *Galen on Jews and Christians*, p. 15.)

Galen comments three times in extant works or fragments on the faith of Jews and Christians: they rely on faith only and not on demonstration. He is very critical of this attitude, cf. the notes on the following passage.

109. CHRISTIAN TEACHING AND CHRISTIAN LIFE

(From Galen's (lost) summary of Plato's *Republic*; preserved in Arabic quotations.)

"Most people are unable to follow any demonstrative argument consecutively; hence they need parables, and benefit from them"—and he (Galen) understands by parables tales of rewards and punishments in a future life—"just as now we see the people called Christians drawing their faith from parables [and miracles], and yet sometimes acting in the same way [as those who philosophize]. For their contempt of death [and of its sequel] is patent to us every day, and likewise their restraint in cohabitation. For they include not only men but also women who refrain from cohabiting all through their lives; and they also number individuals who, in self-discipline and self-control in matters of food and drink, and in their keen pursuit of justice, have attained a pitch not inferior to that of genuine philosophers." (R. Walzer, op. cit., p. 15.)

Galen is dealing with the myth of Er in Book X of Plato's *Republic*. He did not himself believe in rewards and punishments after death, but he is aware of the moral importance of these ideas. He is the earliest pagan who recognizes that the Christians are in some sense philosophers: and thereby shows that the work of Justin and his school bore fruit, cf. 20. "For religious teachers who offered guidance in conduct and a scheme of the universe were so different from the priests of traditional Greek rites and cults that it is not at all astonishing that they should be looked on as philosophers." (R. Walzer, op. cit., p. 51.)

110. THE CHARLATAN ALEXANDER AND THE CHRISTIANS, c. 150–170

(Lucian, *Alexander or The False Prophet*, 25,38.)

Lucian loathed charlatanry, and in this work pilloried Alexander, who had wide influence in the second century even though he came from a small city in remote Paphlagonia. Alexander was among other things an oracle-monger, who plied his trade with great (financial) success.

25   When at last many sensible men, recovering, as it were, from profound intoxication, combined against him, especially all the followers of Epicurus, and when in the cities they began gradu-

ally to detect all the trickery and bunkum of the show, he issued a proclamation designed to scare them, saying that Pontus was full of atheists and Christians who had the hardihood to utter the vilest abuse of him; these he bade them drive away with stones if they wanted to have the god gracious.

*   *   *

38   He established a celebration of mysteries, with torchlight ceremonies and priestly offices, for three days in succession, in perpetuity. On the first day, there was a proclamation, worded as follows as at Athens: "If any atheist or Christian or Epicurean has come to spy upon the rites, let him be off, and let those who believe in the god perform the mysteries, under the blessing of Heaven." Then, at the very outset, there was an "expulsion", in which he took the lead, saying: "Out with the Christians", and the whole multitude chanted in response, "Out with the Epicureans!" (A. M. Harmon, *Lucian* IV (Loeb Library), pp. 209, 225, altered.)

These passages show that, being "atheists", but for very different reasons, Christians and Epicureans were the chief enemies of Alexander. The first passage shows that Christians existed in Pontus in some numbers by 170, and how easily mob-violence might be used against them.

III. THE STORY OF PEREGRINUS

(Lucian, *On the death of Peregrinus*, 11–16.)

Peregrinus or Proteus was a Cynic philosopher who cremated himself on a funeral pyre at the close of the Olympic games in A.D. 165. Lucian believed him to be a charlatan like Alexander (110).

["Lucian relates in a letter to a friend that he was at Olympia at the time, and witnessed the suicide, which he describes with characteristic wit and bitterness. The history of Peregrinus he professes to have heard from a fellow-visitor who was roused to speak by the ridiculous praises which were bestowed by some disciples and friends upon the voluntary martyr. This vainglorious cynic then, as he became at last, had lived, according to this account, a strange and eventful life. In his youth he was obliged to fly from his native country, Parium, near Lampsacus, for parricide and other crimes, and so came after many wanderings to Palestine." (Westcott, *The Two Empires*, pp. 86–7.)]

11   It was then that he learned the wondrous lore of the Christians, by associating with their priests and scribes in Palestine. And— how else could it be?—in a trice he made them all look like children; for he was prophet, cult-leader, head of the synagogue, and everything, all by himself. He interpreted and explained some of their books and even composed many, and they revered him as a god, made use of him as a lawgiver, and adopted him as their patron, next after that other, to be sure, whom they still worship, the man who was crucified in Palestine because he introduced this new cult into the world.

12   Then at length Proteus was apprehended for this and thrown into prison, which itself gave him no little reputation to help him in later life and gratify his passion for imposture and notoriety. Well, when he had been imprisoned, the Christians, regarding the incident as a calamity, left nothing undone in the effort to rescue him. Then, as this was impossible, every other form of attention was shown him, not in any casual way but with assiduity; and from the very break of day you could see aged women lingering about the prison, widows and orphans, while their officials even slept inside with him after bribing the guards. Then elaborate meals were brought in, and sacred books of theirs were read aloud, and excellent Peregrinus—for he still went by that name—was called by them "a new Socrates".

13   Indeed, people came even from the cities in Asia, sent by the Christians at their common expense, to succour and defend and encourage the hero. They show incredible speed whenever any such public action is taken; for in no time they lavish their all. So it was then in the case of Peregrinus; much money came to him from them by reason of his imprisonment, and he procured not a little revenue from it. The poor wretches have convinced themselves, first and foremost, that they are going to be immortal and live for all time, in consequence of which they despise death and even willingly give themselves into custody, most of them. Furthermore, their first lawgiver persuaded them that they are all brothers of one another after they have transgressed once for all by denying the Greek gods and by worshipping that crucified sophist himself and living under his laws. Therefore they despise all things indiscriminately and consider them common property, receiving such doctrines traditionally without any definite evidence. So if any charlatan and trickster, able to profit by occasions, comes among them, he quickly acquires sudden wealth by imposing upon simple folk.

14   However, Peregrinus was freed by the then governor of Syria, a man who was fond of philosophy. Aware of his recklessness and

that he would gladly die in order that he might leave behind him a reputation for it, he freed him, not considering him worthy even of the usual chastisement.

["Thereupon, Lucian continues, in the words of his informant, Peregrinus returned home; but when he found that his crimes were not forgotten, he purchased the goodwill of his countrymen by giving all his property for public uses." (Westcott, *The Two Empires*, p. 89.)]

16   He left home, then, for the second time, to roam about, possessing an ample source of funds in the Christians, through whose ministrations he lived in unalloyed prosperity. For a time he battened himself thus; but then, after he had transgressed in some way even against them—he was seen, I think, eating some of the food that is forbidden them—they no longer accepted him. (A. M. Harmon, *Lucian* V (Loeb Library), pp. 13–19, altered principally from Westcott, op. cit.)

This story shows numerous interesting features of second-century Christianity, e.g. the ease with which a charlatan could impose on the Christians, cf. 103, the respect and care shown to the martyrs, Christian readiness to help each other, their claim to be philosophers, the scorn with which belief in the resurrection was viewed by pagans, the attitude of the authorities.

112. THE "STUBBORNNESS" OF THE CHRISTIANS

(Marcus Aurelius, *Meditations*, XI.3.)

How admirable is the soul which is ready and resolved, if it must this moment be released from the body, to be either extinguished or scattered, or to persist. This resolve, too, must arise from a specific decision, not out of sheer opposition like the Christians, but after reflexion and with dignity, and so as to convince others, without histrionic display. (A. S. L. Farquharson, *The Meditations of the Emperor Marcus Aurelius*, I, p. 217.)

"The most noteworthy point is the implication that the attitude of some Christians at least was so familiar as to be almost proverbial. . . . The remark is parenthetical; Marcus is not condemning the Christians; he is only illustrating a point by an example which has a poignant interest to us." (Farquharson, op. cit., I, pp. 408–9.)

On the "stubbornness" of Christians, viewed from the Roman point of view, cf. the attitude of Pliny (14).

On the attitude of Marcus, cf. his decision in the case of the martyrs of Lyons and Vienne (21), and a rescript of his in the following terms: "if any one has done anything to alarm the unstable minds of men with superstitious fear of the divine, Marcus of blessed memory (*divus*) laid it down that men of this kind were to be transported to an island". (*Dig.* 48.19.30 (Modestinus), Mommsen, *Römisches Strafrecht*, p. 579, n.2.)

113. FRONTO'S SPEECH AGAINST THE CHRISTIANS, c. 180

(Minucius Felix, *Octavius*, 9.6 and 31.2.)

(1) The speaker is the heathen Caecilius:

9.6 What takes place at their banquets is also well known; it is everywhere talked about, as is attested by a speech of our countryman of Cirta.

(2) The speaker is the Christian Octavius:

31.2 Thus also your friend Fronto has not given evidence as one who affirms a thing on oath, but has scattered abuse broadcast like a public speaker; for such practices rather originated amongst people like yourselves. (J. H. Freese, *The Octavius of Minucius Felix*, pp. 42 and 84.)

Fronto's speech against the Christians is lost, but the fact that the most important literary man of his day, to whose kindness and conscientiousness his letters bear witness, could believe the slanders against the Christians shows the extent and depth of the prejudice against which Christianity had to contend.

114. CELSUS: ARE CHRISTIANS MONOTHEISTS?

(Origen, *Against Celsus*, VIII.12,14.)

12 "If these men worshipped no other God but one, perhaps they would have had a valid argument against the others. But in fact they worship to an extravagant degree this man who appeared recently, and yet think it is not inconsistent with monotheism if they also worship His servant."

*   *   *

14   "If you taught them that Jesus is not his Son, but that God is father of all, and that we really ought to worship him alone, they would no longer be willing to listen to you unless you included Jesus as well, who is the author of their sedition. Indeed, when they call him Son of God, it is not because they are paying very great reverence to God, but because they are exalting Jesus greatly." (Chadwick, *Origen, "Contra Celsum"*, pp. 460-1.)

On "Ditheism", cf. 13ᵗ, 136.

115. CELSUS: OBJECTIONS TO THE IDEA OF GOD COMING DOWN TO EARTH

(Origen, *Against Celsus*, IV.2.3.)

2   "The assertion made both by some of the Christians and by the Jews, the former saying that some God or son of God has come down to the earth as judge of mankind, the latter saying that he will come, is most shameful, and no lengthy argument is required
3   to refute it. . . . What is the purpose of such a descent on the part of God? . . . Was it in order to learn what was going on among men? . . . Does he not know everything? . . . If, then, he does know, why does he not correct men, and why can he not do this by divine power? . . . Was he then unable to correct men merely by divine power, without sending some one specially endowed for the purpose?" (Chadwick, *Origen "Contra Celsum"*, pp. 184-6.)

Celsus went on to argue (Origen, IV.5) that the idea of the descent of God implied that he left his throne, and actually changed position in a spatial sense.

116. CELSUS: SLANDERS AGAINST THE VIRGIN

(Origen, *Against Celsus*, I.28,32.)

28   After this he represents the Jew as having a conversation with Jesus himself and refuting him on many charges, as he thinks: first, because "he fabricated the story of his birth from a virgin; and he reproaches him because he came from a Jewish village and from a poor country woman who earned her living by spinning". He says that "she was driven out by her husband, who was a carpenter by trade, as she was convicted of adultery". Then he says that

"after she had been driven out by her husband and while she was wandering about in a disgraceful way she secretly gave birth to Jesus".

* * *

32   Let us return, however, to the words put into the mouth of the Jew, where "the mother of Jesus" is described as having been "turned out by the carpenter who was betrothed to her, as she had been convicted of adultery and had a child by a certain soldier named Panthera" (Chadwick, Origen "Contra Celsum", pp. 28, 31).

On Panthera, a common name for Roman soldiers, see Chadwick, op. cit., p. 31, n. 3.

117. CELSUS: ON THE RESURRECTION

(Origen, Against Celsus, II.55.)

"Come now, let us believe your view that he actually said this. How many others produce wonders like this to convince simple hearers whom they exploit by deceit? They say that Zamolxis, the slave of Pythagoras, also did this among the Scythians, and Pythagoras himself in Italy, and Rhampsinitus in Egypt. The last-named played dice with Demeter in Hades and returned bearing a gift from her, a golden napkin. Moreover, they say that Orpheus did this among the Odrysians, and Protesilaus in Thessaly, and Heracles at Taenarum, and Theseus. But we must examine this question whether anyone who really died ever rose again with the same body. Or do you think that the stories of these others really are the legends which they appear to be, and yet that the ending of your tragedy is to be regarded as noble and convincing—his cry from the cross when he expired, and the earthquake and the darkness? While he was alive he did not help himself, but after death he rose again and showed the marks of his punishment and how his hands had been pierced. But who saw this? A hysterical female, as you say, and perhaps some other one of those who were deluded by the same sorcery, who either dreamt in a certain state of mind and through wishful thinking had a hallucination due to some mistaken notion (an experience which has happened to thousands), or, which is more likely, wanted to impress the others by telling this fantastic tale, and so by this cock-and-bull story to provide a chance for other beggars." (Chadwick, Origen "Contra Celsum", p. 109.)

118. CELSUS: CHARLATANRY AND CREDULITY

(Origen, *Contra Celsum*, I.9.)

After this he urges us to "follow reason and a rational guide in accepting doctrines" on the ground that "anyone who believes people without so doing is certain to be deceived". And he compares those who believe without rational thought to the "begging priests of Cybele and soothsayers, and to worshippers of Mithras and Sabazius, and whatever else one might meet, apparitions of Hecate or of some other daemon or daemons. For just as among them scoundrels frequently take advantage of the lack of education of gullible people and lead them wherever they wish, so also," he says, "this happens among the Christians". He says that "some do not even want to give or to receive a reason for what they believe, and use such expressions as 'Do not ask questions; just believe', and 'Thy faith will save thee'." And he affirms that they say: "The wisdom in the world is an evil, and foolishness a good thing." (Chadwick, *Origen "Contra Celsum"*, p. 12.)

On charlatans, cf. 103, 110; on credulity, cf. 111.

119. CELSUS: MIRACLE AND SORCERY

(Origen, *Against Celsus*, I.28,68.)

28   "Because he was poor he (Jesus) hired himself out as a workman in Egypt, and there tried his hand at certain magical powers on which the Egyptians pride themselves; he returned full of conceit because of these powers, and on account of them gave himself the title of God."

*   *   *

68   After this, suspecting that the great works done by Jesus would be pointed out, of which, although there is much to say, we have only said a little, Celsus pretends to grant that the scriptures may be true when they speak of "cures or resurrection or a few loaves feeding many people, from which many fragments were left over, or any other monstrous tales", as he thinks, "related by the disciples". And he goes on to say: "Come, let us believe that these miracles really were done by you." Then he at once puts them on

a level with "the works of sorcerers who profess to do wonderful miracles, and the accomplishments of those who are taught by the Egyptians, who for a few obols make known their sacred lore in the middle of the market-place and drive daemons out of men and blow away diseases and invoke the souls of heroes, displaying expensive banquets and dining-tables and cakes and dishes which are non-existent, and who make things move as though they were alive although they are not really so, but only appear as such in the imagination". And he says: "Since these men do these wonders, ought we to think them sons of God? Or ought we to say that they are the practices of wicked men possessed by an evil daemon?" (Chadwick, *Origen "Contra Celsum"*, pp. 28, 62–3.)

120. CELSUS: CHRISTIAN PROPAGANDA

(Origen, *Against Celsus*, III.55.)

"In private houses also we see wool-workers, cobblers, laundry-workers, and the most illiterate and bucolic yokels, who would not dare to say anything at all in front of their elders and more intelligent masters. But whenever they get hold of children in private and some stupid women with them, they let out some astounding statements as, for example, that they must not pay any attention to their father and school-teachers, but must obey them; they say that these talk nonsense and have no understanding, and that in reality they neither know nor are able to do anything good, but are taken up with mere empty chatter. But they alone, they say, know the right way to live, and if the children would believe them, they would become happy and make their home happy as well. And if just as they are speaking they see one of the school-teachers coming, or some intelligent person, or even the father himself, the more cautious of them flee in all directions; but the more reckless urge the children on to rebel. They whisper to them that in the presence of their father and their schoolmasters they do not feel able to explain anything to the children, since they do not want to have anything to do with the silly and obtuse teachers who are totally corrupted and far gone in wickedness, and who inflict punishment on the children. But, if they like, they should leave father and their schoolmasters, and go along with the women and little children who are their playfellows to the wool-dresser's shop, or to the cobbler's or the washerwoman's shop, that they may learn perfection. And by saying this they persuade them." (Chadwick, *Origen "Contra Celsum"*, pp. 165–6.)

121. CELSUS: CHRISTIANITY IS FOR FOOLS ONLY

(Origen, *Against Celsus,* III.44.)

"Their injunctions are like this. 'Let no one educated, no one wise, no one sensible draw near. For these abilities are thought by us to be evils. But as for anyone ignorant, anyone stupid, anyone uneducated, anyone who is a child, let him come boldly.' By the fact that they themselves admit that these people are worthy of their God, they show that they want and are able to convince only the foolish, dishonourable and stupid, and only slaves, women, and little children." (Chadwick, *Origen "Contra Celsum"*, p. 158.)

122. CELSUS: CHRISTIANS AND THE EMPIRE

(Origen, *Against Celsus*, VIII.68,69.)

68   Then Celsus next says "that we ought not to disbelieve the ancient man who long ago declared
Let there be one king, him to whom the son of crafty Kronos gave the power."
And he continues: "For, if you overthrow this doctrine, it is probable that the emperor will punish you. If everyone were to do the same as you, there would be nothing to prevent him from being abandoned, alone and deserted, while earthly things would come into the power of the most lawless and savage barbarians, and nothing more would be heard among men either of your worship or of the true wisdom."

*   *   *

69   "You will surely not say that if the Romans were convinced by you and were to neglect their customary honours to both gods and men and were to call upon your Most High, or whatever name you prefer, He would come down and fight on their side, and they would have no need for any other defence. In earlier times also the same God made these promises and some far greater than these, so you say, to those who pay regard to him. But see how much help he has been to both them and you. Instead of

being masters of the whole world, they have been left no land or home of any kind. While in your case, if anyone does still wander about in secret, yet he is sought out and condemned to death." (Chadwick, *Origen "Contra Celsum"*, pp. 504-5.)

68. The quotation is from Homer, *Il.*2. 204-5: for its use later by the Christians, cf. 318 (3).

123. THE EPITAPH OF AVIRCIUS MAR-CELLUS, OF HIEROPOLIS IN PHRYGIA, *c.* 182

(Text in Sir W. M. Ramsay, *Cities and Bishoprics of Phrygia*, II, p. 722-3.)

I, a citizen of the elect city, erected this tomb in my lifetime, that I might have clearly there a place for my body; my name is Avircius, a disciple of the pure Shepherd who feeds the flocks of sheep on mountains and plains, who has great all-seeing eyes; he taught me . . . faithful scriptures. To Rome he sent me to behold sovereignty and to see a queen, golden-robed and golden san-dalled; a people I saw there which has a splendid seal, and I saw the plain of Syria and all the cities, and Nisibis, crossing the Euphrates; but everywhere I met with brethren; with Paul before me, I followed, and Faith everywhere led the way and served food everywhere, the Fish from the spring—immense, pure, which the pure Virgin caught and gave to her friends to eat for ever, with good wine, giving the cup with the loaf. These things I Avircius ordered to be written thus in my presence. I am truly seventy-two years old. Let him who understands these things, and everyone who is in agreement, pray for Avircius. No one is to put anyone else into my tomb; otherwise he is to pay the Roman treasury, 2,000 gold pieces and my good native city of Hieropolis 1,000 gold pieces. (Grant, *Second-century Christianity*, pp. 101-2, altered.)

Avircius Marcellus is mentioned in Eusebius, *H.E.* V.16.3 (85) by the Anony-mous writer against the Montanists, as having asked that author to write a work against these heretics. By *c.* A.D. 400 Avircius had become a legendary figure, portrayed in *Acta S. Abercii*. In these *Acta* his epitaph was quoted, and in 1883 part of the tombstone itself was found by Ramsay and Sterrett. It is now in Rome. The stone itself contains a mere fragment of the whole.

The inscription begins with an elegiac couplet, and then continues in hexa-meters. Christianity is represented cryptically, but to those who understood, the tombstone was a permanent testimony to Avircius' faith in the unity of the Catholic church, a unity which his travels confirmed, as happened in the case of Hegesippus also (47).

the elect city: this was a cryptic way of referring to Christian citizenship in Heaven.

To Rome he sent me . . . golden sandalled: the reading of the inscription is uncertain, but Calder (*J.R.S.*, XXIX (1939), "The Epitaph of Avircius Mar-cellus", pp. 1–2) has shown that, notwithstanding Sir W. M. Ramsay's emphatic statement to the contrary (*Cities and Bishoprics of Phrygia*, II, pp. 725, 728n.), the copy of the stone made by Sterrett in 1883 in Ramsay's company, showed no letter H, as Ramsay asserts, at the broken edge of the stone after ΒΑΣΙΛ. The reading is therefore Βασιλείαν or Βασίλειαν (as in the *Acta*), but not Βασιλῆαν (emperor). "If we read Βασιλείαν Avircius was sent to Rome . . . to look upon Sovereignty and a Sovereign Church. The reading Βασίλειαν of some MSS, implying a visit to the Empress and Princess, need not be considered. It has the advantage of Βασιλείαν in point of metre, but the Epitaph elsewhere is irregular in its scansion." (Calder, loc. cit.) cf. Chavasse, *The Bride of Christ*, p. 117, "The golden robed Queen is evidently the Church as seen in Rome in her royal state; 'her clothing is of wrought gold'."

a splendid seal: ". . . the intentionally mysterious language of the *Epitaph of Abercius* probably refers to Baptism." (Lampe, *The Seal of the Spirit*, p. 189.)

with Paul before me: literally, "Having Paul, I followed", i.e. either "with Paul's teaching and example to inspire me", or "I followed the same routes" (Asia, Syria, Rome).

who understands these things, etc.: Ramsay suggests, op. cit., p. 728, that Avircius is expressing anti-Montanist sentiments.

124. THE SCRIPTURES ACKNOWLEDGED BY THE ROMAN CHURCH, c. 190

(The Fragment of Muratori: Text in Gwatkin, *Selections from Early Christian Writers*, pp. 82–88; Souter, *Text and Canon of the New Testament*, pp. 208–11.)

The fragment begins with the last words of a sentence that obviously refer to St Mark's Gospel.

. . . . but at some he was present, and so he set them down.

The third book of the Gospel, that according to Luke, was compiled in his own name on Paul's authority by Luke the physi-cian, when after Christ's ascension Paul had taken him to be with him like a legal expert. Yet neither did *he* see the Lord in the flesh; and he too, as he was able to ascertain events, begins his story from the birth of John.

The fourth of the Gospels was written by John, one of the disciples. When exhorted by his fellow-disciples and bishops, he said, "Fast with me this day for three days; and what may be revealed to any of us, let us relate it to one another." The same night it was revealed to Andrew, one of the apostles, that John was to write all things in his own name, and they were all to certify.

And therefore, though various ideas are taught in the several books of the Gospels, yet it makes no difference to the faith of believers, since by one sovereign Spirit all things are declared in all of them concerning the Nativity, the Passion, the Resurrection, the conversation with his disciples and his two comings, the first in lowliness and contempt, which has come to pass, the second glorious with royal power, which is to come.

What marvel therefore if John so firmly sets forth each statement in his Epistles too, saying of himself, *What we have seen with our eyes and heard with our ears and our hands have handled, these things we have written to you?*[1] For so he declares himself not an eyewitness and a hearer only, but a writer of all the marvels of the Lord in order.

The Acts, however, of all the Apostles are written in one book. Luke, *to the most excellent Theophilus,*[2] includes events because they were done in his own presence, as he also plainly shows by leaving out the passion of Peter, and also the departure of Paul from the City on his journey to Spain.

The Epistles, however, of Paul themselves make plain to those who wish to understand it, what epistles were sent by him, and from what place or for what cause. He wrote at some length first of all to the Corinthians, forbidding the schisms of heresy; next to the Galatians, forbidding circumcision; then he wrote to the Romans at greater length, impressing on them the rule of the Scriptures, and also that Christ is the first principle of them, concerning which severally it is not necessary for us to discuss. For the blessed Apostle Paul himself, following the rule of his predecessor John, writes only by name to seven churches in the following order—to the Corinthians a first, to the Ephesians a second, to the Philippians a third, to the Colossians a fourth, to the Galatians a fifth, to the Thessalonians a sixth, to the Romans a seventh; although for the sake of admonition there is a second to the

[1] Cf. 1 John 1.1,3-4.   [2] Luke 1.3.

Corinthians and to the Thessalonians, yet *one* Church is recognized as being spread over the entire world. For John too in the Apocalypse, though he writes to seven churches, yet speaks to all. Howbeit to Philemon one, to Titus one, and to Timothy two were put in writing from personal inclination and attachment, to be in honour however with the Catholic Church for the ordering of ecclesiastical discipline. There is in circulation also one to the Laodicenes, another to the Alexandrians, both forged in Paul's name to suit the heresy of Marcion, and several others, which cannot be received into the Catholic Church; for it is not fitting that gall be mixed with honey.

The Epistle of Jude no doubt, and the couple bearing the name of John, are accepted in the Catholic Church; and the Wisdom written by the friends of Solomon in his honour. The Apocalypse also of John, and of Peter only we receive, which some of our friends will not have read in the Church. But the Shepherd was written quite lately in our times in the city of Rome by Hermas, while his brother Pius, the bishop, was sitting in the chair of the church of the city of Rome; and therefore it ought indeed to be read, but it cannot to the end of time be publicly read in the Church to the people, either among the prophets, who are complete in number, or among the Apostles.

But of Arsinous, called also Valentinus, or of Miltiades we receive nothing at all; those who have also composed a new book of Psalms for Marcion, together with Basileides and the Asian founder of the Cataphrygians are rejected. (Gwatkin, *Selections from Early Christian Writers*, pp. 83–8, altered.)

to be with him like a legal expert (*ut iuris studiosum*): the Latin is usually taken to mean "a student of law". (Westcott, *Canon of N.T.*, p. 534, n. 3, believing in a Greek original, regarded the words *ut iuris* as corrupt: Souter, *Text and Canon of the N.T.*, p. 208, prints, with a query, a conjecture "adiutorem", helper.)

"The description of *iuris studiosus* does not only apply to somebody who is being trained in the law, but also to a legal expert who acts on behalf of a Roman official, provincial governor or the like. . . . Such an *adsessor* or *iuris studiosus* issued an *edictum*, *decretum* or *epistula* either in the name of the Roman official to whom he was attached, or else *suo nomine ex opinione* of his superior." (Erhardt, *The Gospels in the Muratorian Fragment*, Ostkirchliche Studien, II.2, 1953, p. 125.)

Thus St Luke's Gospel was written on Paul's authority.

St John's Gospel: "Its, i.e. this document's, account of the origin of the

Fourth Gospel can only be styled 'a cock and bull story'." (Streeter, *The Primitive Church*, p. 205.)

Acts: *the City*, i.e. Rome. This phrase indicates "the Roman character of the document". (Tregelles, *Canon Muritorianus*, p. 40.)

On Paul's visit to Spain, cf. 5.

St Paul: *his predecessor John*. "St John may be called the 'predecessor' of St Paul, either because he was an apostle before him (cf. Galatians 1.17), or because the writer of the fragment placed the composition of the Apocalypse before that of the last of St Paul's Epistles to Churches." (Westcott, op. cit., p. 536, n. 7.)

the couple bearing the name of John: probably 2 and 3 John, as 1 John had been quoted above.

The mention of the *Wisdom of Solomon* is odd, but in Eusebius, *H.E.* VI.13.6, this book appears, with reference to Clement of Alexandria, in a similar context.

of Peter only we receive: there appears to be no mention of 1 Peter. Zahn emended the text (to suit a Greek original), "and of Peter one epistle, which only we receive; there is also a second, which some of our friends, etc." The *Apocalypse of Peter* is an apocryphal work of the second century, which was not without influence on other Christian documents, see, e.g., M. R. James, *The Apocryphal New Testament*, p. 505.

Pius, Bishop from *c.* 140–153: naturally, the inspiration of the *Shepherd* would be a problem at Rome. For the author of the fragment no addition could be made to the numbers of the Apostles and prophets; this would exclude the Montanists.

The text of the last paragraph is hopelessly corrupt. Miltiades (a conjecture) would be the Montanist leader mentioned in 85.

125. THE PASCHAL (QUARTODECIMAN) CONTROVERSY, *c.* 190

(Eusebius, *H.E.* V.23–5.)

23.1 Now a question of no small importance arose in their time. For the communities of the whole of Asia, relying on a tradition of great antiquity, thought that they ought to observe the fourteenth day of the moon—the day on which the Jews were ordered to sacrifice the lamb—as the day for the festival of the Saviour's Pascha; since they deemed it necessary at all costs to put an end to their fast on that day, no matter on what day of the week it should fall. But it was not the custom for the churches throughout all the rest of the world thus to celebrate it, preserving as they did by an apostolic tradition the custom which has prevailed to this

day, that it was not proper to end the fast on any other day than
2 on the day of the resurrection of our Saviour. So then, synods
and assemblages of bishops came together, and unanimously
drew up in letters an ecclesiastical decree for the faithful everywhere, to the effect that the mystery of the Lord's resurrection
from the dead should never be celebrated on any other but the
Lord's day, and that on that day alone we should observe the close
of the paschal fast.

3-4 [Eusebius then enumerates some of the letters that were extant
on this subject, from the bishops assembled (1) in Palestine, (2) at
Rome, (3) in Pontus; (4) from the communities in Gaul, over
which Irenaeus was bishop, (5) from the bishops in Osrohoëne,
(6) from Bachyllus of Corinth: there were also many other letters.
24.1 All these were agreed, but the bishops of Asia, led by Polycrates
of Ephesus, took another view as is set forth in a letter to Victor
of Rome and his church:]

2   As for us, then, we keep the day without tampering with it,
neither adding, nor subtracting. For indeed in Asia great lumin-
aries have fallen asleep, such as shall rise again on the day of the
Lord's appearing, when He comes with glory from heaven to
seek out all his saints: to wit, Philip, one of the twelve apostles,
who has fallen asleep in Hierapolis, [as have] also his two daughters
who grew old in virginity, and his other daughter who lived in
3 the Holy Spirit and rests at Ephesus; and, moreover, [there is]
John too, he who *leant back on* the Lord's *breast*,[1] who was a priest,
wearing the sacerdotal plate, both martyr and teacher. He has
4 fallen asleep at Ephesus. Moreover, Polycarp too at Smyrna, both
bishop and martyr; and Thraseas, both bishop and martyr, of
5 Eumenia, who has fallen asleep at Smyrna. And why need I
mention Sagaris, bishop and martyr, who has fallen asleep at
Laodicea? or the blessed Papirius, or Melito the eunuch who in
all things lived in the Holy Spirit, who lies at Sardis, awaiting the
6 visitation from heaven, when he shall rise from the dead? These
all observed the fourteenth day for the Pascha according to the
Gospel, in no way deviating therefrom, but following the rule
of faith. And moreover I also, Polycrates, the least of you all, [do]
according to the tradition of my kinsmen, some of whom also I
have followed closely. Seven of my kinsmen were bishops, and
I am the eighth. And my kinsmen always kept the day when
7 the people put away the leaven. Therefore I for my part, brethren,
who number sixty-five years in the Lord and have conversed with

[1] John 13.25.

the brethren from all parts of the world and traversed the entire range of holy Scripture, am not *affrighted*[1] by threats. For those better than I have said, *We must obey God rather than men*.[2]

8 Then he goes on to add as follows, with reference to the bishops present at his writing who held the same view as he did:

But I could mention the bishops present with me, whom I summoned when ye yourselves desired that I should summon them. And if I were to write their names, the number thereof would be great. But they who know my littleness approved my letter, knowing that I did not wear my grey hairs in vain, but that I have ever lived in Christ Jesus.

9 Thereupon Victor, the president of the [church] of the Romans, endeavoured to cut off by a single stroke the communities of the whole of Asia, together with the neighbouring churches, from the common union, on the ground of unorthodoxy; and, indeed, denounced them in letters, proclaiming that the brethren in those
10 parts were all wholly excommunicate. Howbeit this did not please all the bishops without exception. On the contrary, they exhorted him in reply to have a mind for *the things which make peace*[3] and neighbourly union and charity. And their words are extant also,
11 in which they censure Victor with unusual severity. One of these was Irenaeus, who wrote in the name of the brethren in Gaul, whose leader he was; and, while holding that the mystery of the Lord's resurrection should be celebrated on the Lord's day and on that alone, he nevertheless gives Victor much suitable counsel besides, not to cut off whole churches of God for observing an ancient custom handed down to them. Then he goes on to add, in these very words:

12 For not only is there a controversy about the day, but also about the very manner of the fast. For some think they ought to fast a single day, but others two, others again even more. And in the opinion of others, the "day" amounts to forty continuous hours.
13 And this variety of observance did not originate in our time, but much further back, in the times of those before us, who, no doubt mistakenly, held closely, in their simplicity and ignorance, to this custom, and have transmitted it to posterity. Yet none the less they all lived in peace, and we live in peace, with one another; and the difference concerning the fast enhances the unanimity of our faith.

14 To these remarks he also adds the following account, which it will not be out of place for me to quote:

. . . among whom the elders before Soter, who presided over

[1] Phil. 1.28.   [2] Acts 5.29.   [3] Rom. 14.19.

the church of which thou art now the leader—we mean Anicetus and Pius, Hyginus and Telesphorus and Xystus—neither themselves observed it nor permitted those [residing] with them [to do so]; and none the less, though themselves not observing it, were they at peace with the members of those communities where it was observed, when the latter came to them. And yet the observance was the more obnoxious to those who did not observe

15 it. And none were ever cast out because of this course of action, but those very elders before thee, though they did not observe it, would send the eucharist to members of those communities who

16 observed it. And when the blessed Polycarp stayed at Rome in the time of Anicetus, although they had some trifling disagreements on other matters, they immediately made peace, nor did they care to quarrel on this head. For neither could Anicetus persuade Polycarp not to observe what he had always observed with John the disciple of our Lord and the other apostles with whom he consorted; nor yet did Polycarp persuade Anicetus to observe it, for he said that he ought to hold to the custom of the elders

17 before him. And though such was the case, they held communion with one another, and in the church Anicetus yielded the [celebration of the] eucharist to Polycarp, manifestly out of respect. So they parted from one another in peace, and the whole Church was at peace, both they who observed and they who did not observe. (Lawlor and Oulton, *Eusebius*, I, pp. 168–70, with one alteration.)

18 [Eusebius comments on the appropriate name of Irenaeus for a peacemaker, and on the letters that he wrote to others besides Victor.

25 He concludes his account by returning to the subject of the Palestinian synod, quoting their letter in which they ask that it should be circulated to others, and emphasize their agreement with Alexandria.]

The importance of the account of the Quartodeciman controversy goes far beyond the actual question at issue. It shows, (1) the difficulty that arose when Churches, of which the orthodoxy and antiquity could not be gainsaid, had diverging traditions, both believed to be derived from Apostles; (2) a change in attitude of the Roman church to a problem which had existed for at least half a century. But Victor's action may only have been that of a harassed and impetuous individual, rather than a desire to impose Rome's will permanently on other churches. At Rome the Quartodeciman Blastus (Eus. *H.E.* V.15, Ps.-Tertullian, *Against all Heresies*, 22) had been deposed from his office as presbyter, and had gone into schism.

23.1.   *the fourteenth day of the moon*: i.e. the fourteenth day of the Jewish month Nisan. "It should be noted that at this period there was apparently no commemoration of the Passion apart from Easter. Eusebius calls Easter Day, including the vigil, the Festival of the Passion of our Saviour (*H.E.* II.17.21, *V.C.* III.18). (Lawlor and Oulton, *Eusebius*, II, p. 185.)

24.1. The Roman Letter was written in the name of the Church, not of Victor personally. It is clear from 24.8 that the synods were summoned on Victor's initiative. The reply of Polycrates consolidated the Asian position: it looks as though the Christians of Asia were uneasy because of their growing isolation, and because their usage gave a handle to Judaizers; Melito, and Apollinarius of Hierapolis both wrote works on the Pascha. The latter is not claimed as a supporter by Polycrates, and some have thought that he took the "Roman" side. Eusebius quotes the beginning of Melito's work in *H.E.* IV.26.3.

It is clear from 24.9 that some churches, contiguous to the province of Asia, supported the Asian position. Victor attempted to excommunicate his opponents "on the ground of unorthodoxy", which here simply means "their different opinion".

24.12. *forty continuous hours*: "From the meal which followed the Friday half-fast till after the Liturgy and Communion on Sunday morning." (Brightman in *J.T.S.* XXV, p. 256, quoted in Lawlor and Oulton, op. cit., II, p. 187.)

24.14. Irenaeus says nothing about Soter's own episcopate, nor about that of Eleutherus his successor. Perhaps the situation had grown worse, and, while avoiding an open breach, their opinion had hardened.

24.16. Polycarp's visit to Rome is generally placed *c.* 154.

126. SERAPION OF ANTIOCH AND THE *GOSPEL OF PETER*, c. 190–200

(Eusebius, *H.E.* VI.12.2–6.)

2 ... another book has been composed by him Concerning the Gospel of Peter, as it is called, which he has written refuting the false statements in it, because of certain in the community of Rhossus, who on the ground of the said writing turned aside into heterodox teachings. It will be reasonable to quote a short passage from this work, in which he puts forward the view he held about the book, writing as follows:

3 For our part, brethren, we *receive* both Peter and the other apostles *as Christ*,[1] but the writings which falsely bear their names we reject, as men of experience, knowing that we did not receive 4 such. For I myself, when I came among you, imagined that all of

[1] Gal. 4.14.

you clung to the true faith; and, without going through the Gospel put forward by them in the name of Peter, I said: If this is the only thing that seemingly causes captious feelings among you, let it be read. But since I have now learnt, from what has been told me, that their mind was lurking in some hole of heresy, I shall give diligence to come again to you; wherefore, brethren, expect me 5 quickly. But we, brethren, gathering to what kind of heresy Marcianus belonged (who used to contradict himself, not knowing what he was saying, as ye will learn from what has been written 6 to you), were enabled by others who studied this very Gospel, that is, by the successors of those who began it, whom we call Docetae (for most of the ideas belong to their teaching)—using [the material supplied] by them, were enabled to go through it and discover that the most part indeed was in accordance with the true teaching of the Saviour, but that some things were added, which also we place below for your benefit. (Lawlor and Oulton, *Eusebius*, I, p. 187, altered.)

This passage shows how a church only thirty miles from Antioch, used, in good faith, a gospel other than one of our canonical four.

On the *Gospel of Peter*, see, e.g., M. R. James, *The Apocryphal New Testament*, pp. 90–4, 507–10, and Lawlor and Oulton, *Eusebius*, II, p. 196, cf. Eusebius, *H.E.* III.25.6.

5. *Marcianus*: otherwise unknown; some think that Marcion is meant, but in that case it is hardly likely that Serapion would have to go to Rhossus to discover the nature of his heresy!

6. The *Docetae*: "This word is not found elsewhere in the *Ecclesiastical History*, but was in common use as indicating persons or sects who denied the reality of our Lord's body or of His sufferings. The docetism of the *Gospel of Peter* is shown in the suppression of all that implies pain in connection with the Crucifixion. In fact the very short account of it begins thus: (c. 4) And they brought two malefactors, and they crucified the Lord between them; but He was silent, since He had no pain." (Lawlor and Oulton, *Eusebius*, II, p. 197.)

127. SERAPION ORDAINS PALUT OF EDESSA, *c.* 200

(*The Doctrine of Addai the Apostle*, ed. Phillips, p. 50.)

Palut himself went to Antioch, and received the hand of the priesthood from Serapion, Bishop of Antioch.

Addai the Apostle (one of the seventy disciples according to Eusebius *H.E.*

I.13.10) was the supposed founder of the Church of Edessa. He ordained Palut deacon, according to the *Doctrine of Addai*, ed. cit., p. 39. But it is most unlikely that Christianity reached Edessa till much later than the Apostolic Age, and that there was confusion is obvious from the introduction of Serapion. "Eusebius (*H.E.* I.13) thought that Addai stood for Thaddeus: a much more probable conjecture is to identify Addai with Tatian, to regard them as the names by which the same man was known to Greeks and Syriac-speaking people respectively." (Burkitt, *C.A.H.* XII, p. 483.)

128. BARDAISAN, c. 200

(Eusebius, *H.E.* IV.30.)

1 Now in the same reign, when the heresies were multiplying in Mesopotamia, Bardesanes, a most able man and an exceedingly skilled disputant in the Syriac language, having composed dialogues against the Marcionites and certain other leaders of various doctrines, committed them to writing in his own tongue, along with very many other treatises of his. These dialogues his disciples (of which he had very many: for he was a powerful defender of the faith) translated from Syriac into Greek. And 2 among them is that able dialogue of his On Fate, to Antoninus, and all the others which, it is said, he composed because of the 3 persecution of that day. Now he formerly belonged to the Valentinian school; but, having abjured it and refuted a great part of this heretic's fictions, he imagined somehow that he had come over to the more correct opinion. Howbeit he did not completely cleanse himself from the filth of the ancient heresy. (Lawlor and Oulton, *Eusebius*, I, p. 135.)

against the Marcionites: "Hippolytus bears witness to the controversy. He says that an Assyrian, named Prepon, wrote a treatise against Bardaisan in defence of Marcion (*Ref.* vii.31)." (Lawlor and Oulton, *Eusebius*, II, p. 152.) This passage shows the ubiquity of the Marcionites, on which Justin also comments (*Apol.* I.26 (74)).

he was a powerful defender of the faith: "This statement is qualified in para. 3 (cf. Eus., *Theoph.* iv.30). But Eusebius regards Bardaisan as at least tolerably orthodox in his later years. Yet there must have been in the system of Bardaisan, 'the teacher of Mani', as Ephraim the Syrian calls him, much which Eusebius would have called deadly error. His cosmogony was heretical, and he did not believe in the resurrection of the body." (Lawlor and Oulton, *Eusebius*, II, p. 152.) Epiphanius, *Haer.* 56, makes Bardaisan secede to Valentinianism.

dialogue' . . . On Fate to Antoninus: Eusebius' dating of Bardaisan in the reign of Marcus Aurelius (sect. 1, above) may be due to the mention of Antoninus, who need not be the Emperor, in the title of this work *On Fate*. An extant work on this subject is probably not by Bardaisan himself, but by a disciple.

129. THE COSMOLOGY OF BARDAISAN

(From Moses bar Kepha, d. 903, in Burkitt, *The Religion of the Manichees*, pp. 76–7.)

Bardaisan held about this world that it is composed of Five Entities or primordial Elements (*īthyē*), viz., Fire and Wind and Water and Light and Darkness. Each of these was standing in its own region, Light in the East, Wind in the West, Fire in the South, Water in the North, the Lord of them all in the Height, and their Enemy the Dark in the Depth below. Once upon a time, whether from some external body or by chance, they were hurled one against the other, and the Dark ventured to come up from the Depth to mingle together with them. Then the pure Entities began to try and keep away from the Dark and appealed to the mercy of the Most High to deliver them from the dirty colour that was being mingled with them, i.e. from the Dark. Then, says he, at the sound of the commotion the Word of the Intention of the Most High, which is the Messiah, came down and cut off the Dark from being in the midst of the pure Elements, and it was hurled down, and He set up the pure Elements again in their places in their symbolic cruciform order. As for that mixture which came into being from the Elements and the Dark their enemy, He constituted from it this World and set it in the midst, that no further mixture might be made, while it is being cleansed by conception and birth till it is perfect.

"Exactly what is meant by the last sentence is obscure. Bardaisan regarded man as naturally mortal and held that only the immortal soul is redeemed by Christ. But unlike Mani and Marcion he was not an ascetic. He was himself a married man, and did not regard generation and birth with abhorrence as a further enmeshing of the Divine substance in matter. On the contrary, he seems to have believed that souls at death who kept the word of Jesus did not taste death, but crossed over into the 'bridal-chamber of Light'; and as fresh generations of men come on, also all containing Souls similar to those which had attained the region of Light, it must have seemed to Bardaisan that they had derived their substance from the primordial Mixture. Conception and birth, therefore, is the process by which something is produced which has the chance of escaping from this mixed world and rejoining the pure region of Light." (Burkitt, loc. cit.)

130. THE BAPTISMAL INTERROGATION
AT ROME, *c.* 200

(Hippolytus, *Apostolic Tradition*, 21, 22.)

21   At the hour set for the baptism the bishop shall give thanks over oil and put it into a vessel: this is called the "oil of thanksgiving". And he shall take other oil and exorcise it: this is called "the oil of exorcism". A deacon shall bring the oil of exorcism, and shall stand at the presbyter's left hand; and another deacon shall take the oil of thanksgiving, and shall stand at the presbyter's right hand. Then the presbyter, taking hold of each of those about to be baptized, shall command him to renounce, saying:

I renounce thee, Satan, and all thy servants and all thy works.

And when he has renounced all these, the presbyter shall anoint him with the oil of exorcism, saying:

Let all spirits depart far from thee.

Then, after these things, let him give him over to the presbyter who baptizes, and let the candidates stand in the water, naked, a deacon going with them likewise. And when he who is being baptized goes down into the water, he who baptizes him, putting his hand on him, shall say thus:

Dost thou believe in God, the Father Almighty?

And he who is being baptized shall say:

I believe.

Then holding his hand placed on his head, he shall baptize him once. And then he shall say:

Dost thou believe in Christ Jesus, the Son of God, who was born by the Holy Ghost of the Virgin Mary, and was crucified under Pontius Pilate, and was dead and buried, and rose again the third day, alive from the dead, and ascended into heaven, and sat at the right hand of the Father, and will come to judge the quick and the dead? And when he says:

I believe,

he is baptized again. And again he shall say:

Dost thou believe in the Holy Ghost; in the holy church, and the resurrection of the flesh?

He who is being baptized shall say accordingly:

I believe,

and so he is baptized a third time.

And afterward, when he has come up [out of the water], he is anointed by the presbyter with the oil of thanksgiving, the presbyter saying:

I anoint thee with holy oil in the name of Jesus Christ.

And so each one, after drying himself, is immediately clothed, and then is brought into the church.

22   Then the bishop, laying his hand upon them, shall pray, saying:

O Lord God, who hast made them worthy to obtain remission of sins through the laver of regeneration of the Holy Spirit, send into them thy grace, that they may serve thee according to thy will; for thine is the glory, to the Father and the Son, with the Holy Spirit in the holy church, both now and world without end. Amen.

Then, pouring the oil of thanksgiving from his hand and putting it on his forehead, he shall say:

I anoint thee with holy oil in the Lord, the Father Almighty and Christ Jesus and the Holy Ghost.

And signing them on the forehead he shall say:

The Lord be with thee;

and he who is signed shall say:

And with thy spirit.

And so he shall do to each one. (Easton, *The Apostolic Tradition of Hippolytus*, pp. 45-8, slightly altered.)

On Baptism, cf. Justin's account in passage 42, and also 103, 107, 156, 157.

21.   The Latin text, the most reliable witness to the original text of Hippolytus, begins at "holding his hand placed on his head".

at the presbyter's left hand: a presbyter performs the anointing, as is shown in the subsequent narrative.

For the renunciation, cf. Tertullian in passage 155.

goes down into the water: at the beginning of Ch. 21, it is stated that the water should, if possible, be running water, cf. 103.

naked: "Every non-Jew in the Graeco-Roman world was so accustomed to the public baths that the baptismal usage would not suggest the slightest impropriety." (Easton, op. cit., p. 90.)

131. DYNAMIC MONARCHIANISM AT ROME

(From *The Little Labyrinth*, in Eusebius, *H.E.* V.28.3–6,8–12, 14.)

3   For they say that all the men of former days, and the apostles themselves, received and taught the things which these men now say, and that the truth of the preaching was preserved until the times of Victor, who was the thirteenth bishop at Rome from Peter; but that the truth was falsified from the days of his successor,

4 Zephyrinus. Now what they say might perhaps have carried weight, were it not, in the first place, that the divine Scriptures were opposed to them. And there are writings of certain of the brethren too, older than the times of Victor, which they wrote both against the Gentiles on behalf of the truth and also against the heresies of that day—I mean [the writings] of Justin and Miltiades and Tatian and Clement and many others— in all of which

5 Christ is spoken of as God. For who does not know the books of Irenaeus and Melito and the rest, proclaiming as they do that Christ is God and man; or all the psalms or songs written from the beginning by faithful brethren, which celebrate the Word of God,

6 even Christ, and speak of Him as God? How then, when the mind of the Church has been thus declared for so many years back, can it be that Christians up to the time of Victor preached in the way that they assert? And how are they not ashamed to ascribe these things falsely to Victor, when they certainly know that Victor excommunicated Theodotus the cobbler, the prime mover and father of this God-denying apostasy, when he was the first to say that Christ was a mere man? For if Victor was of their way of thinking, as their slander affirms, how could he have cast out Theodotus the inventor of this heresy?

*   *   *

   There was a certain confessor named Natalius, who lived not

9 long ago, but in our own time. Once upon a time this man was deceived by Asclepiodotus and another Theodotus, a banker. Both these last were pupils of Theodotus the cobbler, who was the first to be excommunicated by Victor, as I said, the then bishop, on account of this sentiment or, rather, senselessness. So

10 Natalius was persuaded by them to take the title of bishop of this heresy at a salary, and to be paid by them one hundred and fifty

11 denarii a month. When, therefore, he became one of them, he

was frequently admonished by the Lord in visions. For our compassionate God and Lord, Jesus Christ, did not wish that a witness
12 to His own sufferings should perish outside the Church. But when
he paid less regard to the visions, being ensnared by having the
first place among them, and by the greed of filthy lucre which
destroys many, he was finally scourged by the holy angels, and
suffered no light punishment the whole night long; insomuch
that he arose at dawn, put on sackcloth, covered himself with
ashes, and with all haste prostrated himself in tears before Zephyrinus the bishop; and, rolling at the feet not only of the clergy
but also of the laity, he moved with his tears the compassionate
Church of the merciful Christ. And though he used much entreaty
and showed the weals of the stripes he had received, scarcely was
he taken back into communion. (Lawlor and Oulton, *Eusebius*,
I, pp. 172–3.)

13 [A further quotation from *The Little Labyrinth* deals with capri-
14 cious alteration of scripture by these heretics. They used also
dialectical reasoning, and placed a high authority on the ideas of
pagan philosophers.]

Thus, to study Euclid is for some of them a labour of love;
Aristotle and Theophrastus are admired; aye, Galen in like manner
by some is even worshipped. (Lawlor and Oulton, *Eusebius*, I,
p. 174.)

The Logos doctrine had failed to solve the problem of "one God or two".
Hence these educated Christians sought to save monotheism by putting forward an "adoptionist" Christology, i.e. the power of the sole God descended
on the man Christ. It is clear that they were educated Christians, who attempted
to solve this problem with the help of philosophy in a way far different from
Aristeides and Justin.
On Galen, cf. 108, 109 and Walzer, *Galen on Jews and Christians*, p. 78.

132. DYNAMIC MONARCHIANISM: THEODOTUS THE "BANKER"

(Ps.-Tertullian, *Against all Heresies*, 8 (24).)

Another heretical Theodotus arose after him; he too introduced
another sect and said that Christ was only a man, conceived and
born of the Holy Spirit and the virgin. But he was inferior to
Melchizedek, because it was said of Christ, *Thou art a priest for*

ever, *after the order of Melchizedek*.[1] For that Melchizedek is a
heavenly virtue of special grace, because what Christ does for
men, becoming their intercessor and advocate, Melchizedek does
for the heavenly angels and powers. For he is better than Christ,
since he is fatherless, motherless, without genealogy, whose beginning and end is neither comprehended nor comprehensible. (Grant,
Second-century Christianity, p. 140, slightly altered.)

On this Theodotus, see also 131.
after him, i.e. Theodotus the "cobbler", cf. 131.

133. THE HERESY AND EXCOMMUNICA-
TION OF NOËTUS, *c.* 200

(Hippolytus, *Against Noëtus*, 1.)

Some others are secretly introducing another doctrine, who
have become disciples of one Noëtus, a native of Smyrna, who
lived not very long ago. This person was greatly puffed up and
inflated with pride, being inspired by the conceit of a strange
spirit. He alleged that Christ was the Father Himself, and that
the Father Himself was born, and suffered, and died. You see what
pride of heart and what inflation by a strange spirit had insinuated
themselves into him. From his other actions, then, the proof is
already given us that he spoke not with a pure spirit; for he who
blasphemes against the Holy Ghost is cast out from the holy
inheritance. He alleged that he was himself Moses, and that Aaron
was his brother. When the blessed presbyters heard this, they
summoned him before the church, and examined him at length.
But he kept denying that he held such opinions at all. Afterwards,
however, lurking among certain persons, and having gathered
round him others who had embraced the same error, he wished
thereafter to uphold his dogma openly as pure. And the blessed
presbyters called him again before them, and examined him. But
he stood out against them, saying, "What evil, then, am I doing
in glorifying Christ?" And the presbyters replied to him, "We
too know in truth one God; we know Christ; we know that the
Son suffered even as He suffered, and died even as He died, and rose
again on the third day, and is at the right hand of the Father, and
cometh to judge living and the dead. And these things which we
have learned we allege." Then, after examining him, they expelled him from the church. And he was carried to such a pitch
of pride, that he established a school. (A.-N. C. L., altered.)

[1] Heb. 5.6 (Ps. 110.4), 10; 7.1,11,17, cf. Gen. 14.18–20.

Hippolytus further dealt with Noëtus in his *Refutation of all Heresies*, 9.7–10, where he derives the doctrines of Noëtus from Heracleitus of Ephesus (*c.* 500 B.C.).

It is uncertain whether the examination of Noëtus by the presbyters took place at Smyrna or at Rome. The latter appears more likely.

Note the importance of the false spirit as inspiring Noëtus. Hippolytus points out (91) that some Montanists were affected by the Monarchian heresy.

he established a school: cf. 137. In his *Refutation* Hippolytus develops this theme, and gives a succession of "Noëtic" teachers: Noëtus—Epigonus—Cleomenes. The last named bribed Zephyrinus (advised by Callistus, of course, cf. 135) to tolerate them, and "official" support encouraged the development of the school. Hippolytus was relentless in his pursuit of these heretics and, by his own account, argued them temporarily out of their position, but had no permanent success.

134. THE STORY OF CALLISTUS, *c.* 185–192

(Hippolytus, *Refutation of all Heresies*, 9.12.1–13)

1 Callistus was a slave of Carpophorus, a Christian belonging to the household of Caesar. To Callistus, as being of the faith, Carpophorus committed no inconsiderable amount of money, and directed him to bring in profit from banking. He took the money and started business in what is called Fish Market Ward. As time passed not a few deposits were entrusted to him by widows and brethren thanks to the reputation of Carpophorus. Callistus, however, embezzled the lot, and became financially embarrassed. After such conduct, there was not wanting one to tell Carpo-
2 phorus, and the latter stated that he would require an account from him. Callistus got wind of this, and suspected danger from his master. He absconded, intending to make his flight by sea and finding a vessel in the Port ready for a voyage, he went on board, intending to sail wherever she happened to be bound for. But not even in this way could he avoid detection, for there was not
3 wanting one to tell Carpophorus what had taken place. Carpophorus went to the harbour, and following up the information received tried to go on board the ship which was anchored in the middle of the harbour. The ferryman was slow and Callistus, who was in the ship, had time to see his master at a distance. He knew that he had been trapped; he became reckless of life, and, considering his affairs to be in a desperate condition flung himself
4 into the sea. But the sailors leaped into boats and rescued him, though unwilling, while those on shore raised loud shouts. And

thus Callistus was handed over to his master, and brought back to Rome, and his master lodged him in the treadmill.

5   But as time went on, as usually happens, brethren came to Carpophorus, and kept begging him to release the runaway from punishment, on the plea that Callistus acknowledged himself to
6 have money lying to his credit with certain persons. But Carpophorus, as a devout man, said he was indifferent regarding his own property, but that he felt a concern for the deposits; for many used to tell him with tears that it was because of *his* reputation that they had entrusted their deposits to Callistus. Carpophorus yielded to their persuasion, and ordered the release of
7 Callistus. The latter, however, having nothing to pay, and not being able again to abscond, as he was now watched, planned an artifice by which he hoped to meet death. On a Sabbath-day, pretending that he was gone to his supposed debtors, he hurried to the synagogue of the Jews, who were congregated there; he entered and created a disturbance among them. They, however, at this disturbance attacked and struck him, and dragged him
8 before Fuscian, Prefect of the city. Here is their evidence: "The Romans have conceded to us the privilege of publicly reading our ancestral laws. This person, however, came in and tried to stop us by creating a disturbance and alleging that he is a Christian." Fuscian happened at the time to be on the judgement-seat; and on intimating his indignation against Callistus, on account of the statements made by the Jews, there was not wanting one to tell Carpophorus what was going on. He hastened to the
9 judgement-seat of the Prefect and shouted, "I beg you, lord Fuscian, don't believe him; for he is not a Christian, but seeks occasion of death, after embezzling a lot of my money, as I shall prove." The Jews, however, supposing that this was a trick, as if Carpophorus were seeking under this pretext to liberate Callistus, redoubled their hostile clamour before the Prefect. Fuscian was swayed by them, and after scourging Callistus he handed him over to be sent to a mine in Sardinia.

10   But after a time, there being in that place other martyrs, Marcia, the pious concubine of Commodus, desirous of performing some good work, summoned the blessed Victor, who was then bishop of the Church (i.e. of Rome), and inquired of him what martyrs were in Sardinia. And he gave to her the names of all, but did not include that of Callistus, as he knew of his villainous acts.
11 Marcia, obtained her request from Commodus, and gave the letter of emancipation to a eunuch, Hyacinthus, a presbyter. He took it, and crossed to Sardinia, where he delivered the letter to the governor at that time and released all the martyrs except Callistus.

12 But Callistus fell on his knees and wept, and begged that he likewise might obtain release. Hyacinthus, therefore, overcome by
his importunity, asked the governor to release him, saying that
"Marcia had been brought up by himself", and guaranteeing the
governor's security (i.e. for exceeding instructions). The governor
13 was persuaded, and released Callistus also. When the latter arrived
at Rome, Victor was very much annoyed at what had taken place,
but since he was a compassionate man, he did nothing. Guarding,
however, against the reproach of many (for the villainous acts of
Callistus were not distant occurrences), and because Carpophorus
also still objected, Victor sent Callistus to live at Antium, and paid
him a monthly allowance for food. (Based on A.-N. C. L., and
with acknowledgements to the French translation of A. de
Siouville.)

This account of Callistus is included, not because we need accept it all as
accurate history, but because it illustrates the character of Hippolytus, and reveals glimpses of the tangled but fascinating history of the Church in Rome in
the time of Commodus. Hippolytus had stated, at the end of Chapter 11 that
Callistus was regarded as a martyr because of his condemnation by Fuscian.

1. *Carpophorus*: ? the M. Aurelius Carpophorus of *C.I.L.* VI.13040. Fish
Market Ward (*Piscina publica*, lit. public fish pond), one of the fourteen *regiones*
into which Rome was divided. It lay on the south side of the city: the Baths
of Caracalla were built in it.

2. *the Port*, i.e. Portus Romanus, which had superseded Ostia.

4. *the treadmill*: a common punishment for runaway slaves. The Christian
Carpophorus treated Callistus in the normal way that a runaway might expect.

7. *the synagogue of the Jews*: there were a number of synagogues in Rome,
but Hippolytus does not specify further.

Fuscian was Prefect of Rome from 185 or 6 to 189. The scene before his
judgement seat must have been one of great confusion lasting for some time.
The Jews, themselves protected in their worship, knew that they could "get"
Callistus by bringing up his Christianity. When Carpophorus denied that
Callistus was a Christian, he appeared to be saving the accused.

9. *a mine in Sardinia*: convicts sent to the mines were not expected to
return. It was a common punishment for Christians.

10. *Marcia*, "Her life—in such surroundings—could scarcely be in strict
accord with Gospel precepts." (Duchesne, *Early History of the Church*, E. Tr.,
I, p. 183.)

11. *Hyacinthus*: others translate, "a eunuch, rather advanced in life",
giving the literal meaning to πρεσβύτερος.

13. Victor was *a compassionate man*: cf. the impression of Victor given in
125.

sent Callistus to live at Antium, i.e. he paid him to stay away from Rome.

THE INCOMPETENCE OF ZEPHYRINUS

135. THE INCOMPETENCE OF ZEPHYRINUS

(Hippolytus, *Refutation of all Heresies*, 9.12.14; 9.11.1–3.)

This passage follows on the preceding one. As Zephyrinus did not see eye to eye with Hippolytus, he too came under the lash of his invective. There are however definite and suspicious gaps in Hippolytus' narrative, e.g. there is no indication of how or when Callistus secured ordination.

14   After Victor's death, Zephyrinus, having had Callistus as an assistant in the management of his clergy, honoured him to his own damage; he brought him back from Antium, and appointed him over the cemetery.

And Callistus, who was always associating with Zephyrinus, and, as I have previously stated, paying him hypocritical service, put Zephyrinus in the background as a person able neither to form a judgement of things said, nor discerning the design of Callistus, who was accustomed to converse with Zephyrinus on topics which pleased him (i.e. Zephyrinus). (A.-N. C. L., altered.)

The cemetery of Callistus on the *Via Appia*.

Now we go back to the previous Chapter of Hippolytus (i.e. 11) where he had already dealt with the doctrinal issue:

1   Now Callistus led on Zephyrinus, an uneducated simpleton, and a man unskilled in ecclesiastical definitions. And as Zephyrinus was accessible to bribes and covetous, Callistus, by luring him through presents, and by illicit demands, was enabled to seduce him into whatever course of action he pleased. So it was that Callistus succeeded in inducing Zephyrinus continually to create disturbances among the brethren, while he himself took care subsequently, by cunning words, to attach both factions in good-will to himself. And, at one time, to those who entertained true opinions, he would in private allege that they held similar doctrines (with himself), and thus make them his dupes; while at another time he would act similarly towards those who embraced the tenets of Sabellius. But Callistus perverted Sabellius himself, and

2   this, too, though he had the ability to set him right. For during *our* admonition Sabellius did not harden his heart; but as long as he continued alone with Callistus, he was wrought upon to relapse into the system of Cleomenes by this very Callistus, who alleged that he entertained similar opinions. Sabellius, however,

did not then perceive the knavery of Callistus; but he afterwards came to be aware of it, as I shall narrate presently.

3   Now Callistus brought forward Zephyrinus himself, and induced him publicly to say "I know one God, Jesus Christ; nor except Him do I know any other that is begotten and susceptible to suffering". And on another occasion he made the following statement: "The Father did not die, but the Son." Zephyrinus would in this way continue to keep up ceaseless disturbance among the people. And we, becoming aware of his sentiments, did not give place to him, but reproved and withstood him for the truth's sake. And he hurried headlong into folly, from the fact that all consented to his hypocrisy—we, however, did not— and called us worshippers of two gods, disgorging with violence the venom lurking within him. (A.-N. C. L., altered.)

1.   Sabellius gave his name to the form of theological thought which by over-emphasis on the unity of God and the true divinity of Christ, insisted that the "persons" of the Trinity were no more than "modes" of existence of the one deity; hence they were called "Modalist Monarchians".

2.   Cleomenes was another of the Monarchian heretics, cf. p. 160 above.

3.   *worshippers of two gods*: see 136 below.

136. CALLISTUS AS BISHOP: (1) HIS HERETICAL THEOLOGY

(Hippolytus, *Refutation of all Heresies*, 9.12.15–19.)

15   Thus, after the death of Zephyrinus, supposing that he had obtained the position after which he so eagerly pursued, he excommunicated Sabellius, as not entertaining right opinions. He did this from fear of me, and imagining that he could in this manner obliterate the charge against him among the churches, as if he held no different opinions. He was then an impostor and

16   knave, and in process of time carried off many with him. With venom imbedded in his heart, and incapable of thinking straight in any degree, he was ashamed to speak the truth, not only in that he publicly reproached us, saying "You are Ditheists!" but also in that he was frequently accused by Sabellius, as having transgressed his first faith: so he devised some such heresy as the following. Callistus alleges that the Word Himself is Son, and Himself is Father; and, though called by that title, yet God is one indivi-

17   sible Spirit. The Father is not one person and the Son another, but they are one and the same; and that all things are full of the Divine Spirit, both those above and those below. The Spirit, which

became incarnate in the virgin, is not different from the Father, but one and the same. And this is what the saying means: *Believest*
18 *thou not that I am in the Father, and the Father in me?*[1] For that which is seen, which is man, is the Son; whereas the Spirit, which was contained in the Son, is the Father. "For," says Callistus, "I will not say that there are two Gods, Father and Son, but one. For the Father, who existed in Him, after He had taken unto Himself flesh, raised it to the nature of Deity, by bringing it into union with Himself, and made it one; so that Father and Son are styled one God, and that this God being one Person, cannot be two."
19 And in this way the Father suffered *with* the Son; for he does not wish to assert that the Father suffered, and is one Person, being careful to avoid blasphemy against the Father. A senseless and unstable fellow, who improvises blasphemies in every direction, if only he may not seem to speak in violation of the truth! He is not abashed at leaning now towards the doctrine of Sabellius, now towards that of Theodotus! (A.-N. C. L., altered.)

15. *supposing he had obtained the position* . . . : i.e. of Bishop of Rome, a position which Hippolytus could not concede to him.
16. *"You are Ditheists!"*: That was the crux of the matter, which the Logos doctrine had not solved, cf. the views of Celsus on Christian theology (114).
17. *Believest thou not* . . . : our New Testament has the imperative, "Believe me that . . .".
18. *the Father suffered* with *the Son*: . . . "only thinly veiled Patripassianism. By this new subterfuge, Callistus could only further alienate the sympathies of Sabellius without winning those of Hippolytus" (de Siouville, *Hippolyte de Rome, Philosophoumena,* I, p. 60).

137. CALLISTUS AS BISHOP: (2) THE FORGIVENESS OF SINS

(Hippolytus, *Refutation of all Heresies,* 9.12.20–26.)

20   The impostor, i.e. Callistus, after venturing on such opinions, established a school against the Church, adopting the foregoing teaching. And he first invented the device of conniving with men as to their pleasures, saying that sins were forgiven to everyone by himself. For if a person who attends the congregation of any one else, and is called a Christian, should commit any sin, they say that the sin is not reckoned unto him, provided only he
21 hurries off to the school of Callistus. And many persons were

[1] John 14.11.

gratified with his proposition, as being stricken in conscience, and at the same time having been rejected even by numerous heresies; while some of them, in accordance with our sentence, had even been by us forcibly ejected from the Church. Such disciples passed over to them, and served to crowd his school. He laid it down that, if a bishop was guilty of any sin, even a sin unto death,

22 he ought not to be deposed. In his time men who had been twice married, and thrice married, began to be ordained to clerical office as bishops, priests and deacons. If also, however, any one in holy orders should get married, Callistus permitted such a one to continue in holy orders as if he had not sinned. And he alleges that what has been spoken by the Apostle has been declared in reference to this: *Who art thou that judgest another man's servant?*[1] But he asserted that likewise the parable of the tares is uttered in reference to this situation: *Let the tares grow along with the wheat*[2]; or, in

23 other words, let sinners remain in the Church. But also he affirmed that the ark of Noah was made for a symbol of the Church, in which were both dogs, and wolves, and ravens, and all animals clean and unclean; and so he alleges that the case should stand in like manner with the Church. And as many passages bearing on this as he could collect, he so interpreted.

And his hearers, delighted with his tenets, continue deluding both themselves and as many others, and crowds stream into his

24 school. So his pupils multiply, and they rejoice in the crowds attending for the sake of pleasures which Christ did not permit. But in contempt of Him, they place no restraint on the commission of sin, alleging that he pardons those who find favour with him. For he even permitted women, if they were unwedded, and burned with unworthy passion, or if they were not disposed to overturn their own rank through a legal marriage, to have whomsoever they would choose as a bedfellow, whether slave or free, and that a woman, though not legally married, might consider such a one as a husband.

25 [Hippolytus then proceeds to show the awful moral results of Callistus' policy.]

See what a pitch of impiety the lawless one has reached, by inculcating adultery and murder at the same time! And over and above these audacious acts, they—and they are past blushing—attempt to call themselves a "Catholic Church"! And some,

26 thinking to do themselves well, run to them. In his time they first audaciously practised a second baptism! (Based on A.-N. C. L., and on Legge, *Hippolytus: Philosophoumena*, vol. II, pp. 130–2.)

[1] Rom. 14.4.   [2] Matt. 13.30.

24. *on such opinions*, i.e. those mentioned in 136.

a school against the Church: most heretics, among whom Hippolytus reckons Callistus, did not found Churches. Hippolytus regards his own (schismatic) body as the true Church, cf. above "had even been by us forcibly ejected from the Church". On heretical Schools, cf. that of Noëtus, 133.

Whether we side with Callistus or with Hippolytus, it must be admitted that the former's policy was designed to meet an actual situation. The only alternative to the reconciliation of sinners was to allow them to lapse into heathenism. Even the "ecclesiastical" marriages were designed to deal with a situation in which women of good family outnumbered men of like status in the Church, and in which the disadvantages of "mixed" marriages were obvious.

21. *rejected even by numerous heresies*, e.g. the Marcionites.

Clerical transgressions: a *sin unto death*, i.e. unchastity, homicide, apostasy. Tertullian (160) shows us that Callistus forgave the first of these; Hippolytus that he forgave the first and second. On apostasy we cannot be sure, but this sin might be forgiven at Rome long before the time of Callistus, cf. Hermas, *Shepherd*, Vis. II.3.4. "But you shall say to Maximus: 'Behold, persecution is coming, if it seems good to you deny the faith again'." (Lake, *Apostolic Fathers* (Loeb), II, p. 23.) But apostasy cannot have been a serious problem in the time of Callistus; on its seriousness later see passage 202.

24. *burned with unworthy passion* (ἡλικίᾳ γε ἐκκαίοντο ἀναξίᾳ): the text is corrupt and the true reading uncertain.

138. GAIUS OF ROME AND THE BOOK OF REVELATION

(Hippolytus in Dionysius Barsalîbî (twelfth century).)

"A man named Gaius appeared, who said that the Gospel was not John's, nor the Apocalypse, but that they were the work of the heretic Cerinthus." (Lawlor and Oulton, *Eusebius*, II, p. 208.)

We can here catch a glimpse of yet another controversy at Rome in the early third century. It is clear that Eusebius himself had no idea that Gaius held such views.

On Gaius, cf. 6.

139. PERSECUTION IS A LEGAL PARADOX

(Tertullian, *Apology*, 1.11–13.)

11 Why, evil-doers are eager to escape notice; they avoid appearing; they tremble when caught; they deny when accused; even under torture they do not easily or always confess; at all events,

when condemned they lament. They tell how often they have felt the impulses of a mind distraught; they set their deeds down to fate or to the stars; they will not admit to be their own what 12 they recognize as evil. But look at the Christians! There you have quite another story; not a man of them is ashamed of it, not a man regrets—unless, indeed, that he was not a Christian earlier. If he is denounced (as a Christian), he glories in it; if he is accused, he does not defend himself; when he is questioned, he confesses without any pressure; when he is condemned, he renders thanks. 13 What sort of evil is that which has none of the native marks of evil—fear, shame, shuffling, regret, lament? What? is that evil where the criminal is glad, where accusation is the thing he prays for, and punishment is his felicity? It is not for you to call it madness—*you*, a man convicted of sheer ignorance of it. (Tr. T. R. Glover (Loeb Library), pp. 7–9, slightly altered.)

11. *of a mind distraught* (*mentis malae*): the words "may perhaps equally well denote some evil spirit, daemon, or the like, assailing the wretch with solicitation to evil"(Glover, op. cit., p. 6n.).

140. ONLY BAD EMPERORS PERSECUTE
(Tertullian, *Apology*, 5.5–8.)

[In the earlier sections of this chapter, Tertullian argues that the earliest news of Christianity to reach Rome was a report (from Pilate (?)) indicating Christ's divinity which the Emperor Tiberius endorsed, but the Senate rejected.]

("It seems to have been an inference (perhaps from the ways of the Civil Service at the end of the second century) that Pilate must have written to Tiberius." (Glover, op. cit., p. 29n.))

[Tertullian next points out that only the worst Emperors, Nero and Domitian, had been persecutors. He continues:]

5   But from among so many emperors down to to-day, men wise in things divine and human, pick me out one who warred against 6 the Christians! We, however, on the other side, produce a protector, if you will refer to the letters of M. Aurelius, most venerable of Emperors, in which he testifies that the great drought in Germany was broken by rain obtained through the prayers of Christians, who, as it chanced, were among his soldiers. M. Aurelius, indeed, did not openly remove the penalty from Christians, but in another way as openly he got rid of it by attach- 7 ing a condemnation to their accusers, and a harsher one too. What

sort of laws, then, are those which are only used against us by the impious, the unjust, the foul, the fierce, the vain, the demented? laws which Trajan in part frustrated by forbidding Christians to be sought out, laws which never a Hadrian, though the explorer of everything curious, enforced, never a Vespasian, though he warred 8 against the Jews, never a Pius, never a Verus. Yet I should think "the worst of men" might more easily be judged worthy of extermination by the best of men—their enemies, you might say rather than by their fellows! (Tr. T. R. Glover (Loeb Library), pp. 31-3.)

On the story of the "Thundering Legion", see notes on 23, also Tertullian, *To Scapula*, 4, *De Oratione*, 29.

On the general theme, see 44.

On Trajan, see 14, 15, on Hadrian 16.

141. "THE CHRISTIANS TO THE LION!"

(Tertullian, *Apology*, 40.2.)

If the Tiber reaches the walls, if the Nile does not rise to the fields, if the sky doesn't move or the earth does, if there is famine, if there is plague, the cry is at once: "The Christians to the lion!" What, all of them to one lion? (Tr. T. R. Glover (Loeb Library), p. 183.)

Tertullian is dealing with the pagan belief that the existence of the Christians brought the anger of the gods on the world. He has no difficulty in showing that great disasters came on the world before the Christians were heard of.

142. INTRANSIGENCE IN THE FACE OF PERSECUTION, c. 212

(Tertullian, *To Scapula*, 5.)

When Arrius Antoninus was driving things hard in Asia, all the Christians of the city in question, in one united band, presented themselves before his judgement-seat; on which, ordering a few to be led forth to execution, he said to the rest, "You wretches, if you wish to die, you have precipices or halters." If we should take it into our heads to do the same thing here, what will you make of so many thousands, of so many men and women, persons of every sex and every age and every rank, when

they present themselves before you? How many fires, how many
swords will be required? What will be the anguish of Carthage
itself, which you will have to decimate, as each one recognizes
there his relatives and companions, as he sees there it may be
men of your own order, and noble ladies, and all the leading
persons of the city, and either kinsmen or friends of those of your
own circle? Spare yourself, if not us! Spare Carthage, if not yourself! Spare the province, which the indication of your purpose
has subjected to the threats and extortions both of the soldiers
and of private enemies. (A.-N. C. L., altered.)

Scapula, proconsul of Africa, c. 212, was persecuting the Christians: Arrius
Antoninus was proconsul of Asia, probably in the early years of Commodus.
The usual sentiment of the Church in the face of persecution was in accordance
with St Matthew 10.23, but Tertullian and other enthusiasts would have none
of it. Later on Athanasius summed up the situation as follows:

Thus the saints, as I said before, were abundantly preserved in their flight
by the providence of God, as physicians for the sake of them that had need.
And to all men generally, even to us is this law given, that we should flee
when we are persecuted, and hide ourselves when we are sought after, and
not rashly tempt the Lord, but should wait, as I said above, until the appointed,
time of death arrive, or the Judge determine something concerning us,
according as it shall seem to Him to be good: that we should be ready that,
when the time calls for us, or when we are taken, we may contend for the
truth even unto death. This rule the blessed martyrs observed in their several
persecutions. When persecuted, they fled; while concealing themselves, they
showed fortitude; and when discovered, they submitted themselves to
martyrdom. . . . (Athanasius, *Apol. de fuga sua*, 22.)

On the numbers of the Christians, cf. 146.

143. THE TESTIMONY OF THE SOUL
(Tertullian, *Apology*, 17.4–6.)

4   Would you have us prove him to you from His own works, in
their multitude and character, those works that contain us, that
sustain us, that delight us; yes! that affright us? Would you have
us prove Him to you from the witness of the human soul itself?
5   Yes! the soul, be it cabined and cribbed by the body, be it confined by evil nurture, be it robbed of its strength by lusts and
desires, be it enslaved to false gods—none the less, when it recovers
its senses, as after surfeit, as after sleep, as after some illness, when

it recaptures its proper health, the soul names God, and for this reason and no other, because, if language be used aright, He is the one true God. "Good God!" "Great God!" "Which may God

6 give!" is the utterance of all men. That He is also Judge, is shown by such utterance as: "God sees"; "I leave it to God"; "God will repay me." O the witness of the soul by nature Christian! And then, as it says these words, it turns its gaze not to the Capitol, but to heaven. For it knows the abode of the living God; from Him and from heaven it came (Tr. T. R. Glover (Loeb Library), pp. 87–9, slightly altered.)

The testimony of the soul by nature Christian (*testimonium animae naturaliter Christianae*) is a favourite theme of Tertullian's, cf., e.g. Mayor's notes on this chapter, pp. 259–63 of his edition, and in particular Tertullian's work *On the Testimony of the Soul* (tr. T. H. Bindley, *Early Church Classics*).

144. THE INCARNATION OF THE WORD

(Tertullian, *Apology*, 21.10–14.)

10   We have already said that God devised the whole universe by Word, by Reason, by Power. Among your own philosophers, too, it is argued that *Logos*, that is Word and Reason, would seem to be the Artificer of the universe. This *Logos* Zeno defines as the maker who has formed and ordered all; he will have it that this *Logos* is also called fate and God, and mind of Jove, and universal law. All this Cleanthes gathers up into Spirit and affirms

11 it to pervade the universe. We, too, to that Word, Reason and Power (by which we said God devised all things) would ascribe Spirit as its substance; and in Spirit, giving utterance, we should find Word; with Spirit, ordering and disposing all things, Reason; and over Spirit, achieving all things, Power. This, we have been taught, proceeds from God, begotten in this proceeding from God, and therefore called "Son of God" and "God" because of

12 unity of nature. For God too is spirit. When a ray is projected from the sun, it is a portion of the whole, but the sun will be in the ray, because it is the sun's ray, nor is it a division of substance, but an extension. Spirit from Spirit, God from God—as light is lit from light. The parent matter remains whole and undiminished

13 even if you borrow many offshoots of its quality from it. Thus what has proceeded from God, is God and God's Son, and both are one. Thus Spirit from Spirit, God from God—it makes in mode a double number, in order not in condition, not departing

14 from the source but proceeding from it. This ray of God, as was ever foretold in time past, came down into a virgin, and, in her womb fashioned into flesh, is born, man mingled with God. The flesh informed by the spirit is nourished, grows to manhood, speaks, teaches, acts—and is Christ. (Tr. T. R. Glover (Loeb Library), pp. 107–9, altered.)

Tertullian set out his theology also in the early chapters of his work *Against Praxeas*. His language in the *Apology* is simple, with appropriate references to the Stoics.

11. *Spirit as its substance*: i.e. or essence, its ἰδία οὐσία.

145. CHRISTIANS NOT DISLOYAL!

(Tertullian, *Apology*, 30.1,4–5; 32.1; 33.1,2.)

30.1 For we, on behalf of the safety of the Emperors, invoke the eternal God, the true God, the living God, whom the Emperors themselves prefer to have propitious to them beyond all other gods. They know who has given them the empire; they know, as men, who has given them life; they feel that He is God alone, in whose power and no other's they are, second to whom they stand, after whom they come first, before all gods and above all gods. Why not? seeing that they are above all men, and men at any rate live and so are better than dead things.

*　*　*

4 Looking up to heaven the Christians—with hands outspread, because innocent, with head bare because we do not blush, yes! and without one to give the form of words, for we pray from the heart—we are ever making intercession for all the Emperors. We pray for them long life, a secure rule, a safe home, brave armies, a faithful senate, an honest people, a quiet world—
5 and everything for which a man and a Caesar can pray. All this I cannot ask of any other but only of Him, from whom I know I shall receive it, since He it is who alone gives and I am one to whom the answer to prayer is due, His servant, who alone worships Him, who for His teaching am slain, who offer to Him that rich and better sacrifice which He himself commanded—I mean prayer, proceeding from flesh pure, soul innocent, spirit holy.

31 [Tertullian goes on to criticise pagan prayers and offerings. In Ch. 31 he turns to Scripture, pointing out that Christians are bid-

den to pray for enemies, persecutors, and Kings (quoting
1 Tim. 2.2.).]

32.1   There is another need, a greater one, for our praying for the
Emperors, and for the whole estate of the empire and the interests
of Rome. We know that the great force which threatens the whole
world, the end of the age itself with its menace of hideous suffering, is delayed by the respite which the Roman empire means
for us. We do not wish to experience all that; and when we pray
for its postponement are helping forward the continuance of
Rome.

*   *   *

33.1   But why need I say more of the religious awe, the piety, of
Christians, where the Emperor is concerned? We must needs
2   respect him as the chosen of our Lord. So I have a right to say,
Caesar is more ours than yours, appointed as he is by our God.
(Tr. T. R. Glover (Loeb Library), pp. 151–7.)

32.1.   As time went on, the Christian eschatological hope did not in general
die out, but the end merely was pushed a little further back. It eventually
became bound up with the existence of the Roman Empire, which appeared to
be the last of the kingdoms of Daniel 2.36ff.

On Christian prayer for the Emperor, cf. Clement's *Epistle to the Corinthians*,
LX, LXI.

146. THE NUMBERS OF THE CHRISTIANS

(Tertullian, Apology, 37.4–8.)

4   For if we wished to play the part of open enemies, and not
merely hidden avengers, should we lack the power that numbers
and battalions give? Oh, of course, the Moors, the Marcomanni,
yes, and the Parthians—or any other races, as great as you please,
but of one region with their own frontiers—are more numerous
than the race that covers the world! We are but of yesterday, and
we have filled everything you have—cities, tenements, forts,
towns, exchanges, yes! and camps, tribes, palace, senate, forum.
5   All we have left to you is the temples! For what war should we
not have been fit and ready even if unequal in forces—we who
are so glad to be butchered—were it not, of course, that in our
doctrine we are given ampler liberty to be killed than to kill?
6   Why! without taking up arms, without rebellion, simply by
standing aside, by mere ill-natured separation, we could have

fought you! For if so vast a mass of people as we had broken away from you and removed to some recess of the world apart, the mere loss of so many citizens of whatever sort would have brought a blush to your rule—yes, that it would, and punished

7 you, too, by sheer desertion! Beyond doubt, you would have shuddered at your solitude, at the silence in the world, the stupor as it were of a dead globe. You would have had to look about for people to rule. You would have had more enemies left than

8 citizens. For, as things are, you have fewer enemies because of the multitude of the Christians, when nearly all the citizens you have in nearly all the cities are Christian. But you have preferred to call us enemies of the human race rather than of human error. (Tr. T. R. Glover (Loeb Library), pp. 169–71, slightly altered.)

On the numbers of Christians, cf. 142.

147. CHRISTIAN WORSHIP

(Tertullian, *Apology*, 39.1–6.)

1   We are a society with a common religious feeling, unity of
2 discipline, a common bond of hope. We meet in gathering and congregation to approach God in prayer, massing our forces to surround Him. This violence that we do Him pleases God. We pray also for Emperors, for their ministers and those in authority, for the security of the world, for peace on earth, for postponement

3 of the end. We meet to read the books of God—if anything in the nature of the times bids us look to the future or open our eyes to facts. In any case, with those holy words we feed our faith, we lift up our hope, we confirm our confidence; and no less we reinforce our teaching by inculcation of God's precepts. There is, besides, exhortation in our gatherings, rebuke, divine censure.

4 For judgement is passed, and it carries great weight, as it must among men certain that God sees them; and it is a notable foretaste of judgement to come, if any man has so sinned as to be banished from all share in our prayer, our assembly, and all holy intercourse. Our presidents are elders of proved character, men who have reached this honour not for a price, but by character; for nothing that is God's goes for a price.

5   Even if there is a chest of a sort, it is not made up of money paid in entrance-fees, as if religion were a matter of contract. Every man once a month brings some modest coin—or whenever he wishes, and only if he does wish, and if he can; for nobody is

compelled; it is a voluntary offering. You might call them the
6 trust funds of piety. For they are not spent upon banquets nor
drinking-parties nor thankless eating-houses; but to feed the poor
and to bury them, for boys and girls who lack property and
parents, and then for slaves grown old and ship-wrecked mariners;
and any who may be in mines, islands or prisons, provided that it
is for the sake of God's school, become the pensioners of their
confession. (Tr. T. R. Glover (Loeb Library), pp. 175-7.)

On Christian worship, cf. 42.
On the subjects of Christian prayer, cf. 145.

148. THE APOSTOLIC CHURCHES

(Tertullian, *De Praescriptione Haereticorum*, 36.)

Come now, you who would better indulge your curiosity, in
the business of your salvation, run over the apostolic churches,
in which the very thrones of the apostles still have jurisdiction in
their own places, in which their genuine writings are read, uttering
the voice and representing the face of each of them severally. Is
Achaia very near you? You have Corinth. If you are not far from
Macedonia, you have Philippi. If you are able to cross to Asia,
you have Ephesus. But if you are close upon Italy, you have
Rome, from which the authority of the apostles is at hand for us
also. How happy is that church, on which the apostles poured
forth all their doctrine with their blood! where Peter endures a
passion like his Lord's! where Paul wins his crown in a death like
John's! where the Apostle John after suffering no hurt from being
plunged into boiling oil was remitted to his island-exile! Let us
see what she has learned, what taught, what fellowship has had
with churches in Africa also! One Lord God does she acknowledge, the Creator of the universe, and Christ Jesus of the Virgin
Mary, Son of God the Creator, and the Resurrection of the flesh;
the law and the prophets she unites with the writings of evangelists
and apostles, from which she drinks in her faith: this she seals with
the water, arrays with the Holy Ghost, feeds with the eucharist,
exhorts to martyrdom, and she receives no one who opposes
these principles. (A.-N. C. L., altered, with acknowledgements to
Giles, *Documents illustrating Papal Authority*, p. 22.)

This argument is the same as that of Irenaeus (96), though it is expressed more
forcibly, cf. Tertullian, *Against Marcion*, IV.5. . . . "Rome, from which the
authority of the apostles is at hand for us also." We do not know who first
preached the Gospel in Africa; Tertullian naturally appeals to Rome as the

nearest Apostolic church. This passage is the earliest in which the manner of the apostles' deaths is given. The presence of the Apostle John at Rome is not confirmed by any early source.

all their doctrine: "without any reservation such as the heretics asserted" (Bindley, *Tertulliani Praescriptio Haereticorum*, p. 82).

149. THE RULE OF FAITH
(Tertullian, *De Praescriptione Haereticorum*, 13.)

In the preceding chapters Tertullian emphasizes that, after we have believed, search should cease (cf. 151). There is however a "proper seeking after divine knowledge, always within the Rule of Faith" (cf. Origen's views, 182). He proceeds to explain what this "Rule" is.

Now, as to this rule of faith—that we may from this point acknowledge what it is that we defend—it is, you must know, that which prescribes the belief that there is one only God, and that He is none other than the Creator of the world, who produced all things out of nothing through His own Word, first of all sent forth; that this Word is called His Son, and, under the name of God, was seen in divers forms by the patriarchs, ever heard in the prophets, at last brought down by the Spirit and Power of God the Father into the Virgin Mary, was made flesh in her womb, and, being born of her, lived as Jesus Christ; thenceforth He preached a new law and a new promise of the kingdom of heaven, worked miracles, was crucified, and rose again the third day; He was caught up into the heavens, and sat down at the right hand of the Father; He sent instead of Himself the Power of the Holy Ghost to lead such as believe, He will come with glory to take the saints to the enjoyment of everlasting life and of the heavenly promises, and to condemn the wicked to everlasting fire, after the resurrection of both these classes shall have happened, together with the restoration of their flesh. This rule, as it will be proved, was taught by Christ, and raises amongst ourselves no questions except those which heresies introduce, and which make men heretics. (A.-N. C. L., altered, with acknowledgements to T. H. Bindley's translation.)

Cf. Irenaeus on the Rule of Faith, 93.

was seen in divers forms by the patriarchs: this was the usual view, till it was "turned to Arian purposes. Augustine (*On the Trinity* III.11) maintained that 'the Theophanies were not direct appearances of a Person in the Godhead, but self-manifestations of God through a created being'" (Bindley, *Tertulliani De Praescriptione Haereticorum*, p. 49).

150. THE ARGUMENT FROM TRADITION

(Tertullian, *De Praescriptione Haereticorum*, 20,21.)

In Ch. 20 Tertullian sketches the progress of Christianity from Judaea to the Churches founded elsewhere by the Apostles from which yet other Churches derive their faith.

Every sort of thing must necessarily be referred back to its origin. Therefore the churches, although they are so many and so great, comprise but the one primitive church, founded by the apostles, from which they all spring. In this way all are primitive, and all are apostolic, whilst they are all in one unity by their peaceful communion and title of brotherhood and bond of hospitality,—privileges which no other rule directs than the one tradition of the selfsame rule of faith.

21   From this, therefore, do we put in our plea. Since the Lord Jesus Christ sent the apostles to preach, no others ought to be received as preachers than those whom Christ appointed; for *no man knoweth the Father save the Son, and he to whomsoever the Son has revealed.*[1] Nor does the Son seem to have revealed Him to any other than to the Apostles, whom He sent forth to preach—that, of course, which He revealed to them. Now, what that was which they preached—in other words, what it was which Christ revealed to them—can, as I must here likewise make my plea, properly be proved in no other way than by those very churches which the apostles founded in person, by declaring the gospel to them directly themselves, both *vivâ voce*, as the phrase is, and subsequently by their epistles. If, then, these things are so, it follows accordingly that all doctrine which agrees with the apostolic churches—those wombs and original sources of the faith—must be reckoned for truth, as undoubtedly containing that which the said churches received from the apostles, the apostles from Christ, and Christ from God; whereas all doctrine must be prejudged as false which savours of contrariety to the truth of the churches and apostles of Christ and God. (A.-N. C. L., altered.)

21.   *we put in our plea* (*praescriptionem dirigimus*): "It was permitted to anyone who had obtained possession of any property in the provinces in a regular manner, and had been in possession thereof for at least ten years to rebut all claim on the part of the former possessor by means of a plea in demurrer (*longae possessionis praescriptio*)." (Cuq, *Les Institutions juridiques des Romains*,

[1] Matt. 11.27.

Vol. II, 2 ed., p. 248, quoted by de Labriolle. *Latin Christianity*, E. Tr., p. 84.)
If any person claimed such property, the defendant could have inserted in the
written statement of the points on which judgement was requested, a restraint
setting forth that, "if the defendant had in reality possessed the property for
the legal space of time the plaint brought against him would be non suited *a
priori*". (de Labriolle, op. cit., p. 84.)

rule of faith: here *sacramentum*, with the implication of a pledge.

151. PHILOSOPHY IS THE PARENT OF HERESY

(Tertullian, *De Praescriptione Haereticorum*, 7.)

For philosophy is the material of the world's wisdom, the rash
interpreter of the nature and the dispensation of God. Indeed
heresies are themselves instigated by philosophy. From this
source came the "Aeons", and I know not what infinite "forms",
and the "trinity of man" in the system of Valentinus; he was a
Platonist. From the same source came Marcion's better god with
his tranquillity; he came of the Stoics. Then, again, the opinion
that the soul dies is held by the Epicureans; while the denial of the
restoration of the body is taken from the uniform teaching of all
the philosophers; also, when matter is made equal to God, then
you have the teaching of Zeno; and when any doctrine is alleged
touching a god of fire, then Heracleitus comes in. The same
subject-matter is discussed over and over again by heretics and
philosophers; the same arguments are reconsidered. Whence
comes evil? and why? Whence man? and how? Besides the
question which Valentinus has very lately proposed—Whence
comes God? No doubt from *desire* and *abortion!*

* * *

What indeed has Athens to do with Jerusalem? What has the
Academy to do with the Church? what have heretics to do with
Christians? Our instruction comes from *the porch of Solomon*,[1]
who had himself taught that *the Lord should be sought in simplicity
of heart.*[2] Away with all attempts to produce a Stoic, Platonic,
and dialectic Christianity! We want no curious disputation after
possessing Christ Jesus, no inquisition after receiving the gospel!
When we believe, we desire no further belief. For this is our first
article of faith, that there is nothing which we ought to believe
besides. (A.-N. C. L., altered.)

[1] Acts 3.11.   [2] Wisdom 1.1.

desire: the desire of wisdom (Sophia) to have intercourse with Abyss (Bythos): see 64.

abortion: the monstrous creature to which, as a result of her illicit passion, she gave birth.

The Porch of Solomon: in contrast to the porch, the στοὰ ποικίλη at Athens, where Zeno, the founder of Stoicism, taught.

152. MODALIST MONARCHIANISM: THE HERESY AND MISDEEDS OF PRAXEAS, *c.* 213

(Tertullian, *Against Praxeas*, 1.)

In divers ways has the devil shown hostility to the Truth. At times he has tried to shake it by pretending to defend it. He is the champion of the one Lord, the Almighty, the creator of the world, so that he may make a heresy out of the unity. He says that the Father himself came down into the virgin, himself was born of her, himself suffered, in short himself is Jesus Christ. The serpent has forgotten himself: for when he tempted Jesus Christ after the baptism of John it was as Son of God that he attacked him, being assured that God has a son at least from those very scriptures out of which he was then constructing the temptation: *If thou art the Son of God, command that these stones be made bread*[1]: again, *If thou art the Son of God cast thyself down from hence, for it is written that he—the Father, of course—hath given his angels charge concerning thee, that in their hands they should bear thee up, lest in any place thou dash thy foot against a stone.*[2] Or will he accuse the gospels of lying, and say, "Let Matthew and Luke see to it: I for my part approached God himself, I tempted the Almighty hand to hand: that was the reason for my approach, that was the reason for the temptation: otherwise, if it had been (only) God's son, perhaps I should not have demeaned myself (to tempt) him"? Nay but he himself rather is a liar from the beginning,[3] and so is any man whom he has suborned with his own (coin), like Praxeas. For this person was the first to import to Rome out of Asia this kind of wrong-headedness—a man generally of restless character, and moreover puffed up with boasting of his confessorship on account of nothing more than a mere short discomfort of imprisonment: though even if he had given his body to be burned he would have profited nothing, since he had not the love of God,[4] whose

[1] Matt. 4.3.   [2] Matt. 4.6; Ps. 91.11,12.   [3] Cf. John 8.44.
[4] 1 Cor. 13.3.

spiritual gifts he also drove out by assault. For at that time the
bishop of Rome was on the point of recognizing the prophecies
of Montanus and Prisca and Maximilla, and as a result of that
recognition was offering peace to the churches of Asia and
Phrygia; but this man, by false assertions concerning the prophets
themselves and their churches, and by insistence on the decisions
of the bishop's predecessors, forced him both to recall the letters
of peace already issued and to desist from his project of receiving
the spiritual gifts. Thus Praxeas at Rome managed two pieces of
the devil's business: he drove out prophecy and introduced heresy:
he put to flight the Paraclete and crucified the Father. Praxean
tares[1] were sown above (the wheat) and had germinated here
also, while many were asleep in simplicity of doctrine. Thereafter they were brought to light, by whom God would, and
seemed even to have been rooted up. In fact the teacher gave
security for amendment by return to his former opinions, and his
bond remains in the custody of the natural men,[2] in whose
presence the transaction was then carried out. After that, silence.
I for my part was subsequently separated from the natural men by
my acknowledgement and defence of the Paraclete. But those
tares had at that time scattered their seed everywhere, and so for a
time it lay hid, deceptively dissembling its life, and has now burst
forth anew. But it shall also be plucked up anew, if the Lord will,
in the time now at my disposal: if not, then in its due time all
counterfeit grain will be gathered and, along with other offences,
be burned up *in unquenchable fire*.[3] (E. Evans: *Tertullian's Treatise
against Praxeas*, pp. 130–1.)

On the Monarchian heresy see also 131–3, 135–6.

Praxeas: Tertullian and Pseudo-Tertullian (*Against all Heresies*, 8) are the only
writers contemporary with this heretic who mention him, and the silence of
Hippolytus, from whom we learn so much about these doctrinal struggles,
and who must have been at Rome during Praxeas' activity there, is odd. In
consequence, it is possible that Praxeas ("busybody") is a pseudonym used for
some important person like Zephyrinus or Callistus, but, in that case, why
Tertullian—by this time himself a heretic—should wish to spare the Roman
bishops is not clear.

to Rome out of Asia: the Theodoti (131–2), and Noëtus (133) also came from
that part of the world.

The difficulty of gaining accurate information is shown by this recognition
of Montanism by the Roman bishop (? Victor). Praxeas could bring him
firsthand information of the "goings-on": in Asia (see 85–9).

[1] Matt. 13.24ff.   [2] Cf. 1 Cor. 2.14.
[3] Luke 3.17.

the bishop's predecessors: see 92 for the letter sent by the confessors at Lyons to Rome about Montanism in the time of Eleutherus.

the natural men: (ψυχικοί), i.e. the ordinary Christians, the "spiritual" men being the Montanists, cf. 160, whom Tertullian had joined by this time.

153. HERETICS HAVE NO RIGHT TO THE SCRIPTURES

(Tertullian, De Praescriptione Haereticorum, 37.)

Thus, not being Christians, they have acquired no right to the Christian Scriptures; and it may be very fairly said to them, "Who are you? When and whence do you come? As you are none of mine, what are you doing on my property? Indeed, Marcion, by what right do you hew my wood? By whose permission, Valentinus, are you diverting my streams? By what power, Apelles, are you removing my landmarks? This is my property. Why are you, the rest, sowing and pasturing here at your pleasure? This is my property. I have long possessed it; I possessed it before you. I hold sure title-deeds from the original owners themselves, to whom the estate belonged. I am the heir of the apostles. Just as they disposed of it by their will, and committed it to a trust, and adjured the trustees, even so do I hold it. As for you, they have, it is certain, always held you as disinherited, and rejected you as outsiders, as enemies. (A.-N. C. L., altered.)

The interpretation and use of scripture was crucial. Marcion excised—as Tertullian says in the next chapter "used the knife, not the pen"; Valentinus perverted—"he took away the proper significance even of single words and added arrangements of systems that have no existence".

154. THE DISORDER OF HERETICS

(Tertullian, De Praescriptione Haereticorum, 41.)

I must not omit an account of the conduct also of the heretics— how frivolous it is, how worldly, how merely human, without seriousness, without authority, without discipline, as suits their faith. To begin with, it is doubtful who is a catechumen, and who a believer; they have all access alike, they hear alike, they pray alike—even heathens, if any such happen to come among them. *That which is holy they will cast to the dogs, and their pearls*, although (to be sure) they are not real ones, *they will fling to the swine.*[1]

---

[1] Matt. 7.6.

Simplicity they will have to consist in the overthrow of discipline, attention to which on our part they call affectation. They unite in communion anyhow with all comers; for it matters not to them, however different be their treatment of subjects, provided that they can conspire together to storm the citadel of the one only Truth. All are puffed up, all offer you knowledge. Their catechumens are perfect before they are full-taught. The very women of these heretics, how pert they are! For they are bold enough to teach, to dispute, to enact exorcisms, to undertake cures—it may be even to baptize. Their ordinations, too, are carelessly administered, capricious, changeable. At one time they put novices in office; at another time, men who are bound to some secular employment; at another, persons who have apostatized from us, to bind them by vainglory, since they cannot by the truth. Nowhere is promotion easier than in a camp of rebels, where the mere fact of being there is meritorious. And so it comes to pass that to-day one man is their bishop, to-morrow another; to-day he is a deacon who to-morrow is a reader; to-day he is a presbyter who to-morrow is a layman. For even on laymen do they impose the functions of priesthood. (A.-N. C. L., altered, with acknowledgements to the translations of T. H. Bindley (Early Church Classics) and of H. M. Gwatkin, *Selections from Early Christian Writers*.)

without discipline: from what follows, it appears that Tertullian is thinking of the exclusion of catechumens from the Eucharist in the Catholic Church.

have . . . access, i.e. to the altar. Jerome on *Galatians* 6.6 wrote, "Marcion interpreted this passage so as to think that both faithful and catechumens should pray together".

the . . . women of these heretics: Tertullian elsewhere (*On Baptism*, 17, *On the veiling of virgins*, 9) expressly repudiates the idea that women could exercise any ministerial function.

On Holy Orders; "In his later treatises, as a Montanist, Tertullian himself adopted the novel notion of the obliteration of all distinction between cleric and laic. Cf. *On Exhortation to Chastity* 7." (Bindley, *Tertulliani de Praescriptione Haereticorum*, p. 93.) But actually Tertullian is referring only to "cases of necessity".

155. UNWRITTEN TRADITIONS

(Tertullian, *On the soldier's crown*, 3,4.)

3   For how can anything come into use, if it has not first been handed down? Even in pleading tradition, written authority, you say, must be demanded. Let us inquire, therefore, whether

tradition, unless it be written, should not be admitted. Certainly we shall refuse to admit it, unless the example of other observances which, without any document of scripture, we maintain on the ground of tradition alone, and on the support thereafter of custom, affords us a precedent. To deal with this matter briefly, I shall begin with baptism. When we are going to enter the water, but a little before, in the presence of the congregation and under the hand of the president, we solemnly profess that we disown the devil, and his pomp, and his angels. Hereupon we are thrice immersed, making a somewhat ampler pledge than the Lord has appointed in the Gospel. Then, when we are taken up, we taste first of all a mixture of milk and honey, and from that day we refrain from the daily bath for a whole week. We take also, in meetings before daybreak, and from the hand of none but the presidents, the sacrament of the Eucharist, which the Lord both commanded to be eaten at meal-times, and enjoined to be taken by all [alike]. As often as the anniversary comes round, we make offerings for the dead as birthday honours. We count fasting or kneeling in worship on the Lord's day to be unlawful. We rejoice in the same privilege also from Easter to Whitsunday. We feel pained should any wine or bread, even though our own, fall to the ground. At every forward step and movement, at every going in and out, when we put on our clothes and shoes, when we bathe, when we sit at table, when we light the lamps, on couch, on seat, in all the ordinary actions of daily life, we trace upon the forehead the sign of the cross.

4   If, for these and other such rules, you insist upon having positive injunction in Scripture, you will find none. Tradition will be held out to you as their originator, custom as their strengthener, and faith as their observer. (A.-N. C. L., altered.)

On baptism, cf. Justin's account in 42, and 103, 107, 130, 156-7.

156. WHO MAY BAPTIZE

(Tertullian, *On Baptism*, 17.)

The highest priest, who is the bishop, has of course the right to confer it; then the presbyters and deacons, not, however, without the bishop's authority, out of respect to the Church: when this respect is maintained, peace is secure. But besides, even laymen have the right to baptize; for that which is received alike by all, can be by all alike conferred; unless you argue that the name "disciples" belongs only to bishops or presbyters or deacons. The Word of the Lord ought not to be hidden by any one. In like manner Baptism also, which is equally a divine institution, can be practised by all. But how much more is the practice of modesty and obedience binding upon laymen, since those privileges are suited to their superiors, lest they should assume the duty that is assigned to bishops! Jealousy of the bishop's position begets schisms. The most holy Apostle said that *all things were permissible, but that all things were not expedient.*[1] Let it suffice certainly to take advantage of the privilege in cases of necessity, if anywhere the circumstances either of the place or the time or the person compel it. For then is the boldness of the helper welcomed, when the situation of an endangered person is pressing, since he will be guilty of ruining a human being if he refrains from offering what he was freely able to confer. But the forwardness of a woman who has presumed to teach will not of course acquire for her the right of baptizing also, unless some new beast appear like unto the old, so that just as that one took away Baptism, so some beast should by herself confer it. But if they claim writings which are wrongly inscribed with Paul's name— I mean the example of Thecla—in support of women's freedom to teach and baptize, let them know that a presbyter in Asia, who put together that book, heaping up a narrative as it were from his own materials under Paul's name, when after conviction he confessed that he had done it from love of Paul, resigned his position. For how consonant would it seem with faith that he should give woman the power to teach and baptize, who consistently refused permission to woman even to teach? *Let them keep silence*, he says, *and ask their husband's advice at home.*[2] (Souter, *Tertullian on Prayer and Baptism*, pp. 66–8, slightly altered.)

On baptism by laymen, cf. Canon 38 of Elvira (*c.* 305) which lays down that baptism may be administered in case of illness by a layman (but not a twice-married one).

The forwardness of a woman: for Tertullian's views, cf. 154, and *On the veiling of virgins*, 9.

some new beast, etc. This refers back to Ch. 1 where Tertullian states that a woman heretic "had carried away very many with her poisonous teaching, which aimed particularly at the abolition of Baptism" (Souter, op. cit., p. 46).

Writings wrongly inscribed with Paul's name: cf. *Acts of Paul* (*The Story of Paul and Thecla*), 34, 40 (James, *The Apocryphal N.T.*, pp. 279–80).

"Tertullian alone records for us the circumstances of the composition of 'The Acts of Paul', the original form of which exists only in a (fragmentary) Coptic translation. The work was composed in Greek, possibly at Smyrna, about A.D. 160, and was translated into Latin as well as into Coptic, etc. The

---

[1] 1 Cor. 6.12.   [2] 1 Cor. 14.34,35.

book was produced with a worthy enough motive, being based in the main on the canonical Acts of the Apostles. The part of the narrative dealing with Thecla was largely circulated by itself, and survives in numerous copies. She was reported to be a convert of St Paul, belonging to the district of Iconium and Pisidian Antioch, and 'became the type of the female Christian teacher, preacher, and baptizer' (Ramsay, *Church in the Roman Empire*, p. 375)." (Souter, op. cit., p. 67n.)

157. THE CORRECT AGE FOR BAPTISM

(Tertullian, *On Baptism*, 18.)

[But that Baptism is not lightly to be conferred, is known to those whose duty it is to confer it.

Tertullian goes on to show that well-known cases of "hasty" baptism of the Ethiopian in Acts 8, and of St Paul in Acts 9, were owing to special circumstances.]

Consequently in view of the circumstances and will, even the age of each person, a postponement of Baptism is most advantageous, particularly, however, in the case of children. For what need is there, if it is not so urgent, that the sponsors also should be brought into danger, being as they are themselves also by reason of their mortality capable of falling short of their promises and being deceived by the development of an evil disposition? The Lord indeed says: *Forbid them not to come unto Me.*[1] Let them come, then, while they are growing up; let them come while they are learning, while they are being taught whither to come; let them become Christians, when they have been able to know Christ. Why hurries the age of innocence to the remission of sins? Shall we act more cautiously in worldly matters? Shall one to whom earthly substance is not entrusted, be entrusted with heavenly? Let them know how to seek salvation, that you may be seen *to give to him that asketh.*[2] For no less reason the baptism of the unmarried also should be postponed, for in them a testing has been prepared alike for virgins through their maturity and for the widowed through their freedom from the duty of marriage, until they either marry or are hardened for the practice of continence. If any should understand the importance of Baptism, they will be more afraid of its consequences than of its postponement; unimpaired faith is sure of salvation. (Souter, *Tertullian concerning Prayer and Baptism*, pp. 69–70, slightly altered.)

virgins . . . the widowed: Tertullian is speaking of men as well as of women.
[1] Matt. 19.14.   [2] Cf. Matt. 7.7, etc.

158. REPENTANCE FOR SIN AFTER BAPTISM

(Tertullian, *On Repentance*, 7,9.)

7. These poisons of his (i.e. the devil's), therefore, God foresaw, and although the gate of forgiveness has been shut and fastened with the bar of baptism, He has permitted some means of access. In the vestibule He has stationed the second repentance to open to such as knock: but now *once for all*, because now for the second time; but never more, because the last time it had been in vain.

*   *   *

9. The narrower, then, the sphere of action of this second and only [remaining] repentance, the more laborious is its probation; that it may not be exhibited in the conscience alone, but may likewise be carried out in some external act. This act, which is more usually expressed and commonly spoken of under a Greek name, is ἐξομολόγησις (confession) whereby we confess our sin to the Lord, not indeed as if He were ignorant of it, but inasmuch as by confession satisfaction is settled, of confession repentance is born, by repentance God is appeased. And thus *exomologesis* is a discipline for man's prostration and humiliation, enjoining a demeanour calculated to move mercy. With regard also to the very dress and food, it commands the penitent to lie in sackcloth and ashes, to cover his body in mourning, to lay his spirit low in sorrows, to exchange for severe treatment the sins which he has committed; moreover, to know no food and drink but such as is plain—not for the stomach's sake, to wit, but the soul's; for the most part, however, to feed prayers on fastings, to groan, to weep and roar unto the Lord his God; to roll before the feet of the presbyters, and kneel to God's dear ones; to enjoin on all the brethren to be ambassadors to bear his prayer for mercy. All this *exomologesis* does, that it may enhance repentance, may honour God by its fear of the danger incurred, may, by itself pronouncing against the sinner, stand in the stead of God's indignation, and by temporal mortification (I will not say frustrate, but) discharge eternal punishments. Therefore, while it abases the man, it raises him; while it covers him with squalor, it renders him more clean; while it *ac*cuses, it *ex*cuses; while it condemns, it absolves. The less quarter you give yourself, the more (believe me) will God give you. (A.-N. C. L., altered.)

On repentance after baptism, cf. 32, and 137.

The date of Tertullian's work *On Repentance* is *c.* 203; later on when Tertullian became a Montanist, he allowed no second repentance, cf. *On Modesty*, 10: "But I would yield my ground to you, if the scripture of *The Shepherd* (i.e. of Hermas) which is the only one which favours adulterers, had deserved to find a place in the Divine canon; if it had not been habitually judged by every council of churches (even of your own) among apocryphal and false [writings]; itself adulterous, and hence a patroness of its comrades ..." (A.-N. C. L.)

159. THE VISIONS OF A MONTANIST WOMAN

(Tertullian, *On the Soul*, 9.)

From 5 onwards Tertullian had been arguing in favour of the corporeal nature of the soul.

We have now amongst us a sister whose lot it has been to be favoured with gifts of revelation, which she experiences in the Spirit by ecstatic vision amidst the sacred rites of the Lord's Day in the church; she converses with angels, and sometimes even with the Lord; she both sees and hears mysterious communications; some men's hearts she discerns, and she obtains directions for healing for such as need them. Whether it be in the reading of the Scriptures, or in the chanting of psalms, or in the preaching of sermons, or in the offering up of prayers, in all these religious services matter and opportunity are afforded her of seeing visions. Perchance, while this sister of ours was *in the Spirit*,[1] we had discoursed on some topic about the soul. After the people are dismissed at the conclusion of the sacred services, she is in the regular habit of reporting to us whatever things she may have seen in vision; for all her communications are examined with the most scrupulous care, in order that their truth may be probed. "Amongst other things," she says, "there was shown to me a soul in bodily shape, and a spirit appeared to me; not, however, a void and empty illusion, but such as would offer itself to be even grasped by the hand, clear and transparent and of an ethereal colour, and in form resembling that of a human being in every respect." This was her vision, and for her witness there was God; and the apostle is a fitting surety that there were to be Spiritual gifts in the Church.[2] (A.-N. C. L., altered.)

[1] Rev. 1.10.   [2] 1 Cor. 12.1–11.

Amongst us, i.e. among us (?) Montanists. Whether the service described is Catholic or Montanist is disputed, see Waszink, *Tertullianus: De Anima*, pp. 168–169.

160. THE ROMAN BISHOP'S EDICT,
c. 217–222

(Tertullian, *On Modesty*, 1.)

Christian modesty is being shaken to its foundations. . . . I hear that there has even been an edict set forth, and a peremptory one too. The Sovereign Pontiff (!)—the Bishop of Bishops— issues an edict: "I remit, to such as have discharged the require- ments of repentance, the sins both of adultery and of fornication." O edict, on which cannot be inscribed "well done!" And where shall this liberality be posted up? On the very spot, I suppose, on the very gates of lust, beneath the very advertisement of lust. There is the place for such repentance to be published, where the delinquency itself shall haunt. There is the place to read the pardon, where entrance shall be made under the hope thereof. But it is in the Church that this edict is read, and in the Church that it is pronounced: and she is a virgin! Far, far from Christ's betrothed be such a proclamation! . . . This too, therefore, shall be a count in my indictment against the Natural men; against the fellowship of sentiment also which I myself formerly main- tained with them.

Far, far from Christ's betrothed be such a proclamation! She, the true, the modest, the saintly, shall be free from stain even of her ears. She has none to whom to make such a promise; and if she had, she does not make it; since even the earthly temple of God can sooner have been called by the Lord a *den of robbers*,[1] than of adulterers and fornicators. (A.-N. C. L., altered.)

On Callistus' policy regarding the forgiveness of sins see 137, and the notes on that passage.

Sovereign Pontiff (pontifex maximus): this is the earliest occasion on which this title, held at this time by the Emperor, was applied to the Bishop of Rome, to whom it eventually passed, in a Christian sense, when the Christian Em- perors declined to hold a pagan title.

the Natural men (ψυχικοί): i.e. the Catholics, as opposed to the Montanists (πνευματικοί) whom Tertullian had joined, cf. 152.

[1] Matt. 21.13.

161. CONTEMPORARY CIVILIZATION
c. 208–211

(Tertullian, *On the Soul*, 30.)

[Tertullian is arguing against the theory of the transmigration of souls; he says that if we accept this theory, it must be assumed that the numbers of mankind are constant, a thing which history shows to be absurd.]

Surely it is obvious enough, if one looks at the whole world, that it is becoming daily better cultivated and more fully peopled than anciently. All places are now accessible, all are well known, all open to commerce; most pleasant farms have obliterated all traces of what were once dreary and dangerous wastes; cultivated fields have subdued forests; flocks and herds have expelled wild beasts; sandy deserts are sown; rocks are planted; marshes are drained; and where once were hardly solitary cottages, there are now large cities. No longer are islands dreaded, nor their rocky shores feared; everywhere are houses, and inhabitants, and settled government, and civilized life. Our teeming population is the strongest evidence: our numbers are burdensome to the world, which can hardly supply us from its natural elements; our wants grow more and more keen, and our complaints more bitter in all mouths, whilst Nature fails in affording us her usual sustenance. In every deed, pestilence, and famine, and wars, and earthquakes have to be regarded as a remedy for nations, as the means of pruning the luxuriance of the human race. (A.-N. C. L., slightly altered.)

The dating given above is suggested by Waszink, *Tertullianus: De Anima* p. 6.

With this passage, cf. Cyprian in 225 below.

better cultivated and more fully peopled: cf. Tertullian *De Pallio* 2.7 for similar sentiments.

a remedy for nations: cf. Arnobius, *Against the Nations*, I.10, and the references to pagan literature in Waszink, op. cit., pp. 374–5.

162. DOWN WITH THE CHRISTIANS!
(Minucius Felix, *Octavius*, 5.4–5; 6.1; 8.1–4; 9.1.)

The following passages are from the speech of Caecilius, who puts the case against the Christians.

5.4 Surely all must feel grieved and indignant and annoyed that

certain people—people, too, ignorant of learning, unlettered, and unacquainted even with the meanest arts—should pronounce definitely upon the universe and the supreme power, which, after all these ages, still forms the subject of the deliberations of the
5 philosophers and their numerous schools. And this is only natural, since human insignificance is quite incapable of investigating things divine.

*   *   *

6.1 Since, then, either fortune is blind, or nature uncertain, how much more respectful, how much better is it to receive the teaching of our ancestors as the high priest of truth, to reverence the traditional religion, to worship the gods whom your parents taught you to fear before you knew them intimately, and not to pronounce judgement upon the divinities, but to believe our forefathers who, in a still uncivilized age, when the world was only just born, were thought worthy of having the gods as kindly or as kings! Thus it is that in every empire, province, and city each nationality observes the ritual of its own family and worships its local divinities.

*   *   *

8.1 Accordingly, since all peoples are firmly convinced that there are immortal gods, however uncertain our account of them or of their origin, I cannot endure there to be one so audacious and so swollen with impious pretensions to wisdom as to endeavour to destroy or weaken this so ancient, useful, and salutary a religion.
2 Certainly Theodorus of Cyrene and previous to him Diagoras of Melos, called "Atheist" by the ancients, both asserted that there were no gods, a statement which, if believed, would have utterly destroyed the fear and veneration by which human actions are governed; but they will never secure much influence for their impious doctrines under the name and authority of their sham
3 philosophy. Protagoras of Abdera, who discussed the question of the godhead rather as a philosopher than as an atheist, was banished by the Athenians and his writings publicly burnt. Is it not then deplorable that an attack should be made upon the gods by a gang—you must excuse my expressing rather freely the strength of my feeling for the cause I have taken up—a gang, I
4 repeat, of discredited and proscribed desperadoes? They have gathered together from the lowest dregs of the populace ignorant men and credulous women—and women are naturally unstable— and have formed a rabble of impious conspirators; at their nocturnal gatherings, solemn fasts, and barbarous meals the bond of

union is not any sacred rite but crime. They are a secret tribe that
lurks in darkness and shuns the light, silent in public, chattering
in corners.

★   ★   ★

9.1 Ill weeds grow apace, and these vicious habits are spreading
day by day, and these most abominable haunts where this impious
confederacy holds its meetings are multiplying all over the world.
These conspirators must be utterly destroyed and cursed. (J. H.
Freese, *The Octavius of Minucius Felix*, pp. 32–41, altered, with
acknowledgements to the translation of G. H. Rendall (Loeb
Library).)

Caecilius follows with an attack on Christian morals taken up by Fronto,
cf. 113.

5.2–5. This view of the presumptuous ignorance of the Christians is the
same as that of Celsus, cf. 118, 121. Cf. also the opinion of Galen, 108, about
the reliance of the Christians on "faith".

6.1. *to believe our forefathers*: this is a commonplace in ancient religious
thought, cf. Cicero, *De Natura Deorum*, III.2.5, where Cotta says, "I shall
defend them (i.e. the observances of Roman religion) and I always have
defended them, and the argument of any man, be he learned or unlearned,
will not ever deflect me from this view which I have received from our forefathers concerning the worship of the immortal gods." For other passages
dealing with this subject, see J. B. Mayor's note, ad loc., and 165 below, with
note.

as kindly (faciles) or as kings: the idea that the gods had ruled on earth opened
the door to the conception of Euhemerus, that religion was merely the worship
of dead men. This conception of paganism was eagerly taken up by the
Christians.

8.1. *since all peoples are firmly convinced that there are immortal gods*: the
"universal consent" of mankind to religion was a strong argument: professing
atheists in antiquity were a mere handful, cf. Cicero, op. cit., II.2.5, Lactantius, *Div. Inst.* I.2.4.

<h2 style="text-align:center">163. PANTAENUS, c. 180</h2>

(Eusebius, H.E. V.10,1–3.)

1   Now at that time there was a man of great renown for learning
named Pantaenus, who had charge of the school of the faithful at
Alexandria, where it has been a primitive custom that a school
for sacred studies should exist. This school has continued even to

our day, and although we understand that it was filled with men of great learning and zeal for divinity, it is recorded that the said person was especially distinguished at that time, inasmuch as he had come from that sect of philosophers who are called the Stoics.

2 Now, it is said that he displayed such ardent love and zeal for the divine word that he was appointed as a herald of the Gospel of Christ to the nations of the East, and that he journeyed even as far as the land of the Indians. For there were, yes, even still at that time, many evangelists of the word, desirous to contribute an inspired zeal, after the manner of the apostles, for the increase

3 and building up of the divine word. Pantaenus also was one of these, and is mentioned as having gone to India; and the story goes that there he found, in the hands of some persons who had come to know Christ in that land, the Gospel according to Matthew, which had anticipated his arrival; for that Bartholomew, one of the apostles, had preached to them and left behind the writing of Matthew in the actual Hebrew characters, and that it was preserved up to the said time. (Lawlor and Oulton, *Eusebius*, I, pp. 155–6.)

Eusebius regards the "catechetical school" of Alexandria as existing before the time of Pantaenus, but he has no information about it.

2. *even as far as the land of the Indians*: opinions are divided as to whether Pantaenus really reached India, or whether the country intended is South Arabia. The Christians whom he found possessing a Hebrew Gospel according to St Matthew were clearly Jewish Christians. For literature on Christianity and India in the early centuries, see Latourette, *History of the Expansion of Christianity*, I, pp. 157–8.

On Pantaenus, cf. the passage following.

164. THE TEACHERS OF CLEMENT OF ALEXANDRIA

(Clement: *Stromateis*, I.1.11,1–3, quoted by Eusebius, *H.E.* V.11,3–5.)

3   Now this work is not a writing artfully composed for display; but memoirs which I have stored up against old age, a remedy for forgetfulness, simply an image and outlined sketch of those clear and living words which I was privileged to hear, and of those

4 blessed and truly remarkable men. Of these, one—the Ionian— was in Greece, others in Magna Graecia (the one of them came from Coele-Syria, the other from Egypt); there were others in the East, and, in this quarter, the one was from the country of the

Assyrians, the other a Hebrew by origin, in Palestine. But when I fell in with the last (who in ability proved to be the first), having run down my quarry as it lay concealed in Egypt—I took my 5 rest. . . . Now these men, preserving the true tradition of the blessed teaching straight from the holy apostles Peter and James, John and Paul, as son inheriting from father (howbeit few sons are like their fathers), came under God even to our time, to deposit those seeds of their ancestors the apostles. (Lawlor and Oulton, *Eusebius*, I.156, slightly altered.)

Eusebius (*H.E.* VI.13.2) says that Clement in his *Hypotyposeis* (now extant only in fragments) mentioned Pantaenus as his teacher by name. Speculation as to who Clement's teachers were (e.g. Athenagoras, Tatian) does not lead to any firm conclusion.

165. CUSTOM AND CHRISTIANITY

(Clement of Alexandria, *Protrepticus*, X.89.)

1 But, you say, it is not reasonable to overthrow a way of life handed down to us from our forefathers. Why then do we not continue to use our first food, milk, to which, as you will admit, our nurses accustomed us from birth? Why do we increase or diminish our family property, and not keep it for ever at the same value as when we received it? Why do we no longer sputter into our parents' bosoms, nor still behave in other respects as we did when infants in our mothers' arms, making ourselves objects of laughter? Did we not rather correct ourselves, even if we did not happen to have good attendants (παιδαγωγοί) for this purpose?

2 Again, in voyages by sea, deviations from the usual course may bring loss and danger, but yet they are attended by a certain charm. So, in life itself, shall we not abandon the old way, which is wicked, full of passion, and without God? And shall we not, even at the risk of displeasing our fathers, bend our course towards the truth and seek after Him who is our real Father, thrusting away custom as some deadly drug? This is assuredly the noblest of all the tasks we have in hand, namely, to prove to you that it was from madness and from this thrice miserable custom that hatred of godliness sprang. For such a boon, the greatest that God has ever bestowed upon the race of men, could never have been hated or rejected, had you not been clean carried away by custom, and so had stopped your ears against us. (Butterworth, *Clement of Alexandria* (Loeb Library), p. 197.)

The rejection of established custom was a common reproach to the Christians, cf., e.g., the argument of Caecilius in Minucius Felix (162), and Eusebius, *Praeparatio Evangelica*, I.2 (5a, b). "How can men fail to be in every way impious and godless who have apostatized from their ancestral gods? . . . To what kind of punishments would they not justly be subjected, who, deserting their ancestral customs, have become zealous for the foreign myths of the Jews, which are of evil report among all men?" Also *Praep. Ev.* IV.1 (130b–d), "In this present book it will be the right time to examine the third part. And this is what is established in the several cities and countries, and which they call the state religion, and which is also especially enforced by the laws as both ancient and ancestral. . . . (The Greeks) have thoroughly persuaded themselves . . . that we are guilty of the greatest impiety in . . . breaking laws which require everyone to reverence ancestral customs, and not to disturb what should be inviolable, but to walk orderly in the following the religion of their forefathers, and not to be meddlesome through love of innovation. Thus they say that even death has been deservedly fixed by the laws as the punishment of those who transgress." (Lawlor and Oulton, *Eusebius*, II, p. 285.)

This is a favourite theme of Eusebius: cf. also what Galerius says in his edict of toleration in 311 (256 below).

166. THE TRIUMPH OF CHRISTIANITY

(Clement of Alexandria, *Protrepticus*, XI.114.)

1　Away then, away with our forgetfulness of the truth! Let us remove the ignorance and darkness that spreads like a mist over our sight; and let us get a vision of the true God, first raising to Him this voice of praise, "Hail, O Light." Upon us who lay buried in darkness and shut up *in the shadow of death*[1] a *light shone forth* from heaven, purer than the sun and sweeter than the life

2　of earth. That light is life eternal, and whatsoever things partake of it, live. But night shrinks back from the light, and setting through fear, gives place to the day of the Lord. The universe has become sleepless light and the setting has turned into a rising.

3　This is what was meant by *the new creation*.[2] For He who rides over the universe, *the sun of righteousness*,[3] visits mankind impartially, imitating His Father, who *causes His sun to rise upon all men*,[4] and

4　sprinkles them all with the dew of truth. He it was who changed the setting into a rising, and crucified death into life; who having snatched man out of the jaws of destruction raised him to the sky,

---

[1] See Isa. 9.2 (Matt. 4.16 and Luke 1.79).
[2] Gal. 6.15. (R. V. margin.)　　　[3] Mal. 4.2.　　　[4] Matt. 5.45.

transplanting corruption to the soil of incorruption, and transform-
ing earth into heaven. He is God's husbandman, "who gives
favourable omens, and rouses the people to a work" that is good,
"reminding us of the true livelihood,"[1] and granting to us the
Father's truly great, divine and inalienable portion, making men
divine by heavenly doctrine, *putting laws into their minds and*
5 *writing them upon the heart*.[2] To what laws does He allude? *That*
all shall know God from the small to the great; and, God says, *I will*
be gracious to them and not remember their sins.[2] (Butterworth,
Clement of Alexandria (Loeb Library), pp. 243–5.)

Clement has demolished the pagan's case, and now thrusts his opponent on
the defensive.
  1. *Hail, O Light*: cf. the hymn ὦ φῶς ἱλαρόν (*English Hymnal*, 269, *Church*
Hymnary (R. ed.), 281), which belongs to the third century.

167. THE WORD, OUR PAEDAGOGUS

(Clement of Alexandria, *Paedagogus*, I.12.99.1–100.1.)

99.1 Our superintendence in instruction and discipline is the office
of the Word, from whom we learn frugality and humility, and
all that pertains to love of freedom, love of man, and love of
excellence. And so, in a word, being assimilated to God by a participation in virtue, we must not retrograde into carelessness and
2 sloth. But labour, and faint not. Thou shalt be what thou dost
not hope, and canst not conjecture. And as there is one mode of
training for philosophers, another for orators, and another for
athletes; so is there a generous disposition, suitable to the choice
that is set upon moral loveliness, resulting from the training of
Christ. And in the case of those who have been trained according
to this influence, their gait in walking, their sitting at table, their
food, their sleep, their going to bed, their regimen, and the rest
of their mode of life acquire a superior dignity. For such a training
as is pursued by the Word is not overstrained, but is of the right
100.1 tension. Thus, therefore, the Word has been called also
Saviour, seeing He has found out for men those rational medicines
which produce vigour of the senses and salvation; and devotes
Himself to watching for the favourable moment, reproving evil,
exposing the causes of evil affections, and striking at the roots of
irrational lusts, pointing out what we ought to abstain from, and

[1] These words are quoted from Aratus, *Phaenomena*, 6–7.
[2] Jer. 26.33,34 (quoted in Heb. 8.10–12).

supplying all the antidotes of salvation to those who are diseased. For the greatest and most regal work of God is the salvation of humanity. (A.-N. C. L., altered.)

On the office of Paedagogus, see note on 169.

In *Paed.* I.1, Clement summarizes the work of our Paedagogus, the Word: "he first exhorts, then trains, and finally teaches." These stages correspond more or less to the divisions of Clement's work—*Protrepticus* (Exhortation), *Paedagogus* (Moral Training) and *Stromateis* (though we might have expected his final stage to be entitled διδάσκαλος).

99.2 *their gait in walking*, etc.: it is impossible in a book such as this to quote Clement's precepts for the Christian in all the circumstances of life, which fill Books II and III of his *Paedagogus*. There is much sense in them.

168. AN OCCASION FOR SLANDER AGAINST CHRISTIANS

(Clement of Alexandria, *Paedagogus*, III.11.81.2-3.)

2   And if we are called to the kingdom of God, let us walk worthy of the kingdom, loving God and our neighbour. But love is not tested by a kiss, but by kindly feeling. But there are those, that do nothing but make the churches resound with a kiss, not having
3   love itself within. For this very thing, the shameless use of the kiss, which ought to be mystic, has occasioned foul suspicions and evil reports. (A.-N. C. L., slightly altered.)

On the "kiss of peace", cf. 42 (Justin), and for various patristic references, cf. Sanday and Headlam, *Romans*, p. 428 (on 16.16).

169. PHILOSOPHY A PREPARATION FOR THE GOSPEL

(Clement of Alexandria, *Stromateis*, I.5.28.1-3.)

1   Philosophy then before the coming of the Lord was necessary to the Greeks to bring them to righteousness, but now it is profitable to bring them to piety, seeing that it is a sort of training for those who are gaining the fruit of faith for themselves by means of demonstration, for *thy foot shall not stumble*,[1] says he, if thou refer good things to providence, whether they be Greek or Christian.

[1] Prov. 3.23.

2 For God is the cause of all good things, but of some primarily, as of the old and new covenants, and of others consequentially, as
3 of philosophy. Peradventure also it was given primarily to the Greeks in times before the Lord called also the Greeks; for philosophy educated the Greek world as the law did the Hebrews *to bring them to Christ.*[1] Philosophy therefore is a preparation, making ready the way for him who is being perfected by Christ. (Gwatkin, *Selections from Early Christian Writers*, p. 107, altered.)

1. *Philosophy then . . . :* In the previous chapter Clement had been arguing that all "wisdom" is approved by God.

3. *educated . . . to Christ* (ἐπαιδαγώγει): "The paedagogus or tutor, frequently a superior slave, was entrusted with the moral supervision of the child. Thus his office was quite distinct from that of the διδάσκαλος, so that the English rendering 'schoolmaster' (e.g. in the A.V.) conveys a wrong idea" (Lightfoot, *Galatians* (on 3.24)).

It must be noticed that the part of philosophy, while necessary, is yet subordinate.

170. CHARACTERISTICS OF THE GNOSTIC

(Clement of Alexandria, *Stromateis*, IV.22.135.1—137.1: 138.1-3.)

135.1 The man of understanding and perspicacity is, then, a Gnostic. And his business is not abstinence from what is evil (for this is a
2 step to the highest perfection), or the doing of good out of fear.
3 . . . Nor any more is he to do so from hope of promised recom-
4 pense. . . . But only the doing of good out of love, and for the
136.1 sake of its own excellence, is to be the Gnostic's choice. Now, in the person of God it is said to the Lord, *Ask of me, and I will give the heathen for Thine inheritance*[2]; teaching Him to ask a truly regal request—that is, the salvation of men without price, that
2 we may inherit and possess the Lord. For, on the contrary, to desire knowledge about God for any practical purpose, that this may be done, or that may not be done, is not proper to the Gnostic; but the knowledge itself suffices as the reason for con-
3 templation. For I will dare aver that it is not because he wishes to be saved that he, who devotes himself to knowledge for the
4 sake of the divine science itself, chooses knowledge. For the exertion of the intellect through training is prolonged to a perpetual exertion. And the perpetual exertion of the intellect is the essence

[1] Gal. 3.24.   [2] Ps. 2.8.

of an intelligent being, which results from an uninterrupted process of admixture, and remains eternal contemplation, a living
5 substance. Could we, then, suppose any one proposing to the
Gnostic whether he would choose the knowledge of God or everlasting salvation; and if these, which are entirely identical, were
separable, he would without the least hesitation choose the knowledge of God, deeming that property of faith, which from love
137.1 ascends to knowledge, desirable for its own sake. This, then, is
the perfect man's first form of doing good, when it is done not
for any advantage in what pertains to him, but because he judges
it right to do good; and the energy being vigorously exerted in all
things, in the very act becomes good; not, good in some things,
and not good in others; but consisting in the habit of doing good,
neither for glory, nor, as the philosophers say, for reputation, nor
from reward either from men or God; but so as to pass life after
the *image and likeness of the Lord*.[1]

*   *   *

138.1 Such an one is no longer continent, but has reached a state of
2 passionlessness, waiting to put on the divine image. *If thou doest
alms*, it is said, *let no one know it*; *and if thou fastest, anoint thyself,
that God alone may know*,[2] and not a single human being. Not
even he himself who shows mercy ought to know that he does
show mercy; for in this way he will be sometimes merciful,
3 sometimes not. And when he shall do good by habit, he will
imitate the nature of good, and his disposition will be his nature
and his practice. (A.-N. C. L.)

The above extracts only touch the fringe of what Clement has to say about
the Gnostic. The earlier part of Book VII of the *Stromateis* (down to section 88)
is concerned with this subject. See, e.g., the synopsis on pages XCII–XCIX of
Hort and Mayor's edition of Book VII, or Tollinton, *Clement of Alexandria*,
II, pp. 72–101.

171. THE GNOSTIC ON EARTH AND IN HEAVEN

(Clement of Alexandria, *Stromateis*, VI.13.105.1—106.2: 14.114.1–4.)

105.1 He, then, who has first moderated his passions and trained himself for impassibility, and developed to the beneficence of gnostic
perfection, is here equal to the angels. Luminous already, and like

---

[1] Gen. 1.26.   [2] Matt. 6.2–4,16–18.

the sun shining in the exercise of beneficence, he speeds by
righteous knowledge through the love of God to the sacred abode,
like as the apostles. Not that they became apostles through being
chosen for some distinguished peculiarity of nature, since also
Judas was chosen along with them. But they were capable of
becoming apostles on being chosen by Him who foresees even
2 ultimate issues. Matthias, accordingly, who was not chosen along
with them, on showing himself worthy of becoming an apostle,
is substituted for Judas.

106.1 Those, then, even now, who have exercised themselves in the
Lord's commandments, and lived perfectly and gnostically according to the gospel, may be enrolled in the chosen body of the
2 apostles. Such an one is in reality a presbyter of the church, and a
true minister (deacon) of the will of God, if he do and teach what
is the Lord's; not as being ordained by men, nor regarded righteous
because a presbyter, but enrolled in the presbyterate because
righteous. And although here upon earth he be not honoured
with the chief seat,[1] he will sit down on the four-and-twenty
thrones,[2] judging the people, as John says in the Apocalypse.
(A.-N. C. L., slightly altered.)

[In *Strom.* VI.14 Clement sets out his idea that there are different
degrees of glory in Heaven, e.g. 114.1-4:]

114.1 Conformably, therefore, there are various abodes, according
to the worth of those who have believed. To the point Solomon
says, *For there shall be given to him the choice grace of faith, and a*
2 *more pleasant lot in the temple of the Lord.*[3] For the comparative
shows that there are lower parts in the temple of God, which is
the whole church. And the superlative remains to be conceived,
3 where the Lord is. These chosen abodes, which are three, are
indicated by the numbers in the Gospel—the thirty, the sixty,
4 the hundred.[4] And the perfect inheritance belongs to those who
attain to *a perfect man,*[5] according to the image of the Lord.
(A.-N. C. L.)

172. FAITH AND KNOWLEDGE

(Clement of Alexandria, *Stromateis*, VII.10.57.3-5.)

3   Faith, then, is a compendious knowledge of the essentials, but
knowledge is a sure and firm demonstration of the things received
through faith, being itself built up by the Lord's teaching on the

---

[1] Mark 12.39; Luke 20.46.   [2] Rev. 4.4; 11.16.   [3] Wisd. 3.14.
[4] Mark 4.8.   [5] Eph. 4.13.

foundation of faith, and carrying us on to unshaken conviction
4 and scientific certainty. As I mentioned before, there seems to
me to be a first kind of saving change from heathenism to faith,
a second from faith to knowledge; and this latter, as it passes on
into love, begins at once to establish a mutual friendship between
5 that which knows and that which is known. And, perhaps, he
who has arrived at this stage has already *attained equality with
the angels*.[1] At any rate, after he has reached the final ascent in
the flesh, he still continues to advance, as is fit, and presses on
through the holy Hebdomad into the Father's house, to that
which is indeed the Lord's abode,[2] being destined there to be, as
it were, a light standing and abiding for ever, absolutely secure
from all vicissitude. (F. J. A. Hort and J. B. Mayor, *Stromateis*,
VII, p. 101.)

5. *presses on through the holy Hebdomad into the Father's house*: cf. *Excerpta ex
Theodoto*, 63.1. "Now the repose of the spiritual elements on the Lord's Day,
that is, in the Ogdoad, which is called the Lord's Day, is with the Mother, who
keeps their souls, the (wedding) garments, until the end; but the other faithful
souls are with the Creator, but at the end they also go up in the Ogdoad."
(R. P. Casey, *Excerpta ex Theodoto*, p. 83 (Studies and Documents, I)) Clement
is reflecting Gnostic language in his reference to the Hebdomad. The Hebdomad is the abode of the Demiurge, the Ogdoad is the abode of Sophia and the
gateway to the Pleroma, cf. 53.

173. CHURCH AND HERESY

(Clement of Alexandria, *Stromateis*, VII.15.90.1–91.3.)

90.1 What then? If some one is guilty of breaking his engagements
and neglecting his agreement with us, shall we let go the truth
ourselves on account of him who has been false to his agreement?
2 No, the good man must be true to his work and not belie any
promise, however much others may break their engagements.
We ought in no way to transgress the rule of the Church. Above
all, the confession which deals with the essential articles of the
faith is observed by us, but disregarded by the heretics. Those
3 then are to be believed who hold firmly to the truth. Using this
defence broadly, we are now entitled to reply to them that
physicians also, though holding different opinions in accordance
with their particular schools, are still equally engaged in the
4 practice of healing. Does then any one who is suffering in body

1 Luke 20.36.   2 John 14.2.

and needs medical treatment refuse to call in a physician owing
to the diversity of medical schools? So neither should he who
is diseased in soul and full of idols plead the heresies as his
excuse in regard to the recovery of health and conversion to God.
Aye, and we are told that *heresies are for the sake of those who*
5 *are approved*[1]; and by *approved* is meant either those who are
coming to the faith, if they show unusual discrimination in
approaching the teaching of the Lord (like "the approved money-
changers" who distinguish the spurious from the legal coin by
the false stamp), or those who are in the faith itself, and have
already approved themselves therein, both by their life and their
knowledge.

91.1 It is for this reason, therefore, that we need more attention and
consideration to determine how we should live with strictness
2 and what is true piety. For it is evident that the trouble and difficulty of ascertaining the truth have given rise to questionings,
from whence spring vain and self-willed heresies, when men
have not learnt nor really received knowledge, but have merely
3 got a conceit of it. We must therefore spend more thought in
searching for the very truth, which alone has for its subject the
very God. And sweet are the discovery and the remembrance
which attend on toil. (F. J. A. Hort and J. B. Mayor, *Stromateis*,
VII, pp. 157–61.)

Clement argued in section 89 against the view of Greeks and Jews that
diversity of sects was an insuperable obstacle to acceptance of Christianity.
He denied this by thrusting back the argument on his opponents and by referring to the prophecy of the tares and wheat (Matt. 13.25).

90.2. *the rule of the Church*: cf. 93, 149. Clement is as insistent on this as are
Irenaeus and Tertullian.

5. *the approved money changers*: this saying of Christ is quoted by other early
Christian writers also. For references see Hort and Mayor, op. cit., pp. 330–1.
"Paul's words in 1 Thess. 5.21, *Prove all things, hold fast to that which is good* are
really a comment on the saying, and show its meaning." (James, *The Apocryphal
N.T.*, p. 35.)

174. THE RICH MAN'S SALVATION
(Clement, *The Rich Man's Salvation*, 15.1–6; 24.1.24.)

15.1 I for my part would put the matter thus. Since possessions of
one kind are within the soul, and those of another kind outside it,
and these latter appear to be good if the soul uses them well, but
bad if they are badly used, which of the two is it that He, who

[1] 1 Cor. 11.19.

orders us to get rid of what we have, asks us to renounce? Is it those after whose removal the passions still remain, or rather those
2 after whose removal even outward possessions become useful? He who has cast away his worldly abundance can still be rich in passions even though his substance is gone. For his disposition continues its own activity, choking and stifling the power of reasoning and inflaming him with its inbred desires. It has proved no great gain then for him to be poor in possessions when he is
3 rich in passions. For he has cast away not the worthless things but the indifferent, and while depriving himself of what is serviceable he has set on fire the innate material of evil by the lack of out-
4 ward things. A man must say good-bye, then, to the injurious things he has, not to those that can actually contribute to his
5 advantage if he knows the right use of them; and advantage comes from those that are managed with wisdom, moderation and piety. We must reject what is hurtful; but outward things are not injurious.
6 In this way then the Lord admits the use of outward things, bidding us put away, not the means of living, but the things that use these badly; and these are, as we have seen, the infirmities and passions of the soul.

* * *

24.1 Can you also rise superior to your riches? Say so, and Christ does not draw you away from the possession of them; the Lord does not grudge. But do you see yourself being worsted and over-thrown by them? Leave them, cast them off, hate them, say good-bye to them, flee from them. (Butterworth, *Clement of Alexandria* (Loeb Library), pp. 299–301, 319–20.)

It is clear from the works of Clement of Alexandria (if we are to regard them as being of any practical value for their own time) that Christianity was no longer a religion of the slums only, but that it had now a considerable number of wealthy adherents, cf. 175, p. 203. The question of the possession and use of riches was therefore a crucial one. Clement's solution is based on the allegorical interpretation of scripture.

"The wealth He bade His questioner renounce must be taken in a spiritual sense; it was a wealth of passions, a brood of sins in the soul; not money itself, but the love of money. The rich man might have kept his wealth, and by following Jesus have learned to use it rightly. All that rich men in general have to do, therefore, is to eradicate selfishness and to spend their money liberally for the relief of their poorer brethren, who by interceding with God for such benefactors will return an abundant recompense." (Butterworth, op. cit., p. 267.)

175. ORIGEN

(Eusebius, *H.E.* VI.2.12—3.1; 3.3, 8–12.)

In *H.E.* VI.2.2 Eusebius says, "In the case of Origen I think that even the facts from his very cradle, so to speak, are worthy of mention." He describes the youth of Origen in *H.E.* VI.1–8, and then continues his narrative of Origen's life as scholar and teacher from VI.14.10.

The passages quoted deal with some stages in Origen's development.

2.12   But when his father had been perfected by martyrdom, he was left destitute with his mother and six smaller brothers, when
13   he was not quite seventeen. His father's property was confiscated for the imperial treasury, and he found himself, along with his relatives, in want of the necessaries of life. Yet he was deemed worthy of divine aid, and met with both welcome and refreshment from a certain lady, very rich in this world's goods and otherwise distinguished, who nevertheless was treating with honour a well-known person, one of the heretics at Alexandria at that time. He was an Antiochene by race, but the lady we have mentioned kept him at her house as her adopted son, and treated
14   him with especial honour. But although Origen of necessity had to consort with him, he used to give clear proofs of his orthodoxy, at that age, in the faith. For though very great numbers, not only of heretics but also of our own people, were gathered together with Paul (for that was the man's name), attracted by his apparent skilfulness in speech, Origen could never be persuaded to associate with him in prayer, keeping the rule of the Church, even from boyhood, and "loathing"—the very word he himself uses some-
15   where—the teachings of the heresies. His father had brought him forward in secular studies, and after his death he applied himself wholly with renewed zeal to a literary training, so that he had a tolerable amount of proficiency in letters; and, not long after his father's perfecting, by dint of application to these studies, he was abundantly supplied, for a person of his years, with the necessaries of life.
3.1   And while he was devoting himself to teaching, as he himself informs us somewhere in writing, since there was no one at Alexandria set apart for catechetical instruction (for all had been driven away by the threat of the persecution), some of the heathen approached him to hear the word of God.

✶   ★   ★

3   Origen was in his eighteenth year when he came to preside over the catechetical school, and at this time also he came into prominence when the persecutions were going on under Aquila the governor of Alexandria. Then also he won for himself an exceedingly wide reputation among all those who were of the faith, by the kindly help and goodwill that he displayed towards all the holy martyrs, unknown and known alike.

* * *

8   And when he saw still more pupils coming to him (for the task of instruction had been entrusted by Demetrius, the president of the church, to him alone), considering that the teaching of letters was not consonant with training in the divine studies, without more ado he broke off the task of teaching literature, as being unprofitable and opposed to sacred study; and then for a fitting

9   reason, that he might never be in need of others' assistance, he disposed of all the volumes of ancient literature which formerly he so fondly cherished, content if he who purchased them brought him four obols a day. For a great number of years he continued to live like a philosopher in this wise, putting aside everything that might lead to *youthful lusts*[1]; all day long his discipline was to perform labours of no light character, and the greater part of the night he devoted himself to studying the divine Scriptures; and he persevered, as far as possible, in the most philosophic manner of life, at one time disciplining himself by fasting, at another measuring out the time for sleep, which he was careful to take, never

10   on a couch, but on the floor. And above all he considered that those sayings of the Saviour in the Gospel ought to be kept which exhort us *not* [to provide] *two coats nor* to use *shoes*,[2] nor, indeed,

11   to be worn out with thoughts about the future.[3] Yea, he was possessed of a zeal beyond his years, and by persevering *in cold and nakedness*[4] and going to the extremest limit of poverty, he greatly astounded his followers, causing grief to numbers who besought him to share their goods, when they saw the labour that he bestowed on teaching divine things. But he was not one

12   to slacken endurance. He is said, for example, to have walked for many years without using a shoe of any description, yea more, to have refrained for a great many years from the use of wine and all except necessary food, so that he actually incurred the risk of undermining and destroying his constitution. (Lawlor and Oulton, *Eusebius*, I, pp. 177–81.)

[1] 2 Tim. 2.22.   [2] Matt. 10.10.   [3] Cf. Matt. 6. 34.
[4] 2 Cor. 11.27.

2.12. *When his father (Leonides) had been perfected*: in the persecution of Severus, *c.* 202.

2.13-14. These sections afford an interesting sidelight on Alexandrian Christianity: a rich and charitable lady, dabbling in heresy.

3.1. *for all had been driven away*: in particular, Clement.

176. ORIGEN'S SYSTEM OF EDUCATION

(Eusebius, *H.E.* VI.18.)

1 At this time also Ambrose, who held the views of the heresy of Valentinus, was refuted by the truth as presented by Origen, and, as if his mind were illuminated by light, gave his adhesion
2 to the true doctrine as taught by the Church. And many other cultured persons, since Origen's fame was noised abroad everywhere, came to him to make trial of the man's sufficiency in the sacred books. And numbers of the heretics, and not a few of the most distinguished philosophers, gave earnest heed to him, and, one might almost say, were instructed by him in secular philosophy
3 as well as in divine things. For he used to introduce also to the study of philosophy as many as he saw were naturally gifted, imparting geometry and arithmetic and the other preliminary subjects, and then leading them on to the systems which are found among philosophers, giving a detailed account of their treatises, commenting upon and examining into each, so that the man was proclaimed as a great philosopher even among the Greeks them-
4 selves. And many persons also of a more ignorant character he urged to take up the ordinary elementary studies, declaring that they would derive no small advantage from these when they came to examine and study the divine Scriptures. For this reason he deemed especially necessary even for himself a training in secular and philosophic studies. (Lawlor and Oulton, *Eusebius*, I, p. 191.)

On Origen as a scholar, cf. 180-1, 191-2.

177. THE PREACHING AND ORDINATION OF ORIGEN IN PALESTINE
c. 215 and *c.* 231

(Eusebius, *H.E.* VI.19.16-19; 23.4.)

19.16 But after the lapse of some time no small warfare broke out again in the city, and leaving Alexandria secretly he went to Palestine and abode at Caesarea. And although he had not yet

received ordination to the presbyterate, the bishops there requested
him to discourse and expound the divine Scriptures publicly in
17 the church. That this is so is clear from what Alexander, the bishop
of Jerusalem, and Theoctistus, the bishop of Caesarea, write with
reference to Demetrius. They make their defence somewhat as
follows:

And he added to his letter that such a thing had never been
heard of, nor taken place hitherto, that laymen should preach in
the presence of bishops; though I do not know how he comes to
18 say what is evidently not true. For instance, where there are found
persons suited to help the brethren, they also are invited to preach
to the people by the holy bishops, as, for example, in Laranda
Euelpis by Neon, and in Iconium Paulinus by Celsus, and in
Synnada Theodore by Atticus, our blessed brother bishops. And
it is likely that this thing happens in other places also without our
knowing it.

In this way honour was paid to the man of whom we are speaking, while he was still young, not only by his fellow-countrymen
19 but also by the bishops in a foreign land. But since Demetrius
once again recalled him by letter, and by men who were deacons
of the Church urged him to come back with speed to Alexandria,
he returned and continued to labour with his accustomed zeal.
(Lawlor and Oulton, *Eusebius*, I, pp. 193-4.)

16. *After the lapse of some time*: i.e. some time after a visit made by Origen
to Arabia.

no small warfare: this probably refers to the visit of Caracalla in 215; he fell
foul of the people of Alexandria, whose sarcasms and reproaches he resented,
and massacred many.

17. *that such a thing had never been heard of*: it is clear from the precedents
quoted by the Palestinian bishops, precedents drawn from distant and un-
important, though in one case ancient, churches in the interior of Asia Minor
(? based on recollections of Alexander of Jerusalem, who had previously been a
bishop in Cappadocia), that their position was shaky, and this is confirmed by
their action in ordaining Origen (see below). As the organization of the Church,
and the number and power of its clergy increased, the place of laymen declined.

23.4   In their day Origen journeyed to Greece through Palestine because of an urgent necessity in Church matters, and received the
laying-on of hands for the presbyterate at Caesarea from the
bishops there. The agitation that was set on foot concerning him
on this account, and the decisions made by those who presided
over the churches on the matters agitated, as well as the other
contributions that he made as he was reaching his prime to the

study of the divine Word, require a separate composition, and we have given an account in due measure in the second [book] of the Apology that we have written on his behalf. (Lawlor and Oulton, *Eusebius*, I, p. 196, slightly altered.)

4. *In their day*: i.e. in the time of Pontian, and Zebennus, bishops of Rome and of Antioch, *c.* 230.

On the relations of Origen and Demetrius, see 178, and, e.g., McGiffert's note on p. 394 of his edition of Eusebius (N. & P.-N. F.).

the second [*book*] *of the Apology*: the first five books were written jointly by Pamphilus, the teacher of Eusebius, and by Eusebius; the sixth was the work of Eusebius alone, after Pamphilus' martyrdom in 310.

178. ORIGEN ON HIS DEPARTURE FROM ALEXANDRIA, 232

(Origen, *Commentary on St John's Gospel*, VI.2.8–12)

8 As far as the fifth volume, even though the storm at Alexandria appeared to oppose me, I dictated what is given to me, since Jesus rebuked the winds and the waves of the sea. After making some progress with volume six, we were rescued from Egypt, 9 for God who led out his people from that land, saved us. As our opponent warred against me most bitterly by his subsequent letters (which are truly in opposition to the Gospel), and stirred up all the winds of wickedness that are in Egypt against me, the word exhorted me to stand to the contest and guard the supreme part of my soul, lest mistaken arguments prevailed to bring the storm even upon my soul, ere my understanding gained tranquillity, rather than continue with the rest of my writing. Moreover the absence of my usual shorthand writers prevented me 10 from continuing my dictation. But now, when the many fiery darts shot at me have been quenched by God and have lost their force, and my soul now accustomed to what has happened to me because of the heavenly word, is constrained to bear more easily the treacherous plots devised against me, I have gained as it were a great calm and wish, without further delay, to dictate the next portion, praying that God my teacher be present in the sanctuary of my soul to prompt me, that the building of my commentary 11 on the Gospel according to John may be completed. May God hear my prayer that I may be able to fit together the body of my whole discourse, with no circumstances able to interrupt me any longer and cause any intermission whatever of the sequence of my

work. Be assured that I am most eager to begin book six a second time, because, somehow or other what I dictated beforehand in 12 Egypt has not been brought with me. For I decided, that this period also should not pass without any progress in this work, and to make a start now on what remains, and not to lose the great advantage of the ensuing period by waiting without any certainty that my previous dictation would be found.

Origen speaks little in his extant works of the crisis that caused him to leave, or be expelled from, Alexandria; but this passage reveals the bitterness of Demetrius, and the mental anguish of Origen, who was thus badly treated by those with whom he had long lived in mutual confidence.

Eusebius, *H.E.* VI.8.4–5, states that Demetrius actuated by jealousy, raked up Origen's rash act, in literal obedience to Matt. 19.12, an act in which Demetrius had acquiesced at the time.

my usual shorthand writers: these were supplied to him by Ambrose (Eusebius, *H.E.* VI.23), on whom see also 176 above.

179. ORIGEN'S VISIT TO MAMMAEA, MOTHER OF ALEXANDER SEVERUS, *c.* 232

(Eusebius, *H.E.* VI.21.3,4.)

3 Origen's fame was now universal, so as to reach the ears of the Emperor's mother, Mammaea by name, a religious woman if ever there was one. She set great store on securing a sight of the man, and on testing that understanding of divine things which was the 4 wonder of all. She was then staying at Antioch, and summoned him to her presence with a military escort. And when he had stayed with her for some time, and shown her very many things that were for the glory of the Lord and the excellence of the divine teaching, he hastened back to his accustomed duties. (Lawlor and Oulton, *Eusebius*, I, p. 195.)

On the date see Lawlor and Oulton, *Eusebius*, II, p. 219.

At the court of the Severi interest in religion was intense: it was there that the life story of Apollonius of Tyana was worked up by Philostratus, and the Syrian Sun God made supreme over all other deities. The story that Alexander Severus had a statue of Christ, along with those of other religious leaders of mankind in his private chapel comes from the now discredited *Historia Augusta* (*Alex.* 29.2), but he had relations with Julius Africanus, one of the more intellectual Christians of this period, and one need not be surprised that the strong willed and intelligent Mammaea invited Origen to visit her. Later in Origen's life he wrote letters to the Emperor Philip and his wife (Eusebius, *H.E.* VI.36.3).

180. ORIGEN'S DISCUSSIONS WITH HERETICS

(Eusebius, *H.E.* VI.33,1–3; 37.)

1. The case of Beryllus of Bostra, *c.* 243.

33.1 Beryllus, who, as we have mentioned a little above,[1] was bishop of Bostra in Arabia, perverting the Church's standard, i.e. the rule of faith, attempted to introduce things foreign to the faith, daring to say that our Saviour and Lord did not pre-exist in an individual existence of His own before His coming to reside among men, nor had He a divinity of His own, but only the
2 Father's dwelling in Him. Whereupon, after a large number of bishops had held questionings and discussions with the man, Origen, being invited along with others, entered in the first place into conversation with the man to discover what were his opinions, and when he knew what it was that he asserted, he corrected what was unorthodox, and, persuading him by reasoning, established him in the truth as to the doctrine, and restored him to his
3 former sound opinion. And there are still extant to this very day records in writing both of Beryllus and of the synod that was held on his account, which contain at once the questions Origen put to him and the discussions that took place in his own community, and all that was done on that occasion. (Lawlor and Oulton, *Eusebius*, I, p. 202.)

2. Heretics in Arabia, *c.* 248.

37 Once more in Arabia at the above-mentioned time other persons sprang up, introducing a doctrine foreign to the truth, and saying that the human soul dies for a while in this present time, along with our bodies, at their death, and with them turns to corruption; but that hereafter, at the time of the resurrection, it will come to life again along with them. Moreover, when a synod of no small dimensions was then assembled together, Origen was again invited, and there opened a discussion in public on the subject in question, with such power that he changed the opinions of those who had formerly been deluded. (Lawlor and Oulton, *Eusebius*, I, p. 203.)

1. Bostra, a city of "Arabia" about 90 miles NE. of Jerusalem.
Beryllus was clearly some kind of Monarchian, cf. the heresy of Paul of Samosata (239). In *H.E.* VI.20.2 Eusebius speaks highly of him as a writer.

[1] Ch. 20.2.

The procedure adopted was one of which an example is now extant in Origen's *Discussion with Heracleides and his fellow bishops*, discovered in Egypt in 1941 (published by L'institut français d'archéologie orientale, 1949 (*Entretien d'Origène avec Héracleide et les évêques ses collègues*, édité par Jean Scherer), E. tr. by H. Chadwick in *Alexandrian Christianity* (Library of Christian Classics), pp. 437-55).

2. The Arabian heresy appears in Origen's *Discussion with Heracleides*, pp. 144-5, where Origen is asked, "Whether the soul is the blood? (cf. Lev. 17.11)". He replies, "It has come to my ears, and I speak with full assurance, that some here and in the neighbourhood think that after its departure hence, the soul has no perception, but is in the sepulchre, in the body". Origen then recalls a particularly bitter discussion on this subject, which he had with persons known to his present interlocutors. He proceeds to solve their difficulty, as one would expect, by allegorical exegesis; the text of Leviticus is to be referred to the "inner" man, the "vital power of the soul" (op. cit., p. 165).

181. ORIGEN'S WORK ON THE TEXT OF THE OLD TESTAMENT

(Eusebius, *H.E.* VI.16.)

1   And so accurate was the examination that Origen brought to bear upon the divine books, that he even made a thorough study of the Hebrew tongue, and got into his own possession the original writings extant among the Jews in the actual Hebrew characters. Thus, too, he traced the editions of the other translators of the sacred writings besides the Seventy; and besides the beaten track of translations, that of Aquila and of Symmachus and of Theodotion, he discovered certain others, which were used in turn, which, after lying hidden for a long time, he traced and brought

2   to light, I know not from what recesses. With regard to these, on account of their obscurity (not knowing whose in the world they were) he merely indicated this: that the one he found at Nicopolis

3   near Actium, and the other in such another place. At any rate, in the Hexapla of the Psalms, after the four well-known editions, he placed beside them not only a fifth but also a sixth and a seventh translation; and in the case of one of these he has indicated again that it was found at Jericho in a jar in the time of

4   Antoninus the son of Severus. All these he brought together, dividing them into clauses and placing them one over against the other, together with the actual Hebrew text; and so he has left

us the copies of the Hexapla, as it is called. He made a further separate arrangement of the edition of Aquila and Symmachus and Theodotion together with that of the Seventy, in the Tetrapla. (Lawlor and Oulton, *Eusebius*, I, p. 190f., slightly altered.)

1. *a thorough study of the Hebrew tongue*: "thorough" perhaps in that few Christians learned Hebrew at all; on the limitations of Origen's knowledge of Hebrew, see, e.g., McGiffert's note ad loc. (*The Church History of Eusebius*, N. & P.-N. F., p. 262).

Aquila: second century A.D., a proselyte to Judaism from Christianity: translation very close to the Hebrew.

Symmachus: *c*. A.D. 200. An Ebionite (Eus. *H.E.* VI.17). His version "is distinguished from Aquila's by the purity of its Greek and its freedom from Hebraisms" (McGiffert, loc. cit.).

Theodotion: *c*. A.D. 180, a proselyte; his version was based on the Septuagint, and ultimately superseded that translation for the *Book of Daniel*.

None of these versions is now extant *in toto*.

4. *The Hexapla*: "Since Eusebius is not very precise in his language it may be well to say that the six main columns were arranged in the following order from left to right: (1) Hebrew, (2) transliteration of the Hebrew into Greek letters, (3) Aquila, (4) Symmachus, (5) Septuagint, (6) Theodotion. According to this order the two versions which followed the Hebrew most closely—Aquila and Symmachus—immediately followed it, while Theodotion followed the Septuagint, since it was in fact based on that translation." (Lawlor and Oulton, *Eusebius*, II, p. 203.)

The *Hexapla* is no longer extant. It is possible that there was only one complete manuscript of this enormous work, in the library at Caesarea where Jerome saw and used it.

182. THE CHURCH'S TEACHING

(Origen, *De Principiis*, I, Preface 2–8,10.)

LATIN

2   Many of those, however, who profess to believe in Christ, hold conflicting opinions not only on small and trivial questions but also on some great and important ones, I mean on God, or on the Lord Jesus Christ himself, or on the Holy Spirit; not only moreover on these but on others, created beings, I mean on the dominions and the holy powers. In view of this it seems necessary first to lay down a definite line and unmistakable rule in regard to each of these, and to postpone the inquiry into other matters until afterwards. For just as there are many among Greeks and barbarians alike who promise us the truth, and yet we gave up

seeking for it from all who claimed it for false opinions after we had come to believe that Christ was the Son of God and had become convinced that we must learn the truth from him; so because there are many who think that they hold the doctrine of Christ, and some of them differ in their beliefs from the Christians of earlier times, and yet the teaching (i.e. κήρυγμα) of the church is preserved unaltered handed down in unbroken succession from the apostles and existing to this day in the churches, we maintain that that only is to be believed as the truth which in no way conflicts with the tradition of the church and apostles.

3   But the following fact should be understood. The holy apostles, when preaching the faith of Christ, took certain doctrines, those namely which they believed to be necessary ones, and delivered them in the plainest terms to all believers, even to such as appeared to be somewhat dull in the investigation of divine knowledge. The grounds of their statements they left to be investigated by such as should merit the higher gifts of the Spirit and in particular by such as should afterwards receive through the Holy Spirit himself the graces of language, wisdom and knowledge. There were other doctrines, however, about which the apostles simply said that things were so, keeping silence as to how or why; their intention undoubtedly being to supply the more diligent of those who came after them, such as should prove to be lovers of wisdom, with an exercise on which to display the fruit of their ability. The men I refer to are those who train themselves to become worthy and capable of receiving wisdom.

4   The kind of doctrines which are believed in plain terms through the apostolic teaching are the following:

First, that God is one, who created and set in order all things, and who, when nothing existed, caused the universe to be. He is God from the first creation and foundation of the world, the God of all righteous men, of Adam, Abel, Seth, Enos, Enoch, Noah, Shem, Abraham, Isaac, Jacob, of the twelve patriarchs, of Moses and the prophets. This God, in these last days,[1] according to the previous announcements made through his prophets, sent the Lord Jesus Christ, first for the purpose of calling Israel, and secondly, after the unbelief of the people of Israel, of calling the Gentiles also. This just and good God, the Father of our Lord Jesus Christ, himself gave the law, the prophets and the gospels, and he is God both of the apostles and also of the Old and New Testaments.

Then again: Christ Jesus, he who came to earth, was begotten

[1] Heb. 1.1.

of the Father before every created thing. And after he had ministered to the Father in the foundation of all things, for *all things were made through him*,[1] in these last times he emptied himself and was made man, was made flesh, although he was God; and being made man, he still remained what he was, namely, God. He took to himself a body like our body, differing in this alone, that it was born of a virgin and of the Holy Spirit. And this Jesus Christ was born and suffered in truth and not merely in appearance, and truly died our common death. Moreover he truly rose from the dead, and after the resurrection companied with his disciples and was then taken up into heaven.

Then again, the apostles delivered this doctrine, that the Holy Spirit is united in honour and dignity with the Father and the Son. In regard to him it is not yet clearly known whether he is to be thought of as begotten or unbegotten, or as being himself also a Son of God or not; but these are matters which we must investigate to the best of our power from holy scripture, inquiring with wisdom and diligence. It is, however, certainly taught with the utmost clearness in the Church, that this Spirit inspired each one of the saints, both the prophets and the apostles, and that there was not one Spirit in the men of old and another in those who were inspired at the coming of Christ.

5   Next after this the apostles taught that the soul, having a substance and life of its own, will be rewarded according to its deserts after its departure from this world; for it will either obtain an inheritance of eternal life and blessedness, if its deeds shall warrant this, or it must be given over to eternal fire and torments, if the guilt of its crimes shall so determine. Further, there will be a time for the resurrection of the dead, when this body, which is now *sown in corruption*, shall *rise in incorruption*, and that which is *sown in dishonour* shall *rise in glory*.[2]

This also is laid down in the Church's teaching, that every rational soul is possessed of free will and choice; and also, that it is engaged in a struggle against the devil and his angels and the opposing powers; for these strive to weigh the soul down with sins, whereas we, if we lead a wise and upright life, endeavour to free ourselves from such a stain. There follows from this the conviction that we are not subject to necessity, so as to be compelled by every means, even against our will, to do either good or evil. For if we are possessed of free will, some spiritual powers may very likely be able to urge us on to sin and others to assist us to salvation; we are not, however, compelled by necessity to act

[1] John 1.3.   [2] I Cor. 15.42-3.

either rightly or wrongly, as is thought to be the case by those who say that human events are due to the course and motion of the stars, not only those events which fall outside the sphere of our freedom of will but even those that lie within our own power.

In regard to the soul, whether it takes its rise from the transference of the seed, in such a way that the principle or substance of the soul may be regarded as inherent in the seminal particles of the body itself; or whether it has some other beginning, and whether this beginning is begotten or unbegotten, or at any rate whether it is imparted to the body from without or no; all this is not very clearly defined in the teaching.

6   Further, in regard to the devil and his angels and the opposing spiritual powers, the Church's teaching lays it down that these beings exist, but what they are or how they exist it has not explained very clearly. Among most Christians, however, the following opinion is held, that this devil was formerly an angel, but became an apostate and persuaded as many angels as he could to fall away with him; and these are even now called his angels.

7   The Church's teaching also includes the doctrine that this world was made and began to exist at a definite time and that by reason of its corruptible nature it must suffer dissolution. But what existed before this world, or what will exist after it, has not yet been made known openly to the many, for no clear statement on the point is set forth in the Church's teaching.

★ ★ ★

GREEK

LATIN

10   It has also been handed down to us in the teaching that there exist certain angels and good powers, who minister to the salvation of men; but when they were created, and what are their characteristics, no one has in any way made plain.

This also is contained in the church teaching, that there exist certain angels of God and good powers, who minister to him in bringing about the salvation of men; but when these were created, and what they are like, or how they exist, is not very clearly defined. And as for the sun, moon and stars, the tradi-

LATIN

tion does not clearly say whether they are living beings or without life.

Everyone therefore who is desirous of constructing out of the foregoing a connected body of doctrine must use points like these as elementary and foundation principles, in accordance with the commandment which says, *Enlighten yourselves with the light of knowledge*.[1] Thus by clear and cogent arguments he will discover the truth about each particular point and so will produce, as we have said, a single body of doctrine, with the aid of such illustrations and declarations as he shall find in the holy scriptures and of such conclusions as he shall ascertain to follow logically from them when rightly understood. (Butterworth, *Origen on First Principles*, pp. 1–6, altered.)

Where the Greek text of the *De Principiis* is not extant, we have to depend on the Latin translation of Rufinus who modified doctrinal statements in order to defend Origen's orthodoxy.

2. *handed down in unbroken succession from the apostles*: cf. 96, 150.

4. Jerome in the heat of his controversy with Rufinus (*Ep. ad. Avitum*, 2), declared that Origen at the beginning of the *De Principiis*, Book I, regarded the son as "made", and that in regard to the Spirit, the doubts expressed by Origen here were resolved by his insistence that nothing was *uncreated* except God the Father. In his *Commentary on St John*, II.10, Origen clearly regards the Spirit as created through the Word.

183. THE REVOLT OF THE HEAVENLY POWERS

(Origen, *De Principiis*, I.8.1.)

GREEK

... Before the ages minds were all pure, both daemons and souls and angels, offering service to God and keeping his commandments. But the devil, who was one of them, since he possessed free-will, desired to resist God, and God drove him away. With him revolted all the other powers. Some sinned deeply and became daemons, others less and became angels; others still less and became archangels; and thus each in turn received the reward for his individual sin. But there remained some souls who had not sinned so greatly as to become daemons, nor on the other hand so very lightly as to become angels. God therefore made the present world and bound the soul to the body as a punishment. (Butterworth, *Origen on First Principles*, p. 67.)

The Greek of the above is composite, made up from various quotations, and it is possible that it may not accurately represent the language of Origen.

[1] Hos. 10.12 (LXX).

184. THE HOLY TRINITY

I.

(Origen, *De Principiis*, I.3.5.)

GREEK

The God and Father, who holds the universe together, is superior to every being that exists, for he imparts to each one from his own existence that which each one is; the Son, being less than the Father, is superior to rational creatures alone (for he is second to the Father); the Holy Spirit is still less, and dwells within the saints alone. So that in this way the power of the Father is greater than that of the Son and of the Holy Spirit, and that of the Son is more than that of the Holy Spirit, and in turn the power of the Holy Spirit exceeds that of every other holy being. (Butterworth, *Origen on First Principles*, pp. 33–4.)

2. On the Son.

(Origen, *Against Celsus*, V.39.)

Therefore, though we may call him a second God, it should be understood by this that we do not mean anything except the virtue which includes all virtues, and the Logos which includes every logos whatsoever of the beings which have been made according to nature, both those which are primary and those that exist for the benefit of the whole. We say that this Logos dwelt in the soul of Jesus and was united with it in a closer union than that of any other soul, because he alone has been able perfectly to receive the highest participation in him who is the very Logos and the very Wisdom, and the very Righteousness himself. (Tr. Chadwick, *Origen "Contra Celsum"*, p. 296.)

185. CYCLES OF EXISTENCE

(Origen, *De Principiis*, II.8.3.)

GREEK

Those rational beings who sinned and on that account fell from the state in which they were, in proportion to their particular sins were enveloped in bodies as a punishment; and when they are purified they rise again to the state in which they formerly were, completely putting away their evil and their bodies. Then again a second or a third or many more times they are enveloped in different bodies for punishment. For it is probable that different worlds have existed and will exist, some in the past and some in the future. (Butterworth, *Origen on First Principles*, p. 126.)

186. THE POSSIBILITY OF ULTIMATE SALVATION FOR ALL

(Origen, *De Principiis*, I.6.3.)

GREEK

But I think that, from among those that have been made subject to the worse kind of rulers and authorities and world-powers, in each world or in certain worlds, there are some who, by reason of their good deeds and their desire to be transferred from these powers, will speedily attain manhood.

LATIN

But whether among those orders that live under the chieftainship of the devil and conform to his wickedness there are some who will one day in the ages to come succeed in turning to goodness by reason of the power of free-will which is in them, or whether it be true that long-continued and deep-rooted wickedness turns at last from a habit into a

LATIN

kind of nature, you, reader, must judge; whether, that is, this portion of the creation shall be utterly and entirely out of harmony even with that final unity and concord, both in the ages that are *seen* and *temporal* and in those that are *not seen* and *eternal*. But in the meantime, alike in these ages that are *seen* and *temporal* and in those that are *not seen* and *eternal*,[1] all those beings are arranged in a definite order proportionate to the degree and excellence of their merits. And so it happens that some in the first, others in the second, and others even in the last times, through their endurance of greater and more severe punishments of long duration, extending, if I may say so, over many ages, are by these very stern methods of correction renewed and restored, first by the instruction of angels and afterwards by that of powers yet higher in rank, so that they advance through each grade to a higher one, until at length they reach the things that are *invisible* and *eternal*, having traversed in turn, by some form of instruction, every single office of the heavenly powers. It appears to follow from this, in my

[1] 2 Cor. 4.18.

opinion, that every rational nature can, in the process of passing from one order to another, travel through each order to all the rest, and from all to each, while undergoing the various movements of progress or the reverse in accordance with its own actions and endeavours and with the use of its power of free will. (Butterworth, *Origen on First Principles*, pp. 56–7.)

"No opinion of Origen's was more vehemently opposed than this one which gave demons and lost men a chance of restoration" (Butterworth, op. cit., p. 56, n. 4).

The translation of Rufinus fails to indicate that Origen asserted that the devil and his angels could be saved at the last, cf. Jerome. (*Ep. ad Pammachium et Oceanum*, 7); "(Origen teaches that) after many ages and the one restoration of all things Gabriel will be in the same state as the devil, Paul as Caiaphas and virgins as prostitutes" (tr. Butterworth, op. cit., p. 57, n. 1).

187. THE ETERNAL GENERATION OF THE SON

I.

(Origen, *Homilies on Jeremiah*, IX.4.)

So, if I call your attention to the case of the Saviour, that the Father did not beget the Son and release him from his generation but ever is begetting him, I shall present a similar statement in the case of the just man also. But let us see who the Saviour is. He is *effulgence of his* (i.e. *the Father's*) *glory*.[1] The *effulgence of glory* has not once been begotten and is no longer begotten. But as far as the light is productive of the effulgence, to so great an extent the effulgence of the glory of God is being begotten. Our Saviour is the *Wisdom of God*.[2] And Wisdom is the *effulgence of eternal light*.[3] If therefore the Saviour is ever being begotten, and for this reason says, *Before all hills he begets me*[4]—not *before all hills he has begotten me*, but *before all hills he begets me*—and the Saviour is ever being begotten of the Father, so you also if you have the *spirit of adoption*,[5] does God ever beget in himself according to each word, according to each thought, and thus being begotten you are ever being begotten a son of God in Jesus Christ.

[1] Heb. 1.3.   [2] 1 Cor. 1.24.   [3] Wisd. 7.26.
[4] Prov. 8.25.   [5] Rom. 8.15.

2.

(Origen *De Principiis*, I.2.2.)

LATIN

Wherefore we recognize that God was always the Father of his only-begotten Son, who was born indeed of him and draws his being from him, but is yet without any beginning, not only of that kind which can be distinguished by periods of time, but even of that other kind which the mind alone i wont to contemplate in itself and to perceive, if I may so say, with the bare intellect and reason. Wisdom, therefore, must be believed to have been begotten beyond the limits of any beginning that we can speak of or understand. (Butterworth, *Origen on First Principles*, p. 16.)

Cf. also *De Principiis*, I.2.8 for an exposition of Heb. 1.3, and IV.4.1 on the subject generally.

In the passage above from the *Homilies on Jeremiah* Origen is of course not formally presenting this doctrine, but using it as an illustration of the relation of God to the believer.

188. THE MEANING OF SCRIPTURE

(Origen, *De Principiis*, IV.2.4; *Philocalia*, I.11.)

GREEK

4 The right way, therefore, as it appears to us, of approaching the scriptures and gathering their meaning, is the following, which is extracted from the writings themselves. We find some such rule as this laid down by Solomon in the Proverbs concerning the divine doctrines written therein: *Do thou record them threefold in counsel and knowledge, that thou mayest answer words of truth to those who question thee.*[1]

One must therefore record the meaning of the sacred writings in a threefold way upon one's own soul, so that the simple man may be edified by what we may call the flesh of the scripture, this name being given to the obvious interpretation; while the man who has made some progress may be edified by its soul, as it were; and the man who is perfect and like those mentioned by the apostle: *We speak wisdom among the perfect; yet a wisdom not of this world, nor of the rulers of this world, which are coming to nought; but we speak God's wisdom in a mystery, even the wisdom that hath been hidden, which God foreordained before the worlds unto our glory,*[2]

[1] Prov. 22.20–1.   [2] 1 Cor. 2.6–7.

this man may be edified by the spiritual law, which has *a shadow of the good things to come*.[1] For just as man consists of body, soul and spirit, so in the same way does the scripture, which has been prepared by God to be given for man's salvation. (Butterworth, *Origen on First Principles*, pp. 275-6, slightly altered.)

189. THE INTERWEAVING OF THE IMPOSSIBLE WITH THE HISTORICAL IN SCRIPTURE

(Origen, *De Principiis*, IV.3.1, *Philocalia*, I.17.)

GREEK

1   Now what man of intelligence will believe that the first and the second and the third day, and the evening and the morning existed without the sun and moon and stars? And that the first day, if we may so call it, was even without a heaven?[2] And who is so silly as to believe that God, after the manner of a farmer, *planted a paradise eastward in Eden*, and set in it a visible and palpable *tree of life*, of such a sort that anyone who tasted its fruit with his bodily teeth would gain life; and again that one could partake of *good and evil* by masticating the fruit taken from the tree of that name?[3] And when God is said to *walk in the paradise in the cool of the day*,[4] and Adam to hide himself behind a tree, I do not think anyone will doubt that these are figurative expressions which indicate certain mysteries through a semblance of history and not through actual events.

Further, when Cain *goes out from the face of God*[5] it seems clear to thoughtful men that this statement impels the reader to inquire what the *face of God* is and how anyone can *go out* from it. And what more need I say, when those who are not altogether blind can collect thousands of such instances, recorded as actual events, but which did not happen literally?

Even the gospels are full of passages of this kind, as when the devil takes Jesus up into a *high mountain* in order to show him from thence *the kingdoms of the whole world and the glory of them*.[6] For what man who does not read such passages carelessly would fail to condemn those who believe that with the eye of the flesh,

---

[1] Heb. 10.1.   [2] Gen. 1.5-13.   [3] Gen. 2.8-9.   [4] Gen. 3.8.
[5] Gen. 4.16.   [6] Matt. 4.8.

which requires a great height to enable us to perceive what is below and at our feet, the kingdoms of the Persians, Scythians, Indians and Parthians were seen, and the manner in which their rulers are glorified by men? And the careful reader will detect thousands of other passages like this in the gospels, which will convince him that events which did not take place at all are woven into the records of what literally did happen. (Butterworth, *Origen on First Principles*, pp. 288–90.)

Origen's argument is that mingled with the narrative of Scripture are many things "not true, but actually absurd and impossible" (ibid., IV.3.4). These passages portray higher truths and spur on the reader to discover what the meaning is (as, e.g., in the case of Cain). Origen is however much on his guard against wantonly abandoning the literal sense of scripture: "For the passages which are historically true are far more numerous than those interwoven with them which have merely a spiritual sense" (ibid., IV.3.4). He is fully aware of the difficulty of deciding on the sense of certain passages (ibid., IV.3.5) and his answer to the difficulty is to challenge Christians to gain discernment by searching the Scriptures.

190. PORPHYRY ON THE ALLEGORICAL INTERPRETATION OF SCRIPTURE

(Porphyry, *Against the Christians*, III, quoted by Eusebius, *H.E.* VI.19.4.)

[In sections 2 and 3 of Chapter 19 Eusebius explains Porphyry's opposition to Christianity, and his acquaintance with Origen in his (Porphyry's) youth.]

Some, in their eagerness to find an explanation of the wickedness of the Jewish writings rather than give them up, had recourse to interpretations that are incompatible and do not harmonize with what has been written, resulting in approval and praise of their own, rather than in a defence of foreign, goods. For they boast that the things said plainly by Moses are riddles, treating them as divine oracles full of hidden mysteries, and bewitching the mental judgement by their own pretentious obscurity; and so they put forward their interpretations. (Lawlor and Oulton, *Eusebius*, I, p. 192.)

Porphyry's arguments against the Scriptures depended on their being accepted literally. He therefore attacked the current allegorical interpretations of the Alexandrians.

191. PORPHYRY ON ORIGEN

(From Porphyry, *Against the Christians*, III, quoted by Eusebius, *H.E.* VI.19.5–7.)

5   But this kind of absurdity must be traced to a man whom I met when I was still quite young, who had a great reputation, and still holds it, because of the writings he has left behind him, I mean Origen, whose fame has been widespread among the teachers of
6 this kind of learning. For this man was a hearer of Ammonius, who had the greatest proficiency in philosophy in our day; and so far as a grasp of knowledge was concerned he owed much to his master, but as regards the right choice in life he took the
7 opposite road to him. For Ammonius was a Christian, brought up among Christians by his parents, yet, when he began to think and study philosophy, he immediately changed his way of life conformably to the laws; but Origen, a Greek educated in Greek learning, drove headlong towards barbarian recklessness; and making straight for this he hawked himself and his literary skill about; and while his manner of life was Christian and contrary to the law, in his opinions about material things and the Deity he played the Greek, and introduced Greek ideas into foreign fables. (Lawlor and Oulton, *Eusebius*, I, p. 192, slightly altered.)

Porphyry (born *c.* 233) must have been only about twenty-two years old when Origen died. It is unlikely that he ever was a pupil of Origen or a Christian, though Socrates, *H.E.* III.23, says that he renounced Christianity after being beaten by some Caesarean Christians!

6. Ammonius Saccas was an Alexandrian philosopher who died in 243; he was the teacher of Plotinus, and was certainly not a Christian in later life.

Conversely, Origen had never been a heathen.

Eusebius insists in *H.E.* VI.19.10 that Ammonius had remained Christian. But he probably confused the Alexandrian philosopher with another Ammonius who produced a *Harmony of Moses and Jesus* (Eus. *H.E.* VI.19.10) and a *Harmony of the Gospels* (Eus., *Letter to Carpian*, *P.G.* XXII, col. 1276). He may be a bishop of Thmuis, who was, according to Photius (*Interrogatio*, IX, *P.G.*, CIV, col. 1229), deposed by Heraclas for allowing Origen, after his expulsion from Alexandria, to preach in his church.

192. ORIGEN ON THE AUTHORSHIP OF THE EPISTLE TO THE HEBREWS

(Origen in Eusebius, *H.E.* VI.25.11–14.)

11 Furthermore, he thus discusses the Epistle to the Hebrews, in his Homilies upon it:

That the character of the diction of the epistle entitled To the Hebrews has not the apostle's rudeness in speech, who confessed himself *rude in speech*,[1] that is, in style, but that the epistle is better Greek in the framing of its diction, will be admitted by everyone 12 who is able to discern differences of style. But again, on the other hand, that the thoughts of the epistle are admirable, and not inferior to the acknowledged writings of the apostle, to this also everyone will consent as true who has given attention to reading the apostle.

13 Further on, he adds the following remarks:

But as for myself, if I were to state my own opinion, I should say that the thoughts are the apostle's, but that the style and composition belong to one who called to mind the apostle's teachings and, as it were, made short notes of what his master said. If any church, therefore, holds this epistle as Paul's, let it be commended for this also. For not without reason have the men of old time 14 handed it down as Paul's. But who wrote the epistle, in truth God knows. Yet the account which has reached us [is twofold], some saying that Clement, who was bishop of the Romans, wrote the epistle, others, that it was Luke, he who wrote the Gospel and the Acts. . . . (Lawlor and Oulton, *Eusebius*, I, pp. 198–9.)

Elsewhere in his works Origen regards the Epistle as being by Paul.
Eusebius (*H.E.* VI.20.3) says that Gaius of Rome (*c.* 200) rejected the Pauline authorship and adds "even to this day among the Romans there are some who do not consider it to be the Apostle's". In VI.14.2 he gives the opinion of Clement of Alexandria that Paul wrote the Epistle in Hebrew, anonymously, as being primarily Apostle of the Gentiles, whom the Hebrews regarded with suspicion, and that Luke translated the Epistle into Greek.

[1] 2 Cor. 11.6.

193. THE MIRACLES OF JESUS

(Origen, *Against Celsus*, I.68, cf. 119 above.)

You see how by these words he (Celsus) gives his assent, as it were, to the reality of magic. I do not know whether he is the same as the man who wrote several books against magic. But because it happens to be to his advantage for his purpose he compares the stories about Jesus with tales of magic. They might have been comparable if he had first given sufficient proof of the similarity to those who employ trickery. But in fact no sorcerer uses his tricks to call the spectators to moral reformation; nor does he educate by the fear of God people who were astounded by what they saw, nor does he attempt to persuade the onlookers to live as men who will be judged by God. Sorcerers do none of these things, since they have neither the ability nor even the will to do so. Nor do they even want to have anything to do with reforming men, seeing that they themselves are filled with the most shameful and infamous sins. Is it not likely that one who used the miracles that he performed to call those who saw the happenings to moral reformation, would have shown himself as an example of the best life, not only to his genuine disciples but also to the rest? Jesus did this in order that his disciples might give themselves to teaching men according to the will of God, and that the others, who have been taught as much by his doctrine as by his moral life and miracles the right way to live, might do every action by referring to the pleasure of the supreme God. If the life of Jesus was of this character, how could anyone reasonably compare him with the behaviour of sorcerers and fail to believe that according to God's promise he was God who had appeared in a human body for the benefit of our race? (Chadwick, *Origen "Contra Celsum"*, p. 63.)

194. THE SPREAD OF CHRISTIANITY LEADS TO AMBITION IN THE CHURCH

(Origen, *Against Celsus*, III.9.)

I admit that at the present time perhaps, when on account of the multitude of people coming to the faith even rich men and persons in positions of honour, and ladies of refinement and high birth, favourably regard adherents of the faith, one might venture to say that some become leaders of the Christian teaching for the sake of a little prestige. Yet at the beginning when there was great risk attached particularly to teachers, no such suspicion could be reasonably entertained. (Chadwick, Origen "Contra Celsum", p. 134.)

On unworthy clergy, cf. Origen, ibid., III.30 (Chadwick, op. cit., p. 148) and *Comm. in Matt.* XVI.8. "In many so-called Churches, especially those in large cities, one can see rulers of the people of God who do not allow anyone, sometimes not even the noblest of Jesus' disciples, to speak with them on equal terms." (Chadwick, op. cit., p. 148, n. 1.)

195. THE TRAINING OF CHRISTIANS

(Origen, *Against Celsus*, III.51.)

But as far as they can, Christians previously examine the souls of those who want to hear them, and test them individually beforehand; when before entering the community the hearers seem to have devoted themselves sufficiently to the desire to live a good life, then they introduce them. They privately appoint one class consisting of recent beginners who are receiving elementary introduction and have not yet received the sign that they have been purified, and another class of those who, as far as they are able, make it their set purpose to desire nothing other than those things of which Christians approve. Among the latter class some are appointed to inquire into the lives and conduct of those who want to join the community in order that they may prevent those who indulge in secret sins from coming to their common gathering; those who do not do this they whole-heartedly receive, and make them better every day. (Chadwick, Origen "Contra Celsum", p. 163.)

196. THE TREATMENT OF LAPSED CHRISTIANS

(Origen, *Against Celsus*, III.51.)

But Christians mourn as dead men those who have been overcome by licentiousness or some outrageous sin because they have perished and died to God. They admit them some time later as though they had risen from the dead provided that they show a real conversion, though their period of probation is longer than that required of those who are joining the community for the first time. But they do not select those who have fallen after their conversion to Christianity for any office or administration in the

Church of God, as it is called. (Chadwick, *Origen "Contra Celsum"*, pp. 163–4.)

On this subject, cf. 158. Celsus described the Christian penitential system: "the humble man humiliates himself in a disgraceful and undignified manner, throwing himself head-long to the ground upon his knees, clothing himself in a beggar's rags, and heaping dust upon himself". (Chadwick, op. cit., p. 328.)

they do not select those who have fallen: Cyprian, *Ep.* LXVII.8 (217), in dealing with the lapsed Spanish Bishops states it as a rule that lapsed clergy may be admitted to penance, but not to any clerical office, cf. also *Ep.* LXXII.2.

197. CHRISTIANITY AND THE DEFENCE OF THE EMPIRE

(Origen, *Against Celsus*, VIII.73, cf. 122 above.)

We would also say this to those who are alien to our faith and ask us to fight for the community and to kill men: that it is also your opinion that the priests of certain images and wardens of the temples of the gods, as you think them to be, should keep their right hand undefiled for the sake of the sacrifices, that they may offer the customary sacrifices to those who you say are gods with hands unstained by blood and pure from murders. And in fact when war comes you do not enlist the priests. If, then, this is reasonable, how much more reasonable is it that, while others fight, Christians also should be fighting as priests and worshippers of God, keeping their right hands pure and by their prayers to God striving for those who fight in a righteous cause and for the emperor who reigns righteously, in order that everything which is opposed and hostile to those who act rightly may be destroyed? Moreover, we who by our prayers destroy all daemons which stir up wars, violate oaths, and disturb the peace, are of more help to the emperors than those who seem to be doing the fighting. We who offer prayers with righteousness, together with ascetic practices and exercises which teach us to despise pleasures and not to be led by them, are cooperating in the tasks of the community. Even more do we fight on behalf of the emperor. And though we do not become fellow-soldiers with him, even if he presses for this, yet we are fighting for him and composing a special army of piety through our intercessions to God. (Chadwick, *Origen "Contra Celsum"*, p. 509.)

On Christians and military service, cf. 23.

198. CHRISTIANITY AND CIVIL SERVICE

(Origen, *Against Celsus*, VIII.75.)

If Christians do avoid these responsibilities, it is not with the motive of shirking the public services of life. But they keep themselves for a more divine and necessary service in the church of God for the sake of the salvation of men. Here it is both necessary and right for them to be leaders and to be concerned about all men, both those who are within the Church, that they may live better every day, and those who appear to be outside it, that they may become familiar with the sacred words and acts of worship; and that, offering a true worship to God in this way and instructing as many as possible, they may become absorbed in the word of God and the divine law, and so be united to the supreme God through the Son of God, the Logos, Wisdom, Truth, and Righteousness, who unites to Him every one who has been persuaded to live according to God's will in all things. (Chadwick, *Origen "Contra Celsum"*, p. 510.)

Soon after Origen wrote, Christians were freely accepting civil offices, cf. 265, pp. 305–6.

199. THE FAULTS OF UNLETTERED CHRISTIANS

(Origen, *Homilies on Psalm XXXVI*, 5.1.)

Watch this only, brethren, that no one of you be found not only not speaking or meditating wisdom, but even hating and opposing those who pursue the study of wisdom. The ignorant, among other faults, have this worst fault of all, that of regarding those who have devoted themselves to the word and teaching as vain and useless; they prefer their own ignorance to the study and toil of the learned, and by changing titles they call the exercises of the teachers verbiage, but their own unteachableness or ignorance, simplicity.

The intellectual Christianity of Alexandria affected only a few Christians. Clement makes similar complaints.

200. *LIBELLI* OF THE PERSECUTION OF DECIUS, 250

(Text in *Harvard Theological Review*, 16 (1923), pp. 363ff.)

1   *1st Hand.* To the commission chosen to superintend the sacrifices at the village of Alexander's Isle. From Aurelius Diogenes, son of Satabous, of the village of Alexander's Isle, aged 72 years, with a scar on the right eyebrow. I have always sacrificed to the gods, and now in your presence in accordance with the edict I have made sacrifice, and poured a libation, and partaken of the sacred victims. I request you to certify this below. Farewell. I, Aurelius Diogenes, have presented this petition.

2d Hand. I, Aurelius Syrus, saw you and your son sacrificing.

3d Hand. . . . onos . . .

1st Hand. The year one of the Emperör Caesar Gaius Messius Quintus Trajanus Decius Pius Felix Augustus, Epeiph 2 (June 26, 250). (J. R. Knipfing, *Harvard Theological Review*, loc. cit., p. 363, slightly altered.)

2   To the commission chosen to superintend the sacrifices. From Aurelia Ammonous, daughter of Mystus, of the Moeris quarter, priestess of the god Petesouchos, the great, the mighty, the immortal, and priestess of the gods in the Moeris quarter. I have sacrificed to the gods all my life, and now again, in accordance with the decree and in your presence, I have made sacrifice, and poured a libation, and partaken of the sacred victims. I request you to certify this below. (J. R. Knipfing, *Harvard Theological Review*, loc. cit., p. 365, slightly altered.)

All the extant *libelli*, some of which exist only in fragments, come from Egypt. The *libelli* vary slightly in form. Knipfing, loc. cit., writes, "A complete, though hypothetical, text of such a *libellus*, the composite result of a combination of the data of our forty-one texts, would read somewhat as follows:

1st Hand. To the commission of . . . chosen to superintend the (sacred offerings and) sacrifices. From . . . son (*or* daughter) of . . . (and of . . .) (together with his brother and their wives) (and his children), who comes from the village of . . . (in the division of . . .), and is domiciled in the village of . . . (*or* in the . . . quarter of the city) (*or* dwelling beyond the town gates), (aged . . . years with a scar on the right eyebrow) (and member of the household of . . ., who functioned as exegete in the famous city of Alexandria, not to mention the offices he now holds) (*or* priestess of the god Petesouchos the great, the mighty, the immortal, and priestess of the gods in the . . . quarter). I (*or* we) have always and (all my life) without interruption sacrificed and poured libations and manifested piety toward the gods (in accordance with the divine decree), and now (again) in your presence in accordance with the edict, I (*or* we) have made sacrifice and poured a libation (*or* poured a libation and sacrificed) and partaken of the sacred victims (in company with my wife and children) (acting through me). (Wherefore I present this petition and) I (*or* we) request you to certify this (for me, *or* for us) below. Farewell. I (*or* we) have presented this petition (aged . . . and injured) (*or* aged . . .) (and I . . . wrote in his behalf, for he is illiterate) (*or* 2d hand, I . . . presented this petition, I . . . signed for him since he is illiterate).

2d Hand. I . . . (prytanis) (and I . . .) saw you sacrificing (together with your son, *or* sons).

3d Hand. I . . . have signed.

1st Hand. The year one of the Emperor Caesar Gaius Messius Quintus Trajanus Decius Pius Felix Augustus, June 12 (*or any date thereafter up to July 14*).

The second of the *libelli* given above shows that pagans, who *could be under no suspicion of being Christians*, had to secure *libelli*. The priestess has added the words "all my life" to emphasize her declaration.

201. THE WORLDLINESS OF CHRISTIANS
c. 250

(Cyprian, *De lapsis*, 5,6 (*C.S.E.L.*, III.1.240f.).)

5 . . . If we apprehend the cause of our losses, we have then a remedy for the blow. It has pleased the Lord to prove His family; and as a long period of peace had corrupted the discipline which had come down to us from Him, the divine judgement awakened our faith from a declining, and, should I so speak, an almost slumbering state; and whereas we deserved yet more for our sins, the most merciful Lord has so moderated all, that what has passed has seemed rather a trial of what we were, than an actual infliction.

6 Individuals were applying themselves to the increase of wealth; and forgetting both what was the conduct of believers under the Apostles, and what ought to be their conduct in every age, they

with insatiable eagerness for gain devoted themselves to the multiplying of possessions. The bishops were wanting in religious devotedness, the ministers in entireness of faith; there was no mercy in works, no discipline in manners. Men wore their beards disfigured, and the beauty of women was counterfeit. The eyes were changed from what God made them, and a lying colour was passed upon the hair. The hearts of the simple were misled by treacherous artifices, and brethren became entangled in seductive snares; ties of marriage were formed with unbelievers; members of Christ prostituted to the heathen. Not only rash swearing was heard, but even false; persons in high place were swollen with contemptuousness, poisoned reproaches fell from their mouths, and men were sundered by unabating quarrels. Numerous bishops, who ought to be an encouragement and example to others, despising their sacred ministry, engaged themselves in secular vocations, relinquished their Chair, deserted their people, strayed among foreign provinces, hunted the markets for mercantile profits; tried to amass large sums of money, while they had brethren starving within the church, took possession of estates by fraudulent proceedings, and multiplied their gains by accumulated usuries. (L. F., altered.)

5. *a long period of peace*: as far as Africa is concerned, this had lasted from c. 215 onwards.

6. bishops: *sacerdotes*, as usually in Cyprian.

ties of marriage were formed with unbelievers: cf. 19 above, 274 below (Arles can. 12(11)).

engaged themselves in secular vocations (rerum): with the other reading, *regum*, the meaning is, "became ministers of the kings of this world"

202. MASS APOSTASY AT CARTHAGE, 250

(Cyprian, *De lapsis*, 8,9 (*C.S.E.L.*, III.1.242f.).)

8   Alas! there are those, from whom all this is fallen and passed out of memory. They did not even wait to be arrested before they went up, or questioned before they made their denial. Many fell before the fight, many were laid low without meeting the enemy; they did not even give themselves the chance of seeming unwilling to sacrifice to the idols. They ran to the market-place of their own accord, they hasted to death of their own will; as if they had always wished it, as if embracing an opportunity, which they had fervently desired. How many the magistrates put off at the time, as night was at hand! How many who even entreated that their undoing might not be delayed! How can any one make violence

an excuse for his guilt, when the violence was rather on his own part and to his own destruction? When they came, thus willingly, to the Capitol, when they spontaneously submitted themselves to the commission of that dreadful deed, was there no tottering in the limbs, no blackness upon the face, no quaking of the stomach and collapse of the limbs? Did not the senses die, the tongue cleave, and speech fail? Could the servant of God stand there, and speak and renounce Christ, he who before had renounced the Devil and the world? The altar where he went to perish, was it not his funeral pile? Ought he not to shudder at and flee from an altar of the Devil which he had seen in the smoke and redolence of its vile odour, as from the death and sepulchre of his existence? Why bring an offering with you, wretched man, why present a victim? You are yourself an offering at the altar, you are yourself come as a victim; you have slaughtered there your own salvation, your hope; your faith was burnt in those funeral flames.

9   Many, however, were unsatisfied with doing destruction upon themselves; men were urged to their ruin by mutual encouragements, and the fatal cup of death was offered from mouth to mouth. That nothing might be wanting to their load of guilt, even infants in their parents' arms, carried or led, were deprived, while yet tender, of what was granted them in the commencement of life. Will not these children in the day of judgement say: "We did no sin; it was not our will to hasten from the Bread and Cup of the Lord, to an unhallowed pollution. We perish through the treachery of others, and our parents on earth have robbed us of our parentage in heaven: they forfeited for us the Church as a Mother, and God as a Father, and thus, while young and unaware and ignorant of that monstrous act, we are included in a league of sin by others, and perish through their deceit." (L. F., altered.)

203. THE LETTER OF THE CONFESSORS, WRITTEN BY LUCIAN

(Cyprian, *Ep.* XXIII (*C.S.E.L.* III.2.536.).)

Know that we have granted peace to, all of whose behaviour, since the commission of their crime, you are satisfied; and we desire, through you, to make this known to other Bishops also. We wish you to maintain peace with the holy martyrs. Lucian wrote this; there being present of the clergy an exorcist and a reader. (L. F.)

This policy of the confessors was destructive of episcopal authority.

204. THE *LIBELLI PACIS*, 250–251

(Cyprian, *Ep.* XXVII, 1,2 (*C.S.E.L.* III.2.540f.).)

1   Since my former epistle to you, dearest brethren, in which my conduct was explained, and an account given of my discipline and diligence, such as they are, something else has happened, of which also you ought not to be uninformed. For our brother Lucian, himself also one of the confessors, glowing indeed in faith and strong in courage, but insufficiently grounded in the reading of the word of the Lord, has stupidly attempted certain things, making himself for some while past an authority, in that letters written in his hand have been given to many persons indiscriminately, in the name of Paulus. Whereas Mappalicus the martyr, being cautious and modest, regardful of the law and discipline, gave no letter contrary to the Gospel, but, moved by domestic piety, recommended only that peace should be granted to his mother and sister, who had lapsed; Saturninus also, being still in prison after torture, issued no letter of that sort. But Lucian, not only while Paulus was still in prison, gave letters in his name indiscriminately written with his own hand; but even after his decease, continued to do the same in his name, saying that he had been ordered to do so by Paulus; not knowing that the Lord must rather be obeyed than the fellow-servant. In the name of Aurelius too, a youth who had endured torture, many certificates have been given, written by the hand of the same Lucian, because Aurelius did not know how to write.

2   To check this practice in some degree, I wrote a letter which I sent to you under cover of my last Epistle; wherein I did not fail to beg and persuade them to have regard to the law of the Lord and to the Gospel. But after I had sent this letter to them, as though something was being done, more moderately and temperately, the same Lucian wrote a letter in the name of all the Confessors, whereby the whole bond of faith, and the fear of God, and the commandment of the Lord, and the sanctity and strength of the Gospel, were well-nigh dissolved. For he wrote in the name of all, that they had granted peace to all, and that they wished this sentence to be notified through me to other Bishops, a copy of which letter I have transmitted to you. There is added indeed, "of whose behaviour since the commission of their crime you are satisfied". This stirs up greater odium against me, in that when I have begun to hear and examine the cases of individuals,

I must seem to deny to many, what all now insist that they have received from the martyrs and confessors. (L. F.)

3   [Cyprian goes on to show the threatening attitude of the confessors and the lapsed both to himself and to other bishops, some of whom were terrified into acquiescence.]

2. For the letter of Lucian see 203.

205. CYPRIAN'S PROPOSALS TO THE CHURCH OF CARTHAGE ABOUT THE LAPSED, 250

(Cyprian, *Ep.* XVII. 1-3 (*C.S.E.L.* III.2.521ff.).)

1   [Cyprian writes "to his brethren of the laity who stand fast in the faith". He expresses the grief over, and sympathy with the lapsed which both he and his correspondents feel, but] ". . . we I think must not be hasty, nor do any thing incautiously or hurriedly; lest the rash seizure of reconciliation provoke the divine displeasure the more heavily.

. . . The blessed martyrs have written to me about certain persons, requesting that their desires may be considered. When peace is first given to us all by the Lord, and we have begun to return to the Church, each case shall be examined in your presence and with the aid of your judgement.

2   I hear, however, that some of the presbyters, neither mindful of the Gospel nor considering what the martyrs have written to me, nor reserving to the Bishop the honour due to his priesthood and chair, have already begun to communicate with the lapsed and to offer the oblation for them, and to give them the Eucharist; whereas they ought by a due course to attain hereto. For since, in lesser offences, which are not committed against 'God, penance is done for an appointed time, and confession made, with inquiry into the life of him who is doing penance, nor may any come to communion, except hands shall first have been laid on him by the bishop and clergy, how much more in these most grievous and extremest sins, ought all things to be observed with caution and reserve, according to the discipline of the Lord! This our presbyters and deacons ought indeed to have advised you, that so they might tend the sheep committed to them, and instruct them in the way of attaining salvation according to the divine appointment. I know both the meekness and the fear of our people, that

they would have been watchful in appeasing and deprecating the
wrath of God, had not certain of the presbyters, in order to please,
deceived them.

3   Do then even you guide them individually, and by your advice
and restraint temper the minds of the lapsed in accordance with
the divine precepts. Let no one gather prematurely a bitter fruit.
Let no one before he has carefully repaired it, again entrust to
the deep his ship shattered and broken by the waves. Let no one
hasten to recover and put on a tattered garment until he has seen
it mended by a skilful workman, and received it dressed from the
hands of the fuller. I pray they may listen patiently to our advice,
and await our return, that when, by the mercy of God, we shall
come unto you, having summoned many of my colleagues, we
may, after the discipline of the Lord and, in the presence of the confessors, and of your judgements, examine the letters and requests
of the blessed martyrs. On this subject I have written to the
clergy and to the martyrs and confessors, both which epistles I
have ordered to be read to you. (L. F., altered.)

206. AN INSTRUCTION FROM CYPRIAN
TO THE CLERGY OF CARTHAGE

(Cyprian, *Ep.* XVIII.1–2 (*C.S.E.L.* III.2.523f.).)

1   [Cyprian begins by complaining that he has not received replies
to many letters that he had sent. He goes on to instruct the
clergy (he now appears to be writing to those who had remained
faithful to him) as to what they must do with lapsed persons in a
particular case.]

. . . Since I see that there is as yet no opening for my coming
to you, and summer has already begun, a season troubled with
continual and severe sicknesses, I think that the cases of our brethren should be met; so that those who have received letters from
the martyrs, and may be helped by their privilege with God, if
they are seized with any ailment or danger of sickness, may
without waiting for my presence make confession of their sin
before any presbyter at hand, or if a presbyter shall not be found,
and death approaches, then even before a deacon; that so, receiving
imposition of hands unto repentance, they may go to the Lord
with that peace which the martyrs in their letters to me have
requested for them.

2   The rest of the people too that have lapsed, do you cherish

by your presence: and that they abandon not the faith and the Lord's mercy, do you cheer them by your consolation; for neither, if, meek and humble and truly doing penance, they shall continue in good works, will they be left without the help and aid of the Lord, so that they too shall not be helped by divine remedies. To the catechumens also, should any be overtaken by sudden danger, and be near their end, let not your vigilance be wanting, nor let the mercy of the Lord be denied to them that implore the Divine grace. (L. F., altered.)

This letter shows that Cyprian never intended to take up a rigorist position. In his next letter to his clergy (XIX) he has to repeat his instructions as they were harassed by the solicitations of the lapsed.

Cyprian made a great point of being at one with the Roman church in the treatment of the lapsed, cf. *Ep.* XX.3 (209).

207. CYPRIAN'S DEFENCE OF HIS RETIRE-MENT FROM CARTHAGE IN PERSECUTION

(Cyprian, *Ep.* XX.1 (*C.S.E.L.* VIII.2.527.).)

Cyprian to his brethren the Presbyters and Deacons assembled at Rome, greeting.

1   Whereas I have learnt, dearest brethren, that what I have done, and am now doing, has been reported to you in a somewhat garbled and untruthful manner, I have thought it necessary to write this Epistle to you, wherein an account might be given you of my acts, discipline and diligence. For, as the commandments of the Lord direct, as soon as the first onset of disturbance arose and the populace with violent clamour demanded me, I, not regarding so much my own safety, as the general quiet of the brethren, withdrew for a while; lest, by my obstinate presence, the sedition which had begun should be further provoked. Yet, though *absent in body*, neither *in spirit*,[1] nor act, nor advice was I wanting, so as to fail to consult for my brethren to the best of my poor ability, wherein I could, according to the injunctions of the Lord. (L. F., altered from A.-N. C. L.)

[Cyprian goes on to deal with the number of his letters sent for the direction of his flock during his absence, letters that he had already transmitted to Rome.]

[1] 1 Cor. 5.3.

Cyprian's retirement had contrasted unfavourably, in the eyes of the Roman clergy, with the martyrdom of their own bishop Fabian, and led to the abrupt and censorious Roman letter (*Ep.* VIII in Cyprian's correspondence), in the genuineness of which Cyprian could hardly at first believe (*Ep.* IX.2):

> I have also read an Epistle, wherein it is not plainly expressed, either who wrote it, or to whom it was written. And whereas in the same Epistle as well the writing, as its purport, and the very paper itself, led me to suspect that something had either been taken from it, or altered in it; I have sent back to you the very Epistle itself, that you may ascertain whether it be the same which you gave to Crementius the subdeacon to carry: for it is a very serious matter, if the truth of a clerical Epistle has been corrupted by any falsehood or fraud. That we may know this therefore, examine whether the writing and subscription is yours; and write me word what the truth is. (L. F., slightly altered.)

Later however relations became cordial, cf. *Epp.* XXX, XXXI, XXV–XXVII.

208. AFRICAN DOUBTS ABOUT CORNELIUS OF ROME, 251

(Cyprian, *Ep.* XLV.3 (*C.S.E.L.* III.2.602.).)

Cyprian was just about to hold a council on his return to Carthage when letters arrived from Cornelius announcing his election as Bishop of Rome, and from Novatian protesting against this election. In view of the discrepant tone of the two communications he allowed only that of Cornelius to be read to the Council, but the authority of the sender of the other missive ("when such things were written to me against you, coming from a presbyter who sits along with you" (loc. cit. 2)) he took the precaution of sending emissaries to Rome to find out what had happened from bishops who had been present at the consecration.

3 But whereas we wished for written communications from our colleagues who were present at your ordination, we were not forgetful of the ancient practice, nor sought anything new: for it were enough that you by letters announced that you were made Bishop, had there not been a dissentient faction on the opposite side, who by their slanderous and calumnious fictions disturbed the minds and perplexed the hearts of many, as well of our colleagues as of our brethren. For composing which matter, we

deemed it necessary to obtain thence in writing the sure and substantial authority of our colleagues; who in their letters setting forth testimonials worthy of your conversation and life and discipline, have taken away even·from your rivals and from such as delight either in novel or crooked ways, every pretence of doubt or dissent; and according to my advice, pondered over with sound thought, the minds of the brethren, who were tossed on this sea, have sincerely and stedfastly approved your priesthood. (L. F., slightly altered.)

priesthood (*sacerdotium*): "Throughout the letters of Cyprian the bishop is more frequently called *sacerdos* than *episcopus*" (Benson, *Cyprian*, p. 35n.).

209. CYPRIAN AND THE ROMAN CHURCH

(Cyprian, *Ep.* XX.2–3 (*C.S.E.L.* III.2.527f.).)

This continues the letter of which section 1 is given in 207.

2   [Cyprian explains that he had forwarded thirteen of his letters dealing with the lapsed to Rome: these covered his whole policy and showed that he had distributed advice, exhortation and reproof, as necessary. As the situation worsened, owing to the importunity of the lapsed and the susceptibility of the confessors, which led to the issue of "thousands" of *libelli pacis*, he had checked the rashness of certain clergy who were accepting the lapsed into communion, and calmed the people as far as he could.]

3   But afterwards, when some of the lapsed, either of their own accord, or at some one's instigation, broke out into bold demands, so as to endeavour to extort by violence the peace promised them by the Martyrs and Confessors, I twice wrote on this subject also to the Clergy, and ordered my Epistles to be read to them directing, if so I might in some measure mitigate their violence at present, that any who, having received letters from the Martyrs, were departing this life, should, having confessed and received imposition of hands unto repentance, be remitted to the Lord with the peace promised them by the Martyrs. Nor in this did I lay down a law, or rashly make myself its author. (L. F., altered.)

In this letter we see an example of Cyprian's diligence in circulating his correspondence to parties who ought to know its content, and of his anxiety that Rome and Carthage should "keep in step" in ecclesiastical policy.

210. THE DECISIONS OF THE COUNCIL OF CARTHAGE, JUNE 251

(Cyprian, *Ep.* LV.6,17,23 (*C.S.E.L.* III.2.627f.; 635f.; 641f.).)

6   However, according to what had been before determined, when the persecution was lulled, and opportunity given for meeting together, a large number of us bishops whom our own faith and the protection of the Lord had preserved uninjured and safe, met together and, the divine Scriptures being adduced on both sides, we balanced our resolution with wholesome moderation; so that neither should hope of communion and peace be altogether denied to the lapsed, lest through desperation they should fall away still further, and, because the Church was shut against them, following the world, should live as heathens; nor yet on the other hand should evangelical strictness be relaxed, so that they might rush in haste to communion; but that penance should be long protracted, and the Fatherly clemency entreated with mourning, and the cases and purposes and exigencies of each be examined; as is expressed in a tract [*sc.* the *De lapsis*] which I trust has reached you, where the several heads of our determinations are collected together. And lest the number of bishops in Africa should seem insufficient, we wrote to Rome also on this subject to our colleague Cornelius, who himself likewise in a Council held with very many of our fellow-bishops, agreed in the same opinion with us, with like solemnity and wholesome moderation.

* * *

17   But since there is in them what by subsequent penitence may revive . . . it was determined . . . that the cases of each being examined, takers of certificates [*libellatici*] be for the time admitted; that to those who have sacrificed [*sacrificati*] relief should be given in their last moments because *in the grave there is no confession,*[1] nor can any one be urged by us to penitence, if the fruit of penitence is withdrawn. Should the battle first come, strengthened by us he will be found armed for the battle; but should sickness press upon him before the battle, he departs with the consolation of peace and communion.

* * *

23   . . . The Lord in the Gospel pronounces *them that mourn blessed,*[2]

[1] Ps. 6.5.   [2] Matt. 5.4.

because he who mourns invites mercy; he who is froward and proud, heaps up wrath against himself and punishment in the judgement to come. Wherefore ... we have determined, that they who do not repent nor testify sorrow for their sins with all their heart and with open profession of their grief, are to be altogether forbidden the hope of communion and peace, if in sickness and peril they begin to entreat for it; because not repentance for sin, but the warning of impending death, compels them to ask, nor does he deserve to receive solace in death, who has not thought that he should die. (L. F., slightly altered.)

The whole of the long letter of Cyprian to Antonian, from which the above three paragraphs are taken, should be read, as it recapitulates the history of the controversy. The letter was written soon after the Council, which sat from April to June 251. Another passage from this letter, dealing with Cornelius of Rome, will be found in 211.

211. THE CHARACTER OF CORNELIUS: HIS ELECTION TO THE SEE OF ROME, 251

(Cyprian, *Ep.* LV.8 (*C.S.E.L.* III.2.629.).)

8   I come now, dearest brother, to the character of Cornelius our colleague; that you, with us, may more truly know Cornelius, not from the lies of malignants and detractors, but from the judgement of the Lord God, Who made him a bishop, and from the testimony of his fellow-bishops, the whole number of whom throughout the world have unanimously agreed. For—which with praise and honour commends our beloved Cornelius to God and Christ and His Church, and also to all his fellow-priests (i.e. bishops)—he did not on a sudden arrive at the episcopate, but promoted through all ecclesiastical offices, and having often deserved well of the Lord in divine services, he mounted to the lofty summit of the priesthood, along all the steps of holy duty. Moreover, as for the episcopate itself, he neither himself asked nor wished for it, nor as others [*sc.* Novatian] whom the swelling of their own arrogance and pride inflates, seized it; but quiet in all respects and meek, and such as they are wont to be, who are chosen of God to this office, agreeably to the retirement of his virgin-continency, and to the humility of his innate and well guarded modesty, he does not, as some, use violence to be made a bishop; but himself suffered violence so as to receive the episcopate by compulsion. And he was made bishop by very many of

our colleagues then present in the city of Rome, who sent to us letters touching his ordination, remarkable for their high and honourable testimony and praise. Cornelius, moreover, was made bishop by the judgement of God and His Christ, by the testimony of almost all the clergy, by the suffrages of the people who were then present, and by the college of venerable bishops and good men; at a time when no one had been made before him, when the place of Fabian, i.e. when the place of Peter, and the rank of the sacerdotal chair was vacant. This, therefore, being filled by the will of God, and ratified by the consent of all of us, whosoever would thenceforth be made bishop [sc. of Rome, i.e. Novatian], must necessarily be made outside [sc. the Church]; nor can he have ordination of the Church, who does not maintain the unity of the Church. (L. F., altered.)

212. NOVATUS

(Cyprian, *Ep.* LII.1–2 (*C.S.E.L.* III.2.617f.).)

1   [This letter of Cyprian to Cornelius of Rome was a reply to a letter from the latter (*Ep.* L). Cyprian recapitulates what had happened at Carthage some time previously. Novatus had, according to Cyprian, been a thorn in the flesh of previous bishops of Carthage, and only escaped excommunication by the outbreak of the Decian persecution. Before this he had been one of the presbyters who had opposed Cyprian's election. After the persecution he became a leader of the lax party, and then proceeded to Rome where paradoxically he allied himself with, and influenced Novatian.]

2   For of Novatus no news need have been sent from you to us, but rather he should have been made known by us to you, as one ever eager for innovation, frantic with the rapacity of an insatiable avarice, puffed up with the arrogance and stupor of swelling pride, always known for evil to the Bishops here, ever, as a heretic and perfidious, condemned by the voice of the whole priesthood; ever inquisitive in order to betray; a flatterer, to the end that he may deceive; never faithful to love; a torch and fire-brand to light up the flames of sedition; a whirlwind and tempest to make shipwrecks of faith; a foe to quiet; an adversary to tranquillity; an enemy to peace. Lastly, when Novatus departed from among you, that is, when the storm and whirlwind departed, a calm in part succeeded there, and glorious and good confessors who had left

the Church at his instigation, returned to the Church after he had
left the city. It is the same Novatus, who amongst us scattered the
first flames of discord and schism, who separated some of the
brethren here from their bishop, who, amid the very persecution,
was to ours as another persecution in overthrowing the minds of
the brethren. He it is who, without my permission or knowledge,
of his own factiousness and ambition made Felicissimus his follower deacon, and sailed on the storm that he bears with him to
Rome also to overthrow the Church; he there contrived similar
and like plots, rending a portion of the laity from the clergy,
cleaving asunder the concord of the brotherhood who were
closely knit together and mutually loved each other. In short, as
Rome from her greatness ought to have precedency of Carthage,
there he committed greater and more grievous crimes. He who
here made a deacon against the Church, there made a bishop
[*sc.* Novatian]. (L. F.)

Cornelius had informed Cyprian that Novatus, accompanied by various
other doubtful characters, had gone back to Carthage. We know nothing of
his subsequent career.

213. ROME AND THE CARTHAGINIAN DISSIDENTS

(Cyprian, *Ep.* LIX.9,14 (*C.S.E.L.* III.2.676–7,683–4).)

The theme of Cyprian's long letter LIX to Cornelius of Rome is the conduct of his opponents at Carthage, who had set up a pseudo-bishop
Fortunatus, consecrated by a group of five heretical and lapsed bishops. Maximus, a Novatianist envoy, had also been created a bishop at Carthage.

9   But that I did not write to you on the instant, dearest brother,
concerning that Fortunatus the pseudo-bishop, set up by a few,
and those inveterate heretics, the matter was not of such moment
as must needs forthwith and in haste be brought to your knowledge, as though it were great and formidable; especially since
you were already enough acquainted with the name of Fortunatus,
who is one of the five presbyters some time since renegade from
the Church, and lately excommunicated by the sentence of our
fellow-Bishops, many and most grave persons, who wrote to
you on this subject during the past year. You would also recognize
Felicissimus, the standard-bearer of sedition, who is also found in
the same letter sent to you long since by our fellow-Bishops;
who was not only excommunicated by them here, but has lately

been expelled from the Church by you at Rome. Confident that these things were well known to you, and being assured that they had a fixed place in your memory and rule, I did not think it necessary to announce to you with speed and urgency the follies of heretics. For it pertains neither to the majesty nor the dignity of the Catholic Church to be concerned as to the things which the shameless boldness of heretics and schismatics compass among themselves. For Novatian's party also are reported to have made just now Maximus the presbyter, who was lately sent to us as legate from Novatian and rejected from our communion, their pseudo-bishop in these parts; yet I did not write to you about this, because all these things are lightly regarded by us, and I had very recently sent to you the names of the Bishops appointed in these parts, who, in soundness and entireness of faith, preside over the brethren in the Catholic Church. And this, by common consent, we therefore thought good to write to you, that it might be a compendious method for removing error and ascertaining truth, and that you and our colleagues might know to whom to write, and from whom you should receive letters in return; but if any one beside those, whom we included in our letter, should dare to write to you, you should know that he was either polluted by sacrifice or certificate, or that he was one of the heretics, and so perverted and profane.

*   *   *

14   For these too it was not enough to have departed from the Gospel, to have deprived the lapsed of the hope of satisfaction and penance, to have withdrawn those entangled in frauds or stained with adulteries, or polluted by the deadly contagion of sacrifices, from every feeling or fruit of repentance, that they entreat not God, nor make confession of their crimes in the Church; nor yet to have set up for themselves, without the Church and against the Church, a conventicle of their abandoned faction, whither there might stream together a troop of persons of evil consciences who would not entreat and make satisfaction to God. After all this, they yet, in addition, having had a pseudo-Bishop ordained for them by heretics, dare to set sail, and to carry letters from schismatic and profane persons to the chair of Peter, and to the principal Church, whence the unity of the priesthood (i.e. episcopate) took its rise, remembering not that they are the same Romans, whose faith has been commended by the Apostle,[1] to whom faithlessness can have no access.

[1] Rom. 1.8.

But what is the occasion of their going to you, and of their announcing that a pseudo-bishop has been set up against the Bishops? For either they are well pleased with what they have done, and persevere in their wickedness: or if it displeases them and they withdraw, they know whither they should return. For since it has been decreed by our whole body, and is alike equitable and just, that the case of each several person should be there heard where the offence has been committed; and a portion of the flock has been assigned to individual shepherds, which each several one is to rule and govern, having hereafter to give account of his ministry to the Lord; it therefore behoves those over whom we are set, not to run about from place to place, nor, by their crafty and deceitful boldness, break the harmonious concord of Bishops, but there to plead their cause, where they will have both accusers and witnesses of their crime; unless perhaps some few desperate and abandoned men count as inferior the authority of the Bishops appointed in Africa, who have already given judgement concerning them, and have lately by the weight of their judgement condemned those persons' consciences, entangled in the bonds of many sins. Already has their cause been heard: already has sentence been given concerning them, nor does it accord with the authority of Bishops to incur blame for the levity of a changeable and inconstant mind, since the Lord teaches us, and says, *Let your communication be, Yea, yea, Nay, nay.*[1] (L. F., slightly altered.)

14. *the chair of Peter, and to the principal Church (principalis ecclesia)*: *principalis* is rendered by some as "sovereign", by others as "first in order of time", cf., e.g., Giles, *Documents illustrating Papal Authority*, pp. 61-2, Batiffol, *Cathedra Petri*, Ch. V, Ecclesia Principalis.

The church was much exercised by the facility with which persons condemned in one province sought rehabilitation in another, cf., e.g., Canon 5 of Nicaea (300, p. 359).

214. THE UNITY OF THE CHURCH

(Cyprian, *On the Unity of the Catholic Church*, 4-6 (C.S.E.L. III.1.212-15).)

4   If any one consider and weigh this, he will not need length of comment or argument. It is easy to offer proofs to a faithful mind, because in that case the truth may be quickly stated. The Lord speaks to Peter, *I say unto thee*, He says, *that thou art Peter, and upon this rock I will build my Church, and the gates of hell shall not prevail against it. And I will give unto thee the Keys of the Kingdom of heaven,*

[1] Matt. 5.37.

and whatsoever thou shalt bind on earth, shall be bound also in heaven, and whatsoever thou shalt loose on earth shall be loosed in heaven.[1] Upon him, being one, He builds His Church; and though He gives to all the Apostles an equal power, and says, *As my Father sent me, even so send I you; receive ye the Holy Ghost: whosesoever sins ye remit, they shall be remitted to him and whosesoever sins ye retain, they shall be retained*[2]:—yet in order to manifest unity, He has by His own authority so placed the source of the same unity, as to begin from one. Certainly, the other Apostles also were what Peter was, endued with an equal fellowship both of honour and power; but a commencement is made from unity, that the Church may be set before us as one: this one Church in the Song of Songs, the Holy Spirit designs and names in the person of our Lord: *My dove, my spotless one, is but one; she is the only one of her mother, elect of her that bare her.*[3] He who holds not this unity of the Church, does he think that he holds the faith? He who strives against and resists the Church, is he assured that he is in the Church? For the blessed Apostle Paul teaches this same thing, and manifests the sacrament of unity, thus speaking: *There is one body, and one Spirit even as ye are called in one hope of your calling; one Lord, one faith, one baptism, one God.*[4]

5   This unity firmly should we hold and maintain, especially we bishops, presiding in the Church, in order that we may approve the episcopate itself to be one and undivided. Let no one deceive the brotherhood by falsehood; no one corrupt our faith in the truth by a faithless treachery. The episcopate is one; it is a whole in which each bishop enjoys full possession. The Church is likewise one, though she be spread abroad, and multiplies with the increase of her progeny: even as the sun has rays many, yet one light; and the tree, boughs many, yet its strength is one, seated in the deep-lodged root; and as when many streams flow down from one source, though a multiplicity of waters seems to be diffused from the bountifulness of the overflowing abundance, unity is preserved in the source itself. Part a ray of the sun from its orb, and its unity forbids this division of light; break a branch from the tree, once broken it can bud no more; cut the stream from its fountain, the remnant will be dried up. Thus the Church, flooded with the light of the Lord, puts forth her rays through the whole world, with yet one light which is spread upon all places, where "the unity of orb" is not infringed. She stretches forth her branches over the universal earth, in her riches of plenty, and pours abroad her bountiful and onward streams; yet is there one head, one source, one Mother, abundant in the results of her fruitfulness.

[1] Matt. 16.18ff.   [2] John 20.21f.   [3] Cant. 6.8.   [4] Eph. 4.14f.

It is of her womb that we are born; our nourishing is from her milk; our quickening from her breath.

6   The spouse of Christ cannot become an adulteress. She is undefiled and chaste; owning but one home, and guarding with virtuous modesty the sanctity of one chamber. She it is who keeps us for God, and appoints unto the Kingdom the sons she has borne. Whosoever parts company with the Church, and joins himself to an adulteress, is estranged from the promises of the Church. He who leaves the Church of Christ, attains not to Christ's rewards. He is an alien, an outcast, an enemy. He can no longer have God for a Father, who has not the Church for a mother. If any man was able to escape who was outside the ark of Noah, then will that man escape who is out of doors beyond the Church. (L. F., altered.)

The work of Cyprian *On the Unity of the Catholic Church* was read by him at the Council of Carthage in 251, and later sent to Rome (*Ep.* LIV.4). We cannot be sure whether the work, as originally conceived, had wider import than the schism of the five presbyters of Carthage who opposed their bishop on the question of the "lapsed" Christians. But while the text of Chapter 4 quoted above has superior MSS backing, it must be remembered that other versions of Chapter 4 exist containing the celebrated "Roman" additions. It is quite impossible to discuss these here. For a succinct account of the different versions and of the views of modern scholars see Giles, *Documents illustrating Papal Authority*, pp. 50–7, cf. also Fliche et Martin, *Histoire de l'Église*, E. Tr. vol. III, pp. 700–14, vol. IV, pp. 1001–1010.

4. *If any one consider and weigh this*: In Ch. 3 Cyprian had been showing how schism was the newest of the weapons of the devil.

5. *The episcopate is one*: Bévenot (Ancient Christian Writers, XXV, p. 47) translates, "The Authority of the bishops forms a unity, of which each holds his part in its totality."

enjoys full possession (in solidum), i.e. there is a piece of common property, by holding a part of it individually, each owner has common possession of the whole.

215. PESTILENCE AT CARTHAGE, 252

(Pontius, *Life of Cyprian*, 9–10 (*C.S.E.L.* III.1, p. xcixf.).)

9   A dreadful pestilence broke out afterwards, and the extraordinary ravages of a hateful sickness entered house after house of the trembling populace in succession, carrying off with sudden violence numberless people daily, each from his own home. There was a general panic, flight, shrinking from the infection, unnatural exposure of infected friends; as though to carry the dying out of doors, were to rid one's self of death itself.

Meanwhile multitudes lay about the whole city, not bodies, but by this time corpses; and called on the pity of passers-by from the view of a fortune common to both parties. No one looked to aught beyond his cruel gain. No one was alarmed from the recollection of parallel instances. No one did to another what he wished done to himself. It were a crime to pass over what in such circumstances was the conduct of this Pontiff of Christ and God, who had surpassed the Pontiffs of this world as much in benevolence as in truth of doctrine. First he assembled the people in one place, urged on them the excellence of mercifulness, taught them by instances from holy Scripture how much the offices of benevolence avail to merit with God. Then he subjoined that there was nothing wonderful in cherishing our own with the fitting dutifulness of charity; that he became the perfect man, who did somewhat more than publican or heathen, who, *overcoming evil with good*[1] and exercising what resembled a divine clemency, *loved even his enemies*, who *prayed*, as the Lord admonishes and exhorts, for the well-being of *those who are persecuting* him. "*He then makes His sun rise*, and *bestows rain*[2] from time to time to foster the seed, shewing forth all these benefits not only to His own, but to strangers also; and he, who professes himself even God's son, why follows he not the example of his Father? We should answer to our birth," he says; "it is not fit that they should be degenerate who are known to have been born again by God; rather the seed of a good Father should be evidenced in the offspring, by our copying of His good-

10 ness." I pass over many other things and those important, which my limits will not allow me to detail; about which let it suffice to have noticed thus much. If the very Gentiles, had they heard them in the rostrum, would probably have believed forthwith, what should a Christian people do, whose very name begins in faith? Accordingly ministrations are divided among them at once, according to the rank and circumstances of each. Many who from stress of poverty were unable to undertake expenses, undertook more than expenses, by their personal toil doing other services more precious than all riches. Who indeed under such a teacher but must haste to be occupied in some part of that warfare, by which he would be pleasing God the Father, and Christ the Judge, and at the moment so good a Bishop? Accordingly *they did good in the profusion of exuberant works to all*, and not only *to the household of faith*.[3] (L. F., slightly altered.)

For similar conduct of the Christians on a later occasion, cf. Eusebius, *H.E.* IX.3.3ff.

[1] Rom. 12.21.　　[2] Matt 5.44–6.　　[3] Gal. 6.10.

216. MARCIAN OF ARLES, 254

(Cyprian, *Ep.* LXVIII.1,2 (*C.S.E.L.* III.2.744–5).)

Cyprian to his brother Stephen, greeting.

1 Faustinus our colleague, whose see is at Lyons, has more than once written to me, dearest brother, informing me of things, which I well know have been already reported to you as well by him, as by the rest our fellow-bishops in the same province, namely, that Marcian, whose see is at Arles, has joined Novatian, and has departed from the truth of the Catholic Church and from the concord of our body and priesthood, holding to that most harsh perversity of heretical presumption, that to the servants of God who repent and mourn and knock at the Church with tears and groaning and mourning, the solace and aid of Divine mercy and Fatherly lenity are closed, that the wounded are not admitted for the healing of their wounds, but, left without hope of peace and communion, are to be cast to the ravening of wolves and a prey to the devil. Wherein it is ours, dearest brother, to advise and aid, who, considering the Divine clemency, and holding a just balance in the government of the Church, do so exercise towards sinners a vigorous authority, as yet not to deny the medicine of the Divine goodness and mercy in raising the falling and curing the wounded.

2 Wherefore it behoves you to write a very full letter to our fellow-bishops in Gaul, that they no longer suffer the froward and proud Marcian, an enemy both to the mercy of God and the salvation of the brethren, to insult over our college, because he seems as yet not to be excommunicated by us, who this long while boasts and publishes, that, siding with Novatian and following his frowardness, he has separated himself from our communion.

[Cyprian goes on to comment on the repudiation of Novatian "by the priests of God throughout the world", and the absurdity of allowing "his flatterers to mock us".]

Let letters be addressed from you to the Province and to the people dwelling at Arles, whereby Marcian being excommunicated, another may be substituted in his room, and the flock of Christ, which to this day is scattered by him, wounded and despised, be again collected together. Suffice it that many of our brethren in those parts have in these last years departed without peace; at all events, let the rest who survive be aided, who groan day and night, and entreating the mercy of our God and Father, implore the solace of our help. (L. F., slightly altered.)

We do not know what was the upshot of this correspondence. Benson, *Cyprian*, p. 311, thinks that this letter is earlier than *Ep*. LXVII (217): "in his next letter Cyprian has already given Stephen up".

217. THE SPANISH APPEAL, 254
(Cyprian, *Ep*. LXVII.1–6 (*C.S.E.L*. III.2.735–41).)

This letter is written from Cyprian's Fourth Council (254, Autumn), in reply to an appeal from two Spanish Churches.

"The Bishops of Leon and Merida in Spain had accepted testimonials to their orthodoxy as pagans.

*   *   *

The Chairs of these two men had been filled by other two elected by their own churches and approved by the neighbouring prelates. Basilides (of Leon) afterwards recovering from his dejection paid a visit to Rome, and there he and, we must infer, Martial (of Merida) also, by some fraudulent means procured a declaration from the new pope Stephen that he would hold them still to be the lawful occupants of the two sees." (Benson, *Cyprian*, p. 233.)

1   [Cyprian says that answer to the appeal is given "not so much by our counsel as by the divine precepts", i.e. from Ex. 19.22;
2   28.43; Lev. 21.17; Scripture is the sole criterion and the doctrines of men are not to be followed (Isa. 29.13; Mark 7.9).]

Keeping these things before our eyes, and anxiously and religiously considering them, we ought in the ordinations of Bishops to choose none but unblemished and upright ministers, who holily and worthily offering sacrifices to God, may be heard in the prayers which they make for the safety of the Lord's people: since it is written, *God heareth not a sinner; but if any man be a worshipper of God, and doeth His will, him He heareth*.[1] Wherefore with the most careful diligence and impartial examination, must such be chosen to the priesthood as we know will be heard by God.
3   Nor let the people flatter themselves as if they can be free from the contagion of the offence, when communicating with a priest who is a sinner, and lending their consent to the unrighteous and

[1] John 9.31.

unlawful episcopate of their prelate, since the divine censure threatens by the prophet Hosea, and says, *Their sacrifices shall be as the bread of mourning; all that eat thereof shall be polluted*[1]: plainly teaching and shewing that all are altogether bound by sin, who have been polluted by the sacrifices of a profane and unrighteous priest.

[This is proved by the story of Corah, Dathan and Abiram (Num. 16).]

... Wherefore a people, which obeys the precepts of the Lord, and fears God, ought to separate itself from a prelate who is a sinner, nor mingle itself up with the sacrifices of a sacrilegious priest; especially since it has itself the power either of choosing worthy priests or rejecting the unworthy.

4   This, too, we see to be derived from divine authority, that a priest should be chosen in presence of the people, in sight of all, and be approved worthy and fit by public sentence and testimony as in Numbers the Lord commanded Moses [Numbers 20. 25-6]. God commanded a priest to be appointed before all the congregation; that is, He instructs and shows us that the ordinations of priests ought only to be solemnized with the knowledge of the people standing by, that so by their presence either the crimes of the wicked may be detected or the merits of the good proclaimed, and so the ordination be right and lawful, as having been examined with the suffrage and judgement of all. ...

[As was done at the election of a successor to Judas Iscariot (Acts 1.15ff.) and of the deacons (Acts 6.2ff.).]

5   Wherefore the practice received from divine tradition and apostolic observance must be diligently upheld and kept, which is also kept by us and by almost all the provinces, namely that to the due solemnization of ordinations, all the neighbouring bishops of the same province should meet together among the people for whom a prelate is ordained, and the bishop should be chosen in the presence of the people, who know most fully the lives of each, and are thoroughly acquainted with the character of every one from his conversation. This too we see was done among you in the ordination of our colleague Sabinus, so that by the suffrages of the whole brotherhood and by the judgement of the Bishops who had met together in their presence, and who had written to you concerning him, the Episcopate was conferred upon him, and hands were laid on him in the room of Basilides. Nor can it

[1] Hos. 9.4.

rescind an ordination rightly performed, that Basilides, after his crimes had been detected, and his conscience laid bare even by his own confession, canvassing to be unjustly restored to the episcopate from which he had been justly deposed, went to Rome and deceived Stephen our colleague, residing at a distance and ignorant of what had been done and of the real truth. The effect of this is not to efface but to swell the crimes of Basilides, in that to his former sins is moreover added the guilt of deceit and circumvention. For he is not so much to be blamed, who through negligence was imposed upon, as he to be execrated who through fraud imposed upon him. But if Basilides could impose on man, on God he cannot, for it is written, *God is not mocked.*[1] Neither can deceit avail Martial, that he who is also involved in heinous sins, should not forfeit his bishopric; for that the Apostle admonishes and says, *A bishop must be blameless, as the steward of God.*[2]

6   [Besides having sacrificed and obtained certificates of having done so, Basilides had, under stress of illness, blasphemed God. But his conscience had prevailed, he had laid down his office and had undergone penance "and counted himself most happy if he might be allowed to communicate even as a layman". Martial had for some time attached himself to a pagan *collegium*, had buried his sons in *their* burial ground, and had made an even more decisive acknowledgement of paganism before an official . . .]

and since there are many other heinous sins in which Basilides and Martial are held implicated in vain do such attempt to usurp the episcopate, it being evident that men of that mind can neither preside over the Church of Christ, nor ought to offer sacrifices to God: especially since our colleague Cornelius, a peaceable and righteous priest, and by the favour of the Lord honoured also with martyrdom, long since decreed in conjunction with us and with all the bishops constituted throughout the whole world, that such men might indeed be admitted to do penance, but must be kept back from the doors of the clergy and the honour of the priesthood. (L. F., slightly altered.)

Unfortunately we do not know anything of what happened afterwards, but if Stephen persisted in his course of action this must have prepared the way for the breach with Cyprian over heretical baptism.

6.   *certificates (libelli)*: cf. 200.

to communicate even as a layman: This was the usual rule, cf. 196.

collegium: cf. 14, p. 14.

[1] Gal. 6.7.   [2] Tit. 1.7.

218. SCHISMATICAL BAPTISM INVALID

(Cyprian, *Ep.* LXIX.7 (*C.S.E.L.* III.2.756).)

But if any here object and say that Novatian holds the same rule that the Catholic Church holds, baptizes with the same Creed wherewith we also baptize, acknowledges the same God the Father, the same Son Christ, the same Holy Ghost, and therefore can claim the power of baptizing because he seems not to differ from us in the baptismal interrogatory—whoso thinks that this may be objected, let him know in the first place that we and schismatics have not one rule of the Creed, nor the same interrogatories. For when they say, "Dost thou believe remission of sins and eternal life by the holy Church?" they lie in their interrogatory, since they have no Church. Then, moreover, they themselves confess with their own mouths that remission of sins can only be given by the holy Church; and, not having this, they shew that sins cannot be remitted with them. (L. F.)

There was a great deal to be said for admitting Novatianist baptism, for the reasons indicated in the above passage. Cyprian goes on in the succeeding sections of his letter to develop his objections from the fate of Corah, Dathan and Abiram and all who supported them (Num. 16).

their interrogatory: cf. Cyprian *Ep.* LXX.2.

219. HERETICAL BAPTISM INVALID

(Cyprian, *Ep.* LXXI.1 (*C.S.E.L.* III.2.771).)

... I know not on what presumption some of our Colleagues are led to think that such as have been dipped among the heretics ought not to be baptized when they come to us; because, they say, there is *one baptism*.[1] This one baptism is without any doubt in the Catholic Church, because the Church is one, and baptism cannot be out of the Church. For seeing there cannot be two baptisms, if heretics truly baptize, then they have the baptism. And whoso by his own authority allows this privilege to them, yields and allows to them that the enemy and adversary of Christ seems to have the power of washing, purifying and sanctifying man. But we say that such as come thence are not re-baptized but baptized by us. For neither do they receive anything there, where there is nothing; but they come to us that here they may receive where is all grace and truth; for both grace and truth are one. (L. F., altered.)

[1] Eph. 4.5.

220. THE VIEWS OF STEPHEN OF ROME AGAINST REBAPTISM OF HERETICS

(Cyprian, *Ep.* LXXIV.1,2,4 (*C.S.E.L.* III.2.799–800,802).)

1   Although in the letters of which I sent you copies, dearest brother, I have fully expressed all which is to be said upon baptizing heretics; yet since you have desired to be informed what answer our brother Stephen returned to my letter, I have sent you a copy of that answer; on reading which, you will more and more discover his error, in that he endeavours to uphold the cause of heretics against Christians and against the Church of God. For among other things arrogant or extraneous or self-contradictory, which he wrote without due instruction and caution, he moreover added this: "If then any shall come to you from any heresy whatsoever, let there be no innovations beyond what has been handed down, namely that hands be laid on such to repentance, since those who are properly heretics do not baptize such as come to them 2 from one another, but only admit them to communion." He has forbidden one coming from any heresy whatsoever to be baptized in the Church; i.e. he has adjudged the baptisms of all heretics to be right and lawful. And whereas the several heresies have several baptisms and divers sins, he, communicating with the baptism of them all, has heaped up the sins of all in one mass into his own bosom. And he has enjoined "that there be no innovations beyond what has been handed down"; as though *he* innovated who, maintaining unity, claims the one Baptism for the one Church, and not he rather, who, forgetful of unity, adopts the deceitful defilements of a profane immersion.

[Cyprian discusses tradition quoting Josh. 1.8, Matt. 28.20.]

If then it is commanded in the Gospel, or is contained in the Epistles or Acts of the Apostles, that "such as come from any heresy whatsoever should not be baptized, but hands only laid on them in order to repentance"; then let this Divine and holy tradition be observed. But if heretics are everywhere called nothing else than enemies and Antichrists; if they are pronounced to be persons to be *avoided, to be perverse, and condemned of themselves*; why is it that they should not be condemned by us, who it is plain from Apostolical testimony are already *condemned of themselves*?[1]

*   *   *

[1] Tit. 3.10–11.

4   Truly, an excellent and legitimate tradition is propounded by our brother Stephen's teaching, supplying us with an adequate authority! For in the same place of his letter he has added, "since those who are properly heretics do not baptize such as come to them from one another, but only admit them to communion". For to this depth of ill hath the Church of God and spouse of Christ sunk, that she is to follow the example of heretics, that to celebrate the heavenly Sacraments light must borrow her order from darkness, and Christians do the same as Antichrists. (L. F., slightly altered.)

221. THE DECISION OF THE SIXTH COUNCIL OF CARTHAGE (SECOND ON BAPTISM), 256

(From Cyprian, *Ep.* LXXIII.1 (*C.S.E.L.* III.2.778f.).)

You have written to me, dearest brother, desiring to know the bearings of my mind concerning the baptism of heretics, who being placed without, and established outside the Church, claim to themselves a matter over which they have neither right nor power. This we cannot account valid or lawful, since it is agreed that baptism among them is unlawful. And whereas we have already expressed in our letters what we decreed in Council when very many of us were met together, I have sent to you copy of the same letters, to cut a long story short, and in addition what also I afterwards replied to Quintus, our colleague, inquiring of the same matter. And now, too, when we had met together, bishops of the provinces both of Africa and Numidia, to the number of seventy-one, we again confirmed this same by our sentence, ruling that there is one baptism, that appointed in the Catholic Church; and that accordingly whosoever come from the adulterous and profane water to be cleansed and sanctified by the truth of the saving water, are not re-baptized but baptized by us. (L. F.)

What we decreed in council, i.e. in the first council on baptism, 255 (Cyprian, *Ep.* LXX.1-2).

222. THE AFRICAN CUSTOM OF REBAPTISM, 255–256

(Cyprian, *Ep.* LXXIII.3 (*C.S.E.L.* III.2.780).)

But with us it is no new or sudden thing to decide that they are to be baptized, who come from heretics to the Church, in that now many years and a long period of time have elapsed since, under Agrippinus of honoured memory, very many bishops being convened, determined this: and thenceforward until this day, so many thousand heretics in our provinces have been converted to the Church who despised not or hesitated, nay with full consent of reason and will, have been glad to attain the grace of the life-giving laver and saving baptism. (L. F., slightly altered.)

Agrippinus, Bishop of Carthage, *c.* 200.
On this African custom, cf. Tertullian, *On Baptism*, 15.

223. LETTER OF FIRMILIAN, BISHOP OF CAESAREA IN CAPPADOCIA, TO CYPRIAN ON THE REBAPTISM OF HERETICS

(Cyprian, *Ep.* LXXV.5–6,17,22–5 (*C.S.E.L.* III.2.812–14, 821–2, 824–7).)

5   But since your messenger was in haste to return to you, and the winter season was close at hand, we have answered your letter to the best of our power. As regards then what Stephen has said, as though the Apostles forbade those to be baptized who came over from heresy, and that they delivered this to be observed by posterity, you have answered most fully, that no one can be so foolish as to believe that the Apostles delivered this, in that it is known that these very execrable and detestable heresies arose afterwards. For Marcion, the disciple of Cerdon, may be proved to have introduced his profane doctrine against God, much later than the Apostles and long after their times. Apelles, too, consenting to his blasphemy, added many other new and more heinous articles, in enmity to faith and truth. Moreover, the period of Valentinus and Basilides is evidence that they too, after the Apostles and after a long period, rebelled with their wicked falsehoods against the Church of God. It is known also that the other

heretics long after introduced their wicked sects and perverse intentions, as each was led astray by error; of all whom it is evident that they are self-condemned, and that even before the Day of Judgement they have pronounced against themselves an irreversible sentence. Whoso then confirmeth their baptism, what else does he than adjudge himself with them, and condemn himself by making himself a partaker with them?

6   But that they who are at Rome do not in all respects observe the things handed down from the beginning, and that they in vain pretend the authority of the Apostles, any one may know even from this, that in celebrating Easter and in many other divine and sacramental ordinances, we may see that there are certain diversities among them, which are observed at Jerusalem. As in very many other provinces also, there are many differences according to the diversity of places and persons; nor yet has there on this account been any departure from the peace and unity of the Catholic Church. This Stephen has now dared to make, breaking the peace with you which his predecessors ever maintained with you in mutual affection and respect; moreover herein defaming the blessed Apostles Peter and Paul, as if they had handed this down; whereas in their Epistles they execrated heretics, and warned us to avoid them. Whence it is apparent that this tradition is human which upholds heretics, and maintains that *they* have baptism, which belongs to the Church alone.

*   *   *

17   And herein I am justly indignant at such open and manifest folly in Stephen, that he who so boasts of the seat of his episcopate, and contends that he holds the succession from Peter, on whom the foundations of the Church were laid, introduces many other *rocks*, and *builds*[1] anew many Churches, in that by his authority he maintains baptism among them. For they who are baptized, without doubt fill up the number of the Church. But whoso approves their baptism, must needs also maintain of those baptized, that the Church also is with them. Nor does he perceive that he who thus betrays and abandons unity, obscures, and in a manner effaces, the truth of the Christian *Rock*. Yet the Apostle acknowledges that the Jews, though blind through ignorance and bound through that most dreadful sin, have yet *a zeal of God*.[2] Stephen, who proclaims that he occupies by succession the chair of Peter, is roused by no zeal against heretics, conceding to them no small but the very greatest power of grace, so far as to say and

1 Cf. Matt. 16.18.   2 Rom. 10.2.

assert that through the Sacrament of Baptism they wash off the defilement of the old man, pardon the old deadly sins, make sons to God by heavenly regeneration, renew to eternal life by the sanctification of the Divine laver. He who concedes and assigns to heretics such great and heavenly privileges of the Church, what else does he than hold communion with them, for whom he maintains and claims so much grace? And in vain doth he any longer hesitate to consent and be partaker with them in the rest, to join in their assemblies, and mingle his prayers with them, and set up a common altar and sacrifice.

*   *   *

22   And Stephen is not ashamed to assert, that remission of sins can be given by those who are themselves set fast in all kinds of sin, as if the laver of salvation could be in the house of death!

23   What then will become of that which is written, *Abstain from strange water, and drink not from a strange fountain,*[1] if, leaving the *sealed fountain*[2] of the Church, you adopt *strange water* for your own, and pollute the Church with profane fountains? For when you communicate with the baptism of heretics, what else do you do but drink of their mire and mud, and, yourself cleansed with the sanctification of the Church, become defiled with the contagion of others' filth? And do you not fear the judgement of God, when giving testimony to heretics against the Church, though it is written, *A false witness shall not be unpunished?*[3] Why? you are worse than all the heretics; for when many, having discovered their error, come over from them to you, that they may receive the true light of the Church, you abet their errors who come, and obscuring the light of the truth of the Church, increase the darkness of the night of heresy.

*   *   *

24   . . . Holy Scripture says of no one more than of you (Stephen), *An angry man stirreth up strife, and a furious man heapeth up sins.*[4] . . . What *strifes* and dissensions you have *stirred up* through the Churches of the whole world! And how great *sin* you have *heaped up*, when you cut yourself off from so many flocks. For you cut yourself off; do not deceive yourself; for he is truly the schismatic, who has made himself an apostate from the communion of the unity of the Church. For while you think that all may be excommunicated by you, you have excommunicated

---

[1] Prov. 9.17.   [2] Cant. 4.12.   [3] Prov. 19.5.
[4] Prov. 29.22.

yourself alone from all. Nor have even the precepts of an Apostle been able to keep you to the rule of truth and peace, when thus admonishing: *I therefore, the prisoner, . . .*[1]

25   How diligently has Stephen fulfilled these salutary commands and warnings of the Apostle, keeping, in the first place, *lowliness and meekness*! For what can be more *lowly* and *meek* than to have disagreed with so many bishops throughout the whole world, breaking peace with them severally in various modes of discord; now with the Eastern Churches, as we feel confident you are aware, now with yourselves who are in the South! From whom he received episcopal legates with such *long-suffering and meekness* that he would not admit them even to the common intercourse of speech; so mindful, however, of *love* and charity that he commanded the whole brotherhood that no one admit them to their house; so that when they came not only *peace* and communion but shelter and hospitality were denied them. This is to have *kept the unity of the Spirit in the bond of peace* to cut himself off from the unity of charity, and in all things to make himself an alien to the brethren, and with the fury of contumacious discord to rebel against the Sacrament and the Faith. With such an one can there be *one body and one Spirit*; in whom, perhaps, there is not one mind, so slippery is it, so shifting, so uncertain? But as concerns him, let us quit the subject. (L. F., altered.)

5. *we have answered your letter*: i.e. without waiting for the annual synod which Firmilian had mentioned in 4.

In his controversy with Stephen Cyprian sought an ally in Firmilian, one of the most important figures in the Church: it is to be regretted that his letter to Firmilian is lost. The reply of Firmilian, as can be seen from the excerpts quoted, treats Stephen with scorn and contempt. It is clear from other sections of Firmilian's letter that the Asian churches were still being agitated over the baptism of the Montanists and had rejected it at a large synod held at Iconium some time before.

Firmilian's concluding words (apart from final greetings) should be noted:

And yet is not Stephen ashamed to give support to such against the Church, and for the upholding of heretics to divide the brotherhood; nor, further, to call Cyprian *false Christ*,[2] and *false apostle*, and *deceitful worker*.[3] He, conscious that all these marks are in himself, has been beforehand, and falsely hurled at another epithets which he ought, and rightly, to have applied to himself. (L. F., altered.)

[1] Eph. 4.1–6.   [2] Mk. 13.22.   [3] 2 Cor. 11.13.

224. EPISCOPAL AUTHORITY

(Cyprian, at the Seventh Council of Carthage (and Third on
Baptism) 1 September, 256: (*C.S.E.L.* III.1, pp. 435–6).)

It remains that we severally declare our opinion on this same
subject, judging no one, nor depriving any one of the right of
communion, if he differ from us. For no one of us sets himself
up as a bishop of bishops, or by tyrannical terror forces his colleagues to a necessity of obeying; inasmuch as every bishop in the
free use of his liberty and power, has the right of forming his own
judgement, and can no more be judged by another than he can
himself judge another. But we must all await the judgement of
our Lord Jesus Christ, who alone has the power both of setting
us in the government of His Church, and of judging of our acts
therein. (L. F.)

On the opinion expressed here, cf. Cyprian, *Ep.* LXIX.17 where he expresses
the same sentiments.

This council had considered a letter from Jubaianus to Cyprian, the latter's
reply (*Ep.* LXXIII), and Jubaianus' acknowledgement. The bishops are now
about to declare their opinion on heretical baptism and Cyprian enunciates his
view of independent judgement on this matter.

bishop of bishops: cf. 160 for Tertullian's sarcastic use of this phrase.

225. THE DEATH OF THE WORLD

(Cyprian, *To Demetrian*, 3 (*C.S.E.L.* III.1.352–3).)

Herein you must in the first place learn, (since you are ignorant
of the divine teaching, and a stranger to truth), that the world is
now reaching its old age, that it stands no longer in its pristine
strength, no longer is strong with that very vigour and force in
which it once excelled. This, though we ourselves should speak it
not, though we should draw no instructions of it from the holy
Scriptures and the divine teaching, still the world itself declares
it, and attests its own ruin in the tottering estate of things. The
showers of winter fail us for nourishing the seeds; the sun's heat
in summer for ripening the corn; nor in springtide do the fields
display their usual growth, and the trees of autumn are barren of
their accustomed issue. Mountains disembowelled and ransacked
yield a shortened store of marble layers; the exhausted mines send
up but a scanty wealth of silver and of gold; their impoverished

veins day by day are narrowed. The husbandman fails and languishes in the fields, the sailor at sea, the soldier in the camp; honesty fails from the mart, justice from the tribunal, love from friendships, skill from the arts, and discipline from conduct. Do you suppose that the coherence of a thing that is decaying can continue in that strength, wherewith it flourished in its youthful and thriving season? Needful is it that that must weaken which is now drawing near its end, and verges downward to the close. It is thus that the descending sun darts his rays with an obscured and impeded lustre, and that the moon, as her course declines, contracts her exhausted horns; thus that the tree once green and fertile puts on the graceless barrenness of the sere boughs in age, and the fountain which once poured out the large effluence of its overflowing veins, worn out by time, scarcely trickles with an insufficient moisture. It is a sentence passed upon the world, it is God's law, that as things rose so they should fall, as they waxed so should grow old, the strong become weak, and the great become little, and when they have become weak and little, they end. (L. F., slightly altered.)

Demetrian was a persistent opponent of the Christians, to whom Cyprian was at last goaded into replying. He had argued, as pagans so often did, that the calamities of the time were due to Christian neglect of the worship of the gods, cf. 141. On Cyprian's theme, cf. Lucretius, *De Rerum Natura*, II.1105–1173.

226. THE RESCRIPT OF VALERIAN, JULY 258

(Cyprian, *Ep.* LXXX.1 (*C.S.E.L.* III.2.839f.).)

... Many various and uncertain rumours are going about, but the truth is as follows: Valerian had sent a rescript to the Senate directing that bishops, presbyters and deacons should forthwith be punished; that senators and men of rank, and Roman knights should lose their dignity and be deprived of their property, and if, when deprived of their possessions, they should still continue to be Christians, then they should lose their heads also; that matrons should be deprived of their property and banished; that whosoever of Caesar's household had either before confessed, or should now confess, should forfeit their property, and be sent in chains as conscripts to Caesar's estates. (L. F.)

be punished: i.e. with death. This rescript marks the second stage of persecution. The first is represented in 227 below (sections 1,2), where Cyprian is interned, and in 233 where Dionysius of Alexandria receives similar treatment.

227. THE TRIAL OF CYPRIAN, 257, AND HIS MARTYRDOM, 258

(The *Acta Proconsularia* of St Cyprian, (*C.S.E.L.* III.3, pp. CX–CXIV).)

1   When the Emperor Valerian was Consul for the fourth, and Gallienus for the third time, on 30 August, at Carthage, Paternus, the proconsul, in his council-chamber thus spoke to Cyprian, bishop:

P. The most sacred Emperors Valerian and Gallienus have honoured me with letters, wherein they enjoin that all those who do not observe the religion of Rome, shall make profession of their return to Roman rites; I have made accordingly inquiry as to how you call yourself; what answer do you make to me?

C. I am a Christian, and bishop; I know no other gods beside the one and true God, who made heaven and earth, the sea, and all things therein; this God we Christians serve, to Him we pray day and night, for ourselves, for all mankind, for the health of the Emperors themselves.

P. Do you persist in this purpose?

C. That good purpose, which knows God, cannot be changed.

P. You can then, obeying the mandate of the Emperors, go into exile to the city of Curubis.

C. I go.

P. The letters, wherewith I have been honoured by the Emperors, speak of presbyters as well as of bishops; I would know of you, therefore, who be they, who are presbyters in this city?

C. By an excellent and beneficial provision of your laws you have forbidden any to be informers; therefore they cannot be discovered and denounced by me; but they will be found in their own cities.

P. I am today making inquiry here.

C. Our rules forbid any man to offer himself for punishment, and your ordinances discourage the same; they may not therefore offer themselves, but they will be discovered by your inquiries.

P. They shall be discovered by me. They [*sc.* the Emperors] further ordain that no meetings be held in any place, and that the Christians shall not enter their cemeteries; if any transgress this wholesome ordinance, he shall suffer death.

C. Do as you have been instructed.

2   Then Paternus the proconsul bade them lead away the bishop Cyprian into exile. During his long absence in exile on this

account Aspasius Paternus was succeeded by Galerius Maximus, who bade the bishop Cyprian be recalled from exile, and brought before him. Cyprian, the holy Martyr, chosen of God, returned from Curubis, to which he had been exiled by order of Aspasius Paternus, then proconsul, and by official orders abode in his own gardens. There he was in daily expectation that he should be visited as had been shown him. While he remained there, suddenly on 13 September, in the consulship of Tuscus and Bassus, there came to him two chief officials; one the chief equerry on the proconsular staff of Galerius, the other marshal of the guard on the same staff; they placed him between them in a chariot, and carried him to the villa of Sextus, whither Galerius Maximus had retired for the recovery of his health. By order of the proconsul he was reserved for hearing on another day; so the blessed Cyprian withdrew under guard and was privately lodged in the house of the chief equerry of the staff of the most honourable Galerius Maximus, proconsul, in Saturn Street, between the temples of Venus and of Salus. Thither flocked the whole multitude of the brethren; when holy Cyprian knew this, he bade that the girls should be kept in, seeing they all continued in the open street before the gate of the officer's house.

3   So on the next day, 14 September, a great crowd was collected early at the villa of Sextus, as the proconsul commanded. And the same day Cyprian was brought before him as he sat for judgement in the court called Sauciolum.

G. M. Are you Thascius Cyprianus?

C. I am.

G. M. The most sacred Emperors have commanded you to conform to the Roman rites.

C. I refuse.

G. M. Take heed for yourself.

C. Do as you are bid; in so clear a case I may not take heed.

4   Galerius, after briefly conferring with his judicial council, with much reluctance pronounced the following sentence: "You have long lived an irreligious life, and have drawn together a number of men bound by an unlawful association, and professed yourself an open enemy to the gods and the religion of Rome; and the pious, most sacred and august Emperors, Valerian and Gallienus, and the most noble Caesar Valerian, have endeavoured in vain to bring you back to conformity with their religious observances; —whereas, therefore you have been apprehended as principal and ringleader in these infamous crimes, you shall be made an example to those whom you have wickedly associated with you; the authority of law shall be ratified in your blood." He then read the

sentence of the court from a written tablet: "It is the sentence of this court that Thascius Cyprianus be executed with the sword." C. Thanks be to God. (L. F., altered.)

5   After this sentence the crowd of brethren cried: "Let us also be beheaded with him." Hence arose an uproar among the brethren, and a great crowd accompanied him. So Cyprian was led forth on to the land of Sextus, and there he divested himself of his mantle, and kneeled upon the ground, and bowed in prayer to the Lord. And when he had divested himself of his dalmatic and handed it to the deacons, he stood clad in his linen garment, and prepared to await the executioner.

When the executioner arrived Cyprian charged his friends that they should give to the executioner twenty-five golden pieces. Napkins and handkerchiefs were strewn before him by the brethren. Thereafter blessed Cyprian bound his eyes with his own hand, but as he could not fasten the ends of the handkerchief for himself, the presbyter Julian and Julian the sub-deacon fastened them for him.

So the blessed Cyprian suffered, and his body was laid out hard by to content the curiosity of the heathen. Thence it was removed by night, and, accompanied by tapers and torches, was conducted with prayers in great triumph to the burial-ground of Macrobius Candidianus the procurator, which lies on the Mappalian way near the fishponds. A few days later Galerius Maximus the proconsul died.

6   The most blessed martyr Cyprian suffered on the 14th day of September under the Emperors Valerian and Gallienus, but in the reign of our Lord Jesus Christ, to whom is honour and glory for ever and ever. Amen. (E. C. E. Owen, *Some authentic Acts of the Early Martyrs*, pp. 98–9, slightly altered.)

On persecution under Valerian, see 226, 233.

1. Curubis, about forty miles from Carthage, on the Gulf of Hammamet. *Our rules forbid any man*: cf. 142.

2. *by official orders*: lit. by sacred command. As *sacer* was commonly used in such connections, even Christians would feel no incongruity in a phrase like this.

as had been shown him: as related in Pontius, *Life of Cyprian*, 12.

The officers sent would probably be from the cohort of the legion stationed in Africa which was attached to the proconsul. They are called *strator* and *equistrator*. The former had a house large enough to lodge Cyprian, and to entertain Cyprian's friends, as Pontius tells us (*Life of Cyprian*, 15).

4. *with much reluctance*: The words (*vix et aegre*) may simply mean that the ailing proconsul was hardly able to deliver his sentence.

ringleader, lit. standard-bearer.

5. On Cyprian's garments, see Benson, *Cyprian*, pp. 513–16.

The cemetery in which Cyprian was buried was probably named from a former owner of the site.

228. THE CONSECRATION OF NOVATIAN, 251

(Cornelius of Rome, quoted by Eusebius, *H.E.* VI.43.7–10.)

7 How extraordinary a change and transformation, brother beloved, we have beheld to have taken place in him in a little while! For this highly distinguished person, who was in the habit of pledging himself by some terrible oaths in no wise to *seek the office of a bishop*,[1] of a sudden appears as a bishop as if he were cast

8 into our midst by some contrivance. For this master of doctrine, this champion of the Church's discipline, when he was attempting to wrest and filch away the episcopate that was not given him from above, chose to himself two companions who had renounced their own salvation, that he might send them to a small and very insignificant part of Italy, and entice thence by some made-up device three bishops, rough and very simple men. He confidently maintained and affirmed the necessity of their coming quickly to Rome, on the pretext that any dissension whatsoever that had arisen might be ended by their activity as mediators,

9 conjointly with other bishops. When they arrived, inasmuch as they were too simple, as we said before, for the unscrupulous devices of the wicked, they were shut up by certain disorderly men like himself, and at the tenth hour, when they were drunk, and sick with the after effects, he forcibly compelled them to give him a bishop's office by a counterfeit and vain laying on of hands, an office that he assumed by crafty treachery since it did

10 not fall to his lot. One of the bishops not long afterwards returned to the Church, bewailing and confessing his fault; with whom we had communion as a layman, all the laity present interceding for him. And as for the remaining bishops, to these we appointed successors, whom we sent into the places where they were. (Lawlor and Oulton, *Eusebius*, I, pp. 211–12, slightly altered.)

This and other extracts (see also passage 230) from a letter of Cornelius to Fabius of Antioch are given by Eusebius. The spirit shown by Cornelius towards Novatian is similar, *mutatis mutandis*, to that displayed by Hippolytus towards Callistus.

[1] 1 Tim. 3.2

7. *of a sudden appears as a bishop*: Novatian claimed that he had not sought consecration, cf. what Dionysius of Alexandria says in a letter to him (231).

8. *this master of doctrine*: "Cornelius is sarcastic, but he speaks the truth" (Lawlor and Oulton, *Eusebius*, II, p. 232). Novatian was probably far more of a scholar than any of his contemporaries at Rome, as is shown by the illiteracy of their letter to Cyprian (*Ep.* VIII) and by Novatian's surviving works.

9. *when they were drunk*: "We may dismiss the irate and simple-hearted prelate's belief that the rite was performed by them in a state of inebriety, though the assertion illustrates the possibilities of the time." (Benson, *Cyprian*, p. 140, n. 3.)

229. THE CHARACTER OF NOVATIAN BEFORE HIS SCHISM

(Anon., *Ad Novatianum*, 13 (Hartel, *Cyprian* (*C.S.E.L.*), II, Appendix, p. 63.)

. . . who ever in one home, that is the church of Christ, wept over the sins of his neighbours as his own, bore the burdens of his brethren, as the Apostle exhorts, strengthened with his divine preaching those who were unstable in the faith. . . . (Lawlor and Oulton, *Eusebius* II, p. 234.)

This testimony comes from a bitter opponent.

230. THE CHURCH OF ROME, c. 250

(Cornelius of Rome, quoted by Eusebius, *H.E.* VI.43.11–12.)

This passage follows immediately after the passage from Cornelius referring to the consecration of Novatian (228).

11   This vindicator, then, of the Gospel did not know that there should be one bishop in a catholic church, in which he was not ignorant (for how could he be?) that there are forty-six presbyters, seven deacons, seven sub-deacons, forty-two acolytes, fifty-two exorcists, readers and door-keepers, above fifteen hundred widows and persons in distress, all of whom are supported by the grace
12 and loving kindness of the Master. But not even did this great

multitude, so necessary in the Church, that number who by God's providence were rich and multiplying, nor an immense. and countless laity, turn him from such a desperate failure and recall him to the Church. (Lawlor and Oulton, *Eusebius*, I, pp. 211–12.)

11. *This vindicator . . . of the Gospel*: Cornelius is sarcastic, but the Novatianists themselves regarded their sect as *assertores evangelii* (Cyprian, *Ep*. XLIV. 3, cf. *Ep*. XLVI.2.1).

one bishop in a catholic church: In Cyprian (*Ep*. XLIX.2) the confessors who have returned from schism confess among other things "that there should be one bishop in a Catholic Church".

231. DIONYSIUS OF ALEXANDRIA'S APPEAL TO NOVATIAN

(Dionysius of Alexandria, quoted by Eusebius, *H.E.* VI.45.)

Dionysius to his brother Novatian, greeting. If thou wast led on unwillingly, as thou sayest, thou wilt prove it by retiring willingly. For a man ought to suffer anything and everything so as to escape dividing the Church of God, and it were not less glorious to incur martyrdom to avoid schism than to avoid idolatry, nay, in my opinion it were more. For in the one case a man is a martyr for the sake of his own single soul, but in the other for the sake of the whole Church. And if thou wert even now to persuade or compel the brethren to come to one mind, thy recovery will be greater than thy fall, and the one will not be reckoned, while the other will be praised. But if they obey thee not, and thou hast no power, *by all means save thine own soul*.[1] I pray that thou mayest fare well and cleave to peace in the Lord. (Lawlor and Oulton, *Eusebius*, I, p. 214, slightly altered.)

If thou wast led on unwillingly: Novatian had sent letters to other bishops announcing his consecration, and, no doubt, explaining the circumstances. Dionysius of Alexandria clearly takes him at his word, i.e. that Novatian accepted consecration unwillingly, cf. the opinion of Cornelius, 228.

martyrdom: "one may doubt whether Novatian was ever really likely to endure such a fate for withdrawing from his position." (Feltoe, *Dionysius of Alexandria*, p. 38.)

[1] Gen. 19.17 (LXX).

232. THE ESSENCE OF NOVATIAN'S DOCTRINE ABOUT THE LAPSED

(Dionysius of Alexandria, part of a letter to Dionysius of Rome, quoted by Eusebius, *H.E.* VII.8.)

For it is with good reason indeed that we feel enmity towards Novatian, who caused a division in the Church and drew away some of the brethren to impieties and blasphemies, and introduced as well most profane teaching about God, and falsely accuses our most compassionate Lord Jesus Christ of being without mercy; and above all this, he sets at naught the holy washing, and overturns the faith and confession that precede it, and entirely banishes the Holy Spirit from them, even though there was some hope of His remaining with or even returning to them. (Lawlor and Oulton, *Eusebius*, I, p. 222.)

sets at naught the holy washing, etc.: at baptism the Spirit had come upon the believer. By his complete rejection of the lapsed, Novatian defied the experience which, even in the case of Christians who lapsed, had accompanied their baptism. But the Spirit was not to be defeated by the pronouncement of a schismatic; and "there was some hope of His remaining with or even returning to them"; evidence of this would be in their desire to do penance and return to the Church.

233. THE PERSECUTION OF VALERIAN: DIONYSIUS OF ALEXANDRIA BEFORE AEMILIAN, 257

(In Eusebius, *H.E.* VII.11.6–11.)

6   When Dionysius and Faustus and Maximus and Marcellus and Chaeremon were brought into court, Aemilian, the deputy-prefect, said, ". . . And verbally I discoursed with you concerning
7   the kindness that our lords have displayed on your behalf. For they gave you the opportunity of safety if you were willing to turn to that which is according to nature and worship the gods which preserve their Empire, and forget those gods which are contrary to nature. What, therefore, do you say to these things? For I do not expect that you will be ungrateful for their kindness, forasmuch as
8   they urge you on to the better course." Dionysius replied: "Not

all men worship all gods, but each one certain whom he regards as such. We therefore both worship and adore the one God and Maker of all things, who also committed the Empire to the Augusti, most highly favoured of God, Valerian and Gallienus; and to Him we unceasingly pray for their Empire, that it may

9 remain unshaken." Aemilian, the deputy-prefect, said to them: "And who prevents you from worshipping this god also, if he be a god, along with the natural gods? For ye were bidden to worship gods, and gods whom all know." Dionysius replied:

10 "We worship no other God." Aemilian, the deputy-prefect, said to them: "I see that you are at once ungrateful and insensible of the clemency of our Augusti. Wherefore you shall not be in this city but you shall be sent to the parts of Libya and [remain] in a place called Cephro. For this is the place I chose in accordance with the command of our Augusti. And it shall in no wise be permitted either to you or to any others either to hold assemblies

11 or to enter the cemeteries, as they are called. If anyone be proved not to have gone to the place that I commanded, or be found at any assembly, he will bring the peril upon himself, for there shall be no lack of the necessary observation. Be gone therefore whither you were bidden." (Lawlor and Oulton, *Eusebius*, I, p. 225, slightly altered.)

On the two stages in the persecution of Valerian see 226, 227, p. 260. This situation represents the first stage in the persecution in which Cyprian also was interned.

234. THE TOLERATION EDICT OF GALLIENUS, 261

(Eusebius, *H.E.* VII.13.)

The Emperor Caesar Publius Licinius Gallienus Pius Felix Augustus to Dionysius and Pinnas and Demetrius and the other bishops. I have given my order that the benefit of my bounty should be published throughout all the world, to the intent that the places of worship should be given up, and therefore you also may use the ordinance contained in my rescript, so that none may molest you. And this thing which it is within your power to accomplish has long since been conceded by me; and therefore Aurelius Quirinius, who is in charge of the Exchequer, will observe the ordinance given by me. (Lawlor and Oulton, *Eusebius*, I, pp. 228-9.)

Dionysius: probably of Alexandria, possibly of Rome. We do not know anything about Pinnas and Demetrius.

The document given by Eusebius is not an imperial edict but part of a letter to the bishops, following up and clarifying an edict already issued, to the intent that the places of worship should be given up: this appears to imply that the Christians now had buildings specially set apart for worship. Eusebius goes on to add that there was an order of Gallienus addressed to other bishops permitting them to resume possession of cemeteries.

235. DIONYSIUS OF ROME, 259–268, AGAINST THE SABELLIANS

(Dionysius, *Letter against the Sabellians* in Athanasius, *On the decrees of the Council of Nicaea*, 26; text in Feltoe, *Dionysius of Alexandria* (Cambridge Patristic Texts), pp. 177–82.)

The sequence of events presupposed by this document is that Dionysius of Alexandria in his anxiety to suppress Sabellianism used certain expressions indicative of separation in the persons of the Trinity, and of the Son being created. His opponents complained to Dionysius of Rome, who called a synod, cf. Athanasius quoted in notes on 236, and then addressed this letter, naming no one, to the Church at Alexandria.

Next, I may reasonably turn to those who divide and cut to pieces and destroy that most sacred teaching of the Church of God, the Divine Monarchy, making it as it were three powers and separated substances ($\dot{\upsilon}\pi o\sigma\tau\acute{a}\sigma\epsilon\iota s$) and godheads three. I am told that some among you who are catechists and teachers of the Divine Word, instil this notion, who are diametrically opposed, so to speak, to Sabellius' opinions; for he blasphemously says that the Son is the Father, and the Father the Son, but they in some sort preach three Gods, as dividing the sacred Monad into three substances foreign to each other and utterly separate. For it must needs be that with the God of the Universe the Divine Word is united, and the Holy Ghost must repose and dwell in God; thus in one as in a summit, I mean the God of the Universe, the Almighty, must the Divine Triad be gathered up and brought together. For it is the doctrine of the perverse Marcion to sever and divide the Divine Monarchy into three origins—a devil's teaching, not that of Christ's true disciples and lovers of the Saviour's lessons. For they know well that a Triad is preached by Divine Scripture, but that neither Old Testament nor New preaches three Gods.

Equally must one censure those who hold the Son to be a work, and consider that the Lord has come into being, as one of the things which really came to be: whereas the Divine Oracles witness to a generation suitable to Him and becoming, but not to any fashioning or making. A blasphemy then is it, not ordinary but the highest, to say that the Lord is in any sort a handiwork. For if He came to be Son, once He was not; but He was always, if He be in the Father, as He says Himself, and if the Christ be Word, and Wisdom, and Power (which, as you know, divine Scripture says), and these attributes be powers of God. If then the Son came into being, once these attributes were not; consequently there was a season when God was without them; which is most absurd.

And why say more on these points to you, men full of the Spirit and well aware of the absurdities which come to view from saying that the Son is a work? Not attending, as I consider, to this circumstance the authors of this opinion have entirely missed the truth, in explaining contrary to the sense of divine and prophetic Scripture in the passage, the words *The Lord created me a beginning of His ways.*[1] For the sense of *He created*, as you know, is not one, for we must understand *He created* in this place as "He set over the works made by Him," i.e. "made by the Son Himself". And *He created* here must not be taken for "made", for creating differs from making. *Is not He thy Father that hath bought thee? Hath he not made thee and created thee?*[2] says Moses in his great song in Deuteronomy. And one may say to them: "O reckless men, is he a work who is *the firstborn of every creature,*[3] *who is born from the womb before the morning stars,*[4] who said, as Wisdom, *Before all hills he begets me?*"[5]

In many passages of the Divine Oracles is the Son said to have been generated (γεγεννῆσθαι), but nowhere to have come into being (γεγονέναι); which manifestly convicts those of holding what is false about the Lord's generation, who presume to call his divine and ineffable generation a making. Neither then may we divide into three Godheads the wonderful and divine Monad: nor disparage with the name of "work" the dignity and exceeding majesty of the Lord; but we must believe in God the Father Almighty, and in Christ Jesus His Son, and in the Holy Ghost, and hold that to the God of the Universe the Word is united. For *I*, says He, *and the Father are one,*[6] and *I in the Father and the Father in me.*[7] For thus both the Divine Triad and the holy

---

[1] Prov. 8.22.   [2] Deut. 32.6.   [3] Col. 1.15.   [4] Ps. 110.3.
[5] Prov. 8.25.   [6] John 10.30.   [7] John 14.11.

preaching of the Monarchy will be preserved. (Tr. in Athanasius, N. & P.-N. F., slightly altered.)

On οὐσία and on its synonym (at this period) ὑπόστασις, see, e.g., Bethune-Baker, *Introduction to the Early History of Christian Doctrine*, Ch. VIII (The correspondence between the two Dionysii).

Marcion, cf. 82.

creating differs from making : "The Septuagint uses these two verbs in various ways: κτίζειν often represents the Hebrew *bârâ* (*creare*), in Is. 44.2 it stands for Heb. *âsâh* (*facere*), here in Prov. 8.22 it represents *qânâh* (*possidere*), where ἐκτήσατο seems more natural. On the other hand ποιεῖν represents *bârâ* and *âsâh* and other words." (Feltoe, *Dionysius of Alexandria*, p. 181n.)

236. DIONYSIUS OF ALEXANDRIA'S DEFENCE OF HIS THEOLOGY

(From Athanasius, *De Sententia Dionysii*, 18; text in Feltoe, *Dionysius of Alexandria* (Cambridge Patristic Texts), pp. 188–90.)

However, when I spoke of certain things that had an origin and certain things that were made, I did indeed casually mention examples of such things, recognizing that they were not altogether useful for my purpose: for instance, I said that neither was the plant the same as the husbandman, nor the boat as the shipwright. But afterwards I dwelt at length on those which were more to the point and cognate to the subject, and went more into detail about these truer examples, seeking out various additional illustrations which I set out for you also in another letter: and in them I refuted as false the accusation also which they bring against me, as not stating that Christ is of one substance (ὁμοούσιος) with the Father. For even if I say that this word is not found nor read anywhere in Holy Writ, yet these later attempts of mine to explain which they have ignored are not inconsistent with this conception. For I compared human generation, which is clearly a transmission of the parents' own nature, saying that the parents were different from their children in this single point, that they were not themselves the children: or else it must needs be that neither parents nor children should exist. The letter itself I cannot, as I have said before, owing to circumstances, lay my hand on: otherwise I would have sent you my exact words, or rather a copy of the whole letter: and I will do so, if I have the opportunity. But I know from memory that I added several illustrations from things kindred to one another: for instance, I said that a plant coming up

from a seed or a root was different from that whence it sprang
and yet was absolutely of one nature with it: and a river flowing
from a source partakes of a different shape and name; for neither
is the source called river nor the river source, and both these
things exist, and the source is, in a sense, the father and the river
is the water from the source. But these and similar remarks they
pretend never to have seen written, but act as if they were blind.
They only try to pelt me from afar with those two poor ill-
fitting phrases of mine as with stones, failing to recognize that
where a subject is obscure and requires to be brought within our
understanding, not only do diverse but even quite contradictory
illustrations convey the meaning sought for. (Tr. Feltoe, *St
Dionysius of Alexandria* (S.P.C.K.), pp. 103f., slightly altered.)

of one substance (ὁμοούσιος): on this word, cf. 235, 240, 294, 301.

even if I say, etc.: It is clear that not only did Dionysius A. not employ this
word, but also deprecated its use, cf. Athanasius, *De Synodis* 43. "But when
some blamed the bishop of Alexandria to the bishop of Rome because he said
that the Son was a creature, and not of one substance with the Father, the synod
at Rome took these views ill."

Tertullian (*Against Praxeas* 8) uses, as illustrations of the relations of Father
and Son, the sun and the ray, the spring and the river, the root and the shoot.

these two poor ill-fitting phrases: i.e. the two illustrations of the plant and of
the boat, mentioned at the beginning of this passage.

237. DIONYSIUS OF ALEXANDRIA ON THE BOOK OF REVELATION

(Dionysius *On the Promises*, II, in Eusebius, *H.E.* VII.25.)

In the controversies of Dionysius with the Chiliasts, the Book of Revelation
played a very important part. The following extracts give Dionysius' ideas of
the authorship and meaning of the book.

1 Some indeed of those before our time rejected and altogether
impugned the book, examining it chapter by chapter and declaring
2 it to be unintelligible and illogical, and its title false. For they say
that it is not John's, no, nor yet an apocalypse (unveiling), since
it is veiled by its great thick curtain of unintelligibility; and that
the author of this book was not only not one of the *apostles*, nor
even one of the saints or those belonging to the Church, but
Cerinthus, the same who created the sect called "Cerinthian" after
him, since he desired to affix to his own forgery a name worthy
of credit.

3   [Dionysius goes on to describe the tenets of Cerinthus, how the
Kingdom of Christ would be on earth, and afford free satisfaction
of all bodily lusts. Cf. Eus., *H.E.* III.28.2 (71).]

4   But for my part I should not dare to reject the book, since
many brethren hold it in estimation; but, reckoning that my perception is inadequate to form an opinion concerning it, I hold that
the interpretation of each several passage is in some way hidden
and more wonderful.[1] For even although I do not understand it,
5 yet I suspect that some deeper meaning underlies the words. For
I do not measure and judge these things by my own reasoning, but,
assigning to faith the greater value, I have come to the conclusion
that they are beyond my comprehension, and I do not reject that
which I have not grasped, but I marvel the more because I did
not even see it.

6–   [Eusebius inserts a statement of his own that Dionysius exam-
15 ined the whole book and rejected its literal sense. He then quotes
Dionysius again (6–14) on the question "Who was the John who
wrote the book?" He decides that it could not be the son of
Zebedee by contrasting his character, style and anonymity with
those of the writer of the *Apocalypse*. He briefly considers and
rejects John Mark (15) as author.]

16   But I think that there was a certain other [John] among those
that were in Asia, since it is said both that there were two tombs
at Ephesus, and that each of the two is said to be John's.

17   And from the conceptions too, and from the terms and their
arrangement, one might naturally assume that this writer was a
18 different person from the other. For there is indeed a mutual
agreement between the Gospel and the Epistle, and they begin
alike. The one says: *In the beginning was the Word*[2]; the other:
That which was from the beginning.[3] The one says: *And the Word
became flesh, and dwelt among us (and we beheld his glory, glory as of
the only-begotten from the Father)*[4]; the other, the same words
slightly changed: *That which we have heard, that which we have
seen with our eyes, that which we beheld, and our hands handled, con-*
19 *cerning the Word of life; and the life was manifested.*[5] For these words
he employs as a prelude, since he is aiming, as he shows in what
follows, at those who were asserting that the Lord had not *come
in the flesh.*[6] Therefore he was careful also to add: *And that which
we have seen, we bear witness, and declare unto you the life, the eternal
life, which was with the Father, and was manifested unto us; that which*

---

[1] I.e. than appears on the surface.   [2] John 1.1.   [3] 1 John 1.1.
[4] John 1.14.   [5] 1 John 1.1,2.   [6] 1 John 4.2.

we have seen and heard, declare we unto you also.[1] He is consistent
20 with himself[2] and does not depart from what he has proposed,
but proceeds throughout under the same heads and expressions,
21 certain of which we shall mention concisely. But the attentive
reader will find frequently in one and the other "the life",[3] "the
light",[4] "turning from darkness"; continually "the truth",[5]
"the grace",[6] "the joy",[7] "the flesh[8] and blood[9] of the Lord",
"the judgement",[10] "the forgiveness of sins",[11] "the love of God
toward us",[12] the "commandment" that we should "love one
another",[13] that we should "keep all the commandments"[14];
the "conviction" of "the world",[15] of "the devil",[16] of "the
antichrist"[17]; the promise of the Holy Spirit[18]; the adoption of
the sons of God[19]; the "faith"[20] that is demanded of us throughout; "the Father" and "the Son"[21]: these are to be found everywhere. In a word, it is obvious that those who observe their
character throughout will see at a glance that the Gospel and
22 Epistle have one and the same complexion. But the Apocalypse
is utterly different from, and foreign to, these writings; it has no
connection, no affinity, in any way with them; it scarcely, so to
23 speak, has even a syllable in common with them. Nay more,
neither does the Epistle (not to speak of the Gospel) contain any
mention or thought of the Apocalypse, nor the Apocalypse of the
Epistle, whereas Paul in his epistles gave us a little light also on his
revelations,[22] which he did not record separately.
24 And further, by means of the style one can estimate the differ-
25 ence between the Gospel and Epistle and the Apocalypse. For
the former are not only written in faultless Greek, but also show
the greatest literary skill in their diction, their reasonings, and the
constructions in which they are expressed. There is a complete

---

[1] 1 John 1.1,2,3.   [2] The text is probably corrupt.
[3] John 1.4, and *passim*; 1 John 2.25; 3.14f., etc.
[4] John 1–12 *passim*; 1 John 1.5,7; 2.8–10.
[5] John 1.14, and *passim*; 1 John 1.8; 3.19, etc.
[6] John 1.14,16,17; 2 John 3.
[7] John 3.29, etc.; 1 John 1.4; 2 John 12; 3 John 4 (v.l. "grace").
[8] John 1.13,14; 6.53,56, etc.; 1 John 4.2.
[9] John 4.53–56; 19.34; 1 John 1.7; 5.6,8.
[10] John 3.19, etc.; 1 John 4.17; cf. 2.18, etc.
[11] Cf. John 20.23; 1 John 1.9; 2.12; cf. 3.5.
[12] John 3.16; 14.23; 17.23; 1 John 3.1; 4.11, etc.
[13] John 13.34; 15.12,17; 1 John 3.23, etc.
[14] John 15.10; 1 John 2.3; 3.22ff., etc.
[15] John 16.8; 1 John 2.16f.   [16] 1 John 3.8; cf. 2.14, etc.
[17] 1 John 2.18f.   [18] John 14.16, etc.; 1 John 3.24; 4.13; cf. 2.20.
[19] John 1.12; 11.52; 1 John 3.1,2, etc.   [20] John 1.7, etc.; 1 John 5.4.
[21] John 3.36 and *passim*; 1 John 4.14, etc.   [22] 2 Cor. 12.1–4.

274   THE WAY OF LIFE OF PAUL OF SAMOSATA

absence of any barbarous word, or solecism, or any vulgarism
whatever. For their author had, as it seems, both kinds of word,
by the free gift of the Lord, *the word of knowledge* and *the word*[1]

26 of style. But I will not deny that the other writer had seen *revelations* and received *knowledge* and *prophecy*[2]; nevertheless I observe
his language and his inaccurate Greek usage, employing, as he
does, barbarous idioms and in some places committing downright

27 solecisms. These there is no necessity to single out now. For I
have not said these things in mockery (let no one think it), but
merely to establish the dissimilarity of these writings. (Lawlor and
Oulton, *Eusebius*, I, pp. 237–40.)

2.   *For they say that it is not John's*, etc.: Gaius of Rome rejected the book
and the fourth Gospel also, cf. 138.

Cerinthus, cf. 70, 71.

16.   *it is said . . . that there were two tombs at Ephesus . . .*: cf. Eus., *H.E.*
III.39.4 where Eusebius, writing of Papias (31) mentions the two tombs, but
we may doubt whether he had any other source than this passage of Dionysius.

On this passage of Dionysius, cf. Westcott, *Canon of the New Testament*,
p. 367, n. 1; "I do not think there is any other piece of pure criticism in the
early Fathers to compare with it for style and manner".

238. THE WAY OF LIFE OF PAUL OF SAMOSATA, BISHOP OF ANTIOCH, *c.* 260–268

(From the letter of the Synod of 268 in Eusebius, *H.E.* VII.30.
6–16.)

6   But whereas he departed from the canon [of truth], and has
turned aside to spurious and bastard doctrines, we are under no

7 obligation *to judge* the actions of him *that is without*,[3] not even
because, though he was formerly poor and penniless, neither
having received wealth from his fathers nor having got it from
a trade or any occupation, he has now come to possess abundant
wealth, as a result of lawless deeds and sacrilegious plunderings
and extortions exacted from the brethren by threats; for he de-
prives the injured of their rights, and promises to help them for
money, yet breaks his word with these also, and with a light heart
makes his harvest out of the readiness of persons engaged in
lawsuits to make an offer, for the sake of being rid of those that

[1] 1 Cor. 12.8.   [2] 1 Cor. 14.6.   [3] 1 Cor. 5.12.

trouble them; seeing that he considers that *godliness is a way of*
8 *gain.*[1] Neither [do we judge him] because he *sets* his *mind on high
things*[2] and is lifted up, clothing himself with worldly honours
and wishing to be called "ducenarius" rather than bishop, and
struts in *the market-places,*[3] reading and dictating letters as he walks
in public, and attended by a body-guard, some preceding, some
following, and that too in numbers: with the result that the faith
is ill thought of and hated because of his conceit and the over-
9 weening pride of his heart. Nor [do we judge] the quackery in
church assemblies that he devises, courting popularity and posing
for appearance sake, and thus astonishing the minds of the simpler
folk, with the tribunal and lofty throne that he prepared for
himself, not befitting a disciple of Christ, and the "secretum",
which, in imitation of the rulers of the world, he has and so styles.
Also, he smites his hand on his thigh and stamps the tribunal with
his feet; and those who do not applaud or wave their handkerchiefs, as in a theatre, or shout out and jump up in the same way
as do the men and wretched women who are his partizans and
hearken in this disorderly fashion, but who listen, as in God's
house, with orderly and becoming reverence, he rebukes and
insults. And towards the interpreters of the Word who have
departed this life he behaves in an insolent and ill-bred fashion in
the common assembly, and brags about himself as though he
10 were not a bishop but a sophist and charlatan. And as to psalms,
he put a stop to those addressed to our Lord Jesus Christ, on the
ground that they are modern and the compositions of modern
men, but he trains women to sing psalms to himself in the middle
of the church on the great day of the Pascha, which would make
one shudder to hear. Such also is the kind of discourse that he
permits the bishops of the neighbouring country and towns, who
fawn upon him, and the presbyters as well, to deliver in their
11 sermons to the people. For he is not willing to acknowledge with
us that the Son of God has come down from heaven (to anticipate
something of what we are about to write; and this will not be
merely asserted, but is proved from many passages of the notes
that we send, and not least where he says that *Jesus Christ is from
below*); while they who sing psalms to him and utter his praises
in the congregation say that their impious teacher has come down
an angel from heaven. And he does not prevent this, but is even
present when such things are said, arrogant fellow that he is.
12 And as to the "subintroductae", as the Antiochenes call them,
his own and those of the presbyters and deacons in his company,

1 1 Tim. 6.5.   2 Rom. 12.16; 1 Tim. 6.17.
3 Cf. Demosthenes, κατὰ Μειδίου, 158.

with whom he joins in concealing both this and the other incurable
sins (though he knows of, and has convicted, them), that he may
have them under obligation to him, and that they may not dare,
through fear for themselves, to accuse him of his misdemeanours
in word and deed; yea, he has even made them rich, for which
cause he is the beloved and admired of those who affect such

13 conduct—why should we write of these things? But we know,
beloved, that the bishop and the priesthood as a whole should be
a pattern to the people *of* all *good works*[1]; and we are not ignorant
of this: how many have fallen through procuring "subintroductae" for themselves, while others have been under suspicion;
so that even if it be granted that he does nothing licentious, yet
he ought at least to guard against the suspicion that arises from
such a practice, lest he cause someone to stumble, and induce

14 others also to imitate him. For how could he rebuke another, or
counsel him not to consort any further with a woman and so
guard against a slip, as it is written,[2] seeing that he has sent one
away already, and has two in his company in the flower of youth
and beauty, and even if he go away anywhere, he brings them
around with him, living all the while in luxury and surfeiting?

15 Wherefore, though all groan and lament in private, so fearful
have they become of his tyranny and power, that they dare not

16 accuse him. Yet, as we have said before,[3] one might call to account
for these matters a man who has at any rate a catholic mind and is
numbered along with us; but as for one who burlesqued *the
mystery*[4] and strutted about in the abominable heresy of Artemas
(for why should we not bring ourselves to declare his father?)—
from such a one we think that we are under no obligation to
demand a reckoning for these things. (Lawlor and Oulton,
Eusebius, I, pp. 243-4, slightly altered.)

Eusebius tells us practically nothing about the heresy of Paul, and only
fragments of Paul's teaching survive in other sources. For aspects of his teaching
see 239, 240. The heresy of Paul had however roused the episcopate of the neighbouring provinces; the letter from which the above passage is taken was sent
to "Dionysus (of Rome) and Maximus (of Alexandria) and to all our fellow
ministers throughout the world, bishops, presbyters and deacons". (Eus.,
H.E. VII.30.2.)

Dionysius of Alexandria had been asked to come to Antioch, but was prevented by age and illness, and replied by letter (Eus., loc. cit. 3), Firmilian of
Caesarea in Cappadocia came on two occasions and died at Tarsus (Eus., loc.
cit. 4,5), while on his way for a third time.

[1] Tit. 2.7.   [2] Cf. Ecclus. 9.8,9.   [3] Sect. 6.
[4] Cf. 1 Tim. 3.16.

Following the defeat of Valerian by the Persians in 260, Antioch fell into the hands of the Kingdom of Palmyra, and Paul acted both as bishop and as an official of the Palmyrene state.

8. *"ducenarius"*: an imperial procurator who received a salary of 200,000 sesterces, but the title was applied in the third century A.D. and after to many officials of equestrian rank. Paul must have held this title under the kingdom of Palmyra.

9. *"secretum"*: in secular usage this was a part of the *tribunal* or platform on which a magistrate sat; it was separated from the public by barriers or curtains.

charlatan: the word thus translated (γόης) was used by Hippolytus of Callistus (136).

11. *Jesus Christ is from below*: i.e. he is not the same as the Word: for Paul's views, cf. 239.

13. *"subintroductae"*: this is the Latin term (not used by the letter). This problem exercised bishops, cf., e.g., Cyprian *Ep.* IV, and Councils, cf., e.g., Canon 27 of Elvira (265, p. 307), Canon 3 of Nicaea (300, p. 359). For other references see Benson, *Cyprian*, pp. 54–5, Bright, *Canons of the First Four General Councils*, pp. 8–9.

16. *the abominable heresy of Artemas*: In 17 Paul is exhorted to "write to Artemas". In *H.E.* V.28.1 Eusebius links Paul with Artemon, a supposed Monarchian heretic at Rome, but it is quite possible that the Artemas to whom the bishops refer was another heretic, otherwise unknown to us, and a contemporary of Paul.

For subsequent proceedings against Paul, see 241.

239. THE RELATION OF THE DIVINE AND HUMAN IN CHRIST, ACCORDING TO PAUL OF SAMOSATA

(Texts from H. de Riedmatten, *Les actes du procès de Paul de Samosate* (Fribourg en Suisse: Editions St Paul, 1952). The translations have been made from, or altered to conform to, de Riedmatten's text. The references S, 24, etc., conform to his numbering.)

(a) (de Riedmatten, op. cit., S, 24, p. 147, from the Syriac.)

From the encyclical letter of the Synod which condemned Paul of Samosata: He conceived otherwise the conjunction with Wisdom, making it according to friendship and not according to substance.

(b) (de Riedmatten, op. cit., S, 37, p. 158, from Justinian.)

The word was conjoined to him who came from David, i.e.
Jesus Christ who was begotten of the Holy Ghost. And him the
Virgin bore, through the Holy Ghost. But the Word was begotten
of God, apart from the Virgin and apart from any other but God.
Thus it was that the Word took an independent existence. (B. J.
Kidd, *Documents illustrative of the History of the Church*, I, p. 217,
altered.)

(c) (de Riedmatten, op. cit., S, 26, p. 153, from Leontius of
Byzantium.)

A human being is anointed, the Word is not anointed. The
Nazarene our Lord is anointed. For the Word is greater than the
anointed one, i.e. Christ, since the anointed one became great
through Wisdom. For the Word is from above, Jesus Christ is
man from hence. Mary did not give birth to the Word; she was
not before the ages. And Mary is not older than the Word, but
she gave birth to a man like us, though better in every way, since
he was of the Holy Ghost. (B. J. Kidd, op. cit., I, p. 217, altered.)

(d) (de Riedmatten, op. cit., S, 36, p. 158, a fragment of the
examination of Paul by Malchion.)

MALCHION: This Word having thus an independent existence,
himself was born in that body, as you also admitted in the expression "from Mary", since the scriptures say that he shared our
nature, as we participate in it and since *children* (says scripture)
have shared flesh and blood,[1] for this reason the Son of God did so.
I inquire therefore if, even as we men, i.e. as composite beings,
possess a coming together of flesh and of something dwelling in
the flesh, even so the Word Himself, Wisdom Herself was in that
body as the life principle is in us in this life? Even as in our case
we are complete from the conjunction (i.e. of body and the
principle of life) so too it is in His case from the concurrence in
the same person of the Word of God, and the element that came
from the Virgin.
PAUL: You answered for me too from your way of speaking.
MALCHION: I asked you a question. You speak of Wisdom and
Word. But in the case of human beings one is said to participate
in word and wisdom, while another lacks them. Do you mean
that (in the case of Christ) it is by participation or by the Word
itself and Wisdom coming down upon Him? Substance (οὐσία)
and participation are not alike. For the substantial is as a part of
the total person who became our Lord by the intermingling of

[1] Heb. 2.14.

God and man, but participation does not mean being a part of the person in whom it is.

PAUL: All those here agree with what I say. Now *you* tell me—I am asking first (this time). Your argument has tried to put forward as an illustration something in no way analogous. The constitution of humanity is different. We were talking about Word and Wisdom. And all . . . (about the analogy of a human being that you have introduced is irrelevant).

Paul is very wary of being led to admit that the Word took the place of the human soul in Christ, cf. the view put forward by C. E. Raven, *Apollinarianism*, that Paul's opponents, who apparently took this view, were forerunners of Apollinarius' heresy. On the whole question, cf. a fragment of the Synodal Letter in de Riedmatten, op. cit., S, 30, p. 152, from Leontius of Byzantium. (The Bishops ask): "What is the meaning of the assertion that Jesus Christ had a constitution different from ours? We maintain that his constitution differed from ours in but one respect, admittedly of the first magnitude, that the God-Logos was in him what the inner man is in us." (Tr. Chadwick, *J.T.S.*, N.S. IV (1953), p. 93.)

(d) Malchion, who played a leading part in unmasking Paul, was a presbyter, and also head of a school of rhetoric at Antioch. (Eus. *H.E.* VII.29.2.)

240. THE USE OF THE TERM *HOMO-OUSIOS* BY PAUL OF SAMOSATA

(1. Athanasius, *On the Councils of Ariminum and Seleuceia*, 45.)

Athanasius is resolving the apparent contradiction that ὁμοούσιος was rejected by those who condemned Paul, but accepted at Nicaea, see 301.

For they who deposed the Samosatene took co-essential (i.e. consubstantial) (ὁμοούσιος) in a bodily sense, because Paul had attempted sophistry and said "Unless Christ has of man become God, it follows that he is co-essential with the Father; and if so there are of necessity three essences, one the previous essence, and the other two from it" and therefore guarding against this, they said with good reason, that Christ was not co-essential. (N. & P.-N. F.)

(2. Hilary, *De Synodis*, 81.)

: . . our fathers . . ., when Paul of Samosata was declared a heretic, repudiated the expression "of one essence (or substance)", because, in using this expression he declared that Father and Son were a solitary unit.

"If Athanasius is correct, Paul reasoned about the Father and the Son from the nature of material substances, showing that in their case the existence of two articles, such as (let us suppose) two pence, alike made of copper, involves the presupposition of the substance copper—'a previous substance, and the other two derived out of it'." (Prestige, *God in Patristic Thought*, p. 202.)

*   *   *

"Hilary himself appears to imagine that Paul of Samosata actually was a Sabellian (cf. section 82, what Christian can 'follow the man of Samosata in confessing that Christ in Himself is both Father and Son to Himself?'). In this belief Hilary was almost certainly mistaken. Though it has been disputed, nearly all authorities are agreed that Paul was an Adoptionist, and believed, not that the Logos was a transient phase of the divine Person, but that it was a permanent and impersonal attribute of God." (Prestige, op. cit., p. 205.)

241. AURELIAN AND THE CHRISTIANS, 272–275
(Eusebius, *H.E.* VII.30.19–21.)

19   But as Paul refused on any account to give up possession of the church-building, the emperor Aurelian, on being petitioned, gave an extremely just decision regarding the matter, ordering the assignment of the building to those with whom the bishops of the doctrine in Italy and Rome should communicate in writing. Thus, then, was the aforesaid man driven with the utmost indignity from the church by the ruler of this world.

20   Such indeed was the disposition of Aurelian towards us at that time. But as his reign advanced, he changed his mind with regard to us, and was now being moved by certain counsels to stir up persecution against us; and there was great talk about this

21   on all sides. But as he was just on the point of so doing and was putting, one might almost say, his signature to the decrees against us, the divine Justice visited him, and pinioned his arms, so to speak, to prevent his undertaking. (Lawlor and Oulton, *Eusebius*, I, p. 245.)

This is the first occasion of which we have record in which the Church made an appeal to the pagan state. Paul of Samosata, as well as being Bishop of Antioch, had held lucrative office under the kingdom of Palmyra, during the years (261–272) in which that kingdom controlled the East. His final condemnation for heresy was in 268. While he retained the support of Palmyra—and of part at least of the population of Antioch—he could not be ejected from the actual Church building. Aurelian was at Antioch in 272, and, while his judgement on this question was "extremely just" it does not argue any sympathy with Christianity. The continuation of Eusebius' narrative shows how little the Empire was yet prepared for toleration. Lactantius (*On the deaths of the persecutors*, 6) regards Aurelian as having actually sanctioned persecution, but his edict had not reached the more distant provinces.

242. MANI, d. 272

(Eusebius, *H.E.*, VII.31,1–2.)

1   At that time also the madman, who gave his name to his devil-possessed heresy, was taking as his armour mental delusion; for the devil, that is Satan himself, the adversary of God, had put the man forward for the destruction of many. His very speech and manners proclaimed him a barbarian in mode of life, and, being by nature devilish and insane, he suited his endeavours thereto and attempted to pose as Christ: at one time giving out that he was *the Paraclete* and *the* Holy *Spirit*[1] Himself, conceited fool that he was, as well as mad; at another time choosing, as Christ did,

2 *twelve disciples*[2] as associates in his new-fangled system. In short, he stitched together false and godless doctrines that he had collected from the countless, long-extinct, godless heresies, and infected our empire with, as it were, a deadly poison that came from the land of the Persians; and from him the profane name of Manichaean is still commonly on men's lips to this day. (Lawlor and Oulton, *Eusebius*, I, p. 246.)

243. THE MESSAGE OF MANI

(Mani, from Burkitt, *The Religion of the Manichees*, p. 37.)

"In the beginning of the book called *Shābūhrāgan* written by Mani for King Shapur, son of Ardashir, he says:"

Wisdom and deeds have always from time to time been brought to mankind by the messengers of God. So in one age they have been brought by the messenger called Buddha to India, in another by Zarādusht to Persia, in another by Jesus to the West. Thereupon this revelation has come down, this prophecy in this last age, through me, Mani, messenger of the God of truth to Babylonia. (Burkitt, op. cit., p. 37.)

[1] John 14.16f.   [2] Matt. 10.1, etc.

With the above, cf. a statement in *St Ephraim's Prose Refutations of Mani, Marcion and Bardaisan* (ed. Mitchell II, p. XCVIII):

> ... the Manichees "say about Hermes in Egypt, and about Plato among the Greeks, and about Jesus who appeared in Judaea, that 'they are Heralds of that Good One to the world.'" (Burkitt, op. cit., p. 38.)

244. THE UNIVERSALITY OF MANI'S RELIGION

(Mani, *Kephalaion*, CLIV.)

He who has his Church in the West, he and his church have not reached the East: the choice of him who has chosen his Church in the East has not come to the West. ... But my Hope, mine, will go towards the West, and she will go also towards the East. And they shall hear the voice of her message in all languages, and shall proclaim her in all cities. My Church is superior in this first point to previous Churches, for these previous Churches were chosen in particular countries and in particular cities. My Church, mine shall spread in all cities, and my Gospel shall touch every country. (H. C. Puech, *Le Manichéisme*, p. 63.)

245. DIOCLETIAN'S EDICT AGAINST THE MANICHEES, c. 295 (?)

(*Lex Dei sive Mosaicarum et Romanorum Legum Collatio*, XV.iii, ed. Kuebler in *Iurisprudentiae Anteiustinianae Reliquiae*, Ed. 6, II.2, pp. 381–3 (Teubner): A. Adam, *Texte zum Manichäismus* (Kleine Texte 175), pp. 82–3.)

This edict was addressed to Julian, proconsul of Africa. It was probably issued in the name of all four emperors of Diocletian's Tetrarchy, i.e. Diocletian himself, Maximianus Augustus, Constantius Caesar and Galerius Caesar. The text is, in places, very doubtful, and in the version given below the text in Adam, op. cit., has been followed.

1–3 [Peace sometimes allows the spread of most foolish and base doctrines by wicked men, but the gods by their providence have shown mankind what is right and true; they must not be resisted, and "established religion ought not to be criticized by a new one".

It is a very serious charge if one tampers with what has been laid down absolutely and definitely by the ancients. The Emperors regard it as their bounden duty to inflict punishment on those who spread the propaganda of new sects against the revelation of antiquity.]

4   Your Carefulness has written to our Serenity about their activities. We have heard that the Manichees very recently like new and unexpected monstrosities have taken their rise among the race of the Persians which is at enmity with us, and have progressed thence into our empire, and that they commit many crimes there; for our information is that they disturb quiet populations, and even work the greatest harm to whole cities: our fear is that in the course of time as usually happens they will attempt through the accursed morals and savage laws of the Persians to infect men of less wicked nature, i.e. the modest and peaceful race of the Romans and our whole dominion with, as it were, the poison of

5   a malignant serpent. And because all the manifestations of their religion which your Prudence revealed in your account set out the carefully devised and thought out contrivances of obvious malefactors, we therefore set out due and fitting pains and penalties

6   for them. For we order the authors and leaders of the sect, to be subjected to a very severe penalty, namely, to be burnt, along with their abominable scriptures: but their followers, who are persistently obstinate we order to be punished with death, and we

7   ordain that their property be confiscated to our treasury. If any persons of the official classes, or of any rank, no matter what, or of superior status, have betaken themselves to this unheard of, base, and utterly infamous sect, or to the doctrine of the Persians, see that their property is attached to our treasury and that they are themselves committed to the mines (quarries) of Phaeno or

8   Proconnesus. In order that this utter wickedness be rooted out completely from our happy age, let your Devotion not delay to carry out with all haste the orders and regulations of our Tranquillity. Given at Alexandria on 31 March.

The year is uncertain, but outbreak of war with Persia in 293 may have caused the Roman authorities to consider the position of the Manichees. With a certain obtuseness the Romans attacked a sect which came from Persia, but *was itself proscribed there*. The edict divides those to be punished into classes, (1) authors and leaders (*auctores ac principes*) i.e. the Elect, the "true Manichee" (Burkitt, op. cit., p. 44) and (2) the Hearers, who were far more numerous.

4. On Manichaean immorality, cf. the law of Valentinian I (A.D. 372) in *Cod. Theod.* XVI.5.3 (Adam, op. cit., p. 84).

the poison of a malignant serpent: cf. Eusebius in 242 above.

7. *Phaeno*; in Arabia, Christians were sent to these mines (Eus., *H.E.* VIII. 13.5, etc., *Mart. Pal.* 13.1).

Proconnesus an island in the Propontis, where there were extensive quarries.

246. THE EARLY LATIN CHRISTIAN AUTHORS

(Lactantius, *Div. Inst.* V.1.22–7.)

22 Of those who are known to me, Minucius Felix was of no mean rank among pleaders. His book, which is entitled *Octavius*, shows how doughty a champion of the truth he could have been,
23 if he had devoted himself entirely to that occupation. Septimius Tertullianus too was skilled in every sort of literature, but in eloquence he had little readiness, with small polish and much
24 obscurity. So neither did he find much popularity. Cyprian therefore was the one more than others conspicuous and eminent, for he had won to himself much glory from his profession of the art of oratory, and he has written a great number of things in
25 their own sort worthy of admiration. For he was of a ready spirit, fluent, agreeable, and (what is a very great excellence of language) plain, so that you cannot decide whether he was more elegant in language, or happier in explanation, or stronger in
26 persuasion. Yet even he cannot please—further than his words—those who do not know the mystery, since the words he has spoken are mystical, and shaped to the end that they may be understood of the faithful only: in short, by the learned of this world to whom his writings have by chance become known, he is com-
27 monly ridiculed. I heard a man—and an eloquent one too—who by the change of one letter called him Coprian (i.e. from κόπρος, dung), for the reason that he had transferred his stylistic ability, fitted for better things, to old wives tales. (Gwatkin, *Selections from Early Christian Writers*, p. 165, with last sentence added.)

In *Div. Inst.* V.4.3–4 Lactantius recurs to his predecessors. He finds Tertullian's apologetic too legal in form, and limited to defence: he finds Cyprian using the wrong method, e.g. he tried to refute his opponent Demetrian by means of scripture, which the latter rejected.

247. HOW THE GREAT PERSECUTION
BEGAN, 302–303

(Lactantius, *On the deaths of the persecutors*, 11–13.)

11.1 The mother of Galerius, an exceedingly superstitious woman, was a votary of the gods of the mountains. Being of such a character, she made sacrifices with sacred banquets almost every day, and she feasted her servants on the meat offered to idols; but the Christians would not partake, and while she feasted with the
2 Gentiles, they continued in fasting and prayer. On this account she conceived hatred against the Christians, and by woman-like complaints instigated her son, no less superstitious than herself,
3 to destroy them. So during the whole winter Diocletian and Galerius took counsel together; no one else was admitted, and it was the universal opinion that their conferences concerned the most momentous affairs of the empire. The old man long opposed the fury of Galerius, and showed how pernicious it would be to raise disturbances throughout the world and to shed so much blood; that the Christians were wont to meet death with eagerness; and that it would be enough if officials at the court and the
4 armed forces were forbidden to practise Christianity. Yet he could not restrain the madness of that headstrong man. He resolved,
5 therefore, to take the opinion of his friends. Now this was a trait in the evil disposition of Diocletian that whenever he determined to do good, he did it without advice, that the praise might be all his own; but whenever he determined to do ill, which he was sensible would be blamed, he called in many advisers that
6 his own fault might be imputed to other men. A few civil magistrates therefore and a few military commanders were admitted to give their counsel; and the question was put to them according to priority of rank. Some, through personal ill-will towards the Christians, were of opinion that they ought to be destroyed as enemies of the gods and adversaries of the state religion. Others thought differently; but, having understood the will of Galerius, they, either from dread of displeasing him or from a desire of gratifying him, concurred in the opinion given against the
7 Christians. Yet not even then could the Emperor be prevailed upon to yield his assent. He determined that the best plan was to consult his gods, and to that end he despatched a soothsayer to inquire of Apollo of Miletus, whose answer was such as might be

8 expected from an enemy of the divine religion. So Diocletian
was drawn over from his purpose. And although he could struggle
no longer against his friends and against his Caesar (i.e. Galerius)
and Apollo, yet still he attempted to observe such moderation
as to command the business to be carried through without blood-
shed; whereas Galerius would have had all persons burnt alive
who refused to sacrifice.

12.1   A fit and auspicious day was sought for the accomplishment
of this undertaking, and the festival of the god Terminus, celebrated on the twenty-third of February was chosen, in preference
to all others, to "terminate", as it were, the Christian religion.

>That day, the harbinger of death, arose,
>First cause of ill, and long-enduring woes,[1]

2   which befel not only the Christians, but the whole earth.
When that day dawned, in the eighth consulship of Diocletian
and seventh of Maximian, suddenly, while it was yet hardly light,
the prefect, together with chief commanders, tribunes and officers
of the treasury, came to the church in Nicomedia; they forced
the doors and searched everywhere for an image of the god. The
Holy Scriptures were found and burnt; the church was abandoned
3 to general pillage: all was rapine, confusion, tumult. That church,
situated on rising ground, was within view of the palace, and
Diocletian and Galerius stood on a watch-tower, disputing long
4 whether it ought to be set on fire. The sentiment of Diocletian
prevailed, who was afraid that once so great a blaze had started,
some part of the city might be burnt; for there were many large
5 buildings round the church. Then Praetorian Guards came in
battle array, with axes and other tools; they were let loose everywhere, and in a few hours, levelled that very lofty edifice with
the ground.

13   Next day an edict was published, depriving the Christians of
all honours and dignities; ordaining also that, without any distinction of rank or degree, they should be subject to torture, and
that every suit at law should be received against them; while,
on the other hand, they were debarred from being plaintiffs in
questions of wrong, adultery, or theft; and, finally, that they
should neither be capable of freedom, nor have right of suffrage.
(A.-N. C. L., altered.)

13.   The meaning of the last phrase is uncertain. (See note to 248.)

[1] Vergil, *Aen.* IV.169f.

248. THE FIRST EDICTS OF PERSECUTION

(Eusebius, *H.E.* VIII.2.4–5.)

4   It was the nineteenth year of the reign of Diocletian, and the month Dystrus, or March, as the Romans would call it, in which, as the festival of the Saviour's Passion was coming on, an imperial letter was everywhere promulgated, ordering the razing of the churches to the ground and the destruction by fire of the Scriptures, and proclaiming that those who held high positions would lose all civil rights, while those in households, if they persisted in their profession of Christianity, would be deprived of
5   their liberty. Such was the first document against us. But not long afterwards we were further visited with other letters, and in them the order was given that the presidents of the churches should all, in every place, be first committed to prison, and then afterwards compelled by every kind of device to sacrifice. (Lawlor and Oulton, *Eusebius*, I, p. 257.)

4. "Lactantius closes his account of the edict with the words 'libertatem denique ac vocem non haberent'. Eusebius in the same position writes 'Those who were in *oiketiai* (households) if they persisted in their profession of Christianity were to be deprived of their freedom'. The words have been much discussed, and their meaning is uncertain. But the measures taken against the Christians by Valerian may have served as a precedent on this occasion: in the former persecution Christians serving in the imperial bureaux, the Caesariani, were, if they persisted in their faith, reduced to slavery and it may be suggested that this is the meaning of the phrase used by Eusebius." (Baynes in *Cambridge Ancient History*, XII, pp. 665–6.)
    The translation "households" has been allowed to stand, and would mean "Christians in a private station". But the explanation in the *C.A.H.* appears the more likely one.

249. "HAND OVER YOUR BOOKS!"
ACTION AT CIRTA, 19 MAY 303

(*Gesta apud Zenophilum*, *C.S.E.L.* XXVI, pp. 186–8.)

In the eighth and seventh consulships of Diocletian and Maximian, 19th May, from the records of Munatius Felix, high priest of the province for life, mayor of the colony of Cirta. Arrived at the house where the Christians used to meet, the Mayor said to

Paul the bishop: "Bring out the writings of the law and anything else you have here, according to the order, so that you may obey the command."

The Bishop: "The readers have the scriptures, but we will give what we have here."

The Mayor: "Point out the readers or send for them."

The Bishop: "You all know them."

The Mayor: "We do not know them."

The Bishop: "The municipal office knows them, that is, the clerks Edusius and Junius."

The Mayor: "Leaving over the matter of the readers, whom the office will point out, produce what you have."

Then follows an inventory of the church plate and other property, including large stores of male and female clothes and shoes, produced in the presence of the clergy, who include three priests, two deacons, and four subdeacons, all named, and a number of "diggers".

The Mayor: "Bring out what you have."

Silvanus and Carosus (two of the subdeacons): "We have thrown out everything that was here."

The Mayor: "Your answer is entered on the record."

After some empty cupboards had been found in the library, Silvanus then produced a silver box and a silver lamp, which he said he had found behind a barrel.

Victor (the mayor's clerk): "You would have been a dead man if you hadn't found them."

The Mayor: "Look more carefully, in case there is anything left here."

Silvanus: "There is nothing left. We have thrown everything out."

And when the dining-room was opened, there were found there four bins and six barrels.

The Mayor: "Bring out the scriptures that you have so that we can obey the orders and command of the emperors."

Catullinus (another subdeacon) produced one very large volume.

The Mayor: "Why have you given one volume only? Produce the scriptures that you have."

Marcuclius and Catullinus (two subdeacons): "We haven't any more, because we are subdeacons; the readers have the books."

The Mayor: "Show me the readers."

Marcuclius and Catullinus: "We don't know where they live."

The Mayor: "If you don't know where they live, tell me their names."

Marcuclius and Catullinus: "We are not traitors: here we are, order us to be killed."

The Mayor: "Put them under arrest."

They apparently weakened so far as to reveal one reader, for the Mayor now moved on to the house of Eugenius, who produced four books.

The Mayor now turned on the other two subdeacons, Silvanus and Carosus:

The Mayor: "Show me the other readers."

Silvanus and Carosus: "The bishop has already said that Edusius and Junius the clerks know them all: they will show you the way to their houses."

Edusius and Junius: "We will show them, sir."

The Mayor went on to visit the six remaining readers. Four produced their books without demur. One declared he had none, and the Mayor was content with entering his statement on the record. The last was out, but his wife produced his books; the Mayor had the house searched by the public slave to make sure that none had been overlooked. This task over, he addressed the subdeacons: "If there has been any omission, the responsibility is yours." (A. H. M. Jones, *Constantine and the Conversion of Europe*, pp. 51-4.)

250. THE FOURTH EDICT, 304

(Eusebius, *Martyrs of Palestine*, 3.1.)

Such was the course of action in the first year, when the presidents of the Church were alone menaced by the persecution. But when the second year came round and, further, the war against us increased in intensity (Urban being at that time governor of the province), imperial edicts then visited us for the first time, in which by a general ordinance the command was given that in the several cities all the people in a body should sacrifice and offer libations to the idols. (Lawlor and Oulton, *Eusebius*, I, p. 339.)

when the second year came round: i.e. in the spring of 304. By this edict the policy of Decius was taken up again. But it is clear from the narrative of Eusebius in *M.P.* 2 that many Christians found it politic to submit at an earlier date.

251. MELITIUS OF LYCOPOLIS, *c.* 305

(Letter of four Egyptian Bishops; Latin text, from Codex Veronensis LX, in Turner, *Ecclesiae Occidentalis Monumenta Iuris Antiquissima*, I, pp. 634–5; Routh, *Reliquiae Sacrae*, ed. 2., IV, pp. 91–3.)

Hesychius, Pachomius, Theodorus and Phileas, to Melitius our beloved and fellow-minister in the Lord, greeting.

In simplicity of mind we have held rumours about you to be unreliable. Visitors have told us of certain attempts—and even completed actions—alien to divine order and the Church's rule: these we would not credit having regard to the greatness of the audacity and strange temerity involved.

But since many who are visiting us at the present time have certified the truth of these reports, and did not hesitate to attest them as facts, we have been utterly astounded and have been compelled to write this letter to you. What agitation and sadness have been caused to us all in common and to us individually by the report of the ordination carried through by you in parishes wholly unconnected with you, we are unable sufficiently to express. We shall not delay, however, to address a brief rebuke.

There is the law of our fathers and forefathers, of which you are not yourself ignorant, established according to divine and ecclesiastical order—for by them in all respects it has been established and settled with due regard to the good pleasure of God and zealous anxiety for better things—that it is not lawful for any bishop to celebrate ordinations in parishes other than his own; a law which is exceedingly important and wisely devised. For (1) it is but right that the conversation and life of ordinands should be examined with great care; and, (2) that all confusion and turbulence should be done away with. For every one of us will have enough to do in managing his own parish, and in finding with great care and many anxieties suitable ministers among those with whom he has passed his whole life, and who have been trained under his hands. But you, neither taking any account of these things, and with no regard for the future, and the law throughout of our blessed fathers and those who have been taken to Christ in succession, nor the honour of our great bishop and Father Peter, on whom we all depend in the hope which we have in the Lord Jesus Christ, nor softened by our imprisonments and trials, and by the disgraces daily heaped upon us and by the oppression and straits in which all of us are, have ventured on subverting all things at once. What chance of excuse have you got for such acts?

But perhaps you will say: I did this to prevent many being drawn away with the unbelief of many, because the flocks were in need and forsaken, there being no pastor with them. But it is most certain that they are not in such destitution: (1) because there are many going about them and in a position to act as visitors; and (2) even if there was some measure of neglect on their side, then the proper way would have been for representations to be made promptly by the people, and for us to do our duty by them. But they knew that they were in no want of ministers, and therefore they did not come to seek them. They knew that if we made due inquiry, our course, embodied in advice to them, was to dismiss the case, or to have everything done which seemed to be expedient; for † all was done under correction, † and all was considered with well-approved honesty. You, however, giving such strenuous attention to the deceits of certain parties and their vain words, made a stealthy leap to the conducting of ordinations. For if indeed those with you were constraining you to this, and in their ignorance were doing violence to ecclesiastical order, you ought to have followed the common rule and have informed us by letter; and in that way what seemed expedient would have been done. And if perchance some persuaded you to credit their story that it was all over with us (a thing of which you could not have been ignorant, because there were many going to and returning from us who could visit you), even although, I say, this had been the case, yet you ought to have waited for the judgement of the superior father (i.e. Peter of Alexandria), and for his permission to do this. But without giving heed to these matters, but indulging in a different expectation, yea rather, indeed, denying all respect to us, you have provided certain rulers for the people. For already we have learned too that there have been also divisions, because your unwarrantable exercise of the right of ordination displeased many.

And you were not persuaded to delay such procedure or restrain your purpose readily even by the word of the Apostle Paul, the most blessed seer, and the man who put on Christ, who is the Apostle of all of us; for he, in writing to his dearly-beloved son Timothy, says: *Lay hands suddenly on no man, neither be partaker of other men's sins.*[1] And thus he at once shows his own anxious consideration for him, and gives him his example and exhibits the law according to which, with all carefulness and caution, persons are to be chosen for ordination. † He speaks with a view

[1] 1 Tim. 5.22.

to the more distant future. We make this declaration to you, †
that you may study to keep within the safe and salutary limits of
the rule. (A.-N. C. L., much altered.)

The original Greek of this letter is lost. The Latin text appears to be corrupt,
particularly where † † have been inserted.

Eusebius speaks most highly of Phileas (Bishop of Thmuis) in *H.E.* VIII.9.7—
10.1,11, and gives the text of a letter to his church on the sufferings of the
martyrs, in VIII.10.2–10.

Melitius is often called Meletius: Epiphanius, *Haer.* 68.1 suggests that, after
Peter of Alexandria, Melitius was the most important bishop in Egypt. The
events subsequent to the sending of this letter are detailed in 252 and 253 which
follow the letter in Codex Veronensis LX.

252. THE SCHISM OF MELITIUS

(Latin text, from Codex Veronensis LX in Turner, *Ecclesiae
Occidentalis Monumenta Iuris Antiquissima*, I, pp. 635–6; Routh,
Reliquiae Sacrae, ed. 2, IV.94.)

After receiving and perusing this epistle, he neither wrote any
reply nor repaired to them in the prison, nor went to the blessed
Peter. But when all these bishops and presbyters and deacons had
suffered martyrdom in the prison at Alexandria, he at once entered
Alexandria. Now in that city there was a certain person, by name
Isidore, turbulent in character and possessed with the ambition of
finding a teacher. And there was also a certain Arius, who wore
the habit of piety, and was in like manner possessed with the ambition to find a teacher. And when they discovered the object
of Melitius's ambition, and what he wanted, hastening to him and
being envious of the episcopal authority of the blessed Peter, (the
motive of Melitius being disclosed), they discovered to Melitius
certain presbyters, then in hiding, to whom the blessed Peter had
given power to act as parish-visitors. And Melitius recommending
them to improve the opportunity given them, separated them
from Peter's communion, and himself ordained two persons, one
in prison and another in the mines. On learning these things, the
blessed Peter, with much endurance, wrote to the people of Alexandria a letter in the following terms. (A.-N. C. L., much altered.)

The bishops who wrote to Melitius were martyrs, probably in the spring
of 306. The narrative as given above is not entirely clear in the sequence of
events. On Arius and Melitius, cf. 291, but the ordinations carried out by

Melitius ("one in prison and the other in the mines") must surely belong to the period when Melitius himself was imprisoned, "at a later date". (Bell, *Jews and Christians in Egypt*, p. 39, q.v., pp. 38ff. for a succinct account of the schism, and of the authorities for it.)

The letter of Peter follows in 253.

253. THE LETTER OF PETER, BISHOP OF ALEXANDRIA, TO HIS FLOCK

(Latin text, from Codex Veronensis LX, in Turner, *Ecclesiae Occidentalis Monumenta Iuris Antiquissima*, I, p. 636; Routh, *Reliquiae Sacrae*, ed. 2, IV.94.)

Peter, to his beloved brethren, established in the faith of God, greeting. Since I have found out that Melitius acts in no way for the common good—for neither is he contented with the letter of the most holy bishops and martyrs—but, invading my parish has assumed so much to himself as to endeavour to separate from my authority the presbyters and those who had been entrusted with visiting the needy; and, giving proof of his desire for pre-eminence, has ordained in the prison several for himself; now take heed to this and hold no communion with him until I meet him in company with some wise and discreet men, and see what his designs have been. Farewell. (A.-N. C. L., altered.)

254. RESPITE FOLLOWED BY RENEWED PERSECUTION, 308

(Eusebius, *Martyrs of Palestine*, 9.1–3.)

1   These brave deeds on the part of the magnificent martyrs of Christ were followed by a lessening of the fire of persecution, which was being quenched, as it were, by their sacred blood; relief and liberty were now granted those who for Christ's sake were suffering affliction in the mines of the Thebais; and we were just about to regain a breath of pure air, when some agitation (I know not how) caused him, to whom had been assigned the authority to persecute, to be inflamed once more against us.

2   At any rate, all of a sudden an edict of Maximin was again published against us everywhere; and the governors in each province

and, moreover, he who was placed in charge of the troops, urged
by means of proclamations, letters and public ordinances the
curators, together with the duumvirs and registrars in every city,
to put into execution the imperial edict. This ordered that those
idol temples which had fallen should be rebuilt with all speed;
that care should be taken that all the people in a mass, men with
their wives and households, even babes at the breast, should offer
sacrifice and libations and taste with scrupulous care the accursed
sacrifices themselves; that the articles for sale in the market-place
should be defiled by the libations from the sacrifices, and that
guards should be posted before the baths in order to defile with
the abominable sacrifices those whose custom it was to cleanse
3 themselves therein. While these orders, then, were thus being
carried into effect, our people once more fell a prey, as was
natural, to grave anxiety, and the unbelieving heathen found
fault with the absurdity of what was done, on the ground that it
was harsh and unnecessary (for to their mind the thing was dis-
gusting and burdensome). (Lawlor and Oulton, *Eusebius*, I, pp.
371-2, slightly altered.)

This brief respite was probably connected with the positive policy for paganism now instituted by Maximin, cf. 255, to whose dominions alone these
measures given here applied.

1. *These brave deeds . . .*: Eusebius had been relating the sufferings of very
numerous martyrs, by death, torture, mutilation and forced labour in the
mines.

3. *the unbelieving heathen found fault*: they were no more likely to side with
Maximin's policy than they were later with that of Julian.

255. MAXIMIN'S ATTEMPTED REVIVAL
OF PAGANISM, 308-312

(Eusebius, *H.E.* VIII.14.9: IX, 4.2-5.2.)

9   Accordingly, he applied himself to the persecution against us
with more energy and persistence than those before him, ordering
temples to be erected in every city and the sacred groves that had
been destroyed through long lapse of time to be restored with all
diligence; and he appointed idol priests in every locality and city,
and over them as high priest of each province one of those engaged
in state-craft, who was the most manifestly distinguished in every
branch of the public service, with an escort and body-guard of
soldiers; and he recklessly bestowed governments and the greatest

privileges on all charlatans, as if they were pious and dear to the gods. (Lawlor and Oulton, *Eusebius*, I, p. 272, slightly altered.)

It is clear that Maximin's policy lasted and developed during several years, cf. Eusebius *H.E.* IX.4.2—5.2.

4.2   Maximin himself appointed as priests of the images in each city and, moreover, as high priests, those who were especially distinguished in the public services and had made their mark in the entire course thereof. These persons brought great zeal to bear

3   on the worship of the gods whom they served. Certainly, the outlandish superstition of the ruler was inducing, in a word, all under him, both governors and governed, to do everything against us in order to secure his favour; in return for the benefits which they thought to secure from him, they bestowed upon him this greatest of boons, namely, to thirst for our blood and to display some more novel tokens of malice towards us.

5.1   Having forged, to be sure, Memoirs of Pilate and our Saviour, full of every kind of blasphemy against Christ, with the approval of their chief they sent them round to every part of his dominions, with edicts that they should be exhibited openly for everyone to see in every place, both town and country, and that the primary teachers should give them to the children, instead of lessons, for study and committal to memory.

2   While this was thus being carried out, another person, a commander, whom the Romans style "dux", caused certain infamous women to be abducted from the market-place at Damascus in Phoenicia, and, by continually threatening them with the infliction of tortures, compelled them to state in writing that they were once actually Christians, and privy to their unhallowed deeds, and that the Christians practised in the very churches lewdness and everything else that he wished these women to say in defamation of our faith. He also made a memorandum of their words and communicated it to the Emperor, and moreover at his command published this document also in every place and city. (Lawlor and Oulton, *Eusebius*, I, pp. 281–2.)

Lactantius (*On the deaths of the persecutors* 36.4–5) also describes this organization of paganism. He gives the additional information that the new organization was designed as an instrument of persecution also.

5.1. In *H.E.* I.9.3, Eusebius mentions the recent origin of these *Acts of Pilate*, and a mistake in them about the date of the crucifixion.

5.2. Besides the new features in Maximin's policy we may note the effort to revivify the old slanders against the Christians, which were by now an obsolete weapon.

256. THE TOLERATION EDICT OF GALERIUS, 30 APRIL 311

(Lactantius, *On the deaths of the persecutors*, 34.)

1   Amongst our other arrangements, which we are making for the permanent advantage of the state, we had heretofore endeavoured to set all things right according to the ancient laws and public order of the Romans. It has been our special care that the Christians too who had left the persuasion of their forefathers
2   should return to a better mind; since through some strange reasoning such wilfulness had seized the said Christians and such folly possessed them that, instead of following those constitutions of the ancients which peradventure their own ancestors had first established, they were making themselves laws for their own observance, merely according to their own judgement and as their pleasure was, and in divers places were assembling various
3   multitudes. In short, when our order had been set forth to the effect that they should betake themselves to the institutions of the ancients, many of them were subdued by danger, many also
4   exposed to jeopardy. Nevertheless very great numbers held to their determination, and we saw that these neither gave worship and due reverence to the gods, nor yet worshipped the god of the Christians—we therefore in consideration of our most mild clemency, and of the unbroken custom whereby we are used to grant pardon to all men, have thought it right in this case also to offer our speediest indulgence, that Christians may exist again, and may establish their meeting houses, yet so that they do
5   nothing contrary to good order. By another letter we shall signify to magistrates how they should proceed. Wherefore, in accordance with this our indulgence it will be their duty to pray their god for our good estate, and that of the state, and their own, that the commonwealth may endure on every side unharmed, and they may be able to live securely in their habitations. (Gwatkin, *Selections from Early Christian Writers*, pp. 169–71, altered.)

In Chapter 33 Lactantius, with great glee, gives a detailed account of the horrible disease that afflicted Galerius until "beaten by his woes he was compelled to confess God".

1.   On forsaking ancestral custom, cf. 162, 165.

2.   The edict is contemptuous as the words "wilfulness" and "folly" show.

4.   *may establish their meeting-houses*: which had been destroyed, cf. 266, p. 310.

5.   *By another letter*: this letter is lost, but it probably circumscribed the toleration here granted: in the "Edict of Milan" (260), there are several probable references to this letter.

257. A PETITION TO MAXIMIN AGAINST THE CHRISTIANS, 312

(*C.I.L.* III.13132; text in von Gebhardt, *Acta Martyrum Selecta*, p. 185.)

The gods, your kinsmen, most illustrious emperors, having always shown manifest acts of kindness to all who have their religion earnestly at heart and pray to them for the perpetual health of you, our invincible Lords, we have thought it well to have recourse to your immortal sovereignty, and to request that the Christians, who have long been disloyal, and still persist in the same mischievous intent, should at last be put down and not be suffered, by any absurd novelty, to offend against the honour due to the gods. This end will best be attained, if by your divine and perpetual decree, commandment be laid upon all that the villiany of the detestable practices of the atheists be forbidden and prevented; and all be required to attend constantly upon the cult of the gods your kinsmen, on behalf of your eternal and incorruptible sovereignty, as is most patently to the advantage of all your subjects. (Tr. B. J. Kidd, in *Documents Illustrative of the History of the Church*, I, pp. 228-9, altered.)

This inscription comes from Arycanda in Lycia, and is addressed to Maximin, Constantine and Licinius.

According to Eusebius (*H.E.* IX.4.1) Maximinus at first agreed to the policy of toleration promulgated by Galerius in April, 311, but his adherence to it was insincere and he suborned cities to petition him to take measures against the Christians. Lactantius (*On the deaths of the persecutors*, 36.3) agrees. The reply of the Emperor to the petitions is given by Eusebius in *H.E.* IX.7.

258. THE "PAGAN" VISION OF CONSTANTINE, 310

(*Panegyrici Latini*, 6(7).21.3-6.)

This panegyric, delivered at Trier, justified the death of Maximian, revealed the (fictitious) descent of Constantine from Claudius II (268-270), and emphasized his reverence for Apollo (*Sol invictus*).

[After he had disposed of the revolt of his father-in-law Maximian (and of Maximian himself), Constantine had to set out for

the German frontier once more, on account of a revolt there.
3 The news that he was on his way was sufficient to quell this revolt, and he then proceeded to pay his promised vows to the Gods. . . .]

. . . when you had turned aside to the most beautiful temple in
4 the whole world, nay rather to a god present in actuality. For, O Constantine, you saw, I believe, your protector Apollo, in company with Victory, offering you laurel crowns, each of which bear the presage of thirty years. For this is the span of human life
5 that is owed to you, an age beyond that of Nestor. But why indeed do I say, "I believe"? You really saw the god and recognized yourself in the appearance of one to whom the prophecies of poets have declared that the rule of the whole world should
6 belong. These prophecies are, to my mind, fulfilled in you since you are, O Emperor, as he is, young, joyous, health bringing and handsome. (With acknowledgements to the French translation of E. Galletier in the Budé edition II, p. 72.)

Is this to be regarded as (1) an actual vision of which the vision of the cross (259 below) is a Christian counterpart, (2) a recognition by Constantine and his *entourage* of a likeness between the statue of the God and the Emperor, (3) mere flattery by the priests of a victorious Emperor? The crowns each contained the symbol XXX and it has even been suggested that this is the original appearance of the cross. The priests may have offered two crowns, one from each deity, and the remaining thirty is made up from Constantine's own age at the time.

259. THE CONVERSION OF CONSTANTINE, 312

These years, 312–313, are decisive for the history of Christianity and of Europe. No matter what interpretation may be placed on the events of these years, we have reached the turning point in the relations of Church and Empire.

The conviction of Christians and pagans was that Constantine, in his expedition against the usurper Maxentius, was the recipient of divine aid.

I

(Lactantius, *On the deaths of the persecutors* 44, 3–6 (written before 318).)

3   [Constantine had encamped in the neighbourhood of the Milvian Bridge.]

4 The anniversary of Maxentius' accession, the 27th of October, was near, and his (first) five years of rule were drawing to a close.

5 Constantine was directed in a dream to mark the heavenly sign of God on the shields of his soldiers and thus to join battle. He did as he was ordered and with the cross-shaped letter X, with its top bent over, he marked Christ on the shields.

6 [Armed with this sign his army engaged the enemy and was completely victorious.]

Lactantius is talking of the *Latin* letter X. In view of the next passage the "heavenly sign" is interesting. It must be the cross, and Constantine went further by adding a second letter, i.e. ⳩, ☓, or even ☧.

2

(Eusebius, *V.C.* I.26–9 (*c.* 338).)

26 [Constantine saw the oppression of Rome, capital of a universal empire, under the tyrant Maxentius. He had left her liberation to others (i.e. to Severus and Galerius) but they had failed.

27.1 Being convinced that he required greater aid than military force because of the wicked and magical enchantments that were so diligently practised at the tyrant's court, he sought divine aid, counting the possession of arms and of a numerous soldiery of secondary importance . . . but declaring the co-operating power

2 of God to be irresistible and unconquerable. He considered therefore what god he should·choose as his patron . . .

3 Constantine saw the contrast between the gods of paganism who failed to protect their worshippers, and his father Constantius' monotheism, and decided to cleave to the latter.]

28.1 Accordingly he besought his father's god in prayer, beseeching and imploring him to tell him who he was and to stretch out his right hand to help him in his present difficulties. And while he was thus praying with fervent entreaty, a most incredible sign appeared to him from heaven, the account of which it might have been hard to believe had it been related by any other person. But since the victorious emperor himself long afterwards declared it to the writer of this history, when he was honoured with his acquaintance and society, and confirmed his statement by an oath, who could hesitate to accredit the relation, especially since the testimony of aftertime has established its truth? He said that about noon, when the day was already beginning to decline, he saw with his own eyes the trophy of a cross of light in the heavens, above the sun, and an inscription, CONQUER BY THIS attached to it. At this sight he himself was struck with amazement, and his whole army also, which followed him on an expedition, and witnessed the miracle.

He said, moreover, that he doubted within himself what the import of this portent could be. And while he continued to ponder and reason on its meaning, night overtook him; then in his sleep the Christ of God appeared to him with the sign which he had seen in the heavens, and commanded him to make a likeness of that sign which he had seen in the heavens, and to use it as a safeguard in all engagements with his enemies. (Gwatkin, *Selections from Early Christian Writers*, pp. 175-7, and N. & P.-N. F., altered.)

In Eusebius the vision took place *sometime before* the battle of the Milvian bridge: in Lactantius the dream occurred in *the night before it*.

28.1: *CONQUER BY THIS*: the Latin i.e. original form is *In hoc signo vinces*.

260. THE "EDICT OF MILAN", 313
(Lactantius, *On the deaths of the persecutors*, 48.2-12.)

2   When we, Constantine Augustus and Licinius Augustus, had happily met at Milan, and were conferring about all things which concern the advantage and security of the state, we thought that amongst other things which seemed likely to profit men generally, the reverence paid to the Divinity merited our first and chief attention. Our purpose is to grant both to the Christians and to all others full authority to follow whatever worship each man has desired; whereby whatsoever Divinity dwells in heaven may be benevolent and propitious to us, and to all who are placed under 3 our authority. Therefore we thought it salutary and most proper to establish our purpose that no man whatever should be refused complete toleration, who has given up his mind either to the cult of the Christians, or to the religion which he personally feels best suited to himself; to the end that the supreme Divinity, to whose worship we devote ourselves under no compulsion, may continue in all things to grant us his wonted favour and beneficence. 4 Wherefore your Dignity should know that it is our pleasure to abolish all conditions whatever which were embodied in former orders directed to your office about the Christians, that what appeared utterly inauspicious and foreign to our Clemency should be done away and that every one of those who have a common wish to follow the religion of the Christians may from this moment freely and unconditionally proceed to observe the same

5 without any annoyance or disquiet. These things we thought good
to signify in the fullest manner to your Carefulness, that you
might know that we have given freely and unreservedly to the
6 said Christians toleration to practise their cult. And when you
perceive that we have granted this favour to the said Christians,
your Devotion understands that to others also freedom for their
own worship and cult is likewise left open and freely granted, as
befits the quiet of our times, that every man may have complete
toleration in the practice of whatever worship he has chosen.
This has been done by us that no diminution be made from the
7 honour of any religion. Moreover in regard to the legal position
of the Christians we have thought fit to ordain this also, that if
any appear to have bought, whether from our exchequer or from
any others, the places at which they were used formerly to
assemble, concerning which definite orders have been given
before now, and that by a letter issued to your office—that the
same be restored to the Christians, setting aside all delay and
8 doubtfulness, without any payment or demand of price. Those
also who have obtained them by gift shall restore them in like
manner without delay to the said Christians. And those moreover who have bought them, as well as those who have obtained
them by gift, if they request anything of our benevolence,
shall apply to the Vicarius, that order may be taken for them too
by our Clemency. All these things must be delivered over at once
and without delay by your intervention to the corporation of the
9 Christians. And since the said Christians are known to have
possessed, not those places only whereto they were used to
assemble, but others also belonging to their corporation, namely
to their churches, and not to individuals, we comprise them all
under the above law, so that you will order them to be restored
without any doubtfulness or dispute to the said Christians, that
is to their corporation and assemblies; provided always as aforesaid, that those who restore them without price, as we said, shall
10 expect a compensation from our benevolence. In all these things
you must give the aforesaid Christians your most effective intervention, that our command may be fulfilled as soon as may be,
and that in this matter, as well as others, order may be taken by our
11 Clemency for the public quiet. So far we will ensure that, as has
been already stated, the Divine favour toward us which we have
already experienced in so many affairs shall continue for all time
to give us prosperity and successes, together with happiness for
12 the State. But that the tenor of our gracious ordinance may be
brought to the knowledge of all men, it will be your duty by a
proclamation of your own to publish everywhere and bring to

the notice of all men this present document, that the command of this our benevolence may not be hidden. (Gwatkin, *Selections from Early Christian Writers*, pp. 171–5, and A.-N. C. L., altered in accordance with the text of Brandt and Laubmann in *C.S.E.L.*)

There is a translation into Greek of this document in Eusebius, *H.E.* X.5.2–14.

As given by Lactantius, this document is a letter of Licinius directed to the governors of the provinces formerly subject to Maximinus Daia. It probably embodies the toleration already granted by Constantine in the West.

At the meeting at Milan the marriage of Licinius to Constantia, half-sister of Constantine, also took place.

The document embodies, (1) complete religious toleration, a principle on which Constantine never went back, (see 283) though his toleration of paganism became more contemptuous. (2) Provisions for the restoration of property of which the Christians, either individually or corporately, had been deprived during the persecution, with state compensation for any who suffered loss by this measure.

261. THE INSCRIPTION ON THE ARCH OF CONSTANTINE AT ROME, 315

(*C.I.L.* VI.1139.)

To the Emperor Caesar Flavius Constantine, Maximus, Pius, Felix, Augustus, the Roman Senate and People dedicated this arch, decorated with his victories, because, by the prompting of the Divinity, by the greatness of his mind, he with his army, at one moment by a just victory avenged the State both on the tyrant and on all his party.

To the liberator of the city. To the establisher of peace.

The arch is an official war memorial. Its sculptures carry no Christian symbols, even on the shields of the soldiers. The gods of Constantine are the sun god and victory.

262. RESTITUTION OF PROPERTY TO THE CHURCH, 313

(Letter of Constantine to Anulinus, Proconsul of Africa, in Eusebius, *H.E.* X.5.15–17.)

15   Greeting, Anulinus, our most honoured Sir. It is the custom of our benevolence, that we will that whatsoever appertains by right to another should not only not suffer harm, but even be

16 restored, most honoured Anulinus. Wherefore we will that, when
thou receivest this letter, if aught of those things that belonged
to the Catholic Church of the Christians in any city, or even in
other places, be now in the possession either of citizens or of any
others: these thou shouldest cause to be restored forthwith to
these same churches, inasmuch as it has been our determination
that those things which these same churches possessed formerly
17 should be restored to them as their right. Since, therefore, thy
Devotedness perceives that the order of this our command is most
explicit, do thy diligence that all things, whether gardens or
buildings or whatsoever belonged to these same churches by right,
be restored to them with all speed; so that we may learn that thou
hast yielded the most careful obedience to this our order. Fare
thee well, Anulinus, our most honoured and esteemed Sir.
(Lawlor and Oulton, *Eusebius*, I, p. 317.)

Letters such as this were probably sent to governors generally to follow up
the "Edict of Milan". It is improbable that Constantine had yet heard of the
Donatist schism in Africa. Anulinus was soon to hear of it and report on it to
Constantine (270).

263. CONSTANTINE MAKES A GRANT OF MONEY TO THE CATHOLIC CLERGY OF THE AFRICAN PROVINCES, 313

(Constantine to Caecilian of Carthage, in Eusebius, *H.E.* X.6.)

1   Constantine Augustus to Caecilian bishop of Carthage. Forasmuch as it has been our pleasure in all provinces, namely the
African, the Numidian and the Mauretanian, that somewhat be
contributed for expenses to certain specified ministers of the
lawful and most holy Catholic religion, I have despatched a letter
to Ursus, the most distinguished finance minister of Africa, and
have notified to him that he be careful to pay over to thy Firmness
2 three thousand "folles". Do thou therefore, when thou shalt
secure delivery of the aforesaid sum of money, give orders that
this money be distributed among all the above-mentioned persons
3 in accordance with the schedule sent to thee by Hosius. But if,
after all, thou shalt find that there is aught lacking for the fulfilment of this my purpose in respect of them all, thou shouldest
ask without doubting whatsoever thou findest to be necessary
from Heraclides the treasurer of our estates. For indeed when he
was here I gave him orders that if thy Firmness should ask any

money from him, he should be careful to pay it over without any
4 scruple. And since I have learnt that certain persons of unstable
mind are desirous of turning aside the laity of the most holy and
Catholic Church by some vile method of seduction, know that I
have given such commands to Anulinus, the proconsul, and moreover to Patricius, the vicar of the prefects, when they were here,
that they should give due attention in all other matters and especially to this, and not suffer such an occurrence to be overlooked;
5 therefore if thou observest any such men continuing in this madness, do not thou hesitate to go to the above-mentioned judges
and bring this matter before them, so that (as I commanded them
when they were here) they may turn these people from their error.
May the divinity of the great God preserve thee for many years.
(Lawlor and Oulton, *Eusebius*, I, pp. 319–20, slightly altered.)

1. *three thousand "folles"*: the value of this gift is uncertain.
2. *the schedule sent to thee by Hosius* (Ossius): of Cordova in Spain, who was
by now Constantine's religious adviser. This schedule must be a scale of pay-
ments, not a list of names, as Ossius could hardly have possessed such a list.
4 and 5.   The disturbers of the peace to whom Constantine refers are almost
certainly Donatists, cf. 270 for what happened when Anulinus tried to carry
out the Emperor's orders.

264. EXEMPTION FROM PUBLIC OFFICE
FOR THE CATHOLIC CLERGY, 313

(Constantine to Anulinus, in Eusebius, *H.E.* X.7.)

1   Greeting, Anulinus, our most honoured Sir. Since from many
facts it appears that the setting at naught of divine worship, by
which the highest reverence for the most holy and heavenly
[Power] is preserved, has brought great dangers upon public
affairs, and that its lawful restoration and preservation have
bestowed the greatest good fortune on the Roman name and
singular prosperity on all the affairs of mankind (for it is the Divine
Providence which bestows these blessings): it has seemed good
that those men who, with due holiness and constant observance of
this law, bestow their services on the performance of divine
worship, should receive the rewards of their own labours, most
2 honoured Anulinus. Wherefore it is my wish that those persons
who, within the province committed to thee, in the Catholic
Church over which Caecilian presides, bestow their service on this
holy worship—those whom they are accustomed to call clerics—

should once for all be kept absolutely free from all the public offices, that they be not drawn away by any error or sacrilegious fault from the worship which they owe to the Divinity, but rather without any hindrance serve to the utmost their own law. For when they render supreme service to the Deity, it seems that they confer incalculable benefit on the affairs of the State. Fare thee well, Anulinus, our most honoured and esteemed Sir. (Lawlor and Oulton, *Eusebius*, I, p. 320.)

By this letter, and no doubt by others of a similar tenor (cf. *Cod. Theod.* XVI.2.1–3,6.7) the Christian priesthood was put on a level with the pagan one. The Emperor's confidence in the efficacy of Christian worship in saving the state is similar to that of Origen (197).

Immunity from state burdens was a valuable privilege, and "the priesthood soon became a refuge eagerly sought for by the curial class" (Frend, *The Donatist Church*, p. 146, cf. 285 below). The *curiales* in the provincial cities were, e.g., responsible for paying the taxes of their district.

2. *in the Catholic Church over which Caecilian presides*: this phrase may be used to distinguish Catholic from Donatist or, "it may simply mean that the immunity granted was for the territory included in the jurisdiction of the bishop of Carthage, who, according to the reports that came to Constantine, was e.g., named Caecilian". (Lawlor and Oulton, *Eusebius*, II, p. 315).

265. CANONS OF THE COUNCIL OF ELVIRA, *c.* 305

(Text and commentary in Hefele-Leclercq, *Histoire des Conciles* (1907), I.1, pp. 221–64; text in Routh, *Reliquiae Sacrae*, ed. 2, IV, pp. 259–74; in E. J. Jonkers, *Acta et symbola Conciliorum quae saeculo quarto habita sunt*, pp. 5ff.)

Elvira is in Baetica in Southern Spain: this council was attended by nineteen bishops, including Ossius of Cordova, and by twenty-six presbyters.

2   *Flamens* who after the faith of baptism and regeneration have sacrificed, because they have doubled their crime if murder be added, and trebled their sin if immorality be involved, shall not receive communion even at the last.

3   Likewise *Flamens*, who have not sacrificed, but merely given the games (*or* given a simple offering) because they have kept themselves from the fatal sacrifices shall receive communion at the last after the performance of due penance. If these persons after their penance have committed an immoral act, they shall

not again be granted communion lest they seem to have made a mock of the Lord's communion.

Flamens were the priests of Rome and Augustus; the office was frequently hereditary, and Christians must in consequence have been placed in a difficult position. In canon 2 "murder" probably refers to the gladiatorial games, and "immorality" to stage representations. *Flamens* were responsible for the organization of festivals.

5   If any woman, impelled by furious anger, beat her maidservant with a lash so that she gives up the ghost within three[1] days, and it be uncertain whether her death was intentional or accidental, she shall be admitted to communion after seven years if intentional, five years if accidental, after the performance of due penance. But if she fall gravely ill within these stated times, let her receive communion.

Roman mistresses sometimes treated their personal slaves with shocking cruelty, cf. Juvenal, 6.480–3,490–5, Ovid, *Ars Amatoria*, 3.239 (but cf. also Ovid, *Amores*, I.14.15–18). In *Cod. Theod.* IX.12.1 and 2, Constantine legislated on the subject of the death of slaves after punishment in A.D. 319, 326, 329. The master is not guilty of homicide if a slave die after beating or from confinement in chains: he is guilty if he use a lethal weapon on a slave or subject the slave's body to such treatment that he could be presumed to desire the slave's death.

6   But if any one kill another by magic (*maleficium*), a thing which cannot be done without idolatry, communion shall not be granted to him even at the last.

The question of magic appears in other canons of councils, e.g. Ancrya can. 24 where penance is laid on those who admit soothsayers to their houses, no question of murder being involved.

On *maleficium*, cf. 4.

8   Women who, without cause, leave their husbands and marry again, are not to be received into communion even at the last.
9   A baptized woman who leaves a baptized husband on the ground of his adultery and marries again, is to be prohibited from marrying; if she marry, she is not to be received into communion, until the husband whom she has left be departed out of this life, unless perchance extremity of sickness require it to be given her.
13   Virgins who have dedicated themselves to God, if they violate their vow of virginity and give themselves over to lust, without recognizing what they have done, shall not be received into

[1] Cf. Exod. 21.20–1.

communion even at the last. If, however, after having been seduced on one occasion and defiled by a fall due to frailty of the flesh, they do penance all their life and abstain from intercourse, then, inasmuch as they rank rather as lapsed, we decree that they ought to be received into communion at the last.

Ancyra can. 19 deals with virgins who violate their vows by undertaking marriage: they are to be counted as bigamists. Basil, *ad Amphilochium* 4 states that the penalty was exclusion for one year.

18 If bishops, presbyters and deacons, after promotion to the ministry be found guilty of immorality, we decree that, on account of the scandal and the lewdness of the crime, they ought not to be admitted into communion, even at the last.

19 Bishops, presbyters and deacons are not to leave their places in order to engage in trade; nor are they to go the round of the provinces in search of profitable markets. To gain their living, let them send a son, a freedman, an agent, a friend or some other person; and, if they want to trade, let them trade within the province.

On the clergy engaging in trade, *c.* A.D. 250, cf. 201 above.

20 If any cleric be found taking usury, he shall be deposed and excommunicated. If, moreover, a layman be proved to have taken usury, and promise, on being reproved for it, to cease to do so and not exact it further he shall be pardoned; but that, if he persist in that iniquity, he must be cast out of the Church.

Cf. Nicaea can. 17 (300, p. 363).

22 If anyone pass over from the Catholic church to a heresy and again return, an opportunity for penance must not be denied to him, since he has recognized his sin. If anyone has done penance throughout ten years, communion should be granted him after ten years: but if they were carried over to heresy as children (i.e. by their parents), they ought to be received without delay, as they sinned by a fault not their own.

27 A bishop or any cleric whosoever shall have with him only his sister or daughter (and she a virgin dedicated to God): he shall not have any woman not a relative.

Cf. Nicaea can. 3 (300, p. 359), Ancyra can. 19, *Const. Sirm.* 10 (of A.D. 420).

33 Bishops, presbyters and deacons—indeed, all clerics who have a place in the ministry [of the altar]—shall abstain from their wives and shall not beget children—this is a total prohibition: whoever does so, let him forfeit his rank among the clergy.

Hefele, op. cit., I.1, p. 239, points out that the Latin of the Canon is inexact
in that it should be translated *in the opposite sense* to that manifestly intended,
and that a similar inexactitude, again with *prohibere* occurs in canon 80.

37   There shall be no pictures in church, lest what is reverenced and
adored be depicted on the walls.

The exact significance of this prohibition has been much discussed. The
simplest solution appears to be that of Turmel, *Revue du Clergé français*, XLV,
(1906), p. 508 (quoted by Leclercq, op. cit., I, pp. 240-1): "One can think that
the images, for Christians of the third century scarcely freed from the seduc-
tions of paganism, were a constant danger of idolatry, and that the council,
in order to put a stop to this danger believed that it ought to suppress what
was the occasion of it."

49   Landowners are to be warned not to allow their crops, which
they receive from God with giving of thanks, to be blessed by
Jews, lest they make our blessing invalid and weak. If anyone
dares to do this after this prohibition, he shall suffer complete
excommunication.

Canons 16 and 50 also deal with the Jews, the former prohibits the marriage
of Christian girls to Jews, the latter prohibits the taking of food with them.
It is generally agreed that there were many Jews in Spain. The application of
the Canon refers to a blessing of the harvest fields, a ceremony that might be
given a magical interpretation. The Jewish blessing might serve to counteract
the Christian one.

60   If anyone break idols and be killed on the spot, since this is
not written in the Gospel and will never be found happening in
the days of the Apostles, he shall not be received into the number
of the martyrs.

73   If any believer appears as an informer, and through his information someone has been proscribed or killed, he shall not receive
communion even at the last: if the charge was less grave, in five
years he shall be able to receive communion: if he is a catechumen,
after the space of five years he shall be admitted to baptism.
(Translations from various sources.)

266. THE ACTS OF THE COUNCIL OF CIRTA IN NUMIDIA, 4 MARCH 305

(From Augustine, *Contra Cresconium*, III.30; (*P.L.* XLIII.510f.).)

When Diocletian was Consul for the eighth and Maximian
for the seventh time, on March 4, after Secundus, bishop of

Tigisis and Primate (i.e. of Numidia), had taken his seat in the house of Urbanus Donatus, he said:

"Let us first see that all are duly qualified to act, and thus we shall be able to consecrate a Bishop."

Secundus said to Donatus of Mascula: "It is alleged that you have been guilty of Betrayal (i.e. of surrendering the Scriptures)."

Donatus replied: "You know how Florus searched for me to make me offer incense, and God did not deliver me into his hands, my brother; but since God has pardoned me, so do you too leave me to God."

Secundus said: "What, then, are we to do about the Martyrs? They have been crowned because they did not 'betray'."

Donatus said: "Send me to God. Before Him I will render my account."

Secundus said: "Come to one side."

Secundus said to Marinus of the Waters of Tibilis: "It is alleged that you, too, were guilty of Betrayal."

Marinus answered: "I did give papers to Pollus. My codices are safe."

Secundus said: "Stand on one side."

Secundus said to Donatus of Calama: "It is alleged that you were guilty of Betrayal."

Donatus answered: "I gave them medical treatises."

Secundus said: "Stand on one side."

Secundus said to Victor of Rustica: "It is alleged that you 'betrayed' four Gospels."

Victor answered: "Valentianus was Curator. He forced me to throw them into the fire. I knew that they were obliterated (i.e. unusable texts). Pardon me this fault, and God also will pardon me."

Secundus said: "Stand on one side."

Secundus said to Purpurius of Limata: "It is alleged that you killed at Milevis the two sons of your sister."

Purpurius answered: "Do you think that I am frightened of you, like the rest? What have *you* done, who were forced by the Curator and the soldiers to give up the Scriptures? How did you come to be set free by them, unless you surrendered something, or ordered it to be surrendered? For they did not let you go at random. Yes, I did kill, and I intend now to kill those who act against me. So do not now provoke me to say anything more. You know that I interfere with nobody's affairs."

Secundus the Less said to Secundus his uncle: "Do you hear what he is saying against you? He is ready to leave, and make a schism; and not only he, but also all those who are accused by you. I know that they intend to abandon you, and pronounce sentence against you. You will then remain alone, a heretic. So what business is it of yours what any one has done? He has to render an account to God."

Secundus said to Felix of Rotarium, [to Nabor] of Centurio, and Victor of Garba: "What do you think?"

They answered: "They have God, to whom they must render their account."

Secundus said: "You know, and God knows. Sit down."

And they all answered: "Thanks be to God." (O. R. Vassall-Phillips, *St Optatus*, App. XI, pp. 417–19, slightly altered.)

in the house of Urbanus Donatus: "because" (as Optatus, *On the schism of the Donatists* I.14, says) "the churches had not yet been rebuilt".

duly qualified to act: i.e. had committed no sin. The subsequent interrogation by Secundus, and the replies of the bishops show how difficult the situation was. There is no doubt that some saved their scriptures by equivocal conduct (cf. 249), and that there was a fruitful field for accusation and counter accusation.

Purpurius of Limata: "This man was an acknowledged brigand. . . . He inspired terror among the Christians, but he also was prepared to carry the fight into the pagan camp. He and Silvanus (consecrated bishop at this council) had been concerned in robbing the Imperial treasury of vinegar which was stored in a temple of Serapis (*Gesta apud Zenophilum* in Optatus, App. I (*C.S.E.L.* XXVI, pp. 195–6)). Among a population who had suffered cruelly at the hands of the authorities, such a man might well come to the fore as leader. . . ." (Frend, *The Donatist Church*, p. 12.)

267. CANONS OF ANCYRA, c. 314–319

(Text and commentary in Hefele–Leclercq, *Histoire des Conciles*, I.1, pp. 298–326; in Routh, *Reliquiae Sacrae*, ed. 2, IV, pp. 115–77, 212–27; text in R. B. Rackham, *The Text of the Canons of Ancyra*, Studia Biblica et Ecclesiastica, III, pp. 139–216 (with critical commentary), in E. J. Jonkers, *Acta et Symbola Conciliorum quae saeculo quarto habita sunt*, pp. 28–35.)

1   Presbyters who sacrificed and then renewed the struggle, not in pretence but in reality, without any deliberate plan or purpose of persuading officials in order to seem to be subjected to torture (which was applied only in appearance and as a matter of form),

shall share in the honour due to their station, but shall not be allowed to make the offering, or preach, or perform any of the priestly functions.

As Leclercq points out (op. cit., p. 311, n. 2) Canons 1–9 of Ancyra deal with the question of Christians who lapsed in the persecution under Diocletian and his fellow Emperors, and the differentiation between various classes of lapsed Christians. In several canons, e.g. in 2, which deals with lapsed deacons, bishops are given discretionary power to intensify or relax the general regulations in view of special circumstances.

3   Persons who fled in persecution but were arrested or betrayed by their slaves or who in some way have been deprived of their property or endured torture or have been thrown into prison protesting that they were Christians, and †stripped,† where their oppressors had either forced incense into their hands, or compelled them to receive meat (offered to idols)—if such persons have confessed throughout that they were Christians and have ever shown their grief at the occurrence by their dress, their bearing and their humility of life, these being void of offence are not to be hindered from communion, and if they have been hindered through over scrupulousness or ignorance (of the ecclesiastical authorities), they are immediately to be received. This applies to both clergy and laity. The additional problem, whether laity who were subjected to this same trial, can be promoted into the clergy, was discussed. It was decided, that they can be ordained as having committed no fault in the persecution, if their former way of life is found without offence.

[Canons 4 and 5 deal with the attitude of Christians who had been compelled to sacrifice, at the sacrificial banquet: some went gladly in festal garb, others with tears and sorrow. This difference was recognized in their subsequent treatment by the Church.]

9   As many as not only apostasized but rose up against their brethren and compelled them (to sacrifice) and were the agents of compulsion, shall be placed among the "hearers" for three years, among the "prostrators" for six years more; for one year they shall be present at communion but take no part in the offering. When they have completed the period of ten years they shall share in the whole rite, but during this time notice shall be taken of their general conduct.

In his so-called Canonical Letter, 11 (P.G. X.1048) Gregory Thaumaturgus (d. c. 270), divides penitents into four classes (1) the mourners, i.e. those desiring to be admitted to penance, (2) the hearers, who heard, with the catechumens, the exposition of Scripture, (3) the "prostrators", who were admitted into the Christian assembly with the catechumens, (4) participators in the common prayer but not in the Eucharist. This classification was not adopted in Syria, Egypt, or the West.

10   As many as are being ordained deacons if at the time of ordination they have made a declaration and stated that they must marry and cannot remain celibate, such persons, should they marry thereafter can remain in their office, as the bishop had granted them the right to marry at their ordination. But if any held their peace and accepted celibacy at their ordination, and afterwards marry, such persons shall cease from their ministry.

Cf. Neocaesarea can 1. (268).

18   If any chosen to be bishops but not received by the see for which they were named wish to invade other sees and use violence on properly constituted bishops and raise dissensions against them, they are to be excommunicated. If, however, they wish to take their seats among the presbyters, where they formerly were presbyters, they must not be rejected from this honour. If they raise dissensions against the bishops properly constituted in these places they are to lose their dignity of the presbyterate and to be themselves excommunicated.

24   Those who foretell the future and follow the customs of the heathen, or introduce persons into their houses to find out magical remedies or to perform purifications shall under the canon be subject to five years of penitence in accordance with the above-mentioned degrees (of penitence), i.e. they are to be "prostrators" for three years, and for two years they are to join in prayer without taking part in the offering.

Cf. Elvira, can. 6 (265, p. 306).

268. CANONS OF NEOCAESAREA, c. 314–325

(Text and commentary in Hefele–Leclercq, *Histoire des Conciles* I.1, pp. 326–34; in Routh, *Reliquiae Sacrae*, ed. 2, IV, pp. 179–211, 227–48; text in E. J. Jonkers, *Acta et Symbola Conciliorum quae saeculo quarto habita sunt*, pp. 35–8.)

1   If a presbyter marry, he is to be excluded from the clergy; if he fornicate or commit adultery, he is to be completely excommunicated and is to be brought to repentance.

The canon deals with marriage after ordination. On another aspect of the marriage of clergy, cf. Ancyra can. 10 (267, p. 312).

11   No one shall be ordained presbyter under the age of thirty years: even if the person concerned is completely worthy, he must wait. For the Lord Jesus Christ in his thirtieth year was baptized, and began to teach.

thirty years, cf. Num. 4.3, 1 Chron. 23.3.

12   If anyone were baptized in illness he cannot be made a presbyter: for his faith is not from a spontaneous resolve, but from necessity: unless perchance he show his suitability by his subsequent zeal and faith, and there be a shortage of suitable persons.

Cf. the objections raised against Novatian by Cornelius of Rome, quoted by Eusebius, *H.E.* VI.43 (228 above).

15   There ought, according to the ecclesiastical rule, to be seven deacons, even if the city is a very big one. You will find the proof of this in the *Acts of the Apostles.*

269. THE ORIGIN OF DONATISM

(Optatus, *On the schism of the Donatists,* I.15–19.)

15   [The bishops who had taken part in the Council of Cirta (266) came to Carthage and initiated the schism by consecrating Majorinus bishop in opposition to Caecilian.]

* * *

16   No one is unaware that the schism, after the consecration of Caecilian, was effected at Carthage through a certain mischief-making woman named Lucilla. When the Church was still in tranquillity, before her peace had been disturbed by the storms of persecution, this woman could not put up with a rebuke which she received from the archdeacon Caecilian. It was said that she kissed a bone of some martyr or other—if he was a martyr—before she received the spiritual Food and Drink. Having then been corrected for thus touching, before she touched the sacred chalice, the bone of a dead man (if he was a martyr, at least he had not been acknowledged as such), she went away in confusion, full of wrath. While Lucilla was angry and afraid that she might fall under the discipline of the Church, suddenly the storm of persecution sprang up and broke upon us.

17   It was at this time also that a deacon called Felix, who had been summoned before the tribunals on account of a much-spoken-of letter which he had written concerning the usurping Emperor [sc. Maxentius], fearing his danger, is said to have lain hidden in the house of bishop Mensurius. When Mensurius publicly refused to give him up, an account of the matter was despatched. A rescript came back that unless Mensurius would surrender the deacon Felix, he should be himself sent to the palace. On receiving this summons he found himself in no small difficulty, for the Church possessed very many gold and silver ornaments, which he could neither hide underground nor take away with him. So he confided them to the care of some of the seniors, whom he believed to be worthy of trust; not, however, before he had made an inventory, which he is said to have given to a certain old woman. He charged her that, when peace was restored to the Christians, she should hand this over, if he himself did not return home, to whomsoever she found sitting in the bishop's chair. He went away, and pleaded his cause; he was commanded to return, but was not able to reach Carthage.

18   The storm of persecution passed over, and subsided. By the disposition of God, Maxentius sent pardon, and liberty was restored to the Christians. Botrus and Celestius—so it is said— wishing to be consecrated bishops at Carthage, arranged that, without inviting the Numidians, only the neighbouring bishops should be asked to perform the ceremony at Carthage. Then, by the vote of the whole people, Caecilian was chosen and was consecrated bishop, Felix of Aptungi laying his hand upon him. Botrus and Celestius were disappointed of their hope. The inventory of the gold and silver, as had been ordered by Mensurius, was handed over in the presence of witnesses to Caecilian, who was now in possession of the see. The above-mentioned seniors were summoned; but they had swallowed up in the jaws of their avarice, as booty, that which had been entrusted to their keeping. When they were commanded to make restitution, they withdrew from communion with Caecilian. The ambitious intriguers, who had failed to obtain their consecration, did likewise. Lucilla, too, that influential, mischief-making woman, who had before been unwilling to brook discipline, together with all her retainers, separated herself from her bishop. Thus wickedness produced its effect through the meeting together of three different causes and sets of persons.

19   In this way it came to pass that at that time the schism was brought to birth by the anger of a disgraced woman, was fed by ambition, and received its strength from avarice.

It was by these three that the accusations were concocted against Caecilian, so that his consecration might be declared void. They sent to Secundus of Tigisis to come to Carthage, whither the Betrayers, of whom we have already made mention, proceeded. They received hospitality—not from Catholics at whose request Caecilian had been consecrated—but from the avaricious, from the ambitious, from those who had been unable to govern their tempers. Not one of them went to the Basilica, where all the people of Carthage had assembled with Caecilian.

Then Caecilian demanded: "If there is anything to be proved against me, let the accuser come out and prove it." Nothing could at that time be got up against him by all these enemies of his; they imagined, however, that he might be blackened by his consecrator being falsely alleged to have been a Betrayer. So Caecilian gave a second demand—that since—so they thought— Felix had bestowed nothing upon him, they should themselves ordain him, as if he were still a deacon.

Then Purpurius, relying upon his usual spiteful pungency, thus spoke, as though Caecilian had been his sister's son: "Let him stand forth as if he were to be consecrated bishop, and let his head be well smacked in penance."

When the bearing of all this was seen, the whole Church [of Carthage] retained Caecilian, in order not to hand itself over to bandits.

The alternatives were, either that he should be expelled from his see as guilty, or that the Faithful should communicate with him as innocent.

The church was crowded with people; Caecilian was sitting in his episcopal chair; the altar was set in its proper place—that very altar upon which peaceful bishops had in past times offered sacrifice—Cyprian, Carpophorius, Lucian and the rest.

In this manner they went forth, and altar was raised against altar; and there was an unlawful consecration; and Majorinus, who had been reader when Caecilian was archdeacon—Majorinus, a member of the household of Lucilla, at her instigation and through her bribes, was consecrated bishop by Betrayers, who in the Numidian Council had, as we have already said, acknowledged their crimes and granted pardon to one another. It is, therefore, clear that both the Betrayers who consecrated, and Majorinus who was consecrated, went forth from the Church. (O. R. Vassall-Phillips, *St Optatus*, pp. 31-7, slightly altered.)

16. Caecilian was consecrated probably early in 312.
17. Maxentius lost Africa in 308 when the *Vicarius* L. Domitius Alexander

was proclaimed Emperor at Carthage. He recovered it in 311 and treated it with great severity.

some of the seniors (seniores): these are almost certainly clergy, cf. Tertullian, *Apol.* 39.4; Firmilian in Cyprian, *Ep.* LXXV.7 (*maiores natu*); also 279 below.

    18.   *Felix of Aptungi* (in Byzacena) *laying his hand upon him*: Only Felix is mentioned as he was the centre of the long controversy that followed, but two other bishops took part. The method of ordination was a slight on the Numidian bishops, as, "since Cyprian's time the Primate of Numidia had acquired the right of consecrating the new Primate of Africa at Carthage. When is uncertain but the fact is stated by Augustine, *Psalmus contra Partem Donati*, lines 44–6" (Frend, *The Donatist Church*, p. 16).

    19.   *as though Caecilian had been his sister's son*: the reference is to his declaration at the Council of Cirta (266).

270. REPORT OF ANULINUS TO CONSTANTINE, 15 APRIL 313

(Augustine, *Ep.* LXXXVIII.2 (*C.S.E.L.* XXXIV, p. 408).)

2   My duty has caused me, among the acts of my insignificance, to send your Majesty's heavenly letter, after I had received and venerated it, to Caecilian and his subordinate clerics; at the same time I exhorted them that—now that unity has been effected with general consent, since through the condescension of your Majesty their liberty was seen to be in every respect completely secure, and the Catholic Church was protected—they should apply themselves to the service of their holy Law and to the things of God, with due reverence. But a few days afterwards I was approached by certain persons, followed by a great throng of the populace, who held that Caecilian must be opposed, and presented me in my official capacity with two documents, one bound in leather and sealed, the other a document unsealed, and demanded with insistence that I should send them to the sacred and venerable Court of your Highness. This my littleness has been careful to do (preserving Caecilian in his position), and I have forwarded their Acts, that your Majesty may be in a position to determine everything. I have sent the two documents, of which the one bound in leather has been endorsed, *Statement of the Catholic Church of Charges against Caecilian, delivered by the party of Majorinus.* Also the one without a seal together with that in leather. Given on the fifteenth of April at Carthage, when Constantine Augustus was for the third time Consul. (O. R. Vassall-Phillips, *St Optatus*, App. XII, slightly altered.)

The reception of Constantine's letter conferring immunities from civil burdens on the clergy (264), as well as his gifts to the Catholic Church (263), raised the question of what Church was the Catholic one. The Donatists were swiftly on the track, and Anulinus immediately sent this report with the two Donatist petitions. (The unsealed document is 271.)

271. THE PETITION OF THE DONATISTS TO CONSTANTINE

(Optatus, On the schism of the Donatists, I.22.)

O Constantine, most excellent Emperor, since thou dost come of a just stock, and thy father (unlike other Emperors) did not persecute the Christians, and Gaul was immune from this crime, we beseech thee that thy piety may command that we be granted judges from Gaul; for between us and other bishops in Africa disputes have arisen. Given by Lucianus, Dignus, Nasutius, Capito, Fidentius and the rest of the Bishops who adhere to Donatus. (O. R. Vassall-Phillips, *St Optatus*, p. 43, altered.)

This is the document to which Anulinus refers in his letter to Constantine (270).

the rest of the bishops who adhere to Donatus: some think that these words are a later addition to the text as Majorinus was still alive.

272. CONSTANTINE ORDERS AN INVESTIGATION INTO DONATISM, 313

(Letter to Miltiades, Bishop of Rome, in Eusebius, H.E. X.5.18.)

18   Constantine Augustus to Miltiades bishop of the Romans, and to Mark. Inasmuch as documents of such a nature have been sent to me in numbers by Anulinus, the right honourable proconsul of Africa, from which it appears that Caecilian, the bishop of the city of the Carthaginians, is called to account on many charges by some of his colleagues in Africa; and inasmuch as it seems to me to be a very serious matter that in those provinces, which Divine Providence has chosen to entrust to my Devotedness, and where there is a large population, the multitude should be found pursuing the worse course of action, splitting up, as it were, and the bishops
19   at variance among themselves: it seemed good to me that Caecilian himself, with ten bishops, who appear to be his censors, and such ten others as he may deem necessary to his suit, should set sail

for Rome, that there a hearing may be granted him in the presence of yourselves, and moreover of Reticius and Maternus and Marinus also, your colleagues (whom I have ordered to hasten to Rome for this purpose), in such a manner as you may perceive to
20 be in accordance with the most sacred law. Nevertheless, that you may have the fullest knowledge of all these same matters, I have subjoined to my letter copies of the documents that were sent to me by Anulinus, and have despatched them to your aforesaid colleagues. Which when your Firmness reads, you will gauge by what method the most careful investigation can be made of the above-mentioned suit, and a just decision arrived at; since it does not escape the notice of your Carefulness that the respect which I pay to the lawful Catholic Church is so great, that it is my wish that you should leave no schism whatsoever or division in any place. May the divinity of the great God preserve you safely for many years, most honoured Sirs. (Lawlor and Oulton, *Eusebius*, I, pp. 317–18, slightly altered.)

We know nothing about Mark, to whom this letter was sent, as well as to Miltiades.

This letter granted the request of the Donatists that they should be given judges from Gaul (271). The bishops mentioned by name are the Bishops of Autun, Cologne and Arles. Optatus (*On the Schism of the Donatists*, I.23,24) informs us that fifteen Italian bishops took part also, and that the sentence went against the Donatists. They protested and Constantine granted them a second hearing at the Council of Arles (273, 274). See also 273, p. 319 below.

273. INSTRUCTIONS FOR THE APPEAR-ANCE OF CAECILIAN AND HIS OPPONENTS AT ARLES, 314

(Constantine to Aelafius, Vicar of Africa, text in Turner, *Ecclesiae Occidentalis Monumenta Iuris Antiquissima*, I, pp. 376–8; Optatus, *On the schism of the Donatists*, Appendix III (*C.S.E.L.* XXVI, pp. 204–6); Routh, *Reliquiae Sacrae*, ed. 2, IV, pp. 297–9.)

The text of this letter is very corrupt. The translation has been altered to bring it into accord with Turner's text.

Already some time back, since it was brought to my knowledge that many persons in our dominion of Africa had begun to separate from one another with mad fury, and had brought purposeless accusations against each other about the keeping of the most holy

Catholic law, I thought it well, in order to settle this quarrel, that Caecilian, the bishop of Carthage, against whom vehemently different persons often petitioned me, should go to the city of Rome with seven of his supporters, and that some of these who had deemed fit to bring certain charges against him, should appear as well. I also ordered some bishops from the Gauls to proceed to our above-mentioned city of Rome, that, both they and the bishop of the city of Rome, and others who should join them in the inquiry, by the integrity of their lives and praiseworthy manner of living, might bring to a fitting conclusion the matter which seems to have been stirred up. Now they brought to my knowledge, by the written Acts of their meeting, all that had been done in their presence, affirming also by word of mouth that their judgement was based upon equity, and declaring that not Caecilian, but those who thought fit to raise charges against him, were guilty—so that, after their judgement was given, they forbade the latter to go back to Africa. Wherefore, in consequence of all this, I had hoped, in accordance with the probable issue of events, that a fitting end had been made to all the seditions and contentions of every kind which seem to have been suddenly stirred up by the other party. But after I had read the letters which you had deemed it your duty to send to Nicasius and the rest, about the crafty pretext of these men, I recognized clearly that they would not place before their eyes either considerations of their own salvation or (what is of more importance) the reverence which is due to Almighty God—for they are persisting in a line of action which not merely leads to their own shame and disgrace, but also gives an opportunity of detraction to those who are known to turn their minds away from the keeping of the most holy Catholic law. I write thus because—and this is a thing which it is well that you should know—some have come from these men, asserting that the above-mentioned Caecilian is deemed not to be worthy of the worship of our most holy religion, and in answer to my reply that they were making an empty boast (since the affair had been terminated in the city of Rome, by competent men of the highest character who were bishops) they thought fit to answer with persistent obstinacy that the whole case had not been heard, but that these bishops had shut themselves up somewhere and given the judgement as was most convenient to themselves.

Wherefore, since I perceived that these numerous and important affairs were being pertinaciously protracted by discussions, so that it appeared that no end could be made of them without both Caecilian and three of those in opposition against him consenting to come to the town of Arles for the judgement of those questions which they have against Caecilian, I have deemed it well to impose upon your Carefulness to provide, as soon as you receive this letter of mine, that the above-mentioned Caecilian, with some of those whom he himself shall choose—and also one from the provinces of Byzacena, Tripolitania, the Numidias and the Mauritanias (and these must bring a certain number of their clergy whom they shall choose)—and also some of those who have made a schism against Caecilian (public conveyance being provided through Africa and Mauritania), shall travel thence by the short crossing to Spain. In the same way you shall provide in Spain each bishop with an individual travel warrant so that they may all arrive speedily at the above-mentioned place by August 1. Furthermore, you will be pleased to convey to them without delay that it is their duty to provide, before they depart, for suitable discipline in their absence, in order that no sedition or contention of disputing parties may arise—a thing which would be the greatest disgrace. † As to the rest, † after the matter has been fully inquired into, let it be brought to an end. For when they shall all have come together, those things which are now known to be subjects of contention should with reason receive a timely conclusion, and be forthwith finished and arranged.

I confess to your Lordship, since I am well aware that you are a worshipper of the most high God, that I consider it by no means right that contentions and altercations of this kind should be hidden from me by which, perchance, God may be moved not only against the human race but also against me myself to whose care, by His heavenly decree, He has entrusted the direction of all human affairs, and may in His wrath provide otherwise than heretofore. For then shall I be able to remain truly and most fully without anxiety, and may always hope for all most prosperous and excellent things from the ever-ready kindness of the most powerful God, when I shall know that all, bound together in brotherly concord, adore the most holy God with the worship of the Catholic religion that is his due. (O. R. Vassall-Phillips, *St Optatus*, App. III, pp. 384–7, altered.)

It was quite clear that the council of Rome (272) had settled nothing. The agitation against Caecilian was so strong, and the Emperor was so pestered by the Donatists ("different persons often petitioned me") that he decided, notwithstanding his own belief that the case had been fairly judged, to concede a second council (cf. 276), and to give the contending parties and their judges (cf. letter of Constantine to Chraestus of Syracuse, in Eusebius, *H.E.* X.5.21–4) the use of public transport. Why he should choose to send the Africans by the route mentioned is obscure.

274. THE DECISIONS OF THE COUNCIL OF ARLES, 314

(Letter of the Council to Silvester, Bishop of Rome, and the Canons of the Council; text (of both) in C. H. Turner, *Ecclesiae Occidentalis Monumenta Iuris Antiquissima*, I, pp. 381–95; Routh, *Reliquiae Sacrae*, ed. 2, IV, pp. 304–11; of the letter in *C.S.E.L.* XXVI, pp. 206–8; of the Canons in Hefele–Leclercq, *Histoire des Conciles*, 1.1, pp. 275–98 (with commentary); in E. J. Jonkers, *Acta et Symbola Conciliorum quae saeculo quarto habita sunt*, pp. 23–8.)

The letter to Silvester contains Canons 1–8 and then breaks off with *et cetera*: the full list of canons is contained in another document also sent to Silvester. Below the text of the letter is given down to the commencement of the canons: then the canons are given in full. The text of the letter and canons is, in places, very doubtful: such places are marked †.

To the most beloved Pope Silvester: Marinus, etc., (thirty-three in all), eternal health in the Lord.

Being united by the common tie of charity, and by that unity which is the bond of our mother, the Catholic Church, we have been brought to the city of Arles by the wish of the most pious Emperor, and we salute thee with the reverence that is thy due, most glorious Pope. Here we have suffered injury to our law and tradition from some troublesome men of undisciplined mind, whom both the authority of our God, which is with us, and our tradition and the rule of truth reject, because they neither have reasonableness in their argument, nor any moderation in their accusations, nor was their manner of proof to the point. Therefore by the judgement of God and of Mother Church, who knows and approves her own, they have been either condemned or rejected. And would, most beloved Brother, that† you had deemed it well to be present at this great spectacle.† We believe surely that in that case a more severe sentence would have been passed against them; and our assembly would have exulted with a greater joy, had you passed judgement together with us; but since you were by no means able to leave that region where† the Apostles daily sit,† and their blood without ceasing bears witness to the glory of God,† it did not seem to us that by reason of your absence, most well-beloved brother, we ought exclusively to handle those matters, on account of which we had been summoned, but we judged that we also should take counsel for all when doing so for ourselves; because, as the provinces from which we come are different, so events of various kinds will happen which we think that we ought to watch.

Accordingly, we agreed, in the presence of the Holy Spirit and His Angels, that from among the various matters which occurred to each of us, we should make some decisions to provide for the present state of tranquillity. We also agreed to write first to you,† with the approval of him who holds the greater dioceses that by you especially they should be brought to the knowledge of all. What it is that we have determined on, we have appended to this writing of our insignificance. But in the first place we were bound to discuss a matter that concerned our life and what is advantageous to us, namely, that since one *died and rose again for all*,[1] the same season should be observed with a religious mind by all at the same time, lest divisions or dissensions might arise in so great a service of devotion. (O. R. Vassall-Phillips. *St Optatus*, App. IV, altered.)

with the approval of him who holds the greater dioceses (i.e. Constantine): this translates Turner's conjecture (op. cit., p. 383). The text in *C.S.E.L.* (p. 207) is translated, "We agreed to write first to you (i.e. Silvester) who holds the government of the greater dioceses, that by you, etc." Turner points out that the word "diocese" in 313 refers to secular not ecclesiastical administration.

The text of the letter, after breaking off, concludes with a note that Constantine, growing weary of the matter, ordered all to go home.

The Canons of Arles

1 Concerning the Pasch of the Lord: that it be observed by us throughout the whole world on one day and at one time, and that according to custom you send letters to all.

letters: i.e. to indicate the date.

2 Concerning those who have been ordained clerics in any places whatsoever, we have decreed that they remain fixed in the same places.

Cf. can. 21 below, Nicaea can. 15 (300, p. 362).

3 Concerning those, who throw down their arms in time of peace, we have decreed that they should be kept from communion.

The meaning of this canon is uncertain: for various views see e.g. Hefele–Leclercq, ad loc., or C. J. Cadoux, *The Early Church and the World*, p. 588, n. 4.

4 Concerning the charioteers who belong to the faithful, we have decreed that, as long as they continue to drive, they be debarred

[1] 2 Cor. 5.14–15.

5 from communion. Concerning the strolling players, we have
decreed that, as long as they act, they be debarred from com-
6 munion. Concerning these who are ill, and wish to believe, we
have decreed that hands be laid upon them.
7 ' Concerning magistrates, who belong to the Faithful and are
appointed to office, we have determined that, when they are
promoted, they should receive ecclesiastical letters of communion,
but in such a way that in whatever place they may be living, the
bishop of that place shall have a heed to them, and if they begin
to act against discipline, they be then excluded from communion.
8 We have decreed similarly with regard to those who wish to hold
state offices.

Cf. with can. 7 and 8, Elvira can. 2 and 3 (265, p. 305).

9(8) Moreover, with regard to the Africans, forasmuch as they
use their own law of re-baptizing, we have decreed that, if any
heretic comes to the Church, he should be questioned concerning
the Creed; and, if it be found that he has been baptized into the
Father and the Son and the Holy Ghost, hands shall be laid upon
him, and no more. But if, on being questioned as to the Creed,
he does not give the Trinity in answer, then let him rightly be
baptized.

On the baptismal controversy, see 218 to 224.

10(9) Concerning those who bring letters describing them as confessors our decision is that the letters be taken away from them
and they receive other letters of communion.

This canon might refer to *libelli pacis* (204), but it is more likely, as Leclercq
says ad loc. that these letters were the usual letters given to Christians when
travelling: they sometimes called the bearer "confessor" which, as Elvira can.
25 says, assured him of a warm welcome.

11(10) Concerning those who detect their wives in adultery, and
the same are young and are prohibited from marriage, we decree
that, as far as is possible they be dissuaded from taking other
wives, while their (first) wives, though adulteresses, are alive.

No ecclesiastical penalty is laid down in the event of a second marriage.
Elvira can. 9 is far more severe to the women in a similar case, 265, p. 306.

12(11) Concerning Christian maidens who marry heathen, our
decision is that they be kept from communion for some time.

Elvira can. 15 and 16 simply prohibit the marriage of Christian girls to
heathens, obstinate heretics and Jews, with five years' exclusion from communion for parents who allow these marriages.

13(12)   Concerning ministers who lend at interest, we decree that they be kept away from communion, according to the instruction divinely given.

Cf. Elvira can. 20 (265, p. 307), Nicaea can. 17 (300, p. 363).
instruction divinely given: e.g. Ezek. 18.8.

14(13)   Concerning those who are said to have surrendered the Holy Scriptures or communion vessels, or the names of their brethren, we decree that whoever of them has been proved from public documents to have done these things shall be removed from the clergy. For if the same persons are found to have carried out ordinations, and a question † has arisen about those whom they have ordained,† such ordination should not be prejudicial to them. And seeing that there are many who seem to oppose the church, and through bribed witnesses think that they should be allowed to bring accusations, their plea is absolutely disallowed, unless, as we said above, they produce evidence from written documents.

This canon deals with the crucial points in the Donatist controversy.
to have surrendered, etc.: for details, cf. 249.
to have carried out ordinations: cf. 251–2, 269.

15(14)   Concerning those who falsely accuse their brethren, we decree that they are not to communicate to the day of their death.

Cf. Elvira can. 73 (265, p. 308), can. 75.

16(15)   Concerning deacons, whom we have ascertained make the offering in many places, we decree that this must cease.

Cf. Nicaea can. 18 (300, p. 363).

17(16)   Concerning those who in accordance with their sin are separated from communion, we so decree that in whatever places they have been excluded, in the same place they shall resume communion, that one bishop obtrude not upon another.

18   Concerning the city deacons, that they take not so much upon themselves but preserve to the presbyters their order, that they do no such thing (e.g. baptizing and preaching) without the presbyters' knowledge.

Cf. Nicaea can. 18 (300, p. 363). But the exact import of the canon is uncertain. Turner says, ad loc., XVIII *Urbicis*, XVIIII.2 in *urbem nonnisi ad Urbem Romam et ad diacones Romanos (quamvis id multos doctos viros fugerit) referri possunt.*

19   Concerning bishops from elsewhere who are accustomed to come to the city, we decree that a place be granted them to make the offering.

20   Concerning those who claim for themselves alone to have the right of ordaining bishops, we decree that no one take this upon himself, unless he be accompanied by other seven bishops. If seven is impossible that they should not dare to ordain without three others.

Cf. Nicaea can. 4 (300, p. 359).

21   Concerning presbyters and deacons who are accustomed to leave the places in which they were ordained and transfer themselves to other places, we decree that they minister in those places (i.e. where they were ordained). But that if they leave their places and wish to transfer themselves to another place, they are to be deposed.

Cf. can. 2 above.

22   Concerning those who apostasize and never claim readmission, and do not even seek to show repentance, and afterwards when they are ill, ask for communion, we decree that communion be not given to them, unless they recover and produce *fruits worthy of repentance*.[1]

Cf. Nicaea can. 13 (300, p. 362). "The severity of Arles gives greater significance to the tenderness of Nicaea." (Bright, *Canons of the first four General Councils*, ed. 2, p. 54.)

275. THE VINDICATION OF FELIX OF APTUNGI, 15 FEBRUARY 315

(From *Acta Purgationis Felicis* in Optatus, *On the Schism of the Donatists*, App. II (*C.S.E.L.* XXVI, pp. 203–4).)

The Council of Arles had dealt with the Donatists, but in general terms (274). The question was not yet settled whether Felix was a *traditor* or not. These *Acta* are an account of a trial before the Proconsul Aelian. The proceedings hinged upon the evidence of Alfius Caecilian, *duumvir* at Aptungi at the beginning of the persecution. The Donatists had an agent named Ingentius who got from Caecilian a written statement that documents had been taken from the Basilica, but the statement did not implicate Felix. Ingentius then went on to

[1] Luke 3.8.

forge a conclusion which did implicate the bishop. At the trial his forgery was exposed and the proconsul delivered judgement in the following words:

> Aelian the proconsul said: "Through the evidence of Caecilian (not the bishop of Carthage, but the *Duumvir* of Aptungi), who tells us that the Acts have been falsified, and many additions made to his letter, the purpose of Ingentius in doing these things has been made clear. So let him be committed to gaol, for we shall require him for stricter examination. Moreover, it is manifest that Felix the holy Bishop has been cleared from the charge of burning the Divine documents, since no one has been able to prove anything against him to show that he gave up or burned the most sacred Scriptures. For the evidence of all the witnesses, now written down above made it clear that no Divine Scriptures were either discovered, or destroyed, or burnt by him. It is shown by the Acts that Felix the holy Bishop was neither present when these things were done, nor was privy to them, nor did he order anything of the kind." (O. R. Vassall-Phillips, *St Optatus*, App. I, p. 345, altered.)

276. CONSTANTINE CONTINUES THE INVESTIGATION OF DONATISM, 316

(Letter of Constantine to Probian, Proconsul of Africa in Augustine, *Contra Cresconium* III.81 (*P.L.* XLIII.540).)

Your predecessor, Aelian, at a time when he was discharging the duties of that most worthy man, Verus our Vicar, in consequence of his ill-health, thought well (and with reason) amongst other matters to investigate and determine the business—that is, the charges—brought by envy against Caecilian, a bishop of the Catholic Church. For after he had secured the presence of Superius the Centurion, and Caecilian the Magistrate of Aptungi, and Saturninus who was formerly *Curator*, and Calidius the younger *Curator*, and Solon a public official of that city, he gave them a fair hearing—so that when it was alleged as an objection against Caecilian that he had been raised to the episcopate by Felix, who was accused of the betrayal and burning of the Divine Scriptures, the innocence of Felix was proved. Finally, when Maximus charged Ingentius, a decurion of Liqua, with having falsified a letter of Caecilian formerly *Duumvir*, we have learned from the Acts of the Proceedings that this Ingentius was prepared for torture, and was only saved by his statement that he was a decurion of Liqua. Wherefore it is our will that you should despatch this Ingentius, under suitable escort, to my Court of Constantine Augustus, so that it may be made quite clear, in the presence and hearing of those who are concerned with this affair, and for some time past have been incessantly appealing to me, that it is to no purpose that they show their malice against Caecilian the bishop, and have been pleased to bestir themselves against him with violence. So will it be brought to pass that these disputes having ceased, as is right, the people may without any dissension serve their religion with the reverence that is its due. (O. R. Vassall-Phillips, *St Optatus*, App. XIV, pp. 426–7, slightly altered.)

This passage forms a sequel to 275. It is clear that the Donatists were pestering the Emperor and that he hoped that the production of the discredited Ingentius would silence them.

277. CONSTANTINE DECIDES IN FAVOUR OF CAECILIAN, 10 NOVEMBER 316

(Letter of Constantine to Eumalius, Vicar of Africa in Augustine, *Contra Cresconium* III.82 (*P.L.* XLIII.541); Routh, *Reliquiae Sacrae*, ed. 2, IV, p. 317.)

At the trial I clearly perceived, that Caecilian was a man distinguished by entire blamelessness; one who observed the accustomed duties of his religion, and devoted himself to it as was required of him. It was clear also that no fault could be found in him, such as had been attributed to him in his absence, by the inventions of his enemies. (B. J. Kidd, *Documents illustrative of the History of the Church*, Vol. I, p. 275, slightly altered.)

This was the final decision, and the next step had of necessity to be persecution.

278. THE PERSECUTION OF THE DONATISTS, *c.* 320

(*Sermo de passione Donati*, 3 (*P.L.* VIII.752–8).)

Yet the insatiable plunderer, i.e. the devil, takes it ill that he cannot gain possession of all by this artifice: the enemy of salvation has found a more subtle argument to violate the purity of faith. Christ, says he, is a lover of unity, therefore let there be unity. He calls the people which ever was too ready to submit to him—and consequently was deserted by God—Catholic (!) so that by prejudging the meaning of that word, those who are unwilling to communicate with them might be called Heretics (!).

He sends money either to seduce faith or to give an occasion for avarice by pretence of holding to the (Christian) law. But when in the face of all these enticements justice kept her course rigidly and inflexibly, judges are ordered to intervene, they are driven to put the secular power in motion, buildings are surrounded by troops, the rich are threatened with proscription, the sacraments are defiled, a mob of heathen are brought in upon us, sacred edifices become the scenes of hilarious feasts!

This Donatist sermon was preached long after the events that it describes, but the schismatics were determined to keep alive the memory of the "Persecution of Caecilian", who is represented in Ch. 2 as pressing the secular power to act. The Donatus commemorated in the sermon is not of course the leader of the party, but another Donatus, Bishop of Advocata, who was killed in the riots that took place. His "day" was 15 March. "The only distinction between the pre- and post-Constantinian epoch was that in the one the devil used force, now he had allies in the Christian camp itself and could rely on fraud; but for the true Christian the result was the same" (Frend, *The Donatist Church*, p. 321).

by this artifice, i.e. by royal friendship and gifts (as mentioned in Ch. 2 of the *Passio*).

The text of Constantine's edict against the Donatists is not extant.

279. THE UNMASKING OF SILVANUS OF CIRTA, 13 DECEMBER 320

(From *Gesta apud Zenophilum* in Optatus, *On the Schism of the Donatists*, App. I (*C.S.E.L.* XXVI, p. 192f.; Routh, *Reliquiae Sacrae*, ed. 2, IV, pp. 329f.).)

"It is A.D. 320 six years after the vindication of Felix of Aptungi, and another trial is proceeding. Time has amply brought her revenge. Now the accusation is no longer against the consecrator of Caecilian the Catholic Bishop of Carthage, but against Silvanus the Donatist Bishop of Cirta, the consecrator of Majorinus, who had been intruded into Caecilian's Chair. In this trial it is conclusively proved that Silvanus and his abettors had been guilty not merely of Betrayal—the sin falsely alleged against Felix and Caecilian, as a pretext for abandoning communion with Caecilian—but also of theft and simony under peculiarly disgraceful circumstances." (O. R. Vassall-Phillips, *St Optatus*, p. 346.)

Silvanus had been elected bishop of Cirta amid scenes of violence and confusion at the Council of Cirta (266). Silvanus had later on quarrelled with Nundinarius, one of his deacons, who "had a detailed knowledge of his bishop's career and his weak points" (Frend, *The Donatist Church*, p. 161). At this trial before the *Consular* Zenophilus, his guilt was conclusively proved. Victor, who appears in the passage given below, was one of the key personalities: he was a schoolmaster who had bribed Silvanus in order to secure ordination for himself. As a result of this trial Silvanus was exiled, but the Emperor shortly afterwards called off the persecution of the Donatists.

> After these documents had been read, Zenophilus said: "From the acts and letters which have been read aloud, it is clear that Silvanus is a Betrayer."
>
> And he said to Victor: "Frankly confess whether you know that he betrayed anything."
>
> Victor said: "He did betray, but not in my presence."
>
> Z.: "What office did Silvanus hold at the time amongst the clergy?"
>
> V.: "The persecution broke out when Paul was bishop; Silvanus was then a sub-deacon."
>
> Nundinarius the deacon replied: "When he came here, as he said, to be made Bishop, the people answered, 'Let it be another. Hear us, O God.'"
>
> Z. to V.: "Did the people cry out 'Silvanus is a Betrayer'?"
>
> V.: "I myself fought against his being made Bishop."
>
> Z.: "So you did know that he was a Betrayer! Confess to this."
>
> V.: "He was a Betrayer."
>
> Nundinarius the deacon said: "You seniors cried out 'Hear us, O God! We want our fellow-citizen. This man is a Betrayer.'"
>
> Z. to V.: "So you cried out with the people that Silvanus was a Betrayer and ought not to be made Bishop?"
>
> V.: "I did cry out, and so did the people. For we wanted our fellow-citizen, a man of integrity." . . . (O. R. Vassall-Phillips, *St Optatus*, App. II, pp. 365f.)

Seniors: cf. 269 (note).

280. ABANDONMENT OF THE PERSECUTION OF THE DONATISTS, 321

(Letter of Constantine to the Bishops and Laity of Africa in Optatus, *On the Schism of the Donatists*, App. IX (*C.S.E.L.* XXVI, pp. 212–13).)

[Constantine begins by expressing his anxiety for peace and union.]

But whereas the provisions that we have made have not prevailed to subdue the obstinate violence of crime, which has been

implanted in the breasts of certain men—few though they be—
and they still persist in supporting their wickedness, so that they
would not on any account suffer a place in which they were proud
to have sinned to be extorted from them, we must see to it, that
as all this evil affects a few, it may be, through the mercy of
Almighty God, mitigated for the people. For we ought to hope
for a remedy from that source to which all good desires and
deeds are referred. But, until the Heavenly medicine shows itself,
our designs must be moderated so far as to act with patience, and
whatever in their insolence they attempt or carry out, in accordance with their habitual wantonness—all this we must endure
with the strength which comes from tranquillity.

*   *   *

But, if you will give yourselves loyally to this cause (i.e. to endure
with patience), you will speedily bring it about that, by the favour
of God on high, these men who are making themselves the
standard-bearers of this most miserable strife, may all come to
recognize, as their laws or customs fall into decay, that they ought
not through the persuasion of a few to give themselves over to
perish in everlasting death, when they might through the grace
of repentance be made whole again, having corrected their
errors, for everlasting life. (O. R. Vassall-Phillips, *St Optatus*,
pp. 408–9, altered.)

It is clear that the emperor had no idea of the depth of feeling that lay
behind the Donatist movement. It is likely that he never was at ease about the
policy of persecution, and he now abandoned it willingly; it is of course also
likely that the growing expectation of an eventual conflict with Licinius must
have prevented him from giving any more attention to·the problem.

281. WEAKNESS OF AUTHORITY IN THE FACE OF DONATIST ENCROACHMENTS, 330

(Letter of Constantine to the Numidian Bishops in Optatus, *On the
Schism of the Donatists*, App. X (*C.S.E.L.* XXVI, p. 215).)

I have learnt by the receipt of the letter of your Wisdom and
Dignity, that the heretics or schismatics, with their accustomed

wickedness, determined to seize the basilica belonging to the Catholic Church, which I had ordered to be built in the City of Constantine, and that, though they had been often warned, both by us and by our judges at our command, to give up what was not theirs, they have refused to do so, but that you, imitating the patience of the most high God, with a calm mind relinquish to their wickedness what is yours, and ask instead for another site for yourselves in exchange, namely the Custom House. This petition of yours I gladly welcomed, according to my custom, and straightway sent a letter of authorization to the treasurer, commanding him to see that our Custom House should be passed over, with all its rights, to the ownership of the Catholic Church. I have given you this with ready liberality, and have ordered it to be at once delivered to you. I have also commanded a basilica to be built on that spot at the Imperial expense, and have directed letters to be written to the Consular of Numidia, telling him to be of assistance to your Holiness in all things which concern the building of this Church. (O. R. Vassall-Phillips, *St Optatus*, pp. 414–15, altered.)

City of Constantine: Cirta had been renamed.
Constantine was counselling patience with the Donatists, *c.* 321 (280).

282. THE PERSECUTION OF LICINIUS,
c. 319

(Eusebius, *H.E.* X.8.10, 14–18.)

Chapter 8 is a *damnatio memoriae Licinii*, added by Eusebius in a final edition of his work. Sections 1–9 compare Licinius unfavourably with his benefactor Constantine, against whom he began to plot. One of his first steps was (8) persecution of the Christians, forgetful of the calamities that had overwhelmed previous persecutors, some of whom had been destroyed by Licinius himself.

10   First, *he drove* away every Christian from his palace; thus by his own act depriving himself, wretched man, of the prayers *to God on his behalf*,[1] which after the custom of their fathers they are taught *to make for all men*.[2] Then he gave orders that the soldiers in cities were to be singled out and deprived of honourable rank, unless they chose to sacrifice to demons.

[1] A reminiscence of a passage of Dionysius of Alexandria, quoted in *H.E.* VII.1.
[2] I Tim. 2.1,2.

[11–13 describe the harshness, avarice and lust of Licinius—these sections (as Eusebius knows) deal with actions not specifically aimed at Christians.]

14   For example, in the final stage of his madness he proceeded against the bishops, and deeming them opposed to his doings, as being the servants of the supreme God, forthwith plotted against them, not openly as yet (for he feared his superior), but once more with secrecy and guile; and the most highly respected of these, by the contrivance of the governors, he put to death. And the manner in which they were murdered was strange and hitherto unheard

15 of. For instance, the things that were done at Amasea and the other cities of Pontus outdid every excess of cruelty. There some of the churches of God were again thrown down from the top to the bottom; others they shut up, so that none of the accustomed worshippers might assemble or pay to God the service due to Him.

16 For he did not think that the prayers were offered on his behalf —such was the reckoning of an evil conscience—but had been persuaded that we did everything and supplicated God on behalf of the Emperor whom He loved. Hence he hastened to vent his

17 wrath on us. And in truth the sycophants among the governors, persuaded that they were doing what pleased the impious man, plied some of the bishops with penalties suitable for malefactors, and those who had done no wrong were led away and punished, without a pretext, like murderers. And some endured at that time a more novel form of death: their bodies were cut with a sword, into many pieces, and after this cruel and most fearful sight they

18 were cast into the depths of the sea as food for fishes. Thereupon the men of God began again to flee, and once more the fields, once more the deserts, glens and mountains received the servants of Christ. And when the impious man was thus successful in these measures also, he then conceived the idea of stirring up anew the persecution against all. (Lawlor and Oulton, *Eusebius*, I, pp. 321–3.)

It is clear that there was no general persecution. In the last sentence quoted above Eusebius imputes such a design to Licinius, which he was prevented by Constantine from carrying out.

    10. It was natural that Licinius should regard the Christians as disaffected (cf. 16) and that is the reason for their expulsion from the palace, and for the measures taken against the *officers* of "the soldiers in cities", i.e. police. In section 8 Eusebius had already rejected the allegation of disloyalty—"his godly subjects, who had never at any time done any harm to his rule".

    Eusebius dealt with persecution by Licinius in various passages of his *Life of Constantine*. There we find other measures mentioned; that bishops should not communicate with each other or hold synods (*V.C.* I.51), that men and women should not worship together, and that women should be taught only by women (ibid., 53), and that worship should take place out-of-doors (ibid., 53).

283. THE RE-AFFIRMATION OF TOLERATION, 324

(Letter of Constantine to the people of the Eastern provinces, in Eusebius, *V.C.* II.56.)

My own desire is, for the common good of the world and the advantage of all mankind, that thy, i.e. God's, people should enjoy a life of peace and undisturbed concord. Let those, therefore, who still delight in error, be made welcome to the same degree of peace and tranquillity which they have who believe. For it may be that this restoration of equal privileges to all will prevail to lead them into the straight path. Let no one molest another, but let every one do as his soul desires. Only let men of sound judgement be assured of this, that those only can live a life of holiness and purity, whom thou callest to a reliance on thy holy laws. With regard to those who will hold themselves aloof from us, let them have, if they please, their temples of falsehood: *we* have the glorious edifice of thy truth. We pray, however, that they too may receive the same blessing which thou hast given in accordance with thy nature, and thus experience that heartfelt joy which unity of sentiment inspires. (N. & P.-N. F., altered.)

Constantine never went back on this. He weakened paganism, e.g. by plundering temples of their statues to embellish Constantinople, and he suppressed immoral rites, but the general structure of the old religion was left undisturbed.

284. LEGISLATION ABOUT SUNDAY

(*Cod. Theod.* II.8.1.)

Emperor Constantine Augustus to Helpidius.

Just as it appears to Us most unseemly that the Day of the Sun which is celebrated on account of its own veneration should be occupied with legal altercations and with noxious controversies of the litigation of contending parties, so it is pleasant and fitting that those acts which are especially desired shall be accomplished on that day. Therefore all men shall have the right to emancipate and to manumit on this festive day, and the legal formalities thereof are not forbidden. Given on 3 July at Cagliari in the second consulship of Crispus and Constantine Caesars (321). (Pharr, *The Theodosian Code*, p. 44.)

A similar enactment of 321 is found in *Codex Iustinianus* III.12.3. This is directed principally to country-people: they may work in the fields on Sunday, if good weather can speed the spring sowing and planting. City dwellers are, however, to rest.

285. ORDINATION FORBIDDEN TO DECURIONS AND THEIR FAMILIES, 320, (?) 326

(*Cod. Theod.* XVI.2.3.)

Constantine Augustus to Bassus, Praetorian Prefect.

A constitution was issued which directs that thenceforth no decurion or descendant of a decurion or even any person provided with adequate resources and suitable to undertake compulsory public services shall take refuge in the name and service of the clergy, but that in the place of deceased clerics thereafter only those persons shall be chosen as substitutes who have slender fortunes and who are not held bound to such compulsory municipal services. But we have learned that those persons also are being disturbed who became associated with the clergy before the promulgation of the aforesaid law. We command, therefore, that the latter shall be freed from all annoyance, and that the former, who in evasion of public duties have taken refuge in the number of the clergy after the issuance of the law shall be completely separated from that body, shall be restored to their orders and to the municipal councils, and shall perform their municipal duties. 18 July, 320, (?) 326. (Pharr, *The Theodosian Code*, p. 441.)

Constantine reiterated this prohibition in a constitution sent to Ablavius, Praetorian Prefect, in 326, *Cod. Theod.* XVI.2.6 (Pharr, op. cit., p. 441).

The burdens on decurions, or town councillors were so heavy that they were willing to seek any means of evasion. We learn from *Cod. Theod.* XVI.2.1,7 that heretics attempted to have municipal burdens placed on Catholic Clergy: as XVI.2.7 is addressed to the governor of Numidia in 330, it looks as though the Donatists were active in inflicting these burdens on their Catholic opponents, on this cf. also Constantine's letter to the Numidian bishops (Optatus, *On the Schism of the Donatists*, App. X, *C.S.E.L.* XXVI, pp. 213–16) which shows that "heretics" had been instigating the imposition of these burdens on the Catholic clergy.

286. NO IMMUNITIES FOR HERETICS AND SCHISMATICS, 326

(*Cod. Theod.* XVI.5.1.)

Emperor Constantine Augustus to Dracilian (Vicar of the Praetorian Prefect).

The privileges that have been granted in consideration of religion must benefit only the adherents of the Catholic faith (*lex*). It is Our will moreover, that heretics and schismatics shall not only be alien from these privileges but shall also be bound and subjected to various compulsory public services. 1 September, 326. (Pharr, *The Theodosian Code*, p. 450.)

287. CONSTANTINE AND THE NOVATIANISTS, 326

(*Cod. Theod.* XVI.5.2.)

Emperor Constantine Augustus to Bassus (Prefect of the City).

We have not found that the Novatians were precondemned to such an extent that We should suppose that those things which they sought ought not to be granted to them. We direct therefore that they shall firmly possess, without disquietude, their own church buildings and places suitable for burial: that is those properties which they have held for a long time either through purchase or through acquisition in any manner whatsoever. Of course, due provision must be made that they shall not attempt to appropriate to themselves any of the property which manifestly belonged to the Church of perpetual sanctity before the schism. 25 September, 326. (Pharr, *The Theodosian Code*, p. 450.)

The Novatianists, whose orthodoxy was unimpeachable, and whose separation from the Catholics was on a matter of discipline, received more favourable treatment than others. Acesius, a bishop of this sect, was invited by Constantine to the Council of Nicaea (Socrates, *H.E.* I.10, Sozomen, *H.E.* I.22). The Emperor inquired of him about the reasons for his separation, and on hearing of his rigorism towards sinners, replied "Place a ladder, Acesius, and climb up alone into heaven" (Socrates, loc. cit.).

288. GREAT ACHIEVEMENTS AND GREAT EXPECTATIONS: THE CONCLUDING WORDS OF EUSEBIUS' ECCLESIASTICAL HISTORY, 324–325

(Eusebius, *H.E.* X.9.6–9.)

6   Thus was Licinius cast down prostrate. But Constantine the most mighty Victor, resplendent with every virtue that godliness bestows, together with his son Crispus, an Emperor most dear to God and in all respects like unto his father, recovered the East that belonged to them, and formed the Roman Empire, as in the days of old, into a single united whole, bringing under their peaceful rule all of it, from the rising sun round about in the two directions, north as well as south, even to the uttermost limits of

7 the declining day. So then, there was taken away from men all fear of those who formerly oppressed them; they celebrated brilliant festivals; all things were filled with light, and men, formerly downcast, looked at each other with smiling countenances and beaming eyes; with dancing and hymns in city and country alike they gave honour first of all to God the universal King, for this they had been instructed to do, and then to the

8 pious Emperor with his sons beloved of God; old ills were forgotten and oblivion cast on every deed of impiety; present good things were enjoyed, with the further hope of those which were yet for to come. And, in short, there were promulgated in every place ordinances of the victorious Emperor full of love for human-

9 ity, and laws that betokened munificence and true piety. Thus verily, when all tyranny had been purged away, the kingdom

that belonged to them was preserved stedfast and undisputed for Constantine and his sons alone; who, when they had made it their very first action to cleanse the world from hatred of God, conscious of the good things that He had bestowed upon them, displayed their love of virtue and of God, their piety and gratitude towards the Deity, by their manifest deeds in the sight of all men. (Lawlor and Oulton, *Eusebius*, I, pp. 324–5.)

Eusebius had extended his *History* in successive editions from 311 onwards, and his final purpose was achieved with the conclusion of Constantine's war with Licinius in 324, cf. 282 *init*. The final ending of Book X was transferred, *mutatis mutandis*, from the end of Book IX.

6. *Crispus*: son of Constantine and Minervina; the date of his birth is probably *c.* 303: he was his father's right hand man in the war with Licinius; but he was executed by his father in mysterious circumstances in 326 during Constantine's visit to Italy in 325–326. As he is mentioned by Eusebius with approbation, it is clear that Eusebius had finished the history before his downfall.

into a single united whole: cf. 318 (3).

7. *his sons beloved of God*: besides Crispus there were Constantine II (b. 314), Constantius (b. 317), and Constans (b. 320), sons of Constantine by Fausta, who ultimately succeeded their father.

8. *ordinances . . . full of love for humanity, and laws that betokened munificence and true piety*: Eusebius (*V.C.* IV.31) states that Constantine was singularly averse to the death penalty. "One would not say so when one sees the horrible punishments that he ordained against kidnappers of children (A.D. 315), those who seized farm oxen (315), parricides (318), ravishers (326). However, some of his laws are marked with striking care for humanity: he abolished crucifixion; he forbade branding on the face; the finest of his laws, worthy of eternal honour, ordained that prisoners should each day have the right to see the sun." (Piganiol, *L'Empire chrétien*, pp. 70, 71.)

For gifts to the church and immunities to the clergy, cf. 263, 264: for building of churches, cf. 319: for law in favour of virginity, Sozomen, *H.E.* I.9: for law about Sunday, cf. 284.

289. EUSEBIUS ON THE CANON OF THE NEW TESTAMENT

1. The Writings of St Peter and St Paul

(Eusebius, *H.E.* III.3.1–5.)

1   Of Peter, then, one epistle, his former as it is called, is acknowledged; and of this also the elders of olden time have made frequent use, as a work beyond dispute, in their own treatises. But

as for the second extant [epistle], the tradition received by us is that it is not canonical; nevertheless, since it appeared profitable
2 to many, store was set by it along with the other Scriptures. Yet as regards the book of his Acts, as it is entitled, and the Gospel named after him, and his Preaching, as it is called, and The Apocalypse (such is its name): we know that they were not handed down at all among the catholic [writings]; for no Church writer, either in ancient times or even in our day, used testimonies derived from them.

3   But as my history advances I shall deem it profitable to indicate, along with the successions, what Church writers in each period have made use of which of the disputed [books], and what they have said about the canonical and acknowledged writings, and anything that they have said about those that are not such.

4   Now the writings that bear the name of Peter, of which I recognize only one epistle as genuine and acknowledged by the
5 elders of olden time, are so many; while the fourteen epistles of Paul are manifest and clear [as regards their genuineness]. Nevertheless it is not right to be ignorant that some have rejected the Epistle to the Hebrews, saying that it is disputed by the church of the Romans as not being Paul's. And I shall quote at the proper time what those who lived before us have said with reference to this epistle also. Moreover, I have not received his Acts, as they are called, among the undisputed writings. (Lawlor and Oulton, *Eusebius*, I, pp. 65–6.)

5.   On the *Epistle to the Hebrews*, cf. 192.

2. The *Shepherd* of Hermas

(Eusebius, *H.E.* III.3.6.)

6   But since the same apostle, in the concluding salutations of the Epistle to the Romans, has mentioned among the others Hermas also, the author, it is said, of the book of The Shepherd, it should be known that this too has been disputed by some, on whose account it could not be placed among the acknowledged [writings]; while it has been adjudged as most essential by others, especially for those in need of an introduction of an elementary kind. Hence, as we know, it has actually come to be read publicly in churches; and that some of the oldest writers have used it is a fact which I have received by tradition. (Lawlor and Oulton, *Eusebius*, I, p. 66.)

On the *Shepherd*, cf. 124.

3. A summing up of the New Testament writings

(Eusebius, *H.E.* III.25.1–7.)

1   But now that we have reached this point, it is reasonable to sum up the writings of the New Testament already mentioned. Well then, we must set in the first place the holy quaternion of the Gospels; which are followed by the book of the Acts of the

2 Apostles. After this we must reckon the epistles of Paul; following which we must pronounce genuine the extant former epistle of John, and likewise the epistle of Peter. After these we must place, if it really seem right, the Apocalypse of John, the views that have

3 been held as to which we shall set forth at the proper time. These, then, belong to the acknowledged writings. But of those which are disputed, nevertheless familiar to the majority, there is extant the epistle of James, as it is called; and that of Jude; and the second epistle of Peter; and the second and third of John, so named, whether they belong to the evangelist or perhaps to some other

4 of the same name as he. Among the spurious writings there are to be placed also the book of the Acts of Paul, and the Shepherd, as it is called, and the Apocalypse of Peter; and, in addition to these, the extant epistle of Barnabas, and the Teachings of the Apostles, as it is called; and, moreover, as I said, the Apocalypse of John, if it seem right. (This last, as I said, is rejected by some, but

5 others give it a place among the acknowledged writings.) And among these some have reckoned also the Gospel of the Hebrews, a work which is especially acceptable to such Hebrews as received

6 the Christ. Now all these would be among the disputed writings; but nevertheless we have been compelled to make a catalogue of these also, distinguishing those writings which the tradition of the Church has deemed true and genuine and acknowledged, from the others outside their number, which, though they are not canonical but even disputed, yet are recognized by most church-men. [And this we have done] in order that we might be able to know both these same writings and also those which the heretics put forward in the name of the apostles, whether as containing Gospels of Peter and Thomas and Matthias, or even of some others besides these, or as containing Acts of Andrew and John and the other apostles. None of these has been deemed worthy of any kind of mention in a treatise by a single member of successive

7 generations of churchmen; and the character of the style also is far removed from the apostolic manner, and the thought and purport of their contents is so absolutely out of harmony with true ortho-doxy, as to establish the fact that they are certainly the forgeries

of heretics. For this reason they ought not even to be placed among the spurious writings, but refused as altogether monstrous and impious. (Lawlor and Oulton, *Eusebius*, I, pp. 86–7, slightly altered.)

Notwithstanding his interest in the Canon, the account of Eusebius is not entirely satisfactory. In *H.E.* III.25 he enumerates four classes of books, (1) the acknowledged writings, (2) the disputed, (3) the spurious, (4) heretical forgeries. Classes 2 and 3 are orthodox, but Eusebius "draws no clear line of demarcation between them" (Lawlor and Oulton, op. cit., II, p. 101, cf. 25.3 with 25.6 (and with 31.6). By "spurious" he means that the books in 3 were not written by the authors to whom they were attributed; but he has doubts about the authorship of certain books in 2 also.

Yet *Revelation* (cf. 287) is in Class 1 or Class 3, because Eusebius had himself doubts about the value of the book owing to the misconceptions to which it gave rise, cf. *H.E.* III.39.12.

It is curious that I Clement does not appear in his classification. In *H.E.* III.16 he states that it was read publicly down to his own day, in very many churches.

290. THE OUTBREAK OF THE ARIAN CONTROVERSY, c. 318

(Socrates, *H.E.* I.5.)

1   Alexander (Bishop of Alexandria) attempted one day, in the presence of the presbyters and the rest of his clergy, too ambitious a discourse about the Holy Trinity, the subject being "Unity in Trinity".

2   Arius, one of- the presbyters under his jurisdiction, a man possessed of no inconsiderable logical acumen, thinking that the bishop was introducing the doctrine of Sabellius the Libyan, from love of controversy advanced another view diametrically opposed to the opinion of the Libyan, and, as it seemed, vehemently controverted the statements of the bishop. "If," said he, "the Father begat the Son, He that was begotten has a beginning of existence; and from this it is evident, that there was when the Son was not. It therefore necessarily follows that He had His essence from the non-existent." (N. & P.-N. F., altered.)

1.   Alexander became bishop of Alexandria, c. 313.

2.   On Sabellius, cf. 135, 136, 235. That he is called *the Libyan* is probably a deduction from the prevalence of his heresy in the Pentapolis c. 250.

291. ARIUS AND HIS HERESY

(Sozomen, *H.E.* I.15.1–6.)

1 But even though religion was in a flourishing condition in this way and in all other respects, yet the Churches were disturbed by certain sore contentions; for under the pretext of piety, and of seeking a complete discovery of God, certain questions were agitated which had not until then been examined. Arius was the
2 originator of these disputations. He was a presbyter of Alexandria in Egypt. He appeared at first a zealous supporter of truth, though he made common cause with Melitius in his innovations. Eventually however he abandoned Melitius, and was ordained deacon by Peter, Bishop of the Alexandrians, who afterwards cast him out of the church, because, upon Peter's excommunication of Melitius and repudiation of his baptism, Arius denounced what was done, and could not bear to keep quiet. After the martyrdom of Peter, Arius asked forgiveness of Achillas, was allowed to be a deacon, and was elevated to the presbyterate. After this Alexander
3 also held him in high repute. A most expert logician (for he is said to have been not without proficiency even in such studies) he plunged headlong into absurd arguments, and had the audacity to preach in church what no one before him had ever suggested, namely, that the Son of God has come into existence "out of the non-existent" and that "there was when he was not", that as possessing free will he was capable of virtue or of vice, and that he was created and made, and he gave voice to many other similar assertions which one professing such views might utter.
4 Some who heard these doctrines blamed Alexander because he ought not to put up with novelties at variance with the faith, but Alexander deemed it more advisable that each party should state its case in dealing with topics admitting of doubt, so that they might seem to cease their strife not by compulsion, but by persuasion. He sat as judge, with his clergy round him, and
5 brought both parties to a trial. But it happened on this occasion, as is generally the case in a strife of words, that either party aimed at complete victory. Arius defended his views, but the others asserted that the Son is consubstantial and co-eternal with the Father. As points of such importance had been raised, a second meeting was called, but no agreement was reached. While the arguments appeared still evenly balanced, Alexander seemed to incline, first to one party and then to the other. (N. & P.-N. F., altered.)

Arius (b. *c.* 255) appears to have been a deacon under Peter of Alexandria (d. 311), then to have been excommunicated for his support of the Melitians, next to have been allowed by Achillas to resume his functions, and finally to have been ordained presbyter.

With the account given by Sozomen, cf. the account of Socrates (290). The latter represents Arius as opposing Alexander in order to set his bishop right.

Achillas, bishop of Alexandria, 311–312, cf. Eus., *H.E.* VII.32.30.

1. *in this way*: i.e. in the ascetic life.

5. *consubstantial* (ὁμοούσιος): we need not assume from Sozomen's narrative that this word was actually used, but cf. 294 for its use in early stages of the controversy.

292. THE ARIAN HERESY: ENCYCLICAL LETTER OF ALEXANDER OF ALEXANDRIA AND HIS CLERGY, *c.* 319

(Socrates, *H.E.* I.6.4ff., Opitz, *Athanasius Werke*, III.1, Urkunde 4b., pp. 6–11.)

4   I wished indeed to consign this disorder to silence, that if possible the evil might be confined to its supporters alone, and not go forth into other districts and contaminate the ears of some
5   of the simple. But since Eusebius, now in Nicomedia, thinks that the affairs of the Church are under his control because he deserted his charge at Berytus and cast longing glances at the church at Nicomedia (and he did this with impunity) and has put himself at the head of these apostates also, daring even to send commendatory letters in all directions concerning them, if by any means he might inveigle some of the ignorant into this most base heresy which is hostile to Christ, I felt imperatively called on to be silent no longer, knowing what is written in the law, but to
6   inform you of all of these things, that you might understand both who the apostates are, and also the contemptible character of their heresy, and pay no attention to anything that Eusebius
7   should write to you. For now wishing to renew his former malevolence, which seemed to have been buried in oblivion by time, he affects to write on their behalf; while the fact itself plainly shows that he does this for the promotion of his own purposes.
8   These then are those that have become apostates:—Arius,

Achillas, Aïthales, Carpones, another Arius, Sarmates (formerly presbyters), Euzoïus, Lucius, Julian, Menas, Helladius and Gaius (formerly deacons); with these also must be reckoned Secundus and Theonas, who once were called bishops. What they assert

9 in utter contrariety to the Scriptures, and wholly of their own devising, is as follows: "God was not always a father, but that there was when He was not a father; the Word of God was not from eternity, but was made out of nothing; for that the ever-existing God has made Him who did not previously exist, out of the non-existent." Wherefore "there was when He was not", inasmuch as, according to their philosophy, "the Son is a

10 creature and a work; He is neither like the Father in essence, nor is by nature either the Father's true Word or His true Wisdom, but indeed one of His works and creatures, being by a misuse of language called Word and Wisdom since he came into being by God's own Word and the Wisdom which is in God, whereby God both made all things and Him also." Wherefore, "He is as to his nature mutable and susceptible of change, as all

11 other rational things are: hence the Word is alien to, foreign to, and excluded from the essence of God; and the Father is invisible to the Son: for neither does the Son perfectly and accurately know the Father, neither can He perfectly behold him. The Son knows not even the nature of His own essence; for He has been made for us, in order that God might create us by Him, as by an instrument; nor would He ever have existed, unless God had wished to

12 create us." Some one accordingly asked them whether the Word of God could be changed, as the devil has been, and they feared not to say "Yes: He certainly could; for being begotten and created, His nature is susceptible of change." We then, with the

13 bishops of Egypt and Libya, being assembled together to the number of nearly a hundred, anathematized Arius for his shameless avowal of these heresies, together with all such as have countenanced them. (N. & P.-N. F., altered.)

[The rest of the letter is taken up with arguments from scripture against the Arians and further warnings about Eusebius of Nicomedia. It concludes with the signatures of seventeen presbyters and twenty-four deacons (including two named Athanasius) from Alexandria, and of nineteen presbyters and twenty deacons from the Mareotis.]

Eusebius of Nicomedia: with the hint of Alexander that ambition prompted the move of Eusebius from Berytus to Nicomedia, cf. the severe language used by Constantine of Eusebius in 304 below.

The fragments of Arius collected by Bardy, *Recherches sur Saint Lucien d'Antioche et son école*, pp. 216–78 (L'héritage littéraire d'Arius) show identity of phrase with much of what this letter states about his teaching. Opitz has given some of the parallels in his notes: cf. also 296.

The list of signatories is not in Socrates, but is in other sources, Athanasius and Gelasius, that give this letter.

293. LETTER OF ARIUS TO EUSEBIUS, BISHOP OF NICOMEDIA, *c.* 320

(In Theodoret, *H.E.* I.5.1–4, Epiphanius, *Haer.* 69.6; Opitz, Urkunde 1, pp. 1–3.)

1   To his very dear lord, the faithful man of God, orthodox Eusebius, Arius, unjustly persecuted by Pope Alexander on account of that all-conquering truth which you also *defend as with a shield*,[1] sends greeting in the Lord.

As Ammonius, my father, was going to Nicomedia, I thought it right and my bounden duty to greet you by him, and also to make mention of that inborn love and kindly disposition which you bear towards the brethren for the sake of God and of His Christ; I want to tell you that the bishop makes great havoc of us and persecutes us severely, and is in full sail against us: he has driven us out of the city as atheists, because we do not concur in what he publicly preaches, namely, that "God has always been, and the Son has always been: Father and Son exist together: the Son has His existence unbegotten along with God, ever being begotten, without having been begotten: God does not precede the Son by thought or by any interval however small: God has always been, the Son has always been; the Son is from God Himself".

2   Eusebius, your brother in Caesarea, Theodotus, Paulinus, Athanasius, Gregory, Aëtius, and all the bishops of the East, have been made anathema because they say that God has existence without beginning prior to His Son: except Philogonius, Hellanicus, and Macarius, who are heretical fellows, and uncatechized. One of them says that the Son is an effusion, another that He is an emission, another that He is also unbegotten.

3   These are impieties to which we could not listen, even though the heretics should threaten us with a thousand deaths. But as for us, what do we say, and believe, and what have we taught, and what do we teach? That the Son is not unbegotten, nor in

[1] Ps. 47.9

any way part of the unbegotten; nor from some lower essence (i.e. from matter); but that by His own (i.e. the Father's) will and counsel He has subsisted before time, and before ages as God *full ⟨of grace and truth⟩*,[1] only-begotten, unchangeable.

4   And that He was not, before He was begotten, or created, or purposed, or established. For He was not unbegotten. We are persecuted because we say, "the Son had a beginning, but God is without beginning". This is really the cause of our persecution; and, likewise, because we say that He is from nothing. And this we say, because He is neither part of God, nor of any lower essence. For this are we persecuted; the rest you know. Farewell in the Lord. As a fellow-disciple of Lucian, and as a truly pious man, as your name implies, remember our afflictions. (Based on N. & P.-N. F.)

1.   It is clear from what Arius writes that some time had elapsed from the events related in 290 and 291.

2.   The sees of the bishops concerned are as follows; for further information about them, see the articles in *D.C.B.*

Theodotus, of Laodicaea in Syria, cf. 298, 305. He was a friend of Eusebius of Caesarea who pays him a high tribute in *H.E.* VII.32.23, and dedicated to him the *Praeparatio* and *Demonstratio Evangelica*.

Paulinus of Tyre, and later of Antioch, d. *c.* 330, or earlier (?), also a friend of Eusebius of Caesarea, cf. *H.E.* X.4.1.

Athanasius of Anazarbus in Cilicia, a pupil of Lucian of Antioch according to Philostorgius, *H.E.* III.15.

Gregory of Berytus, successor to Eusebius when the latter was translated to Nicomedia.

Aëtius of Lydda (Diospolis).

Philogonius of Antioch, d. 324.

Hellanicus of Tripoli.

Macarius of Jerusalem.

effusion: lit. something belched out (Ps. 44.2 LXX).

3.   *part of the unbegotten*: cf. 4 below; *part of God*: cf. 301, p. 366 (sect. 7).

4.   *a fellow disciple of Lucian*: cf. Bardy, *Recherches sur Saint Lucien d'Antioche et son école*, p. 185. "After the death of Lucian, his disciples remained faithful to his memory. They continued to make use of his name and formed a homogeneous group, perfectly united, which knew, in the face of a thousand difficulties, how to keep him in remembrance. This group comes to the front at the precise moment when the Arian controversy began. It sufficed, so it seems, for Arius to make use of the name of Lucian's school with Eusebius of Nicomedia for the East immediately to be set aflame, and for all the Lucianists to take the part of the priest of Baucalis."

[1] John 1.14.

294. LETTER OF ARIUS TO ALEXANDER, BISHOP OF ALEXANDRIA, c. 320

(Athanasius, *On the Synods of Ariminum and Seleuceia*, 16; Epiphanius, *Haer.* 69.7; Opitz, Urkunde 6, pp. 12–13.)

To our blessed Pope and Bishop Alexander, the Presbyters and Deacons send greeting in the Lord.

Our faith from our forefathers, which we have learned also from thee, Blessed Pope, is this:—We acknowledge One God, alone unbegotten, alone everlasting, alone unbegun, alone true, *alone having immortality*,[1] alone wise, alone good, alone sovereign; judge, governor, and administrator of all, unalterable and unchangeable, just and good, God of Law and Prophets and New Testament; who begat an Only-begotten Son before eternal times, through whom He has made both the ages and the universe; and begat Him not in semblance, but in truth: and that He made Him subsist at His own will, unalterable and unchangeable; perfect creature of God, but not as one of the creatures; offspring, but not as one of things that have come into existence; nor as Valentinus pronounced that the offspring of the Father was an issue; nor as Manichaeus taught that the offspring was a portion of the Father, consubstantial (ὁμοούσιος); or as Sabellius, dividing the Monad, speaks of a Son-and-Father; nor as Hieracas, of one torch from another, or as a lamp divided into two; nor that He who was before, was afterwards generated or new-created into a Son, as thou too thyself, Blessed Pope, in the midst of the Church and in session hast often condemned; but, as we say, at the will of God, created before times and before ages, and gaining life and being and His glories from the Father, who gave real existence to those together with Him. For the Father did not, in giving to Him the inheritance of all things, deprive Himself of what He has ingenerately in Himself; for He is the Fountain of all things. Thus there are Three Subsistences (ὑποστάσεις). And God, being the cause of all things, is unbegun and altogether sole but the Son being begotten apart from time by the Father, and being created and found before ages, was not before His generation; but, being begotten apart from time before all things, alone was made to subsist by the Father. For He is not eternal or co-eternal or co-unoriginate with the Father, nor has He His being together with the Father, as some speak of relations, introducing two ingenerate beginnings, but God is before all things as being Monad and Beginning of all.

[1] 1 Tim. 6.16.

Wherefore also He is before the Son, as we have learned also from thy preaching in the midst of the Church. Even as then from God He has being, and glories and life, and all things are delivered unto Him, in such sense is God His Origin. For He is above Him, as being His God and before Him. But if the terms *from Him*[1] and *from the womb*[2] and *I came forth from the Father and I come*[3] be understood by some to mean as if a part of Him, being consubstantial, or as an issue, then the Father is according to them compounded and divisible and alterable and material, and, as far as concerns them, undergoes what is appropriate to a body, who is the Incorporeal God. (N. & P.-N. F., altered.)

The letter concludes with greetings from Arius and his supporters, in all six presbyters, six deacons and three bishops: the last named are Secundus and Theonas, who remained faithful to him at Nicaea, and Pistus. The inclusion of the latter is odd, as he did not become a bishop until he was obtruded into Alexandria in 337, cf. Athanasius, *Apology against the Arians*, 24. Anyhow the fact that the letter comes from Arius and his clerical supporters indicates that c. 320–321 he was still in Egypt. It is most unlikely that if he "fled to Nicomedia" as is commonly supposed, he took all his supporters with him, cf. Telfer, *J.T.S.* XXXVII (1936), p. 60–3. The views of the heresiarch as to his bishop's teaching should be compared with what he (Arius) said in his letter to Eusebius of Nicomedia (293).

The recurrence of the word ὁμοούσιος (of one essence) *as a word to be avoided* should be noted, cf. Ambrose *De Fide*, III.15 (Opitz, Urkunde 21, p. 42) where Eusebius of Nicomedia is said to have produced a letter to the Council of Nicaea in which he wrote, "If we speak of a true and uncreated Son of God, we begin to confess him 'consubstantial' with the Father." Ambrose adds that the word ὁμοούσιος was included in the Creed *because* the Arians were scared of it! The fear that this word implied division of the divine essence was real both to Arius, and to Eusebius of Caesarea (301).

Hieracas: an Egyptian Christian of the early fourth century, whose manner of life was strongly ascetic. Epiphanius (*Haer.* 69.7) pronounces him as orthodox on the relation of the Father to the Son.

295. THE ARIAN STRATEGY ACCORDING TO ALEXANDER OF ALEXANDRIA, c. 324

(Letter of Alexander in Theodoret, *H.E.* I.4; Opitz, Urkunde 14, pp. 19–28.)

This is a circular letter, as is shown by the use of the plural possessive ὑμέτερος (sect. 2), and I.4.62 where Theodoret states that Alexander wrote in

[1] Rom. 11.36.   [2] Ps. 110.3.   [3] John 16.28.

the same strain to Philogonius of Antioch, to Eustathius of Beroea (later of Antioch), and to the other supporters of his views. The heading of the chapter mentions Alexander "of Constantinople" as the recipient, but it is more likely that Alexander of Thessalonica is meant; it is interesting to note that Constantine may first have heard of the controversy there. He was visited at Thessalonica by Eusebius of Nicomedia (304).

1 Impelled by avarice and ambition knaves are constantly plotting to gain possession of the dioceses that seem greatest. Under various pretexts they trample on the religion of the church. For they are driven mad by the devil *who works in them*,[1] and abandon
2 all reverence and despise the fear of God's judgement. As I suffer from them myself, I had to explain to your Reverence, that you be on your guard against such individuals, lest any of them dare enter your dioceses also, either in person (for the impostors are skilled deceivers), or by false and specious letters. By both means they can delude one who clings to faith, though it be a pure faith.
3 Arius then and Achillas lately made a conspiracy, in which they emulated the ambition of Colluthus—but they are far worse than he. Colluthus reprehended their conduct, and found a means of excusing his own knavish purpose. But they seeing his "making traffic of Christ",[2] could not still remain subject to the Church, but build for themselves *dens of robbers*,[3] in which they constantly assemble and by night and day indulge in slanders against Christ
4 and us. They cry down all the pious apostolic doctrine and, just as the Jews do, have organized a gang to fight Christ. They deny His divinity, and declare Him to be on a level with all mankind. They pick out every saying relative to His saving dispensation, and to His *humiliation*[4] for us, and try to compound from them the proclamation of their own impiety, by abandoning the words showing His divinity *from the beginning*[5] and His ineffable glory
5 with the Father. They make their own the impious view of Greeks and Jews about Christ, and endeavour, as far as they possibly can, to get praised among them. They busy themselves with the parts of our doctrine that excite derision among Greeks and Jews. They daily excite disorders and persecutions against us: on the one hand they have courts assembled (i.e. to accuse us) on the petition of disorderly women whom they have deceived, on the other they discredit Christianity by the younger women who support them running around every street in an indecent fashion. But they have even dared to rend the seamless robe of Christ, which the executioners did not resolve on dividing.[6]

---

[1] Eph. 2.2.   [2] Cf. *Didache* 12.5.   [3] Matt. 21.13.
[4] Cf. Phil. 2.8   [5] Cf. John 1.1.   [6] Cf. John 19.23-4.

6 Because of their subterfuges we only gradually got to know of their teaching which suits their way of life and their unholy project; we drove them by a unanimous vote from the Church which reverences the Divinity of Christ.

7 They tried by running to and fro to reach our fellow ministers who were of one mind with us. They make a show of reverence for the fair name of peace and union, but in fact endeavour to infect some of them with their own disease by means of fair words, and ask them for all too verbose letters, which they read aloud to those that they have deceived, and confirm them as unrepentant in their error, on the ground that they have bishops to agree and

8 be of one mind with them. They do not confess to them the wicked teaching and actions that led to their expulsion, but they either pass these over in silence or deceive by concealing them

9 with specious words and writings. They hide their corrupting teaching with all too persuasive and tricky conversations, and carry away anyone ready to be deceived, and they do not scruple to calumniate *our* religion. And so it comes about that some people sign their letters and receive them into the Church. I think that the greatest blame rests on our fellow ministers who dare to do this: the apostolic canon does not permit it, and their conduct inflames the diabolical activity of our opponents against Christ. (With acknowledgements to the translation in Bohn's Ecclesiastical Library.)

[Alexander then proceeds to a long account of Arian teaching
10ff dwelling on their misinterpretation of scripture, and on the limitation of human intelligence. He is particularly severe on the
23 Arian assertion "there was when he was not": "Is it not incredible to say that he who *made* times, *ages*[1] and seasons, in which 'he was not' must be comprised, 'once was not'"?'

The Arians had made much of Christ's sonship being similar to
35-6 ours: Alexander repudiates this idea. The heresy of Arius is that of Ebion (72) and Artemas (238, pp. 276-7), and resembles the views of Paul of Samosata and Lucian his successor. The leaders of the
37 heresy are Arius and Achillas (36).] And three bishops—ordained in Syria I know not how!—by siding with them inflame them to worse impiety.

(These three were (according to Sozomen, *H.E.* I.15.11) Eusebius of Caesarea, Paulinus of Tyre, and Patrophilus of Scythopolis; by his sneer at them, Alexander repays Arius for his sneer at the three bishops who disagreed with *him* (293).)

[1] Cf. Heb. 1.2.

On the relations of the Father and the Son Alexander stresses that the Son is not the same as the Father, e.g. when He said *I and the Father are one*,[1] "He did not call Himself Father nor did He declare that the persons, two in subsistence (ὑπόστασις), are one, but because the Son of the Father naturally preserves accurately his resemblance to the Father, being personally a copy, a likeness in all respects, being the undistinguishable resemblance of the Father and the truly struck *image*[2] of his prototype" (38). Alexander, just like the Council of Antioch (cf. 298, p. 357), has nothing to say about the divine οὐσία.

He is also careful to deal with the point that rejection of the Arian hypothesis demanded belief in two unbegotten beings, cf. Arius in 294. In Theodoret, *H.E.* I.6.3 Eusebius of Nicomedia, writing to Paulinus of Tyre, says, "We have not heard of two unbegotten beings. . . ." Alexander declares that the "only-begotten" stands between the Father and His creatures (44), and that the expressions used of the Son ("He was", "He has always been", "He existed before the ages") are not the same as saying that He is unbegotten (49).

1. *dioceses*: παροίκιαι. The secular divisions of the Empire were called διοικήσεις, cf. p. 322 above.

3. *Colluthus* (presbyter) was the first signatory to the condemnation of Arius in Alexander's letter of *c.* 319 (292). Wherein his misdemeanour consisted is uncertain, but from Alexander's language here we can assume that he was schismatic rather than heretical. It is possible that he went into schism because he thought that Alexander showed too great toleration to Arius.

296. EXTRACTS FROM THE *THALIA* OF ARIUS

(Athanasius, *On the Synods of Ariminum and Seleuceia*, 15.)

. . . God Himself, then, in His own nature, is ineffable by all men.

Equal or like or one in glory with Himself, He alone has none.

And Ingenerate we call Him because of Him who is generate by nature.

We praise Him as without beginning, because of Him who has a beginning.

And adore Him as everlasting, because of Him who in time has come to be.

He that is without beginning made the Son a beginning of things originated; and advanced Him as a Son to Himself by adoption.

He has nothing proper to God in proper subsistence (καθ' ὑπό-στασιν).

[1] John 10.30.   [2] Heb. 1.3.

For He is not equal, no, nor one in essence (ὁμοούσιος) with Him.

Wise is God, for He is the teacher of Wisdom.

There is full proof that God is invisible to all beings; both to things which are through the Son, and to the Son He is invisible.

I will say it expressly, how by the Son is seen the Invisible; by that power by which God sees, and in His own measure, the Son endures to see the Father, as is lawful.

Thus there is a Triad, not in similar glories. Not intermingling with each other are their subsistences. One is more glorious than the other in glories to infinity.

Foreign from the Son in essence is the Father, for He is without beginning.

Understand that the Monad was; but the Dyad was not, before it was in existence.

It follows at once that though the Son was not, the Father was God. Hence the Son, not being (for He existed at the will of the Father), is God Only-begotten; and He is alien from either. Wisdom existed as Wisdom by the will of the Wise God.

Hence he is conceived in numberless conceptions: Spirit, Power, Wisdom, God's glory, Truth, Image and Word.

Understand that He is conceived to be Radiance and Light.

One equal to the Son, the Superior is able to beget; but one more excellent, or superior, or greater, He is not able.

At God's will the Son is what and whatsoever He is. And when and since He was, from then He has subsisted from God.

He, being a strong God, praises in His degree the Superior.

To speak in brief, God is ineffable to His Son. For He is to Himself what He is, that is, unspeakable. So that nothing which is called comprehensible does the Son know how to speak about; for it is impossible for Him to investigate the Father, who is by Himself. For the Son does not know His own essence: For, being Son, He really existed at the will of the Father.

What argument then allows, that He who is from the Father should know His own parent by comprehension? For it is plain that for that which hath a beginning to conceive Him that is without beginning or to grasp the idea, is not possible. (N. & P.-N. F., altered.)

Athanasius is not quoting the *Thalia* consecutively. Certain doctrines recur several times, but towards the end there is a passage which hangs together on the impossibility of the Son knowing the Father. Athanasius prefixes his quotation by the following: "When Arius had been expelled and was thrown over by the Eusebians, he drew up his heresy on paper, and, as in a Banquet

(*Thalia*), he imitated no grave writer but the Egyptian Sotades in the character and laxity of his verse. For he writes at great length and the following are extracts": (N. & P.-N. F., altered).

In Photius' *Epitome* of Philostorgius, the Arian historian, (II.2) we learn that, in order to attract the unlearned, Arius wrote songs to be sung by sailors, millers and travellers. These should probably be distinguished from the *Thalia*.

The *Thalia* is in verse, but the metre is variously estimated. Bardy regards the lines as degenerate hexametres, but most scholars consider them Sotadic (see, e.g., Puech, *Histoire de la Littérature grecque chrétienne*, III, pp. 59–61, Bardy, *Recherches sur saint Lucien d'Antioche et son école*, pp. 250–2).

Athanasius' reference to the imitation of Sotades "in the character and laxity of his verse" has a double meaning, referring to both metre and content. The obscenities of Sotades were paralleled by the doctrinal errors of Arius.

297. THE MISSION OF OSSIUS: CONSTANTINE'S LETTER TO ALEXANDER AND ARIUS, 324

(Eusebius, *Life of Constantine*, II.63–72; Socrates, *H.E.* I.7; Opitz, Urkunde 17, pp. 32–5.)

63   As soon as the emperor was informed of these facts, which he heard with much sorrow of heart, considering them in the light of a calamity personally affecting himself, he forthwith selected from the Christians in his train one whom he well knew to be approved for the sobriety and genuineness of his faith, and who had in previous times distinguished himself by the boldness of his religious profession, and sent him to negotiate peace between the dissentient parties at Alexandria. He also made him the bearer of a most needful and appropriate letter to the original movers of the strife: and this letter, as exhibiting a specimen of his watchful care over God's people, it may be well to introduce into this our narrative of his life. Its purport was as follows.

64   [In the opening paragraphs of his letter, which is addressed to Alexander and Arius jointly, the Emperor declares his continual anxiety for unity and peace within and without the Church.]

65   "For I was aware that, if I should succeed in establishing according to my wishes, a common harmony of sentiment among all the

servants of God, the general course of affairs would also experience a change correspondent to the pious desires of them all."

66-8 [He comments on his efforts to heal the Donatist schism in Africa and expresses his dismay on finding that the East, from which Christianity had come, was rent by dissension, and that about a trifle.]

69 "I understand, then, that the origin of the present controversy is this. When you, Alexander, demanded of the presbyters what opinion they severally maintained respecting a certain passage in the law, or rather I should say, respecting something connected with an unprofitable question, then you, Arius, inconsiderately insisted on what ought never to have been conceived at all, or if conceived, should have been buried in profound silence. Hence it was that a dissension arose between you, fellowship was withdrawn, and the holy people, rent into diverse parties, no longer preserved the unity of the one body. Now, therefore, do ye both exhibit an equal degree of forbearance, and receive the advice which your fellow-servant righteously gives. What then is this advice? It was wrong in the first instance to propose such questions as these, or to reply to them when propounded. For those points of discussion which are enjoined by the authority of no law, but rather suggested by the contentious spirit which is fostered by misused leisure, even though they may be intended merely as an intellectual exercise, ought certainly to be confined to our own thoughts, and not hastily produced in the popular assemblies, nor unadvisedly intrusted to the ears of the multitude. For of what mental calibre is each individual as to have power either accurately to comprehend, or adequately to explain subjects so sublime and abstruse in their nature? Or, granting that one were fully competent for this, how many of the people will he convince? Or, who, again, in dealing with questions of such subtle nicety as these, can secure himself against a dangerous declension from the truth? It is incumbent therefore on us in these cases to be sparing of our words, lest, in case we ourselves are unable, through the feebleness of our natural faculties, to give a clear explanation of the subject before us, or, on the other hand, in case the slowness of our hearers' understanding disables them from arriving at an accurate apprehension of what we say, from one or other of these causes the people be reduced to the alternative either of blasphemy or schism.

70 "Let therefore both the unguarded question and the inconsiderate answer receive your mutual forgiveness. For the cause of your difference has not been any of the leading doctrines or precepts

of the law, nor has any new heresy respecting the worship of God
arisen among you. You are in truth of one and the same judgement: you may therefore well join in communion and fellowship.
71 "For as long as you continue to contend about these small and
very insignificant questions, I believe it indeed to be not merely
unbecoming, but positively evil, that so large a portion of God's
people which belongs to your jurisdiction should be thus divided."
(N. & P.-N. F., slightly altered.)

72 [Constantine puts forward the plea that they should behave as
philosophers of the same school, united on essentials, but differing
on small points. He urges them to agree and ends with an im-
passioned appeal for the restoration of his own peace of mind,
and that he may be able to visit them, a project which their quarrel
had prevented.]

It is clear from Constantine's letter that he was as yet imperfectly acquainted
with the importance of the controversy. After Nicaea he wrote to the Church
at Alexandria condemning Arius in the strongest terms (Socrates, *H.E.* I.9.17ff.).
  63. Constantine's messenger was Ossius, Bishop of Cordova, who had been
one of his religious advisers from 312 or earlier. Ossius had been a confessor
in the persecution between 303 and 305.
  69. *your fellow-servant*: a description which Constantine liked to use of himself, cf. 303, 304.

298. THE COUNCIL OF ANTIOCH, 325

(Syriac text, with the Greek version of E. Schwartz, in Opitz,
Urkunde 18, pp. 36–41.)

This copy of the letter of the Council is addressed to Alexander (of Thessalonica). The letter (written as from the president of the Council) begins with
a list of those present, and after a few introductory remarks points out that the
writer determined not to try to settle by himself the differences that he found
in the Antiochene Church, but to call a council. (Later on the first person
plural is used.)

When therefore the grace of God assembled us in the community at Antioch, we investigated and busied ourselves with a
policy common, helpful and beneficial for the Church of God.
We found a great deal of disorder, the chief reason being that the
law of the church had been in many respects slighted and despised,
and the canons had in the meantime been wholly invalidated by
worldly men. Since the holding of a synod of bishops had been

hindered in these parts our first care was to investigate a topic that is most important of all and surpasses all others—in fact it comprises the whole mystery of the faith that is in us—I mean what concerns the Saviour of us all, *the Son of the Living God*.[1] For since our brother and fellow servant, the honoured and beloved Alexander, Bishop of Alexandria, had excommunicated some of his presbyters, i.e. Arius and his friends, for the blasphemy which they directed against our Saviour, though they were able by their impious teaching to cause some to stray to such an extent that they were received into communion by them, the holy synod decided to investigate this question first, in order that after a solution had been reached of the supreme points in the mystery as far as lay in our power, so the remaining questions could be investigated in turn individually. At our meeting, and in the presence of some brethren learned in the Church's faith which we were taught by the scriptures and the apostles and which we have received from the fathers, we held a full discussion. We kept before us what Alexander, Bishop of Alexandria, had done against Arius and his friends, that if any clearly were tainted with teaching opposed to these actions, they too should be expelled from the Church, to prevent them by their continued presence from being able to seduce some of the simpler brethren. (From the Greek.)

The faith is as follows ...: to believe in one God, Father almighty, incomprehensible, immutable and unchangeable, providential ruler and guide of the universe, just, good, maker of heaven and earth and of all the things in them, Lord of the law and of the prophets and of the new covenant; and in one Lord Jesus Christ, only begotten Son, begotten not from that which is not but from the Father, not as made but as properly an offspring, but begotten in an ineffable, indescribable manner, because only the Father Who begot and the Son Who was begotten know (for *no one knows the Father but the Son, nor the Son but the Father*[2]), Who exists everlastingly and did not at one time not exist. For we have learned from the Holy Scriptures that He alone is *the sole image*[3], not (plainly) as if He might have remained unbegotten from the Father, nor by adoption (for it is impious and blasphemous to say this); but the Scriptures described Him as validly and truly begotten as Son, so that we believe Him to be immutable and unchangeable, and that He was not begotten and did not come to be by volition or by adoption, so as to appear to be from that which is not, but as befits Him to be begotten; not (a thing which it is not lawful to think) according to likeness or nature

[1] Matt. 16.16.   [2] Matt. 11.27; Luke 10.22.   [3] 2 Cor. 4.4 Col. 1.15.

or commixture with any of the things which came to be through Him, but in a way which passes all understanding or conception or reasoning we confess Him to have been begotten of the unbegotten Father, God the Word, true light, righteousness, Jesus Christ, Lord and Saviour of all. For He is *the image*, not of the will or of anything else, but of His Father's *very substance*[1] (ὑπόστασις). This Son, God the Word, having been born in flesh from Mary the Mother of God and made incarnate, having suffered and died, rose again from the dead and was taken up into heaven, and sits on the right hand of the Majesty most high, and is coming to judge the living and the dead. Furthermore, as in our Saviour, the holy Scriptures teach us to believe also in one Spirit, one Catholic Church, the resurrection of the dead and a judgement of requital according to whether a man has done well or badly in the flesh. And we anathematize those who say or think or preach that the Son of God is a creature or has come into being or has been made and is not truly begotten, or that there was when He was not. For we believe that He was and is and that He is light. Furthermore, we anathematize those who suppose that He is immutable by His own act of will, just as those who derive His birth from that which is not, and deny that He is immutable in the way the Father is. For just as our Saviour is the image of the Father in all things, so in this respect particularly He has been proclaimed the Father's image. (Kelly, *Early Christian Creeds*, pp. 209–10, from the Greek, slightly altered.)

This faith was proposed and the whole of the holy synod agreed and confessed that this is the apostolic and saving teaching. All our fellow ministers were unanimous, except for Theodotus of the church of the Laodiceans (i.e. Laodicea in Syria), and Narcissus of Neronias (in Cilicia) and Eusebius of Caesarea in Palestine who as though forgetful of the Holy Scriptures and the apostolic teaching (though they tried to evade discovery in diverse manners and to conceal their errors by untrue subterfuges) manifestly introduced opposing views. For clearly, from our questions and theirs, they were proved to have the same views as Arius, and hold to opposite views to the above mentioned ones. Through their excessive obtuseness and failure to reverence the holy synod, which rejected their views and regarded them with aversion, we all, fellow ministers in the synod, have judged that we should not communicate with them, and that they are not worthy to communicate with us as their faith is foreign to the Catholic Church. We are writing to you to let you know that you should be on your guard against communicating with them, against

[1] Cf. Heb. 1.3.

writing to them and against receiving letters of communion from them. And know this also that through the great love of the brethren felt by the synod we have given them the great and priestly synod at Ancyra as a place of repentance and recognition of the truth. (From the Greek.)

The letter concludes with a request to Alexander to transmit the letter to others, and final greetings.

The letter of the Council of Antioch was first published by E. Schwartz in *Nachrichten von der kgl. Gesellschaft der Wissenschaften zu Göttingen*, 1905, pp. 272ff. The genuineness of the letter was at first much contested but is now generally accepted. An emendation to the Syriac text makes Ossius president, instead of an unknown Eusebius, i.e. the situation is that Ossius, having failed to reach a settlement in Egypt, was now on his way back to Constantine by land. The troubles which he found at Antioch need not all be connected with Arius. Philogonius, Bishop of Antioch, must recently have died and it may be that Eustathius was consecrated at this council: a party may also have existed that clung to the views of Paul of Samosata. It should be noticed that Ossius had to send out letters to bring the bishops to the Council, and that the participants included bishops from Palestine, Arabia, Phoenicia, Coele Syria, Cilicia and "some from Cappadocia".

On the creed of the Council, cf. Kelly, op. cit., pp. 210–11:

"The patently anti-Arian tone of this tortuous compilation, combined with its transparent ignorance of the Nicene theological solutions, is a powerful argument for its authenticity. All the emphasis is on the assertion that the Son was not created out of nothing, but was begotten in an ineffable way, and that He is the express image of the Father in every respect. Yet there is no mention of the technical phrases FROM THE SUBSTANCE OF THE FATHER or OF ONE SUBSTANCE or anything equivalent. If the creed which Arius submitted to St Alexander is set alongside it, the close relationship between the two documents becomes at once visible. The anathemas at the end deal point by point with matters raised in Arius's *Thalia*, branding such typical theses of his as that Christ was a creature, that there had been a time when He was not, and that His immutability was due to the exercise of His will.

*   *   *

The anathemas are particularly interesting, for they anticipate, with closer attention to the genuine thought of Arius, the ones to be adopted by the Nicene fathers."

The Synod of Ancyra, cf. 299, for Constantine's removal of this synod to Nicaea.

On the position of Eusebius of Caesarea at Nicaea, cf. 301.

299. CONSTANTINE SUMMONS THE COUNCIL OF NICAEA

(Text (Syriac) with Greek version by E. Schwartz in Opitz, Urkunde 20, pp. 41–2.)

That there is nothing more honourable in my sight than the fear of God, is, I believe, manifest to every man. Now because it was agreed formerly that the Synod of Bishops should meet at Ancyra of Galatia, it hath seemed to us on many accounts that it would be well for a Synod to assemble at Nicaea, a city of Bithynia, both because the Bishops from Italy and the rest of the countries of Europe are coming, and because of the excellent temperature of the air, and in order that I may be present as a spectator and participator in those things which will be done. Wherefore I signify to you, my beloved brethren, that all of you promptly assemble at the said city, that is at Nicaea. Let every one of you therefore, regarding that which is best, as I before said, be diligent, without delay in anything, speedily to come, that he may be in his own person present as a spectator of those things which will be done by the same.

God keep you my beloved brethren. (B. H. Cowper, *Syriac Miscellanies*, pp. 5–6, slightly altered to accord with the version of Schwartz.)

300. THE CANONS OF NICAEA, 325

(Text and commentary in Hefele-Leclercq, *Histoire des Conciles*, I.1, pp. 528–620, and in W. Bright, *Canons of the first four General Councils*, ed. 2, pp. IX–XV, 1–89; text in E. J. Jonkers, *Acta et Symbola Conciliorum quae saeculo quarto habita sunt*, pp. 38–47.)

1　If any one has been obliged to undergo a surgical operation from disease, or has been castrated by barbarians, let him continue in the clergy. But if any one in good health has so mutilated himself, it is right that, if he be enrolled amongst the clergy, he should cease from his ministrations; and that from henceforth no such person should be promoted. As, however, it is plain that this is said with reference to those who dare to mutilate themselves, therefore, if any persons have been so mutilated by barbarians, or by their own masters, and in other respects are found worthy, the canon allows them to be admitted to the clerical office.

2   Since many things have been done by men either from necessity, or some other pressing cause, contrary to the canon of the Church, as that persons who have lately come over to the faith from a heathen life, and have been taught for a short time, have been presently brought to the spiritual laver, and at the same time that they have been baptized, have been promoted to the episcopate or presbyterate—it appears right to determine that nothing of the sort shall be done for the future; for some time is necessary for the state of a catechumen, and a fuller probation after baptism; for the Apostolic decree is clear, which says, *Not a novice, lest being lifted up with pride he fall into a snare and the judgement of the devil.*[1] But if, in process of time, any natural fault be discovered about the person, and he be convicted by *two or three witnesses,*[2] let him be deposed from the clergy. Whosoever shall act contrary to these rules will endanger his own orders, as boldly opposing the great Synod.

3   The great Synod altogether forbids any bishop, presbyter or deacon, or any one of the clergy, to have a woman dwelling with him, excepting a mother, or sister, or aunt, or such persons only as are above all suspicion.

Cf. Elvira can. 27 (265, p. 307), Ancyra can. 19, and p. 277 above.

4   It is most proper that a bishop should be constituted by all the bishops of the province; but, if this be difficult on account of some urgent necessity, or the length of the way, that at all events three should meet together at the same place, those who are absent also giving their suffrages and their consent in writing, and then the ordination be performed. The confirming, however, of what is done in each province belongs to the Metropolitan of it.

Cf. Arles can. 20 (274, p. 325).

5   Concerning those, whether of the clergy or laity, who have been excommunicated by the bishops in the different provinces, let the sentence of the canon prevail, which pronounces that those persons who have been cast out by one bishop are not to be received again into communion by any others. Inquiry should, however, be made whether they have been excommunicated[3] through the petty jealousy or contentiousness, or other such-like bitterness, of the bishop. And in order that this inquiry may be conveniently made, it is decreed to be proper that synods should be assembled twice every year in every province, that all the bishops of the province being assembled together, such questions may be examined into,

---

[1] 1 Tim. 3.6.   [2] Matt. 18.16.
[3] John 9.22, R.V. put out of the synagogue.

that so those who have confessedly offended against the bishop may appear to be with reason excommunicated by all the bishops, until it shall seem fit to their general assembly to pronounce a more lenient sentence upon them. And of these synods one is to be held before Lent, that all petty jealousy being removed, a pure gift may be offered to God. The other in the season of autumn.

6   Let the ancient customs hold good which are in Egypt and Libya and Pentapolis, according to which the Bishop of Alexandria has authority over all these places. For this is also customary to the Bishop of Rome. In like manner in Antioch and in the other provinces, the privileges are to be preserved to the Churches. But this is clearly to be understood, that, if any one be made a bishop without the consent of the Metropolitan, the great Synod declares that he shall not be a bishop. If, however, two or three bishops shall from private contention oppose the common choice of all the others, it being a reasonable one and made according to the ecclesiastical canons, let the choice of the majority hold good.

7   Since a custom and ancient tradition has held good, that the Bishop of Aelia should be honoured, let him have his proper honour, saving to the Metropolis (i.e. Caesarea) the honour peculiar to it.

Aelia: Aelia Capitolina was the name of Hadrian's Gentile city, founded on the site of Jerusalem.

8   Concerning those who have formerly called themselves Cathari, i.e. Novatianists, but who come over to the Catholic and Apostolic Church, the holy Synod has decreed that they, having received imposition of hands, shall so remain in the clergy. It is right, however, that they should in the first instance make profession in writing that they will agree to and follow the decrees of the Catholic and Apostolic Church; in particular, that they will communicate with those persons who have been twice married and with those who, having lapsed in persecution, have had a certain period of penitence assigned to them and a time for reconciliation fixed; and, generally, that they will follow in all things the decrees of the Catholic Church. Wherever, therefore, whether in villages or cities, all who have been ordained are found to be of this party only, they shall continue in the clergy in the same rank in which they are found. But if any of these come to a place where there is already a bishop or presbyter of the Catholic Church, it is clear that the bishop of the Church is to have the episcopal dignity, and he who had the name of a bishop amongst those who are called Cathari, shall have the rank of a presbyter, unless it shall seem fit to the bishop to allow him to partake of the honour of the

name. If the bishop is not pleased to do so, he shall assign him the place of a Chorepiscopus or Presbyter, that he may indeed altogether appear to be in the clergy, but that there may not be two bishops in the city.

9   If any have been promoted to be presbyters without inquiry, or if upon examination they have confessed their sins, and, notwithstanding their having confessed, any man has in opposition to the canon laid hands upon them, the canon does not admit persons so ordained. For the Church vindicates only irreproachable characters.

10 If any who have lapsed have been ordained in ignorance, or even if those who ordained them were aware of the fact, this does not prejudice the Ecclesiastical Canon; for upon the circumstances being made known, they are deposed.

11 Concerning those who have fallen away without necessity, or without the spoiling of their goods, or without being in danger, or any other such reason, as happened under the tyranny of Licinius, the Synod has decreed that although they are undeserving of any kindness, they shall nevertheless be dealt with mercifully. As many, therefore, as shall truly repent, shall continue three years amongst the hearers as believers (i.e. as having been already baptized), and seven amongst the prostrators, and for two years they shall communicate with the people in prayer without the offering.

For the persecution of Licinius, cf. 282: for the provisions of the canon, cf. Ancyra can. 9 (267, p. 311).

12 Those who have been called by grace, and have at first displayed their ardour, but afterwards have run like *dogs to their own vomit*[1] (insomuch that some have spent money, and by means of gifts have acquired again their military station), must continue amongst the prostrators for ten years, after having been for three years amongst the hearers. In all such cases, however, it is proper to examine into the purpose and nature of their repentance; for as many as manifest their conversion in deed, and not in appearance only, by their fear, and tears, and patience and good works, these having completed the prescribed time as hearers, may properly communicate in the prayers, and the bishop may be allowed to determine yet more favourably respecting them. But those who hear their sentence with indifference, and think the form of entering into the Church sufficient for their conversion, must complete the whole time.

[1] Prov. 26.11.

13   Concerning those who are likely to depart, the old and canonical law is still to be observed that if any one is about to depart,[1]
he must not be deprived of the perfect and most necessary provision for his journey.[2] If, however, after having been given over,
and having received the Communion, he is again restored to
health, let him continue amongst those who communicate in
prayers only. But generally, and as regards every one who is likely
to die, and who desires to partake of the Eucharist, the Bishop,
after examination, shall impart it to him.

14   Concerning those who are catechumens, and who have lapsed,
the holy and great Synod has decreed that they shall be only three
years amongst the hearers, and after that shall pray with the
catechumens.

15   On account of the great disturbance and disputes which have
occurred, it seems right that the custom which has been admitted
in some places contrary to the canon should by all means be done
away; and that no bishop, presbyter or deacon should remove
from one city to another. But if any person, after the decision of
the holy and great Synod, shall attempt any such thing or shall lend
himself to any such practice, that the arrangement shall be totally
annulled, and he shall be restored to the church in which he was
ordained bishop or presbyter.

15.   This canon was not retrospective, but the cases of Eusebius of Nicomedia (formerly of Berytus) and of Eustathius of Antioch (formerly of Beroea)
must have been in the minds of the Council. This canon was but imperfectly
obeyed (though Constantine commended Eusebius of Caesarea for his refusal
of the see of Antioch, Eus., *V.C.* III.6.1) and the Council of Sardica (343)
"in its very first canon remarked, with a touch of sarcasm, that no bishop had
yet been found to aim at being transferred from a greater city to a lesser"
(Bright, op. cit., p. 49). Cf. Arles can. 2 and can. 21 (274, pp. 322, 325).

16   If any persons recklessly and not having the fear of God before
their eyes, nor regarding the canons of the Church, whether they
be presbyters or deacons, or any others who are enrolled in the
list of the clergy, shall remove from their own Church, they ought
by no means to be received into any other, but they must be
constrained to return to their own parish, or if they continue they
must be without communion. And if any bishop shall dare to
usurp what belongs to another, and to ordain in his church any
such person without the consent of the proper bishop from whom
he has seceded, let the ordination be void.

[1] Cf. 2 Pet. 1.15.   [2] Cf. Deut. 15.14 (LXX).

16. *Without communion* (ἀκοινώνητοι): "not excommunicated in the ordinary sense, but debarred from officiating with their brethren" (Bright, op. cit., p. 53).

17 Since many persons of the ecclesiastical order, being led away by covetousness, and a desire of filthy lucre, have forgotten the Holy Scripture which says, *he gave not his money to usury*,[1] and in lending require their twelve per cent, the holy and great Synod considers it right that if any one after this decision shall be found receiving money by actual arrangement, or going about the business in any other way, as by requiring the whole and a half, or using any other device whatsoever for filthy lucre's sake, he shall be deposed from the clergy, and struck out of the list.

Cf. Elvira can. 20 (265, p. 307), Arles can. 13 (12) (274, p. 324).
their twelve per cent: the usual Roman rate of interest.
the whole and a half: cf. Cod. Theod. II.33.1.

18 It has come to the knowledge of the holy Synod that in certain places and cities, the deacons give the Eucharist to the presbyters, whereas neither canon nor custom allows that they who have no authority to offer should give the Body of Christ to those who do offer. It has also been made known that now some of the deacons receive the Eucharist even before the bishops. Let all such practices be done away, and let the deacons keep within their proper bounds, knowing that they are the ministers of the bishop and inferior to the presbyters. Let them, therefore, receive the Eucharist, according to their order, after the presbyters, either the bishop or presbyter administering it to them. Further, the deacons are not to be allowed to sit among the presbyters; for this is done contrary to the canon and due order. But, if any one even after this decision will not obey, let him be put out of the diaconate.

Cf. Arles can. 18 (274, p. 324).

19 Concerning the Paulianists who have come over to the Catholic Church, the decision is that they must by all means be baptized again. But if any of them have in time past been enrolled amongst the clergy, if they appear to be blameless and without reproach, after they have been rebaptized, let them be ordained by the bishop of the Catholic Church. If, however, upon examination, they are found to be unfit, they must be deposed. In like manner, as regards the deaconesses, and, in short, any who have been enrolled amongst the clergy, the same form shall be observed. And we took note of those deaconesses who are enrolled as far

[1] Ps. 15.5 (LXX).

as concerns dress, since they have not any imposition of hands, so that they are altogether to be reckoned amongst the laity.

19. *be baptized again*: "What is meant is that the persons in question are to be baptized *de novo*. Their former baptism is regarded as void: therefore, strictly speaking, the baptism to be administered to them on their coming over to the Church would be, in the Council's eyes, their only real baptism.

*   *   *

But why was the baptism of Paulianists disallowed? Did they not use the right form, "In the Name of the Father", etc.? Athanasius, who must have been well informed on this point, tells us that they did so; but, he adds, the grossness of their heresy made the sacred words of none effect (*Orat*. II.43)." (Bright, op. cit., pp. 66–7.)

On the question of heretical baptism generally, cf. 218 to 223, and Arles can. 9 (8) (274, p. 323).

And we took note, etc. The last provision of the canon is obscure. The translation given takes the view that there were some deaconesses who had not received any episcopal ordination, as well as others who had.

20   Since there are some persons who kneel on the Lord's Day and in the days of Pentecost; in order that all things may be observed in like manner in every parish, the holy Synod has decreed that all should at those times offer up their prayers to God standing. (W. A. Hammond, *The Definitions of Faith*, 15–22, altered, principally from Bright, op. cit.)

301. LETTER OF EUSEBIUS OF CAESAREA TO HIS CHURCH, ON THE CREED OF NICAEA

(Socrates, *H.E.* I.8; Theodoret, *H.E.* I.12; Opitz, Urkunde 22, pp. 42ff.)

1   What was transacted concerning the faith of the Church at the Great Council assembled at Nicaea, you have probably learned, Beloved, from other sources, rumour being wont to precede the accurate account of what is doing. But lest in such reports the circumstances of the case have been misrepresented, we have been obliged to transmit to you, first, the formula of faith presented by ourselves; and next, the second, which they have published with additions to our words. Our own formulary, then, which was

read in the presence of our most pious Emperor, and declared to be good and unexceptionable:—

2 "As we have received from the Bishops who preceded us, and in our first catechizings, and when we received baptism, and as we have learned from the divine Scriptures, and as we constantly believed and taught as presbyter and bishop, so believing also at the time present, we report to you our faith, and it is this:—

3 "'We believe in One God, Father Almighty, the Maker of all things visible and invisible. And in One Lord Jesus Christ, the Word of God, God from God, Light from Light, Life from Life, Only-begotten Son, first-born of all creation,[1] before all the ages, begotten from the Father, by Whom also all things were made; Who for our salvation was incarnate, and lived among men, and suffered, and rose again the third day, and ascended to the Father, and will come again in glory to judge living and dead. And we' believe also in One Holy Spirit':

"Believing each of these to be and to exist, the Father truly Father, and the Son truly Son, and the Holy Spirit truly Holy Spirit, as also our Lord, sending forth His disciples for the preaching, said, *Go, teach all nations, baptizing them in the Name of the Father and of the Son and of the Holy Spirit.*[2] Concerning whom we confidently affirm that so we hold, and so we think, and so we have held aforetime, and we maintain this faith unto the death, anathematizing every godless heresy. That this we have ever thought from our heart and soul, from the time we recollect ourselves, and now think and say in truth, before God Almighty and our Lord Jesus Christ do we witness, being able by proofs to show and to convince you that, in times past also, we constantly believed and preached thus."

4 On this faith being publicly put forth by us, no room for contradiction appeared; but our most pious Emperor, before any one else, testified that it was most orthodox. He confessed, moreover, that such were his own sentiments; and he advised all present to agree to it, and to subscribe its articles and to assent to them, with the insertion of the single word Consubstantial (ὁμοούσιος) which, moreover, he interpreted himself saying that the Son is consubstantial not according to bodily affections, and that the Son subsisted from the Father neither according to division, nor severance: for the immaterial, and intellectual, and incorporeal nature could not be the subject of any bodily affection, but that it became us to conceive of such things in a divine and ineffable manner. And our most wise and most religious Emperor reasoned

[1] Col. 1.15   [2] Matt. 28.19.

in this way; but they, because of the addition of consubstantial, drew up the following formulary:

"We believe in One God, the Father, Almighty, Maker of all things visible and invisible:

"And in One Lord Jesus Christ, the Son of God, begotten of the Father, Only-begotten, that is, from the substance of the Father; God from God, Light from Light, Very God from very God, begotten not made, Consubstantial with the Father, by Whom all things were made, both things in heaven and things in earth; Who for us men and for our salvation came down and was incarnate, was made man, suffered, and rose again the third day, ascended into heaven, and is coming to judge living and dead.

"And in the Holy Ghost.

"And those who say 'There was when He was not,' and 'Before His generation He was not,' and 'He came to be from nothing,' or those who pretend that the Son of God is 'Of other *hypostasis* or substance,' or 'created,' or 'alterable,' or 'mutable,' the Catholic and Apostolic Church anathematizes."

5 On their suggesting this formula, we did not let it pass without inquiry in what sense they used the expressions "of the substance of the Father" and "Consubstantial with the Father." Accordingly, questions and explanations took place, and the discussion tested the meaning of these phrases. And they professed that the phrase "of the substance" was indicative of the Son's being indeed from the Father, yet without being as if a part of Him. And with this understanding, we thought good to assent to the meaning of the pious teaching suggesting that the Son was from the Father, not, however, a part of His substance. On this account, we assented to the meaning ourselves, without declining even the term "Consubstantial," peace being the aim which we set before us, and fear of deviating from the correct meaning.

6 In the same way, we also admitted "begotten, not made," since they said that "made" was an appellation common to the other creatures which came to be through the Son, to whom the Son had no likeness. Wherefore, He was not a work resembling the things which through Him came to be, but was of an essence which is too high for the level of any work; and which the Divine Oracles teach to have been generated from the Father, the mode of generation being ineffable and inexplicable to every originated nature.

7 And so too on examination there are grounds for saying that the Son is "Consubstantial" with the Father; not in the way of bodies, nor like mortal beings, for He is not such by division of essence, or by severance, no, nor by any affection, or alteration, or

changing of the Father's substance and power (since from all such the unoriginate nature of the Father is alien); but because "Consubstantial with the Father" suggests that the Son of God bears no resemblance to the originated creatures, but that to His Father alone Who begat Him is He in every way assimilated, and that He is not of any other *hypostasis* and substance, but from the Father. To this term also, thus interpreted, it appeared well to assent; since we were aware that even among the ancients some learned and illustrious bishops and writers have used the term "Consubstantial," in their theological teaching concerning the Father and Son.

8   So much then be said concerning the Faith which was published; to which all of us assented, not without inquiry, but according to the specific meanings, mentioned before the most religious Emperor himself, and justified by the fore-mentioned considerations. And as to the anathemas published by them at the end of the Faith, we thought it without offence because it forbade to use words not in Scripture, from which almost all the confusion and disorder in the Church have come. Since then no divinely inspired Scripture has used the phrases, "out of nothing" and "once He was not," and the rest which follow, there appeared no ground for using or teaching them; to which also we assented as a good decision, since it had not been our custom hitherto to use these terms.

9   Moreover, to anathematize "Before His generation He was not" did not seem preposterous, in that it is confessed by all, that the Son of God was before the generation according to the flesh.

10   Nay, our most religious Emperor did, at the time, prove, in a speech, that He was in being even according to His divine generation which is before all ages, since even before He was generated in actuality, He was potentially with the Father ingenerately, the Father being always Father, as King always, and Saviour always, being all things potentially, and being always in the same respects and in the same way.

11   This we have been forced to transmit to you, Beloved, as making clear to you the deliberation of our inquiry and assent, and how reasonably we resisted even to the last minute, as long as we were offended at statements which differed from our own, but received without contention what no longer pained us as soon as, on a candid examination of the sense of the words, they appeared to us to coincide with what we ourselves have professed in the faith which we previously declared. (L. F., altered.)

"Eusebius's sorry letter . . . betrays no change of heart" (F. L. Cross, *The*

Study of Athanasius, p. 14). He regards the Creed of Nicaea with suspicion, and hides its authors in the anonymity of "they". As we know from 298, Eusebius came to Nicaea under the ban of a provisional excommunication, and his reading of the Creed of Caesarea, with the declarations that accompanied the reading, show that he produced his creed to rehabilitate himself. In this he was successful. It is clear that the Emperor was present on this occasion and that in the mind of Eusebius there existed an idea (mistaken, it would seem) that a close connection existed between his Caesarean creed and the creed of the Council. Our knowledge of the actual proceedings is so limited that we cannot follow the discussions that led to the drawing up of the Creed, but comparison makes it clear that the Creed of Nicaea contains little that is distinctively Caesarean. On the whole question see Kelly, *Early Christian Creeds*, Ch. VII, The Creed of Nicaea, and Ch. VIII, The Meaning and Use of the Nicene Creed.

7. At the council the words οὐσία and ὑπόστασις are synonymous. The word ὁμοούσιος was perfectly well known to members of the council, cf. 294, but they applied different senses to it; as Eusebius says, "To this term also *thus interpreted*, it seemed well to assent".

On the use of ὁμοούσιος by "some learned and illustrious bishops and writers", Eusebius could look back to the correspondence of the Dionysii (235–6). Athanasius (*On the Decrees of the Council of Nicaea*, 25) points out that the words ἐκ τῆς τοῦ πατρὸς οὐσίας ἔφυ had been used by Theognostus of Alexandria. On Clement of Alexandria and ὁμοούσιος, see Bethune-Baker, *Introduction to the Early History of Christian Doctrine*, p. 133, n. 2, on Origen, ibid., p. 147, n. 4.

9. Eusebius' statement about, "Before His generation he was not", appears to miss the point at issue completely.

302. THE LETTER OF THE COUNCIL OF NICAEA TO THE EGYPTIAN CHURCH

(Socrates, *H.E.* I.9.1–14; Theodoret, *H.E.* I.9.2–13; Opitz, Urkunde 23, pp. 47–51.)

1   [The letter is addressed to the Alexandrian Church, and to the brethren throughout Egypt, Libya and Pentapolis.]

        *   *   *

2   Since, by the grace of God, a great and holy Synod has been convened at Nicaea, our most pious sovereign Constantine having summoned us out of various cities and provinces for that purpose, it appeared to us indispensably necessary that a letter should be

written to you on the part of the sacred Synod; in order that you may know what subjects were brought under consideration, what rigidly investigated, and also what was eventually determined on and decreed.

3   In the first place, then, the impiety and guilt of Arius and his adherents were investigated, in the presence of our most religious Emperor Constantine; and it was unanimously decided that his impious opinion should be anathematized with all the phrases and expressions that he has uttered blaspheming the Son of God, i.e. that "the Son of God sprang from the non-existent," and that "there was when he was not"; saying, moreover, that "the Son of God was possessed of free-will, so as to be capable either of vice or virtue"; and calling Him a creature and a work. All these sentiments the holy Synod anathematized, having scarcely patience to endure the hearing of such an impious opinion, of such folly and such abominable blasphemies.

4   But the conclusion of our proceedings against him you have either learned already, or will learn; for we would not seem to trample on a man who has received the chastisement which his peculiar crime deserved. Yet so contagious has his impiety proved, as to involve in the same perdition Theonas of Marmarica, and Secundus of Ptolemaïs; for they have suffered the same condemnation as himself.

5   But when the grace of God delivered Egypt from that execrable opinion, with all its blasphemy, and from those persons who had dared to cause discord and division among a people previously at peace, there still remained the contumacy of Melitius to be dealt with, and of those who had been ordained by him; and we now declare to you, beloved brethren, what resolution the Synod came to on this point.

6   Acting with more clemency towards Melitius, although strictly speaking he was wholly undeserving of pardon, the Council permitted him to remain in his own city, and decreed that he should exercise no authority either to nominate for ordination or ordain; and that he should appear in no other district or city on this pretence, but simply retain a nominal dignity.

7   That those who had received appointments from him, after having been confirmed by a more holy ordination, should be admitted to communion on these conditions:—that they should continue to hold their rank and ministry, but regard themselves as inferior in every respect to all those who had been previously approved and nominated in each place and church by our most honoured brother and fellow-minister Alexander. In addition to these things they shall have no authority to propose or nominate

whom they please, or suggest names or to do anything at all without the concurrence of some bishop of the Catholic Church who is one of Alexander's suffragans.

8   Let such as, by the grace of God and your prayers, have been found in no schisms, but have continued in the Catholic and Apostolic Church blameless, have authority to nominate and select names of those who are worthy of the sacred office, and to act in all things according to ecclesiastical law and usage.

9   When it may happen that any of those holding office in the Church die, then let such as have been recently admitted into orders, i.e. Melitians, be preferred to the dignity of the deceased, provided that they should appear worthy, and that the people should elect them, the Bishop of Alexandria also confirming and ratifying their choice.

10   This privilege is conceded to all the others indeed, but to Melitius personally we by no means grant the same licence, on account of his former disorderly conduct; and because of the rashness and levity of his character, he is deprived of all authority and jurisdiction, as a man liable again to create similar disturbances.

11   These are the things which specially affect Egypt, and the most holy Church of the Alexandrians; and, if any other canon or ordinance should be established, our lord and most honoured fellow-minister and brother Alexander being present with us, will on his return to you enter into more minute details, inasmuch as he is a decisive participator in whatever was transacted.

12   We bring you good news relative to unity of judgement on the subject of the most holy feast of Easter; for this point also has been happily settled through your prayers: so that all the brethren in the East who have heretofore kept this festival when the Jews did, will henceforth conform to the Romans, to you and to us all who from the earliest time have observed our period of celebrating Easter.

13   Rejoicing, therefore, in this most desirable conclusion, and in the general unanimity and peace, as well as in the extirpation of all heresy, receive with the greater honour and more abundant love our fellow-minister and your Bishop Alexander, who has greatly delighted us by his presence, and even at his advanced age has undergone extraordinary exertions in order that peace might be re-established also among you.

14   Pray on behalf of us all that the decisions, to which we have so justly come, may be inviolably maintained through Almighty God and our Lord Jesus Christ, together with the Holy Spirit; to whom be glory for ever. Amen. (N. & P.-N. F., altered.)

5.   On the reception of the Melitians by the council, cf. Athanasius' view in 309.

9.   *recently admitted into orders*: i.e. the Melitians referred to in 7 above.

12.   The decision about Easter was the subject of a long letter sent to the churches by Constantine (Eusebius, *V.C.* III.17-18, Socrates, *H.E.* I.9.32ff., Theodoret, *H.E.* I.10.1ff., Opitz, Urkunde 26, pp. 54-7). The issue was not the same as in the Quartodeciman controversy. The point at issue was that at Antioch the Church took the date of the 14 Nisan from the Jews, according to Jewish methods of calculation, at Alexandria the Christians did their own calculations. This led sometimes to a discrepancy of a month in the celebration of Easter in the two great Eastern Churches.

303. CONSTANTINE'S VIEW OF THE WORK OF THE COUNCIL OF NICAEA, 325

(Part of a letter of Constantine to the Catholic Church of the Alexandrians in Socrates, *H.E.* I.9.17ff.; Opitz, Urkunde 25, pp. 52-4.)

17–   [The Emperor begins by greeting the freedom from error and
19   the unity that have been achieved, with the complete rout of the devils.]

But to attain this end, by divine admonition I assembled at the city of Nicaea most of the bishops; with whom I myself who, as one of you, rejoices exceedingly in being your fellow-servant,
20   undertook the investigation of the truth. Accordingly, all points which seemed to produce doubt or excuse for discord have been discussed and accurately examined. And may the Divine Majesty pardon the fearful enormity of the blasphemies which some were shamelessly uttering concerning our Saviour, our life and hope, declaring and confessing that they believe things contrary to the divinely inspired Scriptures and to the holy faith.

21   While more than three hundred bishops remarkable for their moderation and shrewdness were unanimous in their confirmation of one and the same faith, which is in accurate conformity to the truth expressed in the laws of God, Arius alone, beguiled by the subtlety of the devil, was discovered to be the sole disseminator of this mischief, with unhallowed purposes, first among you, and
22   afterwards among others also. Let us therefore embrace that judgement which the Almighty has presented to us: let us return to our beloved brethren from whom a shameless servant of the devil has separated us: let us go with all zeal to the common body and our

23 own natural members. For this is becoming your shrewdness, faith and sanctity; that since the error of him who is an enemy to the truth has been refuted, you should return to the divine favour.

24 For that which has commended itself to the judgement of three hundred bishops cannot be other than the judgement of God; seeing that the Holy Spirit dwelling in the minds of persons of such character and dignity has effectually enlightened them

25 respecting the Divine will. Wherefore let no one vacillate or linger, but let all with alacrity return to the undoubted path of truth; that when I shall arrive among you, which will be as soon as possible, I may with you return due thanks to God, the inspector of all things, for having revealed the pure faith, and restored to you that love for which ye have prayed. (N. & P.-N. F., altered.)

19. *your fellow-servant*: cf. 297 (sect. 69), 304: on Constantine's view of his own relation to Christianity, cf. 317.

21. *more than three hundred bishops*: later consolidated at three hundred and eighteen, cf. Gen. 14.14 (Hilary, *Contra Constantium*, 27). Athanasius in A.D. 350–351 says, "three hundred, more or less" (*On the Decrees of the Council of Nicaea*, 3): in 369 he says, "three hundred and eighteen" (*Ep. ad Afros*, 2).

Arius alone: Constantine ignores the fact that two bishops Secundus of Ptolemais and Theonas of Marmarica had clung to their views, cf. 302, p. 369.

24. *cannot be other than the judgement of God*: herein we see the beginning of the respect in which the decisions of the Council were later held.

25. *when I shall arrive among you*: Constantine never visited Egypt, while he was Emperor, cf. 297 (sect. 72) for his postponement of a proposed visit.

304. THE CONDUCT AND EXILE OF EUSEBIUS OF NICOMEDIA

(From a letter of Constantine to the Church of Nicomedia in Gelasius of Cyzicus, *H.E.* III, Appendix I; Theodoret, *H.E.* I.20 (in part); Opitz, Urkunde 27, pp. 58–61.)

[Constantine begins with a brief sketch of the Christian dispensation. He then comes to the case of the Church of Nicomedia, protesting energetically that he is "their fellow servant", and proclaiming his mission of unity for the world. But there is disunion through false doctrine, and of this Eusebius their "morally abandoned teacher" is the cause.]

Who, I beg of you, is the person who taught this to a guileless people? Eusebius to be sure the participator in the tyrant's savagery (i.e. of Licinius). For that he was constantly a client of the tyrant can be understood from many circumstances. The killing of bishops—I mean true bishops—bears witness to this, the most relentless persecution of Christians proclaims it explicitly.

I shall now say nothing about the outrageous actions against myself. At the moment when the clash of the opposing armies (i.e. of Constantine and Licinius) was at hand, he sent surreptitiously "eyes" to spy on me, and almost afforded armed assistance to the tyrant. Do not imagine that I am not prepared to prove this. There is an accurate proof, because it is well known that the presbyters and deacons who came with Eusebius were publicly arrested by me. But I pass over these incidents, which I now introduce not because I am angry, but to their disgrace. My sole fear and consideration is that I see you brought in as participators in this guilt. For the leadership and crookedness of Eusebius have divorced your conscience from truth. But a cure will not take long if *now at any rate* you receive a faithful and single-minded bishop and you turn your gaze to God. That now rests with you, and should have resulted from your judgement long ago if the aforementioned Eusebius with a turbulent crowd of followers had not come to Nicomedia and shamelessly disturbed the established discipline.

But seeing that I had to say a little to your Love about Eusebius himself, your Forbearance remembers that a council took place at the city of Nicaea at which I was myself present, as became the service of my conscience. My sole desire was to effect universal concord, and in particular to refute and dispose of this question which began through the madness of Arius the Alexandrian, but swiftly gained strength through the wicked and destructive advocacy of Eusebius. But this man Eusebius, dearest and most honoured friends, how pressingly—for conscience itself had convicted him—and how shamelessly he allied himself to this utterly discredited falsehood! He secretly sent different messengers to solicit me, and he asked for my support in some degree, because he was afraid that his being detected in so great a sin would result in his expulsion from his honourable office. God—and may He continue His goodness to me and to you—is my witness of this, since Eusebius perverted my judgement and got round me in an underhand way, as you also shall get to know. For everything was done at that time as he wanted—and he concealed all his evil intention in his own mind.

But—to pass over the rest of his ill behaviour—listen now, I ask you, to what he carried through in company with Theognius, the accomplice in his folly. I had ordered certain Alexandrians who had left our faith to be sent hither, because the fires of discord were blazing up from their activity. But these excellent bishops whom once the truth as expressed by the Council had turned to repentance not only received these and made them welcome, but consorted with them in their depravity of character. So I decided to take action about these ungrateful individuals: I ordered them to be arrested and banished to the most distant region possible. Now it is *your* duty to look to God with that faith which is well known to have existed always, and rightly should exist, and so to act that we may rejoice in the possession of holy, orthodox and philanthropic bishops. And if anyone dares inconsiderately to be roused to remembrance or praise of those corrupters, he will be restrained from his daring by the action of the servant of God, that is to say, of myself. God guard you, beloved brethren. (With acknowledgement to the translation in Bohn's Ecclesiastical Library.)

Eusebius of Nicomedia came as an ambassador from Licinius to Constantine. (*Vit. Const.* from Codex Angelicus A (Philostorgius *H.E.* Anhang V, *G.C.S.*, p. 180).) According to Ammianus Marcellinus, 22.9, Eusebius was remotely related to the Emperor Julian, but we do not know the degree of his relationship. He was closely associated with Constantia, wife of Licinius and half-sister of Constantine.

The killing of bishops . . .: we have no further evidence about such cynicism on Eusebius' part.

you receive a faithful and single-minded bishop: Amphion (Athanasius, *Apology against the Arians*, 7; Socrates, *H.E.* I.14.1; Sozomen, *H.E.* I.21.5).

Theognius (or Theognis): Bishop of Nicaea.

to be banished to the most distant regions: Philostorgius, *H.E.* I.10, says that Eusebius was exiled three months after the conclusion of the Council of Nicaea, and (ibid., II.1b) that he was sent to Gaul. He returned in 328. It should be noted that all our sources do not give the same reasons for the banishment of Eusebius, see *D.C.B.* s.v. Cf. also 307 below.

305. A WARNING FROM CONSTANTINE TO THEODOTUS, BISHOP OF LAODICAEA IN SYRIA, *c.* DECEMBER 325

(Letter of Constantine: Text in *P.L.* VIII, 523;
Opitz, Urkunde 28, p. 63.)

How great the strength of the divine anger is, you too can easily learn from what has happened to Eusebius and Theognius. They behaved like abusive drunkards towards the Most Holy Religion, and even after gaining pardon defiled the name of the

Saviour God in the assembly of their private band of robbers.
For when, after the unanimous concord of the Council (i.e. of
Nicaea) they ought to have amended their former error, at that
very moment they were caught persevering in the same offences.
For this reason Divine Providence thrust them out from her
people. For she could not bear to see innocent souls being corrupted by the madness of a few. She has now demanded from them
a worthy satisfaction, and will take a greater vengeance upon them
for the future throughout eternity.

I thought that this must be made clear to your Sagacity in
order that, if any evil prompting of such men take possession of
your resolution—though I do not think that it will—you may rid
your soul of this, and show eagerness to offer your mind pure—
as is fitting—and your devotion sincere and your faith undefiled
to the Saviour God. For it is indeed right and this be the conduct
of any man if he wishes to be worthy of the prizes of eternal life
that are perfect.

Theodotus of Laodicaea had been claimed by Arius as one of his supporters
(293), and was one of the bishops provisionally excommunicated by the
Council of Antioch (298). He took Constantine's hint.

On the exile of Eusebius of Nicomedia etc., cf. 304, 307.

306. ARIUS' CONFESSION OF FAITH,
c. 327 (or ? *c.* 334)

(Socrates, *H.E.* I.26.2ff.; Sozomen, *H.E.* II.2ff.; Opitz, Urkunde
30, p. 64.)

2   Arius and Euzoïus, to our Most Religious Lord, most beloved
of God, the Emperor Constantine.

In accordance with the command of your devout piety,
Sovereign Lord, we declare our faith, and before God profess in
writing, that we and all our adherents believe as follows:

3   We believe in one God the Father Almighty: and in the Lord
Jesus Christ his only begotten Son, who was begotten of him
before all ages, God the Word through whom all things were
made, both those which are in the heavens and those upon the
earth; who descended, and took flesh, and suffered, and rose
again, ascended into the heavens, and is coming again to judge

4 living and dead. And in the Holy Spirit, and in the resurrection
of the flesh, and in the life of the coming age, and in the kingdom
of the heavens, and in one Catholic Church of God, extending
from one end of the earth to the other.

5   This faith we have received from the holy gospels, the Lord therein saying to his disciples: *Go and teach all nations, baptizing them in the name of the Father, and of the Son, and of the Holy Spirit.*[1]

6   If we do not so believe and truly receive the Father, the Son, and the Holy Spirit, as the whole Catholic Church and the Scriptures teach (in which we believe in every respect), God is our judge

7   both now, and in the coming day of judgement. Wherefore we beseech your piety, Emperor most beloved of God, that we who are persons ordained to the ministry, and holding the faith and sentiments of the church and of the holy Scriptures, may by your pacific and devoted piety be reunited to our mother, the Church, all superfluous questions and the wranglings arising therefrom being avoided: that so both we and the whole Church being at peace, may offer our accustomed prayers for your peaceful and pious reign, and on behalf of your whole family. (N. & P.-N. F., altered.)

The account of Socrates places this letter c. 327, that of Sozomen brings it into connection with the dedication of Constantine's Church of the Holy Sepulchre at Jerusalem, which did not take place till 335. There is no doubt that Arius had not been restored up to the latter date. The reason for this, according to Socrates, was the opposition of Athanasius to whom Constantine wrote in threatening terms (310).

Gelasius, *H.E.* III.15.1, preserves parts of a letter from Constantine *to Alexander*, bidding him receive Arius back. If Alexander is of Alexandria the letter must be c. 327, but he may be Alexander of Constantinople, and the letter could therefore be dated c. 335. Arius' confession is expressed as Sozomen says, "in simple and scriptural terms" and should be compared with 293–4.

Euzoïus was one of the clergy deposed by Alexander of Alexandria c. 320: c. 361 he became bishop of Antioch.

307. LETTER FROM EXILE OF EUSEBIUS OF NICOMEDIA AND THEOGNIUS OF NICAEA, c. 327

(Socrates, *H.E.* I.14.2ff.; Sozomen, *H.E.* II.16.3ff.; Gelasius, *H.E.* III.13.1; Opitz, Urkunde 31, p. 65.)

2   We having been sometime ago condemned by your piety, without a formal trial, ought to bear in silence the decisions of your sacred adjudication. But since it is unreasonable that by silence we should countenance calumniators against ourselves, we on this account declare that we entirely concur with you in the

[1] Matt. 28.19.

faith; and also that, after having closely considered the import of the term consubstantial (ὁμοούσιος), we have been wholly 3 studious of peace, having never followed the heresy. After suggesting whatever entered our thought for the security of the churches, and fully assuring those under our influence, we subscribed the declaration of faith; we did not subscribe the anathematizing; not as objecting to the creed, but as disbelieving the party accused to be such as was represented, having been satisfied on this point, both from his own letters to us, and from personal 4 conversations. But if your holy council was convinced, we, not opposing but concurring in your decisions, by this statement give them our full assent and confirmation: and this we do not as wearied with our exile, but to shake off the suspicion of heresy. 5 If therefore you should now think fit to restore us to your presence, you will have us on all points conformable, and acquiescent in your decrees: especially since it has seemed good to your piety to deal tenderly with and recall even him who was primarily 6 accused (i.e. Arius). It would be absurd for us to be silent, and thus give presumptive evidence against ourselves, when the one who seemed responsible has been permitted to clear himself from the charges brought against him. Vouchsafe then, as is consistent with that Christ-loving piety of yours, to remind our most religious Emperor, to present our petitions, and to determine speedily concerning us in a way becoming yourselves. (N. & P.-N. F., slightly altered.)

This letter does not make it at all clear to whom it is addressed. It is certainly addressed to an ecclesiastical, and not to a secular body, as the reference to the Emperor shows. The petitioners explain their case and ask the recipients to put their case up to Constantine. Many regard this letter as addressed to the (supposed) second session of the Council of Nicaea.

2. *condemned by your piety, without a formal trial*: it looks as though these bishops, after they had been sent into exile by the Emperor (304), had been subject to some episcopal condemnation.

3. *we did not subscribe to the anathematizing*: this is a point which Constantine does not make in 304. Quite possibly he was ignorant of it, or had forgotten. But it does explain why Eusebius and his friends were so ready to associate with Arius on his way to exile. Others, e.g. Eusebius of Caesarea, had been inclined to regard Arius as misrepresented (in a letter which he (Eusebius) wrote to Alexander of Alexandria *c.* 320 (Opitz, Urkunde 7, pp. 14–15). This conviction may have been borne in on Eusebius of Nicomedia when he met Arius on the above mentioned occasion. Anyhow, it was now made clear that the Eusebians did not intend to squabble over doctrine. Arius is represented as already recalled, cf. 306.

308. THE APPOINTMENT OF THE BISHOP AT ALEXANDRIA

(Jerome, *Ep.* CXLVI.1.1, 5-7.)

1   We read in Isaiah, *A fool will speak folly*.[1] I hear that a certain person has broken out into so great madness as to place deacons before presbyters, that is, bishops. For when the apostle plainly teaches that presbyters and bishops are the same, what happens to the server of tables and widows that he sets himself up arrogantly over those at whose prayers the body and blood of Christ are 5 made? Do you ask for authority? Listen to the proof. . . . That afterwards one was chosen to preside over the rest, this was done as a remedy for schism, and to prevent one individual from rend- 6 ing the Church of Christ by drawing it to himself. For even at Alexandria, from the time of Mark the Evangelist to the episcop- ates of Heraclas and Dionysius, the presbyters used always to appoint as bishop one chosen out of their number, and placed on the higher grade, as if an army should make a commander, or as if deacons should choose one of themselves whom they should know to be diligent, and call him archdeacon. For, with the excep- tion of ordaining, what does a bishop do which a presbyter does not? The church of the city of Rome is not to be thought one 7 church, and that of the whole world another. Gaul and Britain, and Africa and Persia, and the East and India, and all foreign nations worship one Christ, and observe one rule of truth. If authority is asked for, the world is greater than the city. Where- ever there is a bishop, whether at Rome, or Eugubium, or Con- stantinople, or Rhegium, or Alexandria, or Tanis, he is of the same dignity and of the same priesthood. The power of riches or the lowliness of poverty does not make him a higher bishop or a lower bishop. But all are successors of the apostles. (D. Stone, *Episcopacy and Valid Orders*, pp. 43ff.)

Jerome is attacking the arrogance of the Roman deacons, as did his con- temporary, the writer called "Ambrosiaster" (in *P.L.* XXXV, 2301-3). Both exalt the office of presbyter.

On the whole question of the appointment of the Bishop of Alexandria, see W. Telfer, *Episcopal Succession in Egypt* (*J. E. H.* 3, pp. 1-13).

6.   *to the episcopates of Heraclas and Dionysius*: if, as Telfer suggests (loc. cit. 4), Jerome's source is Origen, the illustration would be apposite for Origen's

---

[1] Cf. Isa. 9.17.

time, but does not serve as an indication that the custom stopped *then*. Severus, Monophysite Patriarch of Antioch, makes the same statement as Jerome about the appointment of the Bishop of Alexandria by the presbyters, and merely points out that this dissenting practice had ended (*J.T.S.* II, p. 612). According to the *Apophthegmata Patrum*, Ch. 78 (*P.G.* LXV.341), certain heretics accused Athanasius of having received ordination from presbyters, and Eutychius, Melchite Patriarch of Alexandria in the tenth century, states that this custom came to an end with Alexander (*P.G.* CXI.982 B, C). That is very likely, as in the face of Canon 4 of Nicaea (300, p. 359), the Alexandrian church could hardly persist in the practice.

309. ATHANASIUS' VERSION OF THE MELITIAN STORY, TO 328

(Athanasius, *Apology against the Arians*, 59,71.)

59   Peter was bishop among us before the persecution, and during the course of it he suffered martyrdom. When Melitius, who held the title of bishop in Egypt, was convicted of many crimes and in particular of offering sacrifice to idols, Peter deposed him in a general council of the bishops. Whereupon Melitius did not appeal to another council, or attempt to justify himself before those who should come after. He made a schism instead and they who espoused his cause are even yet called Melitians instead of Christians. He began immediately to revile the bishops and made false accusations, first against Peter himself, and against his successor Achillas, and, after Achillas, against Alexander. . . . While Melitius was doing this, the Arian heresy began. But in the Council of Nicaea, while the heresy was anathematized, and the Arians were cast out, the Melitians, on whatever grounds (for it is not necessary now to mention the reason), were received. Five months, however, had not passed when, the blessed Alexander having died, the Melitians, who ought to have remained quiet, and to have been grateful that they were received on any terms, like dogs unable to forget their vomit, began to trouble the churches.

Upon learning this, Eusebius, who had the lead in the Arian heresy, sent and bought the Melitians with large promises; he became their secret friend, and arranged with them for their assistance on any occasion when he might wish for it. . . .

71   . . . When Melitius was admitted into communion (I wish that he had never been) the blessed Alexander, who knew his craftiness, required of him a schedule of the bishops whom he said he

had in Egypt, and of the presbyters and deacons that were in Alexandria itself, and if he had any in the country district attached to the city. This the Pope Alexander has done lest Melitius, having received the freedom of the Church, should tender many and thus, continually, by a fraudulent procedure, foist upon us whomsoever he pleased. Accordingly he has made out the following schedule of those in Egypt. "I, Melitius, of Lycopolis," etc. [twenty-nine bishops in Egypt, four presbyters and three deacons in Alexandria, and one country-presbyter]. (N. & P.-N. F., altered.)

59. *in particular of offering sacrifice*: no particular reliance should be placed on this accusation which was all too promiscuously made.

On the decision of the Council of Nicaea about the Melitians, see 302, section 9.

Five months . . . had not passed, etc.: this does not mean that there was only a period of five months between the Council of Nicaea and the death of Alexander of Alexandria (328), but that Alexander died *c*. four to five months after his reconciliation with the Melitians, to which section 71 infra refers. But if we do relate the "five months" to the Council of Nicaea, they must refer to the (supposed) second session of 327, an idea supported by many modern scholars.

Upon learning this, Eusebius, etc.: Epiphanius, one of the keenest heresy hunters of the early centuries, states quite unequivocally in *Haer.* 68.1 that Melitius himself was orthodox. "The faults of Melitius were above all faults of conduct, and, if the Melitian schism compromised itself with Arianism, that was after the death of its author. St Epiphanius is not indulgent to Arians or to the supporters of Arians. But he takes great care to separate the personal case of Melitius from that of his posthumous disciples, who became all too docile instruments in Arian hands" (D'Alès, *Le Dogme de Nicée*, p. 214).

71. The precaution taken by Alexander was most natural and necessary. In the list submitted to him the name of Ischyras (314, 315) does not appear.

310. THE RELIGIOUS POLICY OF CONSTANTINE, *c*. 328

(Part of a letter of Constantine to Athanasius in Athanasius, *Apology against the Arians* 59.)

Having therefore knowledge of my will, grant free admission to all who wish to enter the Church. For if I learn that you have hindered any who lay claim to membership, or debarred them from entrance, I will immediately send someone to depose you at my command and remove you from your place (i.e. send you into exile). (N. & P.-N. F., altered.)

This attitude of Constantine is very significant. It is now Athanasius who is the excluding force, preventing the Emperor from his realization of one united Catholic Church. His opponents, like Eusebius of Nicomedia, did not argue about doctrine and discipline! (cf. 307).

According to Athanasius, the Emperor sent this letter at the instigation of Eusebius of Nicomedia.

311. ATHANASIUS AND THE MELITIANS, c. 335

(From a letter of Callistus, a Melitian: text in Bell, *Jews and Christians in Egypt*, pp. 53ff.)

"The situation revealed is roughly as follows: Athanasius was anxious and despondent, partly in consequence of reports which reached him from abroad. Among these was one concerning a Macarius, whom apparently the Emperor had ordered to be taken into custody. A certain Archelaus, a second person whose name is lost, and Athanasius son of Capito . . . set out from Egypt with the intention of carrying off Macarius, i.e., apparently, of delivering him from justice, and also bearing defamatory letters against an Alexandrine named Heraiscus; but "Apa Johannes" (i.e. John Arcaph, successor to Melitius) hearing a report of this at Antioch, came and seized them and placed them in custody." (Bell, op. cit., p. 55.)

> So Athanasius heard this news, that Archelaus was arrested, and Athanasius is very despondent. Often (?) did they come for him, and till now he has not left the country; but he had his baggage embarked at sea as though he would leave the country, and then again he took his baggage off the ship, not wishing to leave the country. . . . I have written to you in order that you might know in what affliction we are; for he carried off a Bishop of the Lower Country and shut him in the Meat Market, and a priest of the same region he shut in the lock-up, and a deacon in the principal prison, and till the twenty-eighth of Pachon (=23 May) Heraiscus too has been confined in the Camp—I thank God our Master that the scourgings which he endured have ceased— and on the twenty-seventh he caused seven Bishops to leave the country. . . . (Bell, op. cit., p. 62.)

This letter shows that the accusations of violence brought against Athanasius were not without foundation. This letter is probably to be dated shortly before the Council of Tyre (314 below).

312. THE DEPOSITION OF EUSTATHIUS OF ANTIOCH, *c.* 330 (?)

The exile of Eustathius, bishop of one of the greatest churches, was an event important in itself and fraught with serious consequences for the Church of Antioch because of the schism which it engendered. But divergent reasons, not necessarily incompatible, are given by various authors, and it is clear that there was no authoritative account of what took place. For an earlier dating of the fall of Eustathius, see H. Chadwick in *J.T.S.* XLIX (1948), pp. 27–35.

I

(Athanasius, *History of the Arians* 4.)

There was one Eustathius, Bishop of Antioch, a Confessor, and sound in the Faith. This man, because he was very zealous for the truth, and hated the Arian heresy, and would not receive those who adopted its tenets, is falsely accused before the Emperor Constantine, and a charge invented against him, that he had insulted his mother. And immediately he is driven into banishment, and a great number of presbyters and deacons with him. (N. & P.-N. F.)

The insult to Helena, if true, may be referred to some word or action of Eustathius on the visit of Helena to the East in 326–327.

2

(Socrates, *H.E.* I.23.8–24.1)

23.8 Eustathius, bishop of Antioch, accused Eusebius Pamphili of perverting the Nicene faith, Eusebius on the other hand denied that he violated that exposition of the faith, and recriminated, saying that Eustathius was a defender of the opinion of Sabellius. In consequence of these misunderstandings, each of them wrote as if contending against adversaries: and although it was admitted on both sides that the Son of God has a distinct subsistence and existence, and all acknowledged that there is one God in three subsistences, yet from what cause I am unable to divine, they could not agree among themselves, and therefore could in no way endure to be at peace.

24.1 Having therefore convened a Synod at Antioch, they deposed Eustathius, as a supporter of the Sabellian heresy, rather than of the doctrines which the council at Nicaea had formulated. As some affirm, they took this course for other reasons implying moral turpitude, though none other have been openly assigned. (N. & P.-N. F., altered.)

[Socrates, after tilting at the obscurity of the reasons for which bishops depose other bishops, refuses to believe in the charge of Sabellianism and takes the view that there must have been other grounds.]

Eusebius of Caesarea (called *Eusebius Pamphili* from his master Pamphilus, martyr in 310) was no enthusiast for the Creed of Nicaea (cf. 301), and as time went on such lack of enthusiasm would become obvious. The accusation of Sabellianism, which the opponents of Nicaea regarded as more or less implicit in the creed, was a perfectly natural one. But other reasons must have operated also, and we may judge it likely that Eusebius resented the strong language used by Eustathius about Origen, e.g. in his still extant work *De Engastrimytho contra Origenem* (*On the Witch of Endor*). For examples of his language see Sellers, *Eustathius of Antioch*, p. 32.

Sozomen, *H.E.* II.19, does not add much to our knowledge except that the strife engendered by Eustathius' deposition injured the accused in the eyes of the Emperor.

For when he (Constantine) understood what had happened, and that the people of that church were divided into two parties, he was much enraged, and regarded him with suspicion as the author of the tumult. (N. & P.-N. F.)

Theodoret, *H.E.* I.41, represents Eustathius as the victim of a plot engineered by Eusebius of Nicomedia and his friends, and the accusation against Eustathius as entirely moral (cf. Philostorgius *H.E.* II.7). In Ch. 22, however, Theodoret significantly points out that all those chosen as Bishops of Antioch in the years immediately following the deposition of Eustathius were pro-Arian.

3

That the Emperor was much involved in the matter is shown particularly by Eusebius, *V.C.* III.59–62, chapters in which three letters from Constantine to the Antiochenes, to Eusebius himself and to the assembled bishops are included. Eusebius had refused to accept the bishopric of Antioch himself and was warmly commended by Constantine.

(Eusebius, *V.C.* III.62.)

Now the letters of Eusebius himself on this subject appeared to be strictly accordant with the order prescribed by the Church, and set out the contrary opinion, that he would not on any account abandon the church entrusted to him by God. It is my decision therefore that this so justly expressed statement of the case—and one which you should all observe—should be made authoritative, and that he should not be separated from his own church. Nevertheless it is expedient that your Prudence should be made acquainted with my opinion also. For I am informed that Euphronius the presbyter, who is a citizen of Caesarea in Cappadocia, and George of Arethusa, likewise a presbyter, and appointed to that office by Alexander at Alexandria, are men of tried faith. It was right, therefore, to intimate to your Prudence, that in proposing these men and any others whom you may deem worthy the episcopal dignity, you should decide this question in a manner conformable to the tradition of the apostles. (N. & P.-N. F., altered.)

The candidates selected by Constantine show the limits of the Emperor's knowledge, and how he could be imposed upon. He does not know that George, whose ordination by Alexander *appeared to be a guarantee of his faith*, had also been deposed by Alexander. For this individual's chequered history see *D.C.B.* s.v.

313. CONSTANTINE'S PROSCRIPTION OF THE WORKS OF PORPHYRY AND ARIUS, *c.* 333

(Letter of Constantine *To the bishops and people*, in Socrates, *H.E.* I.9.30–31, and Gelasius, *H.E.* II.36.)

30   Since Arius has imitated wicked and impious persons, it is just that he should undergo the like ignominy. Wherefore as Porphyry, that enemy of piety, for having composed licentious treatises against Religion, found a suitable recompense, and such as thenceforth branded him with infamy, overwhelming him with deserved reproach, his impious writings also having been destroyed; so now it seems fit both that Arius and such as hold his sentiments should be denominated Porphyrians, that they may take their appellation from those whose conduct they have imitated. And in addition to this, if any treatise composed by Arius should be discovered, let it be consigned to the flames, in order that not only his depraved doctrine may be suppressed, but

31   also that no memorial of him may be by any means left. This therefore I decree, that if any one shall be detected in concealing a book compiled by Arius, and shall not instantly bring it forward

and burn it, the penalty for this offence shall be death; for immediately after conviction the criminal shall suffer capital punishment. May God preserve you! (N. & P.-N. F.)

This proscription of books is the first to be made in the interests of the Church. The prohibition in the case of Porphyry was ineffective as his work required refutation by Apollinarius of Laodicaea (c. 370) and Philostorgius (c. 425), and was again proscribed by Theodosius II and Valentinian III in 448.

314. THE COUNCIL OF TYRE, 335: ACCUSATIONS AGAINST ATHANASIUS

(Sozomen, H.E. II.25.3–8,12.)

3 Of John's party, Callinicus, a bishop, and a certain Ischurias accused him of breaking a mystical chalice and of throwing down an episcopal chair; and of often imprisoning Ischyras, although he was a presbyter; and by falsely informing Hyginus, governor of Egypt, that he had cast stones at the statues of the emperor;
4 of occasioning his being thrown into jail; of deposing Callinicus, bishop of the Catholic Church at Pelusium and a friend of Alexander, and of saying he would debar him from fellowship unless he could remove certain suspicions concerning his having broken a mystical chalice; of committing the Church of Pelusium to Mark, a deposed presbyter; and of placing Callinicus under a military guard, and of inflicting tortures and judicial trials on him.
5 Euplus, Pachomius, Isaac, Achillas and Hermaeon, bishops of
6 John's party, accused him of inflicting blows. They all concurred in maintaining that he obtained the episcopal dignity by means of the perjury of certain individuals, it being a universal principle that no one should receive ordination, who could not clear himself of any crime laid to his charge. They further alleged that after being deceived by him they had separated themselves from communion with him, and that, so far from satisfying their scruples, he had treated them with violence and thrown them into prison.
7 Further, the affair of Arsenius was again agitated; and as generally happens in such a studiously concocted plot, many even of those considered his friends loomed up unexpectedly as accusers. A document was then read containing popular complaints that the people of Alexandria could not continue their attendance at
8 church on his account. Athanasius was ordered to justify himself

and presented himself repeatedly before the tribunal; he success-
fully repelled some of the allegations, and requested a postponement for investigation of the others. He was exceedingly perplexed
when he reflected on the favour in which his accusers were held
by his judges, on the number of witnesses belonging to the sects
of Arius and Melitius who appeared against him, and on the
indulgence that was manifested towards the informers, whose
allegations he had overcome particularly in the indictment concerning Arsenius, whose arm he was charged with having cut
off for the purposes of magic, and in the indictment concerning
a certain woman to whom he was charged with having given
gifts for immoral purposes, and with having corrupted her by
night although she was unwilling.

*   *   *

12   As to the second (i.e. the charge about Arsenius), the accusers
strove to justify themselves by saying that a bishop under the
jurisdiction of Athanasius, named Plusian, had, at the command
of his chief, burnt the house of Arsenius, fastened him to a column,
and maltreated him with thongs, and then imprisoned him in a
cell. They further stated that Arsenius escaped from the cell
through a window, and while he was sought for remained a while
in concealment; that as he did not appear, they naturally supposed
him to be dead; and because he was a well-known man and a
confessor, the bishops of John's party kept up a search for him
and applied to the magistrates for help. (N. & P.-N. F., altered.)

The passages of Sozomen quoted above are probably based on a collection
of documents relating to Synods made by Sabinus, Bishop of Heraclea in
Thrace, c. 373–378.

3. *of John's party*: i.e. John Arcaph whom Melitius had appointed as his own
successor.
4. As is clear from 311, there is probably some truth in the accusations of
violence made against Athanasius; the present passage shows the variety of the
accusations, extending to cases of others than Melitians, and apparently extending back to the time before Athanasius' election as Bishop of Alexandria.
7. *was again agitated*: Athanasius, *Apology against the Arians*, 65, states that
the Emperor had already acquitted him of this charge.
8. The accusation of immorality was all too common, cf. 312 (2, note).
Athanasius' rebuttal is contained in sections 9–11 of the present passage. It is
probably not derived from Sabinus.
12. For the interesting, but probably unhistorical story about Athanasius
and Arsenius at the Council of Tyre, see Socrates, *H.E.* I.29.

315. ATHANASIUS' APPEAL TO CONSTANTINE: HIS EXILE, 336

(Letter of Constantine to the Council of Tyre in Athanasius, *Apology against the Arians*, 36; Socrates, *H.E.* I.34; Sozomen, *H.E.* II.28; narrative of Socrates, *H.E.* I.35.)

I

1-4 [The Emperor begins by rebuking the Synod for its disorderly and partisan decisions, and demands the attendance of its members before him, for the following reason.]

5   As I was returning on horseback to that city which bears my name, my all-blessed country, Constantinople, Athanasius, the bishop, presented himself so unexpectedly in the middle of the road, with certain priests who accompanied him, that I felt exceed-
6 ingly surprised at beholding him. God, who sees all things, is my witness, that at first I did not recognize who he was, but that some of my attendants having ascertained this point, and the injustice which he had suffered, gave me as you would expect
7 the necessary information. I did not on this occasion have any conversation with him or grant him an interview. He, however, persevered in requesting an audience; and although I refused him, and was on the point of commanding that he should be removed from my presence, he declared with more boldness, that he sought no other favour of me than that I should summon you hither, in order that he might in your presence complain of
8 what necessarily he had suffered. As this request appears reasonable and timely, I gladly gave orders for this letter to be written to you, and to command all of you who were convened at the Synod of Tyre to hasten to the court of our Clemency, so that you may demonstrate by your works the purity and integrity of your decisions before me, whom you cannot refuse to acknowledge as a genuine servant of God. (N. & P.-N. F. (Sozomen), altered.)

9- [Constantine concludes by recalling the prosperity of his time,
12 the fear that the barbarians have of him and their conversion through him, the necessity for forbearance, his care for unity and his desire to preserve the law of God against its enemies.]

2

(Socrates, *H.E.* I.35.1-4)

1   This letter caused anxiety to those who constituted the Synod,
2 and most of them returned to their respective cities. But Eusebius,
Theognis, Maris, Patrophilus, Ursacius, Valens and their friends
went to Constantinople, and would not permit any further
inquiry to be instituted concerning a broken cup, or table, or the
murder of Arsenius; but they had recourse to another calumny,
informing the emperor that Athanasius had threatened to prohibit the sending of corn which was regularly conveyed from
Alexandria to Constantinople. They affirmed also that these
menaces were heard from the lips of Athanasius by the bishops
3 Adamantius, Anubion, Arbathion and Peter, for slander is most
prevalent when the assertor of it is a person worthy of credit.
Hence the emperor being deceived, and excited to indignation
against Athanasius by this charge, at once condemned him to
4 exile, ordering him to reside in the Gauls. Now some affirm that
the emperor came to this decision with a view to the establish-
ment of unity in the church, since Athanasius was inexorable in
his refusal to hold any communion with Arius and his adherents.
He accordingly took up his abode at Trèves, a city of Gaul.
(N. & P.-N. F., altered.)

An account from *one* of the Church historians about these events is at best a
partial one. That of Socrates is based on Athanasius, *Apology against the Arians*,
87. Athanasius withdrew from the Council of Tyre, but Theodoret adds
(*H.E.* I.30) that he was taken into protective custody by the imperial officials
to save him from physical violence.

The bishops named by Socrates, i.e. Eusebius, etc., had all been, or were to
be (like Ursacius of Singidunum and Valens of Mursa) prominent supporters
of Arius.

a broken cup, or table: the chalice of a Melitian presbyter Ischyras, which
Macarius, one of Athanasius' presbyters was said to have broken; the table
was his altar, overturned by the same Macarius. For a list of accusations against
Athanasius see Sozomen, *H.E.* II.25 (314 above).

the murder of Arsenius: cf. 314.

The accusation about the corn ships was a *capital* one. The Neo-Platonist
philosopher Sopater, who had presided at the inaugural ceremonies of Constantinople in 330, was accused (? in 331) of stopping the corn ships by means
of magic, and was beheaded. See, e.g., A. Piganiol, *L'Empire chrétien*, p. 51,
who connects the fall of Sopater with the events mentioned in 313 above.

316. MARCELLUS OF ANCYRA

(Text of the fragments of Marcellus in *Eusebius Werke* IV
(*G.C.S.*), ed. Klostermann, pp. 183–215.)

The vicissitudes of Marcellus of Ancyra began before the death of Constantine, and continued for long after. He was "the chief representative of the
supposed Sabellian tendencies of the Nicene Christology" (Bethune-Baker,
Introduction to the Early History of Christian Doctrine, p. 190), and was deposed
from his see in 336. See Socrates, *H.E.* I.36, Sozomen, *H.E.* II.33. The fragments quoted are an attempt to indicate some of the main lines of Marcellus'
thought. They are drawn from the works of Eusebius of Caesarea *Against
Marcellus*, and *On the Theology of the Church*.

66 It is impossible for three subsistencies (ὑποστάσεις) to be
united to a monad, unless the trinity (i.e. the three ὑποστάσεις)
was to have its beginning from the monad.

76 If you wish to hear another prophecy of Isaiah confirming for
us, ONE GOD, *I am God*, he says, *at the first, and unto the last, I
am he.*[1] The word *I* is indicative of one person (πρόσωπον). For
the two expressions signify one person. He begins with *I* and
continues with *am*, so that through the two parts of speech,
pronoun and verb, the fact that the Divinity is a monad is
confirmed.

6 Therefore this most holy Word had not been named *first born
of all creation*[2] before he became man (for how could the ever-
existent be first born of anything?) but the first *new man*[3] unto
whom God wished *to sum up all things*,[4] him the divine scriptures
name *first born of all creation*.

42 For the Word was *in the beginning*,[5] being nothing else than
Word. But the human being united to the Word, not previously
existing, came into being as John teaches us saying, *And the
Word became flesh.*[6] Thus therefore he obviously mentions the
Word alone. For if Holy Scripture mentions the name Jesus or
Christ, it clearly means the Word of God with human flesh. If
anyone even before the new covenant were to announce that he
can show the name Christ or Jesus used of the Word alone, he
will find this spoken prophetically, e.g. *The kings of the earth
gathered together, and the rulers were assembled against the Lord and
against his Christ.*[7]

67 If therefore the Word clearly comes forth from the Father and
has come to us, and the Holy Spirit (as Asterius also agreed)

[1] Isa. 41.4.   [2] Col. 1.15.   [3] Eph. 2.15.   [4] Eph. 1.10.
[5] John 1.1.   [6] John 1.14.   [7] Ps. 2.2.

proceeds from the Father,[1] and in another place the Saviour says of the Spirit, *He shall not speak from himself, but whatsoever things he shall hear these shall he speak and he shall declare unto you the things that are to come. He shall glorify me, for he shall take of mine and shall declare it unto you,*[2] not clearly and openly, but in an ineffable word the monad appears, widening out into a trinity, but in no way whatsoever submitting to division. For if the Word proceeds from the Father, and the Spirit himself also is agreed *to proceed from the Father,* and in another place the Saviour says, *He shall take of mine and shall declare it unto you,* is it not perfectly clear that some hidden mystery is being revealed? For how, unless the monad, being indivisible, widens out into a trinity, is it possible for him at one time to say about the Spirit that *he proceeds from the Father,* at another, *He shall take of mine and shall declare it unto you,* and on another occasion, breathing on his disciples to say, *Receive ye the Holy Spirit?*[3] For how if he proceeds from the Father is he declared as receiving this service from the Son? For of necessity if there are two divided persons, as Asterius said, either the Spirit, proceeding from the Father does not require the service of the Son (for of necessity everything proceeding from the Father must be perfect, not requiring help from another in any way whatsoever) or if he takes from the Son and from his power ministers grace, he no longer proceeds from the Father.

67. Asterius was an Arian sophist against whom Marcellus wrote. Like other leading Arians, he had been a pupil of Lucian of Antioch. For an account of him, and the text of the surviving fragments of his works, see G. Bardy, *Recherches sur Saint Lucien d'Antioche et son École,* pp. 316–57.

317. CONSTANTINE AS BISHOP

(Eusebius, *V.C.* IV.24.)

Hence it was not without reason that once, on the occasion of his entertaining a company of bishops, he let fall the expression, "that he himself too was a bishop," addressing them in my hearing in the following words: "You are bishops whose jurisdiction is within the Church: I also am a bishop, ordained by God to over-look those outside the Church." And truly his measures corresponded with his words; for he watched over all his subjects with an episcopal care, and exhorted them as far as in him lay to follow a godly life. (N. & P.-N. F., altered.)

[1] John 15.26. [2] John 16.13–14. [3] John 20.22.

Hence, etc.: because of his personal religious devotion, his benefactions to the Church, and his opposition to paganism.

The occasion of this remark of Constantine was probably at his Tricennalia (336). For his "episcopal" care, cf. 318 (1), where the pastoral care of Constantine is compared with that of the Word.

318. THE CHRISTIAN EMPIRE

(From Eusebius, *Oration on the Tricennalia of Constantine*, A.D. 336.)

I

The Word of God and the Christian Emperor
(2.1-5)

1   The only begotten Word of God reigns, from ages which had no beginning, to infinite and endless ages, the partner of his Father's kingdom. And our emperor ever beloved by him, who derives the source of imperial authority from above, and is strong in the power of his sacred title, has controlled the empire of the 2 world for a long period of years. Again, that Preserver of the universe orders the whole heaven and earth, and the celestial kingdom, consistently with his Father's will. Even so our emperor whom He loves, by bringing those whom he rules on earth to the only begotten and saving Word renders them fit subjects for his 3 kingdom. And as He who is the common Saviour of mankind, by his invisible and Divine power as a good shepherd, drives far away from his flock, like savage beasts, those apostate spirits which once flew through the airy tracts above this earth, and fastened on the souls of men; so this His friend, graced by His heavenly favour with victory over all his foes, subdues and chastens the open adversaries of the truth in accordance with the 4 usages of war. He who is the pre-existent Word, the Saviour of all things, imparts to His followers the seeds of true wisdom and salvation, makes them at the same time truly wise, and understanding the kingdom of their Father. Our emperor, His friend, acting as interpreter to the Word of God, aims at recalling the whole human race to the knowledge of God; proclaiming clearly in the ears of all, and declaring with powerful voice the laws of 5 truth and godliness to all who dwell on the earth. Once more, the universal Saviour opens the heavenly gates of His Father's kingdom to those whose course is thitherward from this world. Our emperor, emulous of his Divine example, having purged his

earthly dominion from every stain of impious error, invites each holy and pious worshipper within his imperial mansions, earnestly desiring to save with all its crew that mighty vessel of which he is the appointed pilot.

2

The Imperial Sacrifice
(2.5–6)

5 He does not, in imitation of ancient usage, defile his imperial mansions with blood and gore nor propitiate the infernal deities with smoke and fire, and sacrificial burnt offerings; but dedicates a sacrifice pleasant and acceptable to the universal Sovereign, even his own imperial soul, and a mind truly fitted for the service of

6 of God. For this sacrifice alone is grateful to Him: and this sacrifice our emperor has learned, with purified mind and thoughts, to present as an offering without the intervention of fire and blood; while his own piety is strengthened by the truthful doctrines with which his soul is stored, and he sets forth in magnificent language the praises of God, and imitates his Divine philanthropy by his own imperial acts. Wholly devoted to Him, he dedicates himself as a noble offering, a first-fruit of that world, the government of which is intrusted to his charge.

3

The Excellence of Monarchy
(3.5–7)

5 Lastly, invested as he is with a semblance of heavenly sovereignty, he directs his gaze above, and frames his earthly government according to the pattern of that Divine original, feeling strength in its conformity to the monarchy of God. And this conformity is granted by the universal Sovereign to man alone of the creatures of this earth: for He only is the author of sovereign power, who

6 decrees that all should be subject to the rule of one. And surely monarchy far transcends every other constitution and form of government: for that democratic equality of power, which is its opposite, may rather be described as anarchy and disorder. Hence there is one God, and not two, or three, or more: for to assert a plurality of gods is plainly to deny the being of God at all. There is "one King"; and his Word and royal Law is one: a Law not expressed in syllables and words, not written or engraved on tablets, and therefore subject to the ravages of time; but the

living and self-subsisting Word, who Himself is God, and who administers His Father's kingdom on behalf of all who are under him and subject to his power.

5. *he directs his gaze above*: the uplifted eyes are a feature of Constantinian coinage, at any rate from 324. Eusebius (*V.C.* IV.15) speaks of coins and pictures where the Emperor is represented with his eyes upraised to heaven. Cf. also L'Orange, *Apotheosis in Ancient Portraiture*, pp. 116–17, on the colossal head of Constantine in Rome from a statue originally in the Basilica of Constantine. "The eyes express . . . the transcendence of the ruler's personality. In the gaze he travels far beyond his physical surroundings, and attains his goal in a higher sphere, in contact and identity with the governing powers." L'Orange dates this statue as after 324.

6. *monarchy far transcends*, etc.: cf. Eusebius, *Martyrs of Palestine*, 1.1, where Procopius, the first martyr at Caesarea in the Diocletianic persecution, quotes Homer, *Il.* 2.204–5, lines that had become proverbial, cf. also Celsus' use of the same passage (Origen, *Contra Celsum*, VIII.68) *against* the Christians (122).

Eusebius' reverence for monarchy is not far seeing. He did not see that in the division of the Empire, organized by Constantine himself—an arrangement that he praises (ibid., 3.4)—between the sons and nephews of the Emperor, the seeds of separate rule were already sown.

4

The Virtues of the Christian Emperor
(5.1–4)

1   And in this hope (i.e. of the heavenly kingdom) our divinely-favoured emperor partakes even in this present life, gifted as he is by God with native virtues, and having received into his soul the outflowings of His favour. His reason he derives from the universal Reason (i.e. the Word): he is wise by communion with wisdom; good by participation in good; just by sharing in justice; prudent by fellowship with prudence, and brave by sharing in
2   the heavenly power. And truly may he deserve the imperial title, who has formed his soul to royal virtues, according to the standard of that celestial kingdom.

2–3   [On the other hand, a non-Christian ruler will display vices where Constantine displays virtues.]

4   Let then our emperor, on the testimony of truth itself, be declared alone worthy of the title; who is dear to the Supreme Sovereign himself; who alone is free, nay, who is truly lord: above the thirst of wealth, superior to sexual desire; victorious even over natural pleasures, controlling, not controlled by, anger and passion. He

is indeed an emperor, and bears a title corresponding to his deeds; a VICTOR in truth, who has gained the victory over those passions which overmaster the rest of men: whose character is formed after the Divine original of the Supreme Sovereign, and whose mind reflects, as in a mirror, the radiance of His virtues. Hence is our emperor perfect in prudence, in goodness, in justice in courage, in piety, in devotion to God: he truly and only is a philosopher since he knows himself, and is fully aware that supplies of every blessing are showered on him from a source quite external to himself, even from heaven itself. Declaring the august title of supreme authority by the splendour of his vesture, he alone worthily wears that imperial purple which so well becomes him.

4. ... *that imperial purple which so well becomes him*: cf. *Epitome de Caesaribus* 41 (end of the fourth century). "He (Constantine) was greedy for praise beyond all measure ... he adorned his imperial robes with jewels, and his head with a diadem which he constantly wore."

5

Constantine's Dependence on the Word
(18.1–3)

1   These words of ours, however, may well appear superfluous in your ears, convinced as you are, by frequent and personal experience, of our Saviour's Deity; yourself also, in actions still more than words, a herald of the truth to all mankind. Yourself, it may be, will vouchsafe at a time of leisure to relate to us the countless manifestations which your Saviour has accorded you of Himself, and the countless occasions of His presence with you
2   while you sleep. I speak not of those secret suggestions which must not be told to us: but of those principles which He has instilled into your own mind, and which are fraught with general interest
3   and benefit to the human race. You will yourself relate in worthy terms the visible protection which your Divine shield and guardian has extended in battle; the ruin of your open and secret foes; and His ready aid in time of peril. To him you will ascribe relief in the midst of perplexity; defence in solitude; expedients in extremity; foreknowledge of events yet future; your forethought for the general weal; your power to investigate uncertain questions;. your conduct of most important enterprises; your administration of civil affairs; your military arrangements, and correction of abuses in all departments; your ordinances respecting public right; and, lastly, your legislation for the common benefit

of all. You will, it may be, also detail to us those particulars of
His favour which are secret to us, but known to you alone, and
treasured in your royal memory as in secret storehouses. (N. &
P.-N. F., altered.)

The swift arrival of the "Christian" Empire compelled Christians to reshape
their thinking. The whole question is dealt with by K. M. Setton, *The Christian
Attitude towards the Emperor in the fourth Century*, and the attitude of Eusebius in
particular by Baynes in *Byzantine Studies* (1955), pp. 168ff. The new attitude
of Christians is ultimately derived from the political thought of the Hellenistic
monarchies.

319. THE LAST DAYS OF CONSTANTINE, 537

(Eusebius, *V.C.* IV.60–73.)

60   All these edifices the emperor consecrated with the desire of
perpetuating the memory of the apostles of our Saviour before
all men. He had, however, another object in erecting this building
(i.e. the Church of the Apostles at Constantinople): an object at
first unknown, but which afterwards became evident to all. He
had in fact made choice of this spot in the prospect of his own
death, anticipating with extraordinary fervour of faith that his
body would share their title with the apostles themselves, and
that he should thus even after death become the subject, with
them, of the devotions which should be performed to their honour
in this place, and for this reason he bade men assemble for worship
there at the altar which he placed in the midst. He accordingly
caused twelve coffins to be set up in this church, like sacred pillars
in honour and memory of the apostolic band, in the centre of
which his own was placed, having six of theirs on either side of
it. Thus, as I said, he had provided with prudent foresight an
honourable resting-place for his body after death, and, having
long before secretly formed this resolution, he now consecrated
this church to the apostles, believing that this tribute to their
memory would be of no small advantage to his own soul. Nor did
God disappoint him of that which he so ardently expected and
desired.

61   [Immediately after Easter the Emperor became indisposed:
indisposition developed into illness, and Constantine, becoming
convinced of the approach of death,] felt that the time was come at

which he should seek purification from the sins of his past career, firmly believing that whatever errors he had committed as a mortal man, his soul would be purified from them through the efficacy of the mystical words and the saving waters of baptism. [He then proceeded from Helenopolis (Drepanum) in Bithynia to the suburbs of Nicomedia where he summoned "the bishops" 62 and addressed them]: "The hour is come in which I too may have the blessing of that seal which confers immortality; the hour in which I may receive the seal of salvation." [The Emperor had hoped to be baptized in Jordan but he now accepted God's will in this respect. He promised that if his life should be prolonged,]

"I will prescribe to myself from this time such a course of life as befits his service." After he had thus spoken, the prelates performed the sacred ceremonies in the usual manner, and, having given him the necessary instructions, made him a partaker of the mystic ordinance. Thus was Constantine the first of all sovereigns who was regenerated and perfected in a church dedicated to the martyrs of Christ; thus gifted with the Divine seal of baptism, he rejoiced in spirit, was renewed, and filled with heavenly light: his soul was gladdened by reason of the fervency of his faith, and astonished at the manifestation of the power of God. At the conclusion of the ceremony he arrayed himself in shining imperial vestments, brilliant as the light, and reclined on a couch of the purest white, refusing to clothe himself with the purple any more.

63– [After thanking God he completed various secular arrangements 64 and died on Whitsunday.

65– His death was received with universal manifestations of grief, 72 and his reign was regarded as continuing after his death: his funeral, conducted after the arrival of his second surviving son Constantius, was a magnificent spectacle.]

73 A coinage was also struck which bore the following device. On one side appeared the figure of our blessed prince, with the head closely veiled: the reverse exhibited him sitting as a charioteer, drawn by four horses, with a hand stretched downward from above to receive him up to heaven. (N. & P.-N. F., altered.)

62. Constantine was baptized, according to Jerome (*Chron. ad annum* 2353) by Eusebius of Nicomedia.
73. For reproductions of this coinage, see, e.g., F. Maurice, *Numismatique constantinienne*, II, Plate XVI, Nr. 16; K. Hönn, *Konstantin der Grosse*, Plate XXVII.

NOTES ON SOURCES

Acta Iustini et Sociorum (20). See *Acta Martyrum*.

Acta Martyrum: the very extensive Christian literature dealing with martyrdom begins in the second century. Some of the genuine *Acta* are, or are based on, the official accounts of the trial and condemnation of Christians, e.g. 20, 22; others are accounts by eyewitnesses or other contemporary sources, which were sometimes in the form of letters addressed to other churches, e.g. 18, 19, 21. We are not here concerned with the numerous spurious *Acta* which are quite unhistorical.

AGRIPPA CASTOR, fl. *c.* 140, wrote against the heresy of Basileides. We know nothing of him beyond what Eusebius tells us in 60.

ALEXANDER, d. 328, Bishop of Alexandria from 313, during which period that church was rent by the Arian heresy and the Melitian schism. He was the author of various letters dealing with the Arians, see 292, 295.

AMBROSE, 339–397, Bishop of Milan from 374, had an influence on the history of his time exceeded by that of no other western churchman. In the present volume he figures only indirectly in 83, where he is quoting Origen, and in 294 for a detail about the Council of Nicaea.

THE ANONYMOUS against the Montanists wrote three books of which fragments are preserved in Eusebius, *H.E.* V.16–17. He was a friend of Avircius Marcellus (85–7, 89).

ANULINUS, proconsul of Africa in 313, had to administer Constantine's first legislation in favour of the Church, and to handle the situation caused by the Donatist schism (270). He *may* be the Anulinus who was proconsul in 303, and in this case he had been a violent persecutor.

APOLLINARIUS, CLAUDIUS, fl. *c.* 180, Bishop of Hierapolis, wrote apologetic works, and also against the Montanists. Only a few fragments survive. He is probably the source of the information given by Eusebius in 23.

APOLLONIUS, fl. *c.* 200, Asian writer against the Montanists, quoted by Eusebius in *H.E.* V.18 (88).

ARISTEIDES, fl. *c.* 140, of Athens, Apologist, represents himself as a "philosopher". His *Apology*, mentioned by Eusebius (34), was rediscovered in a Syriac version in 1889, a discovery which revealed that a great part of Aristeides' work had been embodied in the Byzantine *Life of Barlaam and Josaphat*, which was formerly attributed to St John of Damascus (*c.* 675–749). Two papyrus fragments of the original have been found and also a fragment of an Armenian version (34, 35).

ARIUS, d. 335, presbyter of Alexandria and heresiarch, was a pupil of Lucian of Antioch (see 293). His known works deal only with the controversy which he stirred up. They consist only of letters, e.g. 293, 294, 306, and the *Thalia* or *Banquet* in which his theology was expounded in verse (296).

ATHANASIUS, *c.* 295–373, Bishop of Alexandria from 328, tenaciously maintained the faith of Nicaea through all vicissitudes. In this book only the earlier part of his career comes under consideration. His "historical" works are really propaganda in his own favour, but they contain numerous original documents (235–6, 240, 294, 296, 308–10, 312, 315); cf. also 142.

ATHENAGORAS, fl. *c.* 180, of Athens, Apologist, addressed his *Plea for the Christians* to Marcus Aurelius and Commodus. A. is the most conciliatory of all the apologists (45, 46). He is the author also of another extant work, *On the Resurrection of the Body*.

AUGUSTINE, 354–430, Bishop of Hippo Regius from 395, appears in this volume only as a source for documents illustrating the early history of Donatism (270, 276–7).

AVIRCIUS MARCELLUS, fl. *c.* 180, see 123.

BARDAISAN, 154–222, of Edessa, is the "father" of Christian Syriac literature, but we know very little about him, cf. 128. He was, according to Epiphanius, *Haer.* 56.1, a confessor. His orthodoxy, notwithstanding what Eusebius says, is suspect. It is not certain that any work now extant should be attributed to him (129).

BASILEIDES, fl. *c.* 140, of Alexandria, Gnostic teacher, wrote extensively, but only some fragments remain. 59 is an extract from his *Exegetica*. For an account of his system, see 50–59, and also 60.

CALLISTUS, a Melitian, writer of a letter, *c.* May–June, 335, on the sufferings of the Melitians at the hands of Athanasius. Nothing further is known of him (311).

CASSIUS DIO, *c.* 160–post 229, consul in 211 and 229, wrote, in Greek, a History of Rome from the beginning to A.D. 229 in 80 books, now only partially extant. Passage 10 is from an *Epitome* of Dio made by Xiphilinus in the eleventh century. Christianity is not mentioned in the extant portions of Dio's work.

CELSUS, fl. *c.* 180, was a redoubtable opponent of Christianity (114–122). A large portion of his work, the *True Word*, can be reconstructed from the refutation of it written by Origen, *c.* 245 (193–8).

CLEMENT OF ALEXANDRIA, d. *c.* 214, was converted in adult life, and, after a long spiritual pilgrimage (164), settled in Alexandria as a pupil of Pantaenus (163), whom he succeeded as head of the Catechetical School. He left Alexandria, *c.* 202, in the persecution of Severus, and died in Asia Minor, *c.* 214. Clement possessed wide knowledge of Greek literature and philosophy, which he regarded as a true forerunner of Christianity (169). He was devoted to the allegorical method of interpreting Scripture, which he applied even to straightforward passages of the N.T. The "learned" Christianity of Clement is very different from the faith of simple believers, and to him the highest type of Christian is the Gnostic (170–172). But Clement was completely committed to the Church, in which he may have been a presbyter (164–74).

CLEMENT OF ROME. In the lists of Roman bishops Clement appears as an early Bishop of Rome. The *First Epistle of Clement* is a letter sent by the Church of Rome to the Church of Corinth, *c*. 96, and in early tradition (Dionysius of Corinth, Irenaeus) is regarded as being sent by Clement. The *Second Epistle of Clement* is a work of the mid-second century. The extensive "Clementine" literature which grew up in the third century has no authentic connection whatsoever with Clement of Rome (5, 12, 13).

Codex Theodosianus, a collection of imperial edicts from 313 onwards, published in 438 under the Emperor Theodosius II (284–7).

Codex Veronensis LX is a Latin MS. written *c*. 700 containing a collection of documents connected, generally speaking, with councils and creeds of the fourth and fifth centuries. The collection may in origin be Carthaginian. The documents on the Melitian schism (251–3) which are found in this MS. would be included because they have a bearing on canon law, and may have been sent by Cyril of Alexandria to Carthage *c*. 420. (For a full description of the MS. and its contents see W. Telfer in *Harvard Theological Review*, XXXVI (1943), pp. 169–246.)

CONSTANTINE THE GREAT, *c*. 274–337, Emperor from 306, sole Emperor from 324. His laws and letters are a chief primary source for the relations of Christianity and the State from 313 onwards (260, 262–4, 272–3, 276–7, 280–1, 283–7, 297, 299, 303–5, 310, 312–3; 315).

CORNELIUS, Bishop of Rome, 251–253, corresponded with Cyprian and with Fabius of Antioch about the controversy over "lapsed" Christians, and the schism of Novatian, who had disputed the election of Cornelius (228, 230).

CYPRIANUS, THASCIUS CAECILIUS, *c*. 200–258, of Carthage, a rhetorician, converted *c*. 246 and chosen as Bishop of Carthage *c*. 249. The period of his episcopate was troubled by the persecutions of Decius and of Valerian, by pestilence, and by the controversies over lapsed Christians and over the rebaptism of heretics. Cyprian wrote treatises on various subjects, all of which were apposite to the circumstances of his time, in an excellent style (cf. 246); his letters are a most important historical source. He died a martyr on 14 September, 258 (201–14, 216–22, 224–7).

Dêr Balyzeh Papyrus, see 106.

The *Didache* or *Teaching of the Twelve Apostles* or, in full, *The Teaching of the Lord, through the Twelve Apostles, to the Gentiles*, was known to Eusebius (*H.E.* III.25.4) but was regarded as lost till it was published by the Metropolitan Bryennius of Nicomedia in 1883. The *Teaching* consists of instruction in ethics, on church order and on the eschatological hope. Notwithstanding the labour and ingenuity expended on this work, its date and provenance are still uncertain. It has been variously regarded as a primitive Christian document or as a production or compilation of an archaizer of as late as the third century (103).

DIONYSIUS (THE GREAT), d. 264–265, was head of the Catechetical School at Alexandria from *c*. 232, and Bishop from *c*. 248. He took a leading part, distinguished by his moderation and good sense, in the controversies of his time (236–8). He wrote extensively, but only fragments of his works are now extant (231–3, 236–7).

DIONYSIUS BARSALÎBÎ, d. 1171, Jacobite, bishop from 1145, "the star of the century among the Jacobites" (Wright, *Short History of Syriac Literature*, p. 246), wrote extensively on a great variety of subjects. In his commentary on *The Apocalypse*, *Acts* and *Epistles* traces are found of the arguments about the *Apocalypse* between Hippolytus and Gaius at Rome (138).

DIONYSIUS OF CORINTH, Bishop *c.* 180, wrote letters to various churches (Eus., *H.E.* IV.23), and clearly was an individual of great influence (6). Only fragments survive.

DIONYSIUS, Bishop of Rome 259–268, corresponded with his namesake of Alexandria: he criticized theological expressions used by the latter in combating Sabellianism (235).

The Doctrine of Addai is a Syriac document, composed in its present form *c.* 400, which deals with the early history of Christianity in Edessa. On these legends, see Eusebius, *H.E.* I.13, with Lawlor and Oulton's notes, or *D.C.B.* s.v. Thaddaeus, but one need not suspect that the information given in 127 is false.

EPHRAIM THE SYRIAN, *c.* 306–373, born at Nisibis, is the most famous writer, preacher and poet of the Syriac church. He wrote against Bardaisan, Marcion and Mani (243).

EPIPHANIUS, *c.* 315–403, of Eleutheropolis near Gaza in Palestine, acquired a great reputation for knowledge and sanctity as head of a monastery which he established near his native place. In 367 he was chosen as bishop of Constantia (Salamis) in Cyprus, and Metropolitan of the island. He was a violent defender of orthodoxy, but his undoubted learning is not matched by clarity of thought and by tact. According to Jerome he knew Greek, Syriac, Hebrew, Coptic and some Latin. His work against heresies—eighty in number—is the *Panarion* (medicine chest), usually cited in abbreviated form as *Haer.* It preserves many extracts from works no longer extant (69, 90, 294).

The Epistle of the Apostles, an apocryphal work dated *c.* 150–180, originally in Greek but now extant only in Ethiopic (106).

The Epistle to Diognetus is an apology of early but uncertain date by an unknown author. The sole MS. containing it was destroyed in the siege of Strasburg in 1870. It has been suggested that the *Epistle* is the *Apology* of Quadratus (q.v.), or that it is by Hippolytus (q.v.) or Pantaenus. Diognetus may be a Stoic philosopher who was one of the teachers of Marcus Aurelius (36).

EUSEBIUS OF CAESAREA IN PALESTINE, *c.* 260–*c.* 339, Bishop of Caesarea from *c.* 313; pupil of Pamphilus (martyr in 310) and through him of Origen. He wrote voluminously as apologist, exegete and historian. His *Ecclesiastical History* is our chief primary source for the history of the Church down to *c.* 300. This work in its original form was completed *c.* 303 and enlarged in successive editions to continue the history down to 324. It ends with the final victory of Constantine over Licinius, cf. 288. Eusebius' view of history was annalistic, and his *Chronicle*, also first completed *c.* 303, supplied him with a rigid chronological framework which continually interrupts his narrative. In his *History* Eusebius quotes many works by earlier authors, some of which are no longer extant. For Eusebius' halting and equivocal position in the Arian Controversy, see 301. After the death of Constantine in 337, Eusebius wrote the *Life of Constantine*, a panegyric which is not without historical value in itself and which contains numerous original documents. In this work, and in his *Oration on the Tricennalia of Constantine*, Eusebius works out a theory of the Christian Empire (318), derived ultimately from Hellenistic theories of kingship. Passages in this book written by or derived from Eusebius are 6, 8, 11, 23, 31, 34, 44, 47, 60, 71, 82, 85–90, 92, 102, 105, 125–6, 128, 131, 163, 175–7, 179–81, 190–2, 228, 230–4, 237–8, 241–2, 248, 250, 254–5, 259 262–4, 272, 282–3, 288–9, 297, 301, 312, 316–19.

EUSEBIUS OF NICOMEDIA, d. 341 or 342, Bishop successively of Berytus, Nicomedia and Constantinople, had, like Arius, been a pupil of Lucian of Antioch (see 293). He wrote numerous letters on the Arian controversy. From *c.* 328 he became a leading adviser of Constantine, and led energetically the reaction against the bishops who were the leading supporters of the faith of Nicaea (307).

EUZOÏUS, friend of Arius, joint author of 306. See note on 306.

FIRMILIAN, d. 268, Bishop of Caesarea in Cappadocia, was a man of great influence, of whose career we know all too little. He was a friend of Origen, who spent a considerable period *c.* 235 in Cappadocia. Firmilian took a leading part in the controversies of the period, but his sole extant work is a letter to Cyprian on the baptismal controversy (223), in which he supported Cyprian against Stephen of Rome.

FRONTO, M. CORNELIUS, *c.* 90–168, see 113.

GAIUS, fl. *c.* 210, a Roman writer of whose *Dialogue with the Montanist Proclus* only a few fragments are preserved by Eusebius. Gaius held views, of which Eusebius does not apparently know, about the authorship of the *Fourth Gospel* and of the *Apocalypse*, and for which he was attacked by Hippolytus (6, 138).

GALEN, *c.* 130–*c.* 200, of Pergamum, was the most famous doctor of the second century. He spent the latter part of his life at Rome. He was philosopher as well as physician, and he is the first pagan author of whom we know who has anything good to say about the Christians (108, 109).

GELASIUS, fl. *c.* 475, of Cyzicus, author of a Church History, in three books, dealing with the reign of Constantine. It is of little value, but contains some original documents (304, 307).

HEGESIPPUS, fl. *c.* 120–180, was according to Eusebius, *H.E.* IV.22.8, of Jewish origin. He wrote *c.* 180 five books of *Hypomnemata* (8, 11, 47), which were the principal and perhaps only source of information for Eusebius on the early Church of Jerusalem. H. journeyed to Rome; he was much preoccupied with the identity of faith held by different churches. On Hegesippus and his list of Roman bishops, see 47.

HERMAS, fl. *c.* 110–*c.* 150 at Rome, a freedman, author of *The Shepherd* (a work so named from one of his celestial informants). Hermas is a prophet and moral reformer. If the autobiographical details in his work are to be trusted, he is, as Streeter says (*The Primitive Church*, p. 203), "a timid, fussy, kindly, incompetent, middle-aged freedman, delightfully naïve, just a little vain of his prophetic gift, and with a wife and children decidedly out of hand." His work is regarded as scripture by Irenaeus, Origen and Tertullian (while still a catholic), but it is not so regarded by the *Muratorian Fragment* (124) (32, 33).

HILARY, *c.* 315–367, Bishop of Poitiers from *c.* 350, was an energetic defender of the faith of Nicaea. He was sent into exile by Constantius II, and lived in the East from 356–359. His extensive writings contribute one passage only, on Paul of Samosata, to this book (240).

HIPPOLYTUS, *c.* 160–235, Presbyter, and later schismatic bishop at Rome, was one of the most energetic controversialists and versatile writers of the early centuries—his works include exegesis, liturgy and chronology. Not only did he defend Christianity against the heretics, following in the footsteps of Irenaeus, but he also attacked Zephyrinus and Callistus, Bishops of Rome, for moral and theological incompetence. Eventually he became head of a schismatic body, and was sent into exile, with Pontian, Bishop of Rome, to Sardinia in 235, where he died. A statue of H., unfortunately headless, was found in a cemetery at Rome in 1551. Eusebius and Jerome knew very little about H., and it is only in recent times that his importance has been recognized. See also under Pseudo-Tertullian (130, 133–8).

IGNATIUS, d. *c.* 115 (?), Bishop of Antioch, wrote seven letters, four from Smyrna and three from Troas, when on his way to martyrdom at Rome. Five of his letters are addressed to churches in the province of Asia, one (from Troas) to Polycarp, Bishop of Smyrna (q.v.) and one to the church at Rome, to inform the Christians there of his coming, and to warn them against any efforts to save him. No contemporary evidence is available to support the date usually assigned to Ignatius—Eusebius says that he was a martyr under Trajan—but this need occasion no surprise as Christian documents of this period are rare. Ignatius vigorously champions the threefold ministry as the only possible church order (24–30).

IRENAEUS, *c.* 130–*c.* 200, Bishop of Lugdunum (Lyons) from *c.* 178, came originally from Asia, where he had in his youth been instructed by Polycarp of Smyrna. In the severe persecution of 177, Irenaeus carried a letter concerning Montanism from Gaul to the Roman Church; later he rebuked Victor of Rome for his attitude in the Quarto-deciman Controversy (125). His work *Against Heresies* is a shattering refutation of the Gnostics and of Marcion. The five books of this work are fully extant only in a Latin translation, probably made in the third century; part of the original Greek is extant, as are portions of Armenian and Syriac translations (58, 62–7, 70, 72, 73, 77, 81, 93–102, 125).

JEROME, of Stridon in Dalmatia, *c.* 347–*c.* 420, the friend and later the enemy of Rufinus (q.v.), was one whose eminence in scholarship was unfortunately matched by his virulence in controversy. He was one of the western leaders of Monasticism and lived for over 30 years as head of a (western) monastery at Bethlehem. Jerome was commissioned by Pope Damasus, whose secretary he was from 382-385, to revise the Latin text of Holy Scripture: the ensuing text (the Vulgate) is partly revision but in great measure a new translation, particularly of the O.T. In the present volume Jerome is the source of one passage only (308).

JOSEPHUS, FLAVIUS, c. 38-post 100, Jewish historian, descended from a priestly family; he commanded Jewish forces in Galilee in 66-67; he was taken prisoner and later befriended by Vespasian and Titus, whom he accompanied to Rome. He assumed the family name of Vespasian, "Flavius", in addition to his own. He wrote his historical works at Rome, and is in particular our chief source for the great Jewish revolt of 66-70 (1).

JUSTIN MARTYR, d. 165, of Flavia Neapolis (Shechem) in Palestine, was converted in adult life after a spiritual pilgrimage that led him through various schools of philosophy. After his conversion he still regarded himself as a philosopher and set up a school of Christian instruction at Rome. He is the most important of the apologists of the second century. Eusebius, *H.E.* IV.18.1-6, enumerates eight works by Justin, but only three of these are now extant, his *First Apology*, his *Second Apology* which is an appendix to the first, and his *Dialogue with Trypho*, a learned Jew. Justin died a martyr, with six of his pupils, at Rome in 165 (20, 37-43, 48, 74).

LACTANTIUS, L. CAELIUS FIRMIANUS, c. 240-c. 320, native of Africa, pupil of Arnobius, rhetorician, was summoned to Nicomedia to teach there c. 295, and remained there till c. 305. Later, in extreme old age, he became tutor, in Gaul, to Crispus, eldest son of Constantine. His *Divine Institutes*, written between 303 and 313, is designed to be a complete vindication of Christianity against paganism on religious, philosophical and ethical grounds. The work *On the deaths of the persecutors*, on the authorship of which many doubts have been cast, is now generally regarded as being by L., and is a leading primary source for the persecution from 303 onwards (246-7, 259-60).

Letter of the Gallic Churches (21), see *Acta Martyrum*.

The Little Labyrinth, a work quoted, though not named by Eusebius in *H.E.* V.28., on the Monarchian heresy at Rome. The name of the work is found in Theodoret, *Haer. Fab.* II.5, who quotes one of the passages given by Eusebius. Some scholars regard Hippolytus as its author (131).

LUCIAN, c. 120-post 180, of Samosata, travelling lecturer and rhetorician, is superficial in his thought, but gives us many sketches of contemporary life in his numerous surviving works. He hated charlatanry, cf. 110, and the story of Peregrinus well illustrates features of Christianity, a subject in which Lucian had no direct interest himself (110-111).

MANI, founder of the Manichaean sect, began his preaching at Ctesiphon in 242, and suffered martyrdom in 272. His aberrant form of Christianity had great success. He wrote seven books, of which fragments survive, six in Syriac, and one, addressed to King Shapur, in Persian (243-4).

MARCELLUS, d. 374, Bishop of Ancyra before 325, was a strong supporter of the Creed of Nicaea, and hence was hated by the party of Eusebius of Nicomedia. He was accused of Sabellianism, and was deposed in 336. Eusebius of Caesarea attacked him in his two works, *Against Marcellus* and *On the Theology of the Church*, in which fragments of Marcellus' work survive (316). He was vindicated by Julius of Rome in 340, and by the Council of Sardica in 343.

MARCUS AURELIUS ANTONINUS, 121–180, Emperor from 161, was marked out for high office by Hadrian and Antoninus Pius. Stoic philosophy was the inspiration of his life. In his *Meditations* he mentions the Christians incidentally, once only (112).

Martyrdom of Polycarp (18), see *Acta Martyrum*.

MELITO, fl. *c.* 180, Bishop of Sardis, was a versatile writer of whose works fragments are extant and also a recently discovered *Homily on the Passion*. He is regarded by Polycrates of Ephesus (125) as one of his supporters in the Quartodeciman Controversy. His *Apology* (44) was addressed to Marcus Aurelius.

MINUCIUS FELIX, M., fl. *c.* 200. Roman lawyer, but originally from Africa, author of the *Octavius*, an apology constructed in dialogue form and written in an excellent style, cf. 246. The work obviously has close connection with the *Apology* and *Ad Nationes* of Tertullian, but the question of priority has found no clear solution. It would appear however more likely that Minucius weaves the vigorous thought of Tertullian into his dialogue than that Tertullian copied the work of an author far inferior to himself in force and originality (113, 162).

MOSES BAR KEPHA, d. 903, Jacobite bishop in Mesopotamia for 40 years, wrote commentaries on all the books of the Bible, homilies and against heresies (129).

The Muratorian Fragment, *c.* 200, so called from L. A. Muratori who first published it in 1740, is an account, in Latin, of the Canon of the N.T. The beginning and end are lost. It may be based on a Greek original, and in view of the references in it to Paul's leaving "the City", and to the *Shepherd* of Hermas, may be of Roman origin (124).

Ad Novatianum, a polemic against Novatian written *c.* 253–257, probably by an African bishop (229).

OPTATUS, fl. *c.* 365, Bishop of Milevis in Numidia, attacked the Donatists in his work *On the Schism of the Donatists* or *Against Parmenian*. To this work there was subjoined a collection of documents compiled between 330 and 347, and dealing with the early history of the sect, from which 271, 273, 275, 279–81 are taken (269).

ORIGEN, *c.* 185–254, of Alexandria, became head of the Catechetical School *c.* 203. He lived an ascetic life, and, following literally Matt. 19.12, unmanned himself. As scholar, teacher and writer, and (in later life) as preacher, Origen was unequalled in the early church. His advice and help were sought by distant churches (cf. 180), though his philosophical background led him into doctrinal errors which became the subject of controversy in his lifetime and long after. Following on his ordination in Palestine (177), Origen was expelled from Alexandria (178), and moved to Caesarea where he continued his work. He was tortured in the persecution of Decius. For his views on scripture, see 188–90, 192, his work on the text of the O.T., 181, his theological system, 182–7, and his reply to Celsus, 193–8, cf. 114–22, also 199.

Panegyrici Latini is the name given to twelve speeches in praise of Roman Emperors. The earliest in date is that of Pliny on Trajan; nine others, dated from 289–321 are of the time of Diocletian and Constantine, one belongs to the reign of Julian (362) and one to that of Theodosius (381). These speeches are in a large measure imperial propaganda, and are valuable historical documents for contemporary events and tendencies (258).

PAPIAS OF HIERAPOLIS, fl. *c.* 130, author of an *Exposition of the Oracles of the Lord*, in five books, now no longer extant. For the passages quoted by Eusebius about the composition of the Gospels, see 31.

Passio Martyrum Scillitanorum (22), see *Acta Martyrum*.

PAUL OF SAMOSATA, fl. *c.* 260, about which year he became bishop of Antioch. Paul also acted as a secular official for the Kingdom of Palmyra, which controlled Antioch after the capture of Valerian by the Persians. He was deposed for heresy in 268 (238), but not ejected from Antioch till the reign of Aurelian (241). For his theological views see 239, 240.

PETER, d. 311, Bishop of Alexandria from 300, withdrew from Alexandria in the persecution of 303ff., and his absence encouraged the activities of Melitius (251–3). Peter suffered martyrdom in 311. Of his writings little survives, but it is known that in theology he was a critic of Origen (253).

PHILOSTORGIUS, a Cappadocian, wrote a history of the Church from *c.* 300–425 in twelve books. Only fragments are now extant. He was an Arian, and his work reflects the Arian point of view. He is mentioned in 296, 304.

PLINIUS CAECILIUS SECUNDUS, C. (the younger Pliny); *c.* 61–*c.* 114, friend of Tacitus and Suetonius, barrister, consul in 100; sent as a special commissioner to govern Bithynia *c.* 111. His letters to Trajan cover 16 months of his governorship (14, 15).

POLYCARP, d. 155 (? later), Bishop of Smyrna, was a disciple of "John" in Asia and himself taught Irenaeus (96, p. 119; 102). He must have been a bishop for many years. Ignatius addressed one of his letters to him. Irenaeus informs us that P. was the author of various letters, but of these only one, that *To the Philippians*, has survived (30). About 154 Polycarp visited Rome, to confer with Anicetus; they failed to reach agreement on the celebration of Easter, but did not on that account break communion. By his long life Polycarp was a most important witness to the Apostolic Tradition. The *Martyrium Polycarpi* is the earliest extant account of the death of a martyr (18).

POLYCRATES, *c.* 125–post 190, Bishop of Ephesus, is known to us only through the fragments of his letter to Victor of Rome about the Quartodeciman Controversy (125).

PONTIUS, deacon of Cyprian, author of a life, or rather panegyric, of his bishop (215).

PORPHYRY, c. 230–c. 305, of Tyre, Neoplatonist, disciple and successor of Plotinus. He was not, like his master, an original thinker. He was the most serious literary opponent of Christianity in the ancient world. In his youth he had close association with Christians, cf. 191n., and in particular with Origen (191). His work against the Christians is no longer extant. Constantine gave orders for it to be burnt (313) (also 190).

PSEUDO-TERTULLIAN, *Against all Heresies*, is a brief work attached, in certain manuscripts to the end of Tertullian, *De Praescriptione Haereticorum*. This work is certainly not by Tertullian and is probably an Epitome of the *Synatagma* of Hippolytus, a work written before his longer and more elaborate refutation called the *Philosophoumena* (131).

PTOLEMY, fl. c. 180, Gnostic, a disciple of Valentinus (69).

QUADRATUS, fl. c. 130, Apologist and Prophet, addressed an *Apology* to Hadrian, of which only a single fragment is preserved (34). The theory has been put forward that the *Epistle to Diognetus* is the *Apology* of Quadratus, of which the surviving fragment fits into a *lacuna* in the text of the *Epistle* (34).

RHODO, fl. c. 180, of Asia, a disciple of Tatian at Rome, wrote against the Marcionites and particularly against Apelles (82). We know of him only from Eusebius, *H.E.* V.13.

RUFINUS, TYRANNIUS, of Aquileia, d. 410, the friend and later the enemy of Jerome, spent part of his life in the East, in Egypt and Palestine. He was strongly attracted to Origen's theology, and this led him into conflict with Jerome. His chief importance for Christian literature is as a translator into Latin of Origen (cf. 182, p. 211; 186, p. 217) and of Eusebius (16).

SERAPION, fl. c. 200, Bishop of Antioch, is mentioned by Eusebius, *H.E.* V.19, as having written against the Montanists. Beyond this nothing more is known of him except for the information given in 126, 127.

Sermo de Passione Donati, see 278.

SOCRATES, c. 380–post 439, of Constantinople, a lawyer, wrote a history of the Church from 305–439, in seven books. He has preserved many original documents and his general attitude on ecclesiastical questions is impartial (290, 306–7, 312–13, 315).

SOZOMEN, fl. c. 440, from near Gaza in Palestine, wrote a history of the Church from 324–425 in nine books, at Constantinople. He is very dependent on Socrates, but also quotes original documents not used by the latter, and his history is embellished with more legendary material than that of Socrates. For a case in which they disagree, cf. 290 with 291 (291, 306–7, 314–15).

SUETONIUS TRANQUILLUS, C., c. 75–c. 140, friend of Pliny (the younger), private secretary to Hadrian. Of his extensive works only the *Lives of the Caesars* and part of *On Famous Men* survive. His *Lives* are biography, not history, and abound in scandalous and other anecdotes. But he had access to many documents and used these freely, and "within his limits he preserves material of great value" (*C.A.H.* X, p. 873) (2, 4).

SULPICIUS SEVERUS, d. c. 420, belonged to a distinguished family of Aquitaine. He received an excellent education and was a well known barrister when the death of his wife and the influence of Martin of Tours and of Paulinus of Nola led him to forsake the world for the life of a solitary. His *Chronicle* is a sketch of Jewish and Ecclesiastical History down to 400. His extensive writings on Martin of Tours are a leading source for the spread of Monasticism in Gaul (7).

TACITUS, P. CORNELIUS, c. 58–c. 116, Roman historian, consul in 97, governor of Asia under Trajan, friend of Pliny the Younger. His chief historical works are the *Histories* (from 68 onwards) and the *Annals* (from 14–68). The latter work, in which the famous chapter on the Neronian persecution occurs, was being composed in the last years of his life. The loss of that part of the *Histories* that dealt with the siege of Jerusalem is much to be regretted (3).

TATIAN, c. 120–post 174, born in Assyria, became a travelling sophist. According to his own testimony he was converted by reading the Scriptures. At Rome he was a disciple of Justin, after whose martyrdom he returned to the East and fell into some form of ascetic Gnosticism (104). His *Address to the Greeks* is a work of scornful polemic rather than an apology. T. compiled the earliest known Harmony of the Gospels, the *Diatessaron* (105), a work widely used in the Church of Syria. It is uncertain whether this work, now extant only in Arabic and other versions, was originally compiled in Greek or in Syriac.

TERTULLIANUS, Q. SEPTIMIUS FLORENS, c. 160–post 220, of Carthage, born a heathen and converted in adult life, was well trained in the Roman rhetorical system of education, and may be the lawyer Tertullian who belongs to this period. After his conversion he wrote apologetic works defending Christianity, polemical works attacking heretics, Jews and pagans, and works on a variety of moral and ethical topics. These works are written in a style of extraordinary vigour, but sometimes also of considerable obscurity (cf. 246). Ultimately he become a Montanist and thereafter used the same vigour in attacking the Catholic Church as he had previously shown in defending it. The last that we see of him is between 217 and 222, when he criticized Callistus, Bishop of Rome (160), for his views on sin and penitence. T. exercised very great influence on the theological vocabulary of the Latin church. He knew Greek also and wrote works (no longer extant) in Greek. Notwithstanding Jerome's statement (*De Vir. Ill.* 53) that T. was a presbyter, some modern scholars are doubtful about his having belonged to the clergy (139–161).

THEODORET, c. 393–c. 460, Bishop of Cyrrhus in Syria from 423, wrote, among many other works, a history of the Church from 324–428. The similarities of his work with those of Socrates and Sozomen are perhaps best explained by the use of the same sources. In Christology Theodoret was an upholder of the Antiochene school, and took a leading part in the controversies of his time (293, 295).

THEOGNIUS or THEOGNIS, Bishop of Nicaea, fl. c. 325, friend of Eusebius of Nicomedia and Arius, joint author of 307.

CHRONOLOGICAL TABLES

SYNOPSIS OF CHURCH HISTORY IN THE SECOND CENTURY

Roman Emperors and General History	Bishops of Rome	Imperial Rescripts	Martyrs and Confessors	Christian Writers (works wholly or partly extant are in italics)	Heretics	Pagan Thinkers and Writers
TRAJAN, 98–117 101–6. Conquest of Dacia 113 ff. Eastern Conquests c. 112. Tacitus governor of Asia 115. Revolt of the Jews (Mesopotamia, Cyprus, Egypt, Cyrene). Revolts in Mauretania and Britain	Clement (?) Evarestus (?) Alexander (?)	c. 112 to Pliny in Bithynia	c. 107 (?) Symeon of Jerusalem c. 112 In Bithynia under Pliny Ignatius of Antioch (at Rome) (? date)	Ignatius (7 letters) Polycarp, *To the Philippians* Hermas, *The Shepherd* (part)	Cerinthus Satorninus (?)	Pliny d. c. 113 Tacitus d. c. 117
HADRIAN, 117–138 Destruction of Legio IX in Britain; Hadrian's Wall Temples dedicated, to Olympian Zeus at Athens, to Venus and Roma at Rome 132–135 Revolt of the Jews under Bar-Cochba Foundation of Aelia Capitolina	Sixtus I Telesphorus d. c. 136 Hyginus	c. 125 to Minucius Fundanus in Asia	In Asia c. 124 At Rome *The Shepherd* of Hermas shows that persecution had taken place Telesphorus c. 136 Persecution by the Jews in Bar-Cochba's revolt	Papias (*fragments*) *Epistle of Barnabas* Aristo of Pella (v. Jews) Agrippa Castor (v. Basileides) Quadratus (Apologist) *Apocryphal Gospels, etc.*	Carpocrates Basileides Valentinus (at Rome c. 136–165) Cerdo	Epictetus fl. Suetonius fl. Arrian fl. Plutarch d. c. 125
ANTONINUS PIUS, 138–161 147. 900th anniversary of the founding of Rome. Rampart of Antoninus between Forth and Clyde	Pius I, c. 140–154 Anicetus, c. 154–(?)	To various cities: Larissa, Thessalonica, Athens: to the assembly of the province of Achaea	Polycarp and others at Smyrna, 156 (? later) (*Martyrium Polycarpi*) Ptolemy and Lucius at Rome (?) Peregrinus (pseudo-confessor)	Aristeides (*Apology*) (?) *Epistle to Diognetus* Justin (*Apologist* and v. Heretics) Hermas (*continued*)	Valentinus Marcion c. 144+ at Rome: Marcellina at Rome c. 155+ Montanus c. 157	Juvenal d. c. 140 Fronto fl. Gellius fl. Apuleius fl.

Roman Emperors and General History	Bishops of Rome	Persecutions and Martyrs	Christian Authors	Other prominent Christians	Heretics, Schismatics Controversies	Pagan Thinkers and Writers
MARCUS AURELIUS, 161–180 (*Meditations* written *post* 166). 161–166. Parthian War. 166 ff. Barbarian war on Danube frontier. (Episode of the "Thundering Legion") Pestilence. 175. Revolt of Avidius Cassius	Soter, (?)–175 Eleutherus, 175–189	To the governor at Lyons, 177. Edict on those disturbing men's minds by spreading superstition. At Rome Justin and others c. 163–7. At Athens: Publius. Martyrs in Crete; Christians sent to Greece to the mines. In Asia, Sagaris, Thraseas and others. At Lyons, 177. (?) Theodotus of Byzantium	Justin (v. Jews also) Tatian, Athenagoras } *Apologies*, Melito (*fragments*). Apollinarius, Miltiades (writers v. Montanists and Jews)		Great success of Marcionites and Montanists. Marcus (in Rhone valley)	Celsus' "True word". Lucian fl. Pausanias fl. Ptolemy fl. Numenius fl.
COMMODUS, 180–192. Execution of many senators	Victor, 189–199	Under the influence of Marcia, Commodus grants toleration. In Africa, Martyrs of Scilli (180). In Asia, under Arrius Antoninus. At Rome: Apollonius, Natalius; Roman Christians in the mines in Sardinia	Theophilus of Antioch, *Apology*. Pantaenus. Irenaeus (v. *Heretics*)		Monarchian Heresy in Asia and at Rome	

SYNOPSIS OF CHURCH HISTORY, A.D. 193–284

Roman Emperors and General History	Bishops of Rome	Persecutions and Martyrs	Christian Authors	Other prominent Christians	Heretics, Schismatics Controversies	Pagan Thinkers and Writers
193–235. Dynasty of the Severi. 193–211. SEPTIMIUS SEVERUS. d. at York, 4 Feb. 211. Siege of Byzantium, 193–6. Sack of Lyons, 197		c. 197 in Africa 202+ In Egypt (Leonides). In Africa (Perpetua, Felicitas and others), 211–213. By Scapula in Africa	c. 190–202 ff. Clement of Alexandria. c. 197 *Apology* of Tertullian. Serapion of Antioch. c. 203 Origen head of catechetical school at Alexandria	Demetrius, Bishop of Alexandria d. c. 232. Apollonius (v. Montanists)	Monarchians (at Rome, particularly; the Theodoti (2), Sabellius, Noëtus, Praxeas). Quartodeciman Controversy. c. 211 Council at Carthage on rebaptism of Heretics	Galen d. c. 199. Plotinus b. c. 205. Cassius Dio fl. fl. Ammonius Saccas. Philostratus, *Life of Apollonius of Tyana*

Roman Emperors and General History	Bishops of Rome	Persecutions and Martyrs	Christian Authors	Other prominent Christians	Heretics, Schismatics, Controversies	Pagan Thinkers and Writers
198–217. CARACALLA Constitutio Antoniniana	Zephyrinus, 199–217		Gaius fl. at Rome	Heraclas at Alexandria	c. 217 The Roman bishop's Edict. Controversies of Hippolytus with Zephyrinus and Callistus	Ulpian (jurist) fl.
218–222. ELAGABALUS Syrian Sun-worship at Rome	Callistus, 217–222		c. 218 Origen visits Rome c. 220 Minucius Felix	Bardaisan fl. Sextus Julius Africanus fl.	Tertullian becomes Montanist Hippolytus goes into schism	
222–235. ALEXANDER SEVERUS 226. Revival of Persia as a great power 232. Persian War	Urban, 222–230 Pontian, 230–235		c. 231 Origen, ordained in Palestine, expelled from Alexandria, settles at Caesarea	Heraclas, Bp. of Alexandria, 233–247		c. 232 Porphyry b. 233–244 Plotinus at Alexandria Herodian (historian) fl.
235–238. MAXIMINUS	Anterus 235–236 Fabian 236–250	Attack on higher clergy Pontian and Hippolytus sent to the mines Persecution in Cappadocia and Palestine	Origen, On Martyrdom	fl. Gregory Thaumaturgus		
242–244. GORDIAN III Persian Expedition				fl. Firmilian of Caesarea in Cappadocia	Origen deals in conferences with various heresies	
PHILIP, 244–249 248. Secular games celebrate 1000 years of Rome			c. 245 Origen, Contra Celsum Novatian, Roman presbyter, De Trinitate	Dionysius, Bp. of Alexandria, 247–264 Cyprian, Bp. of Carthage, 249–258*	242, Mani begins his preaching in Persia	

412

* For details see table p. 417.

		General Persecution	Cyprian: De Unitate			
DECIUS, 249–251 Gothic war	(250–251 No Bp. at Rome) 251–253, Cornelius (exiled) Lucius, 253–4	Fabian, Babylas of Antioch: Pionius, Origen (d. 254 or 5) etc., etc.	Cyprian: De Unitate Catholicae Ecclesiae		"lapsed" Christians: Schisms (1) of Carthage, (2) of Novatus at Rome	
VALERIAN GALLIENUS } 253–260 260. Valerian defeated and captured by the Persians Rise of Kingdom of Palmyra (Zenobia)	Stephen, 254–257 Sixtus II, 257–258	257, First stage, attacks on clergy and on corporate life of the Church 258, Second stage, Martyrdoms of Sixtus, Lawrence, Cyprian, etc.			Controversy about re-baptism of heretics Dionysius of Alexandria v. Chiliasts and Sabellians	
GALLIENUS, 260–268, Sole Emperor Empire of the Gauls (Postumus) Persian War	Dionysius, 259–268	Toleration	264–280 Theognostus head of catechetical school at Alexandria	Paul of Samosata, Bp. of Antioch, c. 260	Controversy of the two Dionysii about the Trinity c. 268 Condemnation of Paul of Samosata, Bp. of Antioch (Malchion's disputation with Paul)	Plotinus at Rome c. 263 Porphyry at Rome Dexippus (historian) fl.
CLAUDIUS II, 268–270 Defeat of the Goths		? Renewal of persecution				270 Plotinus d.
AURELIAN, 270–275 Defeat of Zenobia and destruction of Palmyra Temple of Sol Invictus at Rome. New walls of Rome built	Felix, 270–275	Aurelian intends to renew persecution	Commodian (poet) fl. (?)		c. 274 Aurelian's decision about Paul of Samosata 272, Martyrdom of Mani	273 Longinus d. c. 274 Porphyry, Against the Christians
PROBUS, 276–282 Constant wars v. Persians and northern barbarians	Eutychian, 275–283		c. 280 fl. Pierius at Alexandria			
Accession of DIOCLETIAN, 284	Gaius, 283–296					

SYNOPSIS OF CHURCH HISTORY, A.D. 284–337

Roman Emperors and General History	Bishops of Rome	Bishops of Alexandria, etc.	Persecutions and Martyrs	Christian Teachers and Authors	Heresies, Schisms, Councils	Pagan Thinkers and Writers
DIOCLETIAN, 284–305 Decentralization of authority MAXIMIAN, 285–305 Epoch of reform: wars with barbarians 288. Revolt of Carausius; Britain separated from the Empire 293. THE TETRARCHY Diocletian and Maximian are Augusti; CONSTANTIUS and GALERIUS, Caesars	Gaius, 283–296	Theonas, 282–300		Pierius and Achillas presbyters of Alexandria fl. Anatolius of Laodicaea in Syria fl.		
296. Constantius recovers Britain; revolt in Egypt suppressed 297. Persian War Roman victories followed by peace 301. Edict on Prices	Marcellinus, 296–304		c. 295 Edict against the Manichees	c. 290 Lucian of Antioch fl. c. 295 (?) Lactantius goes to Nicomedia		
		Peter, 300–311	Persecution of Christians in the army [Failure of Diocletian's sacrifice] 303 Feb., 1st Edict (Books, buildings, certain classes), 2nd Edict (Imprisonment of clergy), 3rd Edict (Torture and death for clergy) 304, 4th Edict (General Persecution)	c. 300 Gregory the Illuminator (Conversion of Armenian Royal House) Literary activity of Eusebius of Caesarea, and of Pamphilus Methodius fl.	c. 305 Council of Elvira	Literary attacks on Christianity in Bithynia
305. Abdication of Diocletian and Maximian				c. 305 Lactantius leaves Bithynia	305, Council of Cirta. Melitian Schism in Egypt	

...AND ...GALERIUS Augusti: SEVERUS and MAXIMINUS Caesars					
306. Constantius d. at York Constantine hailed as Augustus by his army, recognized as Caesar [Coup d'etat of MAXENTIUS, son of Maximian]					
307. Severus d.: LICINIUS Augustus Betrothal of Constantine and Fausta					
308. Revolt of Africa: Conference at Carnuntum fails to end confusion	308–9 Marcellus		308 Persecution slackens but is renewed [Pagan church of Maximinus] 310 Pamphilus		312 Donatist schism in Africa
310. Death of Maximian 311. Death of Galerius. Africa reconquered	309 Eusebius [Disturbances, both bishops exiled] Miltiades 311–314	311–312 Achillas	311 Toleration edict of Galerius. Renewed persecution in the lands ruled by Maximinus 311 Methodius Peter of Alexandria Lucian of Antioch		313 Council of Rome
312. Constantine invades Italy: Battle of the Milvian Bridge		312 Caecilian of Carthage	313 "Edict of Milan" grants universal toleration	c. 313 Lactantius Divinae Institutiones	314 Council of Arles c. 314–319 Council of Ancyra c. 314–325 Council of Neocaesarea c. 316 Final decision on Donatism by the Emperor
313. Meeting of Constantine and Licinius at Milan		312–328 Alexander			
313. Death of Diocletian Licinius defeats Maximinus: death of Maximinus	314–335 Silvester I	c. 312–339 Eusebius of Caesarea		c. 316 Sermon of Eusebius at Tyre	
314. First War of Constantine and Licinius		c. 316–342 Eusebius of Nicomedia	c. 317 Persecution of the Donatists in N. Africa		
315. Decennalia of Constantine Arch of Constantine at Rome				c. 318 Lactantius De Mortibus Persecutorum	
317. Crispus, Constantine II and Licinius II become Caesars			c. 320 Toleration for Donatists c. 321 Licinius begins to persecute in his dominions	c. 320 First works of Athanasius	c. 319 Beginning of the Arian Controversy

415

SYNOPSIS OF CHURCH HISTORY, A.D. 284–337—continued

Roman Emperors and General History	Bishops of Rome	Bishops of Alexandria, etc.	Persecutions and Martyrs	Christian Teachers and Authors	Heresies, Schisms, Councils	Pagan Thinkers and Writers
324. Second War of Constantine and Licinius. Defeat and (later) execution of Licinius 324–330. Foundation and building of Constantinople		324 Philogonius of Antioch d. 325–330 Eustathius of Antioch	324 Constantine extends religious toleration to the East	325 Final edition of Eusebius' *Ecclesiastical History* *c.* 332 Juvencus (poet) fl.	324 Council of Antioch 325 Council of Nicaea	
326. *Vicennalia* of Constantine Condemnation of Crispus and of Fausta		328–373 Athanasius			Exile of Arius, etc. and (later) of Eusebius of Nicomedia, etc. [327 (?) Second Session of Council of Nicaea] Return of Eusebius etc. 327 Temporary reconciliation of the Melitians	331 Execution of Sopater (Neo-Platonist) *c.* 333 Works of Porphyry proscribed
332. Victory over the Goths		[*c.* 330 ff. Confusion and schism at Antioch]	*c.* 330 Athanasius uses violence toward the Melitians		331–2 Athanasius visits Constantine 334 (Abortive) Council of Caesarea	
335. (Nominal) division of the Empire between Constantine's sons and nephews					335 Council of Tyre Athanasius flees to Constantine and is sent to Trier	
335–336. *Tricennalia* of Constantine 337. War with Persia 337. Baptism and death of Constantine	336 Mark 337–352 Julius I			336 The *Oration* of Eusebius of Caesarea. Eusebius *Contra Marcellum* and *De Ecclesiastica Theologia*	336 Exile of Marcellus of Ancyra	

CYPRIAN

249. Cyprian becomes Bishop of Carthage (? early in the year).

250. January: Persecution of DECIUS. Cyprian retires from Carthage. [20 Jan.: Martyrdom of Fabian, Bishop of Rome.] Nov.: Persecution relaxed at Carthage.

251. March: [Cornelius becomes Bishop of Rome; Novatian's schism.] After Easter (23 March) Cyprian returns to Carthage. April: First Council of Carthage confirms Cyprian's excommunication of his opponents (Novatus, etc.). Cyprian's *De Unitate Catholicae Ecclesiae*. Council sat till June. July: Arrival of envoys from Novatian announcing his election as Bishop of Rome.

252. April: Persecution of Gallus. Plague at Carthage. May: Second Council. Readmission of the lapsed. Consecration of Fortunatus and Maximus (Novatianist) as pseudo-bishops at Carthage.

253. [Exile and (June) death of Cornelius.] Sept.: Third Council of Carthage. [Lucius, Bishop of Rome.] [VALERIAN becomes Emperor.]

254. [March: death of Lucius. May: Stephen becomes Bishop of Rome.] Fourth Council of Carthage. The apostate Spanish Bishops. The case of Marcian of Arles.

255. First Council of Carthage on Baptism (Council 5).

256. (Spring) Second and (autumn) Third Councils on Baptism (Councils 6 and 7).

257. Persecution of Valerian. Internment of Cyprian. [Death of Stephen. Aug.: Sixtus II (Xystus), Bishop of Rome.]

258. [6 Aug.: Martyrdom of Sixtus.] 14 Sept.: Martyrdom of Cyprian.

INDEX

Proper names, personal and geographical, that appear only incidentally are not included in the index.

Cirta—*contd.*
308–10, 313, 316–17; renamed Constantine, 331; Donatists seize Church at, 331

Cittinus, martyr at Carthage, 41, 43

Cleanthes, Stoic, 171

Clement (1), Bishop of Rome, 118, 121, 157, 223, 340, 399; on the persecution of Nero, 4–5; his letter to Corinth, 10, 118; on the Ministry, 11–12

Clement (2), of Alexandria, 202, 223, 227, 398; his teachers, 192–3; on philosophy, 196–7; on the Gnostics, 197–9; on Church and heresy, 200–1

Cleomenes, Monarchian, 160, 163–4

Codex Theodosianus, 399

Codex Veronensis LX, 399

Colluthus, schismatic(?) at Alexandria, 348, 350

Constantia, half-sister of Constantine the Great, 374

Constantine the Great, Emperor, 399; his father, his family, 317, 337; fictitious descent of, 297; reverence for Apollo, 297–8; conversion of, 298–300; and religious toleration, 300–2, 333; Arch of, 302; gifts of, to the Church, 303–4, 317, 328; receives appeals from Donatists, 316–17; investigates Donatism, 317–18, 326–7; persecutes Donatism, 327–30; weakness of, in the face of Donatism, 330–1; legislation of, 333–6; and the Arian controversy, 352–4; summons Council of Nicaea, 358, 368, 371; and the Creed of Nicaea, 365, 367–8, 369, 375; on Eusebius of Nicomedia, 372–4; religious policy of, 380–1; and the Church of Antioch, 382–4; and Athanasius, 387–8; as Bishop, 390; his dependence on the Word, 391–5; baptism of, 396; received into heaven, 396

Constantinople, 333, 387–8; Church of the Apostles at, 395

Corinth, Church of, 5, 73, 175; schism at, 10–12, 118

Cornelius, Bishop of Rome, 238–41, 250, 399; election of, 236

Cotta, 191

Councils: on Montanism, 109; on the Quartodeciman question, 148–9; of Ancyra, 310–12; of Antioch, (1) 354–7, 375; (2) 382–3; of Arles, 318–25; of Carthage, (1) 238–9, (2) 253, (3) 254, (4) 258; of Cirta, 308–10, 313, 316–17; of Elvira, 305–8; of Iconium, 254; of Neocaesarea, 312–13; of Nicaea, 347, 358–72; of Rome, 317–18; of Tyre, 381, 385–6; provincial, 359–60

Creeds and Rules of Faith: in Aristides, 56; in Justin, 66; early creeds, 131; at Rome, *c.* 200, 155, 175; in Irenaeus, 115; in Tertullian, 175–6, 183; in Cyprian, 257; of Arius, 346, 375–6; of the Council of Antioch, 355–6; of Caesarea, 365; of Nicaea, 366; of Eusebius of Nicomedia, 376–7

Crispus, eldest son of Constantine, 336–7

Curubis, Cyprian exiled to, 260–1

Cyprian, Bishop of Carthage, 315, 399; his conduct in pestilence, 246; and Stephen of Rome, 247–50, 252–7; on the election of bishops, 249; on baptism, 251; trial and martyrdom of, 260–3; Lactantius on, 284

DECIUS, Emperor: persecution of, 228–9, 289; events during persecution of, in Africa, 230–6, in Italy, 236, in Egypt, 228–9

Decurions, ordination forbidden to, 335

Demetrian, pagan opponent of Cyprian, 259, 284

Demetrius, Bishop of Alexandria, 204, 206–8

Demons, Devils: instigate persecution, 62; misrepresent baptism in *their* rites, 66; inspire Marcion, 98; in Origen's *De Principiis*, 215, 217–18; stir up wars, etc., 226

Devil, the, 214–15, 281, 327–8, 343, 371

Diagoras of Melos, atheist, 190

Demiurge, the, 89, 94–5

Diatessaron of Tatian, 131–2

Didache (Teaching of the twelve Apostles), 339, 399: on Baptism, Prophets, etc., 126–9

Diocletian, Emperor, 311; edict against the Manichees, 282–3; begins persecution, 285–6; his edicts against the Christians, 286–7

Dionysius (1), Bishop of Alexandria, 259, 267, 378, 399–400; in persecution of Valerian, 266–7; and Sabellianism, 268–271

Dionysius (2) Barsalîbî, 400

Dionysius (3), Bishop of Corinth, 5, 400

Dionysius (4), Bishop of Rome, 276, 400; against the Sabellians, 268–70

Ditheism, Ditheists, 138, 164

Docetism, Docetae, 45, 47, 82, 89–90, 101, 152

Doctrine of Addai, 400

Domitilla, 8, 9; Cemetery of, 8

Donata, martyr at Carthage, 41–3

Donatists, Donatist Schism, 303–4, 325–6, 335, 353; origins of, 313–16; agitation against Caecilian, 316–17; Constantine orders investigation into, 317–18, 326–7; Constantine persecutes, 327–30; encroachments of, at Cirta, 331